A History of Philosophy by Frederick Copleston, S.J.

VOLUME I: GREECE AND ROME
From the Pre-Socratics to Plotinus

VOLUME II: MEDIEVAL PHILOSOPHY
From Augustine to Duns Scotus

VOLUME III: LATE MEDIEVAL AND RENAISSANCE PHILOSOPHY
Ockham, Francis Bacon, and the Beginning of the Modern World

VOLUME IV: MODERN PHILOSOPHY
From Descartes to Leibniz

VOLUME V: MODERN PHILOSOPHY
The British Philosophers from Hobbes to Hume

VOLUME VI: MODERN PHILOSOPHY
From the French Enlightenment to Kant

*VOLUME VII: MODERN PHILOSOPHY
From the Post-Kantian Idealists to Marx, Kierkegaard, and Nietzsche

*VOLUME VIII: MODERN PHILOSOPHY
Empiricism, Idealism, and Pragmatism in Britain and America

*VOLUME IX: MODERN PHILOSOPHY
From the French Revolution to Sartre, Camus, and Lévi-Strauss

*Available March 1994

A HISTORY
OF
PHILOSOPHY

A HISTORY
OF
PHILOSOPHY

VOLUME IV

Modern Philosophy: From Descartes to Leibniz

Frederick Copleston, S.J.

IMAGE BOOKS

DOUBLEDAY

New York   London   Toronto   Sydney   Auckland

AN IMAGE BOOK

PUBLISHED BY DOUBLEDAY

a division of Bantam Doubleday Dell Publishing Group, Inc.

1540 Broadway, New York, New York 10036

IMAGE, DOUBLEDAY, and the portrayal of a deer drinking from a stream are
trademarks of Doubleday, a division of Bantam Doubleday Dell
Publishing Group, Inc.

First Image Books edition of Volume IV of *The History of Philosophy* published
1963 by special arrangement with The Newman Press and Burns & Oates, Ltd.

This Image edition published January 1994.

De Licentia Superiorum Ordinis: J. D. Boyle, S.J., Praep. Prov. Angliae

Nihil Obstat: J. L. Russell, S.J., Censor Deputatus

Imprimatur: Franciscus, Archiepiscopus Birmingamiensis Birmingamiae die
25 Julii 1957

Library of Congress Cataloging-in-Publication Data

Copleston, Frederick Charles.
A history of philosophy.

Includes bibliographical references and indexes.
Contents: v. 1. Greece and Rome—[etc.]—
v. 4. From Descartes to Leibniz—v. 5. The British
philosophers from Hobbes to Hume—v. 6. From the
French Enlightenment to Kant.
1. Philosophy—History.   I. Title.
B72.C62   1993   190   92-34997

ISBN 0-385-47041-X

CONTENTS

CONTENTS

PREFACE

AT the end of Volume III of this *History of Philosophy* I expressed the hope of covering the period from Descartes up to and including Kant in the fourth volume. I meant, of course, that I hoped to discuss the whole of this part of modern philosophy in one book. This hope, however, has not been fulfilled. I have found myself compelled to devote three books to the period in question. And for the sake of convenience I have made each of these three books a separate volume. Volume IV, *Descartes to Leibniz*, deals with the great rationalist systems of philosophy on the Continent in the pre-Kantian period. In Volume V, *Hobbes to Hume*, I discuss the development of British philosophy from Hobbes up to and including the Scottish philosophy of common sense. In Volume VI, *Wolff to Kant*, I shall treat of the French Enlightenment and of Rousseau, of the German Enlightenment, of the rise of the philosophy of history from Vico to Herder, and finally of the system of Immanuel Kant. The title, *Wolff to Kant*, is certainly not ideal; but in view of the fact that in his pre-critical days Kant stood in the Wolffian tradition there is at least something to be said in its favour, whereas a title such as *Voltaire to Kant* would be extremely odd.

As in former volumes, I have divided the matter according to philosophers rather than by following out the development of first one and then another philosophical problem. Furthermore, I have treated some philosophers at considerable length. And though I think that division of the matter according to philosophers is the most convenient division for the readers whom I have principally in mind, this method certainly has its disadvantages. Faced by a number of different thinkers and by more or less detailed descriptions of their ideas, the reader may fail to grasp the general picture. Further, though I think that the old division into continental rationalism and British empiricism is justified, provided that a number of qualifications are added, a rigid adherence to this scheme is apt to give the impression that continental philosophy and British philosophy in the seventeenth and eighteenth centuries moved on two sets of parallel straight lines, each developing in entire independence of the other. And this is an erroneous impression. Descartes exercised a modest

influence on British thought; Berkeley was influenced by Malebranche; Spinoza's political ideas owed something to Hobbes; and
the philosophy of Locke, who wrote in the seventeenth century,
exercised a great influence on the thought of the French Enlightenment in the eighteenth century.

As a partial remedy for the disadvantages attending the method
of division which I have chosen I decided to write an introductory
chapter designed to give the reader a general picture of the
philosophy of the seventeenth and eighteenth centuries. It thus
covers the matter discussed in Volumes IV, V and VI, which, as
I have said, I originally hoped to deal with in one volume. I have,
of course, placed this introduction at the beginning of Volume IV;
and there will therefore be no introductory chapters in Volumes
V and VI. A descriptive introduction of this sort inevitably
involves a good deal of repetition. That is to say, ideas which are
discussed in later chapters at greater length and in more detail
are roughly outlined in the introduction. None the less, I consider that the advantages to be gained by including a general
descriptive introduction greatly outweigh the accompanying
disadvantages.

At the end of each of the three previous volumes I have added
a 'Concluding Review'. But just as the introduction covers the
matter dealt with in Volumes IV, V and VI, so will the Concluding
Review. It will therefore be placed at the end of Volume VI, that
is, after the exposition of Kant's philosophy. In the course of this
Concluding Review I propose to discuss, not only from an historical but also from a more philosophical point of view, the
nature, importance and value of the various styles of philosophiz-
ing of the seventeenth and eighteenth centuries. I think that it is
better to reserve such discussion until after the historical exposition
of the thought of the period than to interrupt this exposition
with general philosophical reflections.

Finally a word about references. References such as 'Vol. II, ch.
XL' or 'See vol. III, pp. 322-4' refer to this *History of Philosophy*.
As for references to the writings of the philosophers with whom
I deal, I have tried to give these in a form which will be of use to
the student who wishes to look them up. Some historians and
expositors have the practice of giving references according to
volume and page of the recognized critical edition, when such
exists, of the writings of the philosopher in question. But I am
doubtful of the wisdom of adhering exclusively to this practice in

a volume such as the present. In the chapters on Descartes, for example, I have indeed cited the volume and page of the Adam-Tannery edition; but I have also given references, where feasible, according to chapter and section or part and section of the work in question. The number of people who have easy access to the Adam-Tannery edition is extremely limited, just as few people possess the recent splendid critical edition of Berkeley. But cheap editions of the more important writings of the leading philosophers are easily obtainable; and in my opinion references should be given with a view to the convenience of students who possess such editions rather than to that of the few who possess or have access to the recognized critical editions.

CHAPTER I

INTRODUCTION

*Continuity and novelty: the early phase of modern philosophy
in its relation to mediaeval and Renaissance thought—Continental rationalism: its nature, its relation to scepticism and
to neo-Stoicism, its development—British empiricism: its nature
and its development—The seventeenth century—The eighteenth
century—Political philosophy—The rise of the philosophy of
history—Immanuel Kant.*

1. MODERN philosophy is generally said to have begun with
Descartes (1596–1650) or with Francis Bacon (1561–1626) in
England and with Descartes in France. It is not perhaps immediately evident with what justification the term 'modern' is
applied to the thought of the seventeenth century. But its use
clearly implies that there is a break between mediaeval and post-mediaeval philosophy and that each possesses important characteristics which the other does not possess. And the seventeenth-century philosophers were certainly convinced that there was a
sharp division between the old philosophical traditions and what
they themselves were trying to do. Men like Francis Bacon and
Descartes were thoroughly persuaded that they were making a
new start.

If for a long time the views of Renaissance and post-Renaissance
philosophers were accepted at their face value, this was partly due
to a conviction that in the Middle Ages there was really nothing
which merited the name of philosophy. The flame of independent
and creative philosophical reflection which had burned so brightly
in ancient Greece was practically extinguished until it was revived
at the Renaissance and rose in splendour in the seventeenth
century.

But when at last more attention came to be paid to mediaeval
philosophy, it was seen that this view was exaggerated. And some
writers emphasized the continuity between mediaeval and post-mediaeval thought. That phenomena of continuity can be observed in the political and social spheres is obvious enough. The
patterns of society and of political organization in the seventeenth
century clearly did not spring into being without any historical

antecedents. We can observe, for instance, the gradual formation of the various national States, the emergence of the great
monarchies and the growth of the middle class. Even in the field
of science the discontinuity is not quite so great as was once
supposed. Recent research has shown the existence of a limited
interest in empirical science within the mediaeval period itself.
And attention was drawn in the third volume of this *History*[1]
to the wider implications of the impetus theory of motion as
presented by certain fourteenth-century physicists. Similarly, a
certain continuity can be observed within the philosophical sphere.
We can see philosophy in the Middle Ages gradually winning
recognition as a separate branch of study. And we can see lines of
thought emerging which anticipate later philosophical developments. For example, the characteristic philosophical movement
of the fourteenth century, generally known as the nominalist
movement,[2] anticipated later empiricism in several important
respects. Again, the speculative philosophy of Nicholas of Cusa,[3]
with its anticipations of some theses of Leibniz, forms a link
between mediaeval, Renaissance and pre-Kantian modern thought.
Again, scholars have shown that thinkers such as Francis Bacon,
Descartes and Locke were subject to the influence of the past to
a greater degree than they themselves realized.

This emphasis on continuity was doubtless needed as a corrective to a too facile acceptance of the claims to novelty advanced by
Renaissance and seventeenth-century philosophers. It expresses
an understanding of the fact that there was such a thing as
mediaeval philosophy and a recognition of its position as an
integral part of European philosophy in general. At the same time,
if discontinuity can be over-emphasized, so can continuity. If we
compare the patterns of social and political life in the thirteenth
and seventeenth centuries, obvious differences in the structure of
society at once strike the eye. Again, though the historical factors
which contributed to the occurrence of the Reformation can be
traced, the Reformation was none the less in some sense an
explosion, shattering the religious unity of mediaeval Christendom.
And even though the seeds of later science can be discovered in
the intellectual soil of mediaeval Europe, the results of research
have not been such as to necessitate any substantial change of
view about the importance of Renaissance science. Similarly,
when all that can legitimately be said to illustrate the continuity

[1] pp. 165–7.   [2] Vol. III, chs. III–IX.   [3] Vol. III, ch. XV.

between mediaeval and post-mediaeval philosophy has been said, it remains true that there were considerable differences between them. For the matter of that, though Descartes was undoubtedly influenced by Scholastic ways of thought, he himself pointed out that the use of terms taken from Scholastic philosophy did not necessarily mean that the terms were being used in the same senses in which they had been used by the Scholastics. And though Locke was influenced in his theory of natural law by Hooker,[1] who had himself been influenced by mediaeval thought, the Lockean idea of natural law is not precisely the same as that of St. Thomas Aquinas.

We can, of course, become the slaves of words or labels. That is to say, because we divide history into periods, we may tend to lose sight of continuity and of gradual transitions, especially when we are looking at historical events from a great distance in time. But this does not mean that it is altogether improper to speak of historical periods or that no major changes take place.

And if the general cultural situation of the post-Renaissance world was in important respects different from that of the mediaeval world, it is only natural that the changes should have been reflected in philosophic thought. At the same time, just as changes in the social and political spheres, even when they seem to have been more or less abrupt, presupposed an already existing situation out of which they developed, so also new attitudes and aims and ways of thought in the field of philosophy presupposed an already existing situation with which they were in some degree linked. In other words, we are not faced with a simple choice between two sharply contrasted alternatives, the assertion of discontinuity and the assertion of continuity. Both elements have to be taken into account. There are change and novelty; but change is not creation out of nothing.

The situation, therefore, seems to be this. The old emphasis on discontinuity was largely due to failure to recognize that there was in the Middle Ages any philosophy worthy of the name. Subsequent recognition of the existence and importance of mediaeval philosophy produced an emphasis on continuity. But we now see that what is required is an attempt to illustrate both the elements of continuity and the peculiar characteristics of different periods. And what is true in regard to our consideration of different periods is true also, of course, in regard to different

[1] See vol. III, pp. 322–4.

individual thinkers. Historians are beset by the temptation to depict the thought of one period as simply a preparatory stage for the thought of the next period, and the system of one thinker as no more than a stepping-stone to the system of another thinker. The temptation is, indeed, inevitable; for the historian contemplates a temporal succession of events, not an eternal and immutable reality. Moreover, there is an obvious sense in which mediaeval thought prepared the way for post-mediaeval thought; and there is plenty of ground for looking on Berkeley's philosophy as a stepping-stone between the philosophies of Locke and Hume. But if one succumbs entirely to this temptation, one misses a great deal. Berkeley's philosophy is much more than a mere stage in the development of empiricism from Locke to Hume; and mediaeval thought has its own characteristics.

Among the easily discernible differences between mediaeval and post-mediaeval philosophy there is a striking difference in forms of literary expression. For one thing, whereas the mediaevals wrote in Latin, in the post-mediaeval period we find an increasing use of the vernacular. It would not, indeed, be true to say that no use was made of Latin in the pre-Kantian modern period. Both Francis Bacon and Descartes wrote in Latin as well as in the vernacular. So too did Hobbes. And Spinoza composed his works in Latin. But Locke wrote in English, and in the eighteenth century we find a common use of the vernacular. Hume wrote in English, Voltaire and Rousseau in French, Kant in German. For another thing, whereas the mediaevals were much given to the practice of writing commentaries on certain standard works, the post-mediaeval philosophers, whether they wrote in Latin or in the vernacular, composed original treatises in which the commentary-form was abandoned. I do not mean to imply that the mediaevals wrote only commentaries; for this would be quite untrue. At the same time commentaries on the *Sentences* of Peter Lombard[1] and on the works of Aristotle and others were characteristic features of mediaeval philosophical composition, whereas when we think of the writings of seventeenth-century philosophers we think of free treatises, not of commentaries.

The growing use of the vernacular in philosophical writing accompanied, of course, its growing use in other literary fields. And we can associate this with general cultural, political and social changes and developments. But we can also see in it a symptom

[1] See vol. II, p. 168.

of the emergence of philosophy from the confines of the Schools. The mediaeval philosophers were for the most part university professors, engaged in teaching. They wrote commentaries on the standard texts in use at the universities, and they wrote in the language of the learned, academic world. The modern philosophers in the pre-Kantian period, on the contrary, were in the majority of cases unconnected with the work of academic teaching. Descartes was never a university professor. Nor was Spinoza, though he received an invitation to Heidelberg. And Leibniz was very much a man of affairs who refused a professorship because he had quite another kind of life in view. In England Locke held minor posts in the service of the State; Berkeley was a bishop; and though Hume attempted to secure a university chair, he did not succeed in doing so. As for the French philosophers of the eighteenth century, such as Voltaire, Diderot and Rousseau, they were obviously men of letters with philosophical interests. Philosophy in the seventeenth and eighteenth centuries was a matter of common interest and concern among the educated and cultured classes; and it is only natural that the use of the vernacular should have replaced the use of Latin in writings designed for a wide public. As Hegel remarks, it is only when we come to Kant that we find philosophy becoming so technical and abstruse that it could no longer be considered to belong to the general education of a cultured man. And by that time the use of Latin had, of course, practically died out.

In other words, the original and creative philosophy of the early modern period developed outside the universities. It was the creation of fresh and original minds, not of traditionalists. And this is one reason, of course, why philosophical writing took the form of independent treatises, not of commentaries. For the writers were concerned with developing their own ideas, free from regard for the great names of the past and for the opinions of Greek and mediaeval thinkers.

To say, however, that in the pre-Kantian period of modern philosophy the vernacular came to be employed in place of Latin, that independent treatises were written rather than commentaries, and that the leading philosophers of the period were not university professors, does not do very much to elucidate the intrinsic differences between mediaeval and post-mediaeval philosophy. And an attempt must be made to indicate briefly some of these differences.

It is often said that modern philosophy is autonomous, the

product of reason alone, whereas mediaeval philosophy was sub-ordinate to Christian theology, hampered by subservience to dogma. But if it is expressed in this bold way, without qualification, the judgment constitutes an over-simplification. On the one hand we find St. Thomas Aquinas in the thirteenth century asserting the independence of philosophy as a separate branch of study, while in the fourteenth century we find theology and philosophy tending to fall apart as a result of the nominalist criticism of traditional metaphysics. On the other hand we find Descartes in the seventeenth century trying to harmonize his philosophical ideas with the requirements of Catholic dogma,[1] while in the eighteenth century Berkeley explicitly says that his ultimate aim is to lead men to the saving truths of the Gospel. The facts of the case, therefore, do not warrant our stating dogmatically that all modern philosophy was free from any theological presuppositions and from the exercise of any controlling influence by the Christian faith. Such a statement would not be applicable to Descartes, Pascal, Malebranche, Locke or Berkeley, even if it fits Spinoza, Hobbes, Hume and, of course, the materialist thinkers of the eighteenth century in France. At the same time it is undoubtedly true that we can trace a progressive emancipation of philosophy from theology from the beginnings of philosophical reflection in the early Middle Ages up to the modern era. And there is an obvious difference between, say, Aquinas and Descartes, even though the latter was a believing Christian. For Aquinas was first and foremost a theologian, whereas Descartes was a philosopher and not a theologian. Indeed, practically all the leading mediaeval philosophers, including William of Ockham, were theologians, whereas the leading philosophers of the seventeenth and eighteenth centuries were not. In the Middle Ages theology was esteemed as the supreme science; and we find theologians who were also philosophers. In the seventeenth and eighteenth centuries we find philosophers, some of whom were believing Christians while others were not. And though their religious beliefs doubtless exercised some influence on the philosophical systems of men such as Descartes and Locke, they were fundamentally in the same position as any philosopher today who happens to be a Christian but who is not, in the professional sense, a theologian. That is one reason why philosophers like Descartes and Locke appear to us 'modern' if we compare them with St. Thomas or St. Bonaventure.

---

[1] For example, his theory of substance with the dogma of transubstantiation.

One should, of course, distinguish between a recognition of the facts and an evaluation of the facts. Some would say that in proportion as philosophy was separated from its close connection with theology and was freed from any external control, it became what it ought to be, a purely autonomous branch of study. Others would say that the position accorded to philosophy in the thirteenth century was the right one. That is to say, the rights of reason were recognized; but so were the rights of revelation. And it was a benefit to philosophy if recognition of revealed truth warned it off erroneous conclusions. Here we have different evaluations of the facts. But however we evaluate the facts, it seems to me to be indisputably true that philosophy became progressively emancipated from theology, provided that the word 'emancipated' is understood in a neutral sense from the valuational point of view.

It is customary to associate the change in the position of philosophy in regard to theology with a shift of interest from theological themes to a study of man and of Nature without explicit reference to God. And there is, I think, truth in this interpretation, though there is also room for exaggeration.

The humanistic movement of the Renaissance is often mentioned in this connection. And, indeed, to say that the humanistic movement, with its extension of literary studies and its new educational ideals, was concerned primarily with man is to utter an obvious truth, in fact a tautology. But as was pointed out in the third volume of this *History*,[1] Italian humanism did not involve any very decisive break with the past. The humanists denounced barbarity in Latin style; but so had John of Salisbury in the twelfth and Petrarch in the fourteenth century. The humanists promoted a literary revival; but the Middle Ages had given to the world one of Europe's greatest literary achievements, the *Divina Commedia* of Dante. An enthusiasm for the Platonic or rather neo-Platonic tradition in philosophy accompanied Italian humanism; but neo-Platonism had also exercised an influence on mediaeval thought, even though the neo-Platonic themes in mediaeval philosophy were not based on a study of the variety of texts which were made available in the fifteenth century. Italian Platonism, in spite of its strong feeling for the harmonious development of the human personality and for the expression of the divine in Nature, can hardly be said to have constituted a direct antithesis to the

[1] Ch. XIII.

mediaeval outlook. Humanism doubtless developed, intensified, widened and placed in a much more prominent position one strand in mediaeval culture; and in this sense it involved a shift of emphasis. But it would not have been sufficient by itself to prepare the background for the early phase of modern philosophy.

A change from the theocentric character of the great mediaeval systems to the centring of interest on Nature as a unified, dynamic system can be observed much more clearly in the writings of philosophers such as Giordano Bruno[1] and Paracelsus[2] than in those of Platonists such as Marsilius Ficinus and John Pico della Mirandola.[3] But though the speculative philosophies of Nature of Bruno and kindred thinkers expressed and promoted the transition from mediaeval to modern thought, as far as the centre of interest is concerned, another factor was also required, namely, the scientific movement of the Renaissance.[4] It is not, indeed, always easy to draw a clear line of division between speculative philosophers of Nature and scientists when one is treating of the period in question. But nobody is likely to deny the propriety of placing Bruno in the first class and Kepler and Galileo in the second. And though the speculative philosophies of Nature formed part of the background of modern philosophy, the influence of the scientific movement of the Renaissance was of great importance in determining the direction of philosophical thought in the seventeenth century.

In the first place it was Renaissance science, followed later by the work of Newton, which effectively stimulated the mechanistic conception of the world. And this conception was obviously a factor which contributed powerfully to the centring of attention on Nature in the field of philosophy. For Galileo, God is creator and conserver of the world; the great scientist was far from being either an atheist or an agnostic. But Nature itself can be considered as a dynamic system of bodies in motion, the intelligible structure of which can be expressed mathematically. And even though we do not know the inner natures of the forces[5] which govern the system and which are revealed in motion susceptible of mathematical statement, we can study Nature without any immediate reference to God. We do not find here a break with

---

[1] Vol. III, ch. XVI.   [2] Ibid., ch. XVII.
[3] Ibid., ch. XVIII.   [4] Ibid.
[5] According to Galileo, there are in Nature 'primary causes', namely, forces such as gravity, which produce distinct and specific motions. The inner natures of the former are unknown, but the latter can be expressed mathematically.

mediaeval thought in the sense that God's existence and activity
are either denied or doubted. But we certainly find an important
change of interest and emphasis. Whereas a thirteenth-century
theologian-philosopher such as St. Bonaventure was interested
principally in the material world considered as a shadow or remote
revelation of its divine original, the Renaissance scientist, while
not denying that Nature has a divine original, is interested
primarily in the quantitatively determinable immanent structure
of the world and of its dynamic process. In other words, we have
a contrast between the outlook of a theologically-minded metaphysician who lays emphasis on final causality and the outlook
of a scientist for whom efficient causality, revealed in mathemati-
cally-determinable motion, takes the place of final causality.

It may be said that if we compare men who were primarily
theologians with men who were primarily scientists, it is so obvious
that their interests will be different that it is quite unnecessary to
draw attention to the difference. But the point is that the combined influence of the speculative philosophies of Nature and of
Renaissance science made itself felt in the philosophy of the
seventeenth century. In England, for example, Hobbes eliminated
from philosophy all discourse about the immaterial or spiritual.
The philosopher is concerned simply and solely with bodies,
though Hobbes included under bodies in the general sense not
only the human body but also the body politic or State. The
continental rationalist metaphysicians from Descartes to Leibniz
did not, indeed, eliminate from philosophy the study of spiritual
reality. The assertion of the existence of spiritual substance and
of God is integral to the Cartesian system, and in his theory of
monads Leibniz, as will be seen later, practically spiritualized
body. At the same time Descartes seemed to Pascal to employ
God simply to get the world going, as it were, after which he had
no further use for Him. Pascal's accusation may well be unjust;
and in my opinion it is unjust. But it is none the less significant
that Descartes' philosophy was able to give an impression which
one can hardly imagine being given by the system of a thirteenth-
century metaphysician.

It was not, however, simply a question of direction of interest.
The development of physical science not unnaturally stimulated
the ambition of using philosophy to discover new truths about the
world. In England Bacon emphasized the empirical and inductive
study of Nature, pursued with a view to increasing man's power

over and control of his material environment, a study which
should be carried on without regard to authority or to the great
names of the past. In France one of Descartes' main objections
against Scholasticism was that it served, in his opinion, only to
expound systematically truths already known and that it was
powerless to discover new truths. In his *Novum Organum* Bacon
called attention to the practical effects of certain inventions
which, as he put it, had changed the face of things and the state
of the world. He was conscious that new geographical discoveries,
the opening up of fresh sources of wealth and, above all, the establishment of physics on an experimental basis heralded the opening
of a new era. And though much of what he anticipated was not
to be realized until long after his death, he was justified in noting
the beginning of a process which has led to our technical civilization. Men such as Bacon and Descartes were doubtless unaware
of the extent to which their minds were influenced by former ways
of thought; but their consciousness of standing at the threshold of
a new era was not unjustified. And philosophy was to be pressed
into the service of the ideal of extending human knowledge with a
view to progress in civilization. True, the Cartesian and Leibnizian ideas of the appropriate method to be employed in this
process were not the same as that of Francis Bacon. But this does
not alter the fact that both Descartes and Leibniz were profoundly impressed and influenced by the successful development
of the new science and that they regarded philosophy as a means
of increasing our knowledge of the world.

There is another important way in which the scientific development of the Renaissance influenced philosophy. At the time no
very clear distinction was made between physical science and
philosophy. The former was known as natural philosophy or
experimental philosophy. Indeed, this nomenclature has survived
in the older universities to the extent that we find at Oxford, for
example, a chair of experimental philosophy, though the occupant
is not concerned with philosophy as the term is now understood.
None the less it is obvious that the real discoveries in astronomy
and physics during the Renaissance and in the early modern
period were made by men whom we would class as scientists and
not as philosophers. In other words, on looking back we can see
physics and astronomy attaining adult stature and pursuing their
paths of progress more or less independently of philosophy, in
spite of the fact that both Galileo and Newton philosophized (in

our sense of the term). But in the period of which we are treating there was no really empirical study of psychology in the sense of a science distinct from other sciences and from philosophy. It was only natural, therefore, that the successful developments in astronomy, physics and chemistry should arouse in philosophers the idea of elaborating a science of man. True, the empirical study of the human body was already being developed. We have only to recall the discoveries in anatomy and physiology which were made by men like Vesalius, author of the *De fabrica humani corporis* (1543) and Harvey, who discovered the circulation of the blood about 1615. But for the study of psychology we have to turn to the philosophers.

Descartes, for instance, wrote a work on the passions of the soul, and he proposed a theory to explain the interaction between mind and body. Spinoza wrote on human cognition, on the passions and on the reconciliation of the apparent consciousness or awareness of freedom with the determinism demanded by his system. Among the British philosophers we find a marked interest in psychological questions. The leading empiricists, Locke, Berkeley and Hume, all deal with problems about knowledge; and they tend to treat these problems from a psychological rather than from a strictly epistemological point of view. That is to say, they tend to concentrate their attention on the question, how do our ideas arise? And this is obviously a psychological question. Again, in English empiricism we can see the growth of the associationist psychology. Further, in his introduction to the *Treatise of Human Nature* Hume speaks explicitly of the need for developing the science of man on an empirical basis. Natural philosophy, he says, has already been established on an experimental or empirical basis; but philosophers have only just begun to put the science of man on a like footing.

Now, a scientist such as Galileo, who was concerned with bodies in motion, could, of course, confine himself to the material world and to questions of physics and astronomy. But the view of the world as a mechanical system raised problems which the metaphysical philosopher could not evade. In particular since man is a being within the world, the question arises whether or not he falls wholly within the mechanical system. Obviously, there are two possible general lines of answer. On the one hand the philosopher may defend the view that man possesses a spiritual soul, endowed with the power of free choice, and that in virtue of this spiritual and free soul he partly transcends the material world and the system of mechanical causality. On the other hand he may extend the scientific conception of the material universe to include man as a whole. Psychical processes will then be probably interpreted as epiphenomena of physical processes or, more crudely, as being themselves material, and human freedom will be denied.

Descartes was convinced of the truth of the first answer, though he spoke of mind rather than of soul. The material world can be described in terms of matter, identified with geometrical extension, and motion. And all bodies, including living bodies, are in some sense machines. But man as a whole cannot be simply reduced to a member of this mechanical system. For he possesses a spiritual mind which transcends the material world and the determining laws of efficient causality which govern this world. At the very threshold of the modern era, therefore, we find the so-called 'father of modern philosophy' asserting the existence of spiritual reality in general and of man's spiritual mind in particular. And this assertion was not merely the relic of an old tradition; it was an integral part of Descartes' system and represented part of his answer to the challenge of the new scientific outlook.

Descartes' interpretation of man gave rise, however, to a particular problem. For if man consists of two clearly distinguishable substances, his nature tends to fall apart and no longer to possess a unity. It then becomes very difficult to account for the evident facts of psycho-physical interaction. Descartes himself asserted that the mind can and does act on the body: but his theory of interaction was felt to be one of the least satisfactory features of his system. And Cartesians such as Geulincx, who are generally known as 'occasionalists', refused to admit that two heterogeneous types of substances can act on one another. When interaction apparently takes place, what really occurs is that on the occasion of a psychic event God causes the corresponding physical event, or conversely. Thus the occasionalists had recourse to the divine activity to explain the apparent facts of interaction. But it is not immediately evident how, if the mind cannot act on the body, God can do so. And in the system of Spinoza the problem of interaction was eliminated, because mind and body were regarded as two aspects of one reality. In the philosophy of Leibniz, however, the problem reappears in a somewhat different form. It is no longer the question how can there be interaction between two heterogeneous types of substances, but rather how there can be interaction between numerically distinct and independent monads, between, that is to say, the dominant monad which constitutes the human mind and the monads which constitute the body. And Leibniz's answer was similar to, though not precisely the same as, that of the occasionalists. God so created the monads that their activities are synchronized in a manner analogous to that in which the movements of the hands of two perfectly constructed clocks would correspond, though the one clock does not act on the other.

The occasionalists began, of course, with Descartes' idea of spiritual and material substances; and their peculiar theory presupposes this idea. But there were other philosophers who attempted to extend to man as a whole the new scientific conception of the world. In England Hobbes applied the fundamental ideas of Galileo's mechanics to all reality, that is, to all reality which can be significantly considered in philosophy. He equated substance with material substance, and he would not allow that the philosopher can envisage or treat of any other kind of reality. The philosopher, therefore, must consider man as purely material being, subject to the same laws as other bodies. Freedom is eliminated, and consciousness is interpreted as motion, reducible to changes in the nervous system.

On the Continent a number of eighteenth-century philosophers adopted a similarly crude materialism. For example, La Mettrie, author of *Man a Machine* (1748), represented man as a complicated material machine and the theory of a spiritual soul as a fable. In proposing this view he claimed Descartes as his direct ancestor. The latter had started to give a mechanistic interpretation of the world; but he had abandoned it at a certain point. He, La Mettrie, was concerned to complete the process by showing that man's psychical processes, no less than his physical processes, could be explained in terms of a mechanistic and materialist hypothesis.

The challenge of the new science, therefore, raised a problem in regard to man. True, the problem was in a sense an old problem; and in Greek philosophy we can find solutions which are analogous to the divergent solutions offered by Descartes and Hobbes in the seventeenth century. We have only to think of Plato on the one hand and of Democritus on the other. But though the problem was an old one, it was also a new one, in the sense that the development of the Galilean and Newtonian science placed it in a new light and emphasized its importance. At the end of the period covered in Volumes IV–VI we find Immanuel Kant attempting to combine an acceptance of the validity of Newtonian science with a belief in man's moral freedom. It would, indeed, be very misleading to say that Kant restated the position of Descartes; but if we draw a general line of division between those who extended the mechanistic outlook to include man in his totality and those who did not, we must place Descartes and Kant on the same side of the line.

When we are considering the shift of interest from theological themes to a study of Nature and of man without explicit reference to God, the following point is relevant. When Hume in the eighteenth century spoke about the science of man, he included moral philosophy or ethics. And in British philosophy in general during the period between the Renaissance and the end of the eighteenth century we can observe that strong interest in ethics which has continued to be one of the leading characteristics of British thought. Further, it is generally true, though there are certainly exceptions, that the English moralists of the period endeavoured to develop an ethical theory without theological presuppositions. They do not start, as did St. Thomas Aquinas[1] in the thirteenth century, with the idea of the eternal law of God and then descend to the idea of the natural moral law, considered as an expression of the former. Instead they tend to treat ethics without reference to metaphysics. Thus British moral philosophy in the eighteenth century illustrates the tendency of post-mediaeval philosophical thought to pursue its course independently of theology.

Analogous remarks can be made about political philosophy. Hobbes in the seventeenth century certainly writes at some length about ecclesiastical matters; but this does not mean that his political theory is dependent on theological presuppositions. For Hume in the eighteenth century political philosophy is part of the science of man, and in his eyes it has no connection with theology or, indeed, with metaphysics in general. And the political theory of Rousseau in the same century was also what one may call a secularist theory. The outlook of men such as Hobbes, Hume and Rousseau was very different from that of St. Thomas Aquinas[2] and still more from that of St. Augustine.[3] We can,

---

[1] For St. Thomas's moral theory, see vol. II, ch. XXXIX.
[2] See vol. II, ch. XL.   [3] Ibid., ch. VIII.

indeed, see their outlook prefigured in the writings of Marsilius of Padua[1] in the first half of the fourteenth century. But Marsilius was scarcely the typical political philosopher of the Middle Ages.

In this section I have emphasized the influence of physical science on the philosophy of the seventeenth and eighteenth centuries. In the Middle Ages theology was regarded as the supreme science, but in the post-mediaeval period the natural sciences begin to occupy the centre of the stage. In the seventeenth and eighteenth centuries, however, we are still in a period when the philosopher is confident that he, like the scientist, can add to our knowledge of the world. True, this statement stands in need of considerable qualification if we bear in mind the scepticism of David Hume. But, generally speaking, the mood is one of optimistic confidence in the power of the philosophical mind. And this confidence is stimulated and intensified by the successful development of physical science. The latter has not yet so completely dominated the scene as to produce in many minds the suspicion, or even the conviction, that philosophy can add nothing to our factual knowledge of reality. Or to put the matter in another way, if philosophy has ceased to be the handmaid of theology, it has not yet become the charwoman of science. It receives a stimulus from science, but it asserts its autonomy and independence. Whether or not the results encourage one to accept its claims, is another question. It is in any case not a question which can be profitably discussed in an introduction to the history of philosophy in the period of which we are treating.

2. It is customary to divide pre-Kantian modern philosophy into two main streams, the one comprising the rationalist systems of the Continent from Descartes to Leibniz and his disciple Christian Wolff, the other comprising British empiricism down to and including Hume. This division has been adopted here. And in this section I wish to make some introductory remarks about continental rationalism.

In the broadest sense of the term a rationalist philosopher would presumably be one who relied on the use of his reason and who did not have recourse to mystical intuitions or to feelings. But this broad sense of the term is quite insufficient for distinguishing the great continental systems of the seventeenth and

[1] See vol. III, ch. XI.

eighteenth centuries from British empiricism. Locke, Berkeley and Hume would all maintain that they relied on reasoning in their philosophical reflections. For the matter of that, the term, if understood in this broad sense, will not serve for distinguishing the metaphysics of the seventeenth and eighteenth centuries from mediaeval metaphysics. Some critics may accuse St. Thomas Aquinas, for example, of wishful thinking, in the sense that in their opinion he found inadequate reasons for accepting conclusions which he already believed on non-rational grounds and which he wished to defend. But Aquinas himself was certainly convinced that his philosophy was a product of rational reflection. And if the accusation against him were valid, it would apply equally well to Descartes.

In common parlance a rationalist is now generally understood to be a thinker who denies the supernatural and the idea of the divine revelation of mysteries. But, quite apart from the fact that this use of the term presupposes that there is no rational evidence for the existence of the supernatural and no rational motives for believing that there is any divine revelation in the theological sense, it would certainly not provide us with a distinctive characteristic of continental pre-Kantian philosophy as contrasted with British empiricism. The term, as used in this sense, would fit, for example, a number of French philosophers of the eighteenth century. But it would not fit Descartes. For there is no adequate reason for denying or even doubting his sincerity either in elaborating proofs of the existence of God or in accepting the Catholic faith. If we wish to use the term 'rationalism' to distinguish the leading continental systems of the seventeenth and eighteenth centuries from British empiricism, we have to assign some other meaning to it. And perhaps this can most easily be done by referring to the problem of the origin of knowledge.

Philosophers such as Descartes and Leibniz accepted the idea of innate or *a priori* truths. They did not think, of course, that a newly-born infant perceives certain truths from the moment when it comes into the world. Rather did they think that certain truths are virtually innate in the sense that experience provides no more than the occasion on which the mind by its own light perceives their truth. These truths are not inductive generalizations from experience, and their truth stands in need of no empirical confirmation. It may be that I perceive the truth of a self-evident principle only on the occasion of experience; but its truth does not depend on experience. It is seen to be true in itself, this truth being logically antecedent to experience even though, from the psychological point of view, we may come to an explicit perception of its truth only on the occasion of experience. According to Leibniz, such truths are prefigured, in some undetermined sense, in the mind's structure, even though they are not known explicitly from the first moment of consciousness. They are, therefore, virtually rather than actually innate.

But a belief in self-evident principles is not sufficient by itself to characterize the continental metaphysicians of the seventeenth and eighteenth centuries. The mediaeval metaphysicians too had believed in self-evident principles, though Aquinas saw no adequate reason for calling them innate. The point which characterizes Descartes, Spinoza and Leibniz is rather their ideal of deducing from such principles a system of truths which would give information about reality, about the world. I say 'their ideal' because we cannot assume, of course, that their philosophies do in fact constitute pure deductions from self-evident principles. If they did, it would be extremely odd that their philosophies should be mutually incompatible. But their ideal was the ideal of a deductive system of truths, analogous to a mathematical system but at the same time capable of increasing our factual information. Spinoza's chief work is entitled *Ethica more geometrico demonstrata* (*Ethics demonstrated in a geometrical manner*), and it purports to expound the truth about reality and man in a quasi-mathematical manner, beginning with definitions and axioms and proceeding through the orderly proving of successive propositions to the building up of a system of conclusions, the truth of which is known with certainty. Leibniz conceived the notion of a universal symbolic language and of a universal logical method or calculus, by means of which we could not only systematize all existing knowledge but also deduce hitherto unknown truths. And if the fundamental principles are said to be virtually innate, the entire system of deducible truths can be considered as the self-unfolding of the reason itself.

It is obvious that the rationalist philosophers were influenced by the model of mathematical reasoning. That is to say, mathematics provides a model of clarity, certainty and orderly deduction. The personal element, subjective factors such as feeling, are eliminated, and a body of propositions, the truth of which is assured, is built up. Could not philosophy attain a like objectivity and certainty, if an appropriate method, analogous to that of mathematics, were employed? The use of the right method could make metaphysical philosophy, and even ethics, a science in the fullest sense of the word instead of a field for verbal wrangling, unclarified ideas, faulty reasoning and mutually incompatible conclusions. The personal element could be eliminated, and philosophy would possess the characteristics of universal, necessary and impersonal truth which is possessed by pure mathematics. Such considerations, as will be seen later, weighed heavily with Descartes.

It is commonly maintained today that pure mathematics as such does not give us factual information about the world. To take a simple example, if we define a triangle in a certain way, it must possess certain properties, but we cannot deduce from this the conclusion that there exist triangles possessing these properties. All that we can deduce is that if a triangle exists which fulfils the definition, it possesses these properties. And an obvious criticism of the rationalists is that they did not understand the difference between mathematical and existential propositions. This criticism is not, indeed, altogether fair. For, as will be shown later, Descartes endeavoured to found his system on an existential proposition and not on what some writers call a 'tautology'. At the same time it can scarcely be denied that there was a tendency on the part of the rationalists to assimilate philosophy, including natural philosophy or physics, to pure mathematics and the causal relation to logical implication. But it is arguable that the background of Renaissance science encouraged them to think in this way. And I wish now to illustrate this point.

That Nature is, as it were, mathematical in structure was the tenet of Galileo. 'As a physicist he tried to express the foundations of physics and the observed regularities of Nature in terms of mathematical propositions, so far as this was possible. As a philosopher he drew from the success of the mathematical method in physics the conclusion that mathematics is the key to the actual structure of reality.'[1] In *Il saggiatore*[2] Galileo declared that philosophy is written by God in the book of the universe, though we cannot read this book until we understand the language, which is that of mathematics. If, therefore, as Galileo maintained, the structure of Nature is mathematical in character, so that there is a conformity between Nature and mathematics, it is easy to

[1] Vol. III. p. 287.   [2] 6.

understand how philosophers who were dominated by the ideal of the mathematical method came to think that the application of this method in the philosophical field could lead to the discovery of hitherto unknown truths about reality.

In order, however, to appreciate the significance of Descartes' quest for certainty and of his looking to mathematics as a model for reasoning, it is desirable to bear in mind the revival of scepticism which was one of the aspects of Renaissance thought. When one thinks of French scepticism in the last part of the sixteenth century the name which comes first to mind is that of Montaigne (1533–92). And this is only natural, given his eminent position in the field of French literature. As was pointed out in the third volume of this *History*,[1] Montaigne revived the ancient arguments in favour of scepticism; the relativity and unreliable character of sense-experience, the mind's dependence on sense-experience and its consequent incapacity for attaining absolute truth, and our inability to solve the problems which arise out of the conflicting claims of the senses and the reason. Man lacks the power to construct any certain metaphysical system; and the fact that metaphysicians have arrived at different and incompatible conclusions bears witness to this. To exalt the powers of the human mind as the humanists did is absurd: rather should we confess our ignorance and the weakness of our mental capacities.

This scepticism about the possibility of attaining metaphysical and theological truth by the use of reason was eventually accepted by Charron (1541–1603), a priest. At the same time he insisted on man's obligation to humble himself before divine revelation, which must be accepted on faith. In the field of moral philosophy he accepted an ethics of Stoic inspiration. In the previous volume[2] mention was made of Justus Lipsius (1547–1606), one of the revivers of Stoicism during the Renaissance. Another was William Du Vair (1556–1621) who tried to harmonize the Stoic ethics with the Christian faith. It is understandable that at a time when scepticism in regard to metaphysics was influential the Stoic ideal of the morally independent man should exercise an attraction on some minds.

But scepticism was not confined to the elegant, literary version represented by Montaigne or to the fideism of Charron. It was represented also by a group of free-thinkers who had little difficulty in showing the inconsistencies in Charron's combination of

[1] pp. 228–30.   [2] Vol. III, p. 228.

scepticism with fideism. This combination had existed already in the fourteenth century; and some religiously-minded people are undoubtedly attracted by it. But it is scarcely a satisfactory position from the rational point of view. Further, the free-thinkers or 'libertines' interpreted the term 'nature', which plays such an important role in the Stoic ethic, in a very different sense from that in which Charron understood it. And the term is, indeed, ambiguous, as can be seen by considering the different senses in which it was taken by the Greeks.

The revival of scepticism, ranging from Montaigne's Pyrrhonism and Charron's fideism to scepticism combined with moral cynicism, is relevant to Descartes' attempt to set philosophy on a sure basis. In meeting the challenge he looked to mathematics as the model of certain and clear reasoning, and he desired to give to metaphysics a similar clarity and certainty. Metaphysics must here be understood as including philosophical, as distinct from dogmatic, theology. In Descartes' opinion the proofs which he offered of God's existence were absolutely valid. And he believed, therefore, that he had provided a firm foundation for belief in the truths revealed by God. That is to say, he believed that he had shown conclusively that there exists a God who is capable of revealing truths to mankind. As for ethics, Descartes was himself influenced by the revival of Stoicism, and though he did not develop a systematic ethics, he at any rate contemplated incorporating into his philosophy those Stoic principles which he recognized as true and valuable. In the moral philosophy of Spinoza too we can see a distinct flavour of Stoicism. Indeed, Stoicism was in certain important respects much better adapted for use in the philosophy of Spinoza than in that of Descartes. For Spinoza, like the Stoics, was both a monist and a determinist, whereas Descartes was neither.

Mention of differences between Descartes and Spinoza leads us to consider briefly the development of continental rationalism. To speak at length about this theme in an introductory chapter would be inappropriate. But a few words on the subject may serve to give the reader some preliminary, if necessarily inadequate, idea of the scheme of development which will be treated more at length in the chapters devoted to individual philosophers.

We have already seen that Descartes affirmed the existence of two different types of substances, spiritual and material. In this sense of the word he can be called a dualist. But he was not a dualist in the sense that he postulated two ultimate, independent ontological principles. There is a plurality of finite minds and there is a plurality of bodies. But both finite minds and bodies depend on God as creator and conserver. God is, as it were, the link between the sphere of finite spiritual substances and the corporeal sphere. In several important respects the philosophy of Descartes differs very much from the systems of the thirteenth-century metaphysicians; but if we attend merely to the statement that he was a theist and a pluralist who recognized an essential difference between spiritual and material substances, we can say that he preserved the tradition of mediaeval metaphysics. To say this alone would be, indeed, to give a very inadequate idea of Cartesianism. For one thing, it would leave out of account the diversity of inspiration and aim. But it is none the less worth bearing in mind the fact that the first outstanding continental philosopher of the modern era preserved a great deal of the general scheme of reality which was current in the Middle Ages.

When we turn to Spinoza, however, we find a monistic system in which the Cartesian dualism and the Cartesian pluralism are discarded. There is only one substance, the divine substance, possessing an infinity of attributes, two of which, thought and extension, are known to us. Minds are modifications of the one substance under the attribute of thought, while bodies are modifications of the same unique substance under the attribute of extension. The Cartesian problem of interaction between the finite mind and the finite body in man disappears, because mind and body are not two substances but parallel modifications of one substance.

Although the monistic system of Spinoza is opposed to the pluralistic system of Descartes, there are equally obvious connections. Descartes defined substance as an existent thing which requires nothing but itself in order to exist. But, as he explicitly acknowledges, this definition applies strictly to God alone, so that creatures can be called substances only in a secondary and analogical sense. Spinoza, however, adopting a similar definition of substance, drew the conclusion that there is only one substance, God, and that creatures cannot be more than modifications of the divine substance. In this limited sense his system is a development of that of Descartes. At the same time, in spite of the connections between Cartesianism and Spinozism, the inspirations and atmospheres of the two systems are very different. The latter system may perhaps be regarded as being partly the result of a speculative application of the new scientific outlook to the whole of reality; but it is also suffused with a quasi-mystical and pantheistic colouring and inspiration which shows through the formal, geometrical trappings and which is absent from Cartesianism.

Leibniz, with his ideal of a logical deduction of hitherto unknown truths about reality, might perhaps be expected to adopt a similar monistic hypothesis. And he evidently saw this himself. But in point of fact he put forward a pluralistic philosophy. Reality consists of an infinity of monads or active substances, God being the supreme monad. Thus as far as pluralism is concerned, his philosophy is more akin to that of Descartes than to that of Spinoza. At the same time he did not believe that there are two radically different types of substances. Each monad is a dynamic and immaterial centre of activity; and no monad can be identified with geometrical extension. This does not mean, however, that reality consists of an anarchic chaos of monads. The world is a dynamic harmony, expressing the divine intelligence and will. In the case of man, for example, there is a dynamic or operational unity between the monads of which he is composed. And so it is with the universe. There is a universal harmony of monads conspiring together, as it were, for the attainment of a common end. And the principle of this harmony is God. The monads are so knit together that, even though one monad does not act directly on another, any change in any monad is reflected throughout the whole system in the divinely pre-established harmony. Each monad reflects the whole universe: the macrocosm is reflected in the microcosm. An infinite mind, therefore, could read off, as it were, the whole universe by contemplating one single monad.

If, therefore, we wish to regard the development of continental rationalism as a development of Cartesianism, we can say perhaps that Spinoza developed Cartesianism as viewed from a static point of view, while Leibniz developed it from a dynamic point of view. With Spinoza Descartes' two kinds of substances become so many modifications of one substance considered under two of its infinite attributes. With Leibniz the Cartesian pluralism is retained, but each substance or monad is interpreted as an immaterial centre of activity, the Cartesian idea of material substance, identifiable with geometrical extension and to which motion is added from without, as it were, being eliminated. Or one can express the development in another way. Spinoza resolves the Cartesian dualism by postulating a substantial or ontological monism, in which Descartes' plurality of substances become modifications or 'accidents' of one divine substance. Leibniz, however, eliminates the Cartesian dualism by asserting a monism of quite a different type from that asserted by Spinoza. All monads or substances are in themselves immaterial. We thus have monism in the sense that there is only one kind of substance. But at the same time the Cartesian pluralism is retained, inasmuch as there is a plurality of monads. Their dynamic unity is due, not to their being modifications or accidents of one divine substance, but to the divinely pre-established harmony.

A further way of expressing the development would be this. In the Cartesian philosophy there is a sharp dualism in the sense that the laws of mechanics and of efficient causality hold good in the material world, whereas in the spiritual world there is freedom and teleology. Spinoza eliminates this dualism by means of his monistic hypothesis, assimilating the causal connections between things to logical implication. As in a mathematical system conclusions flow from the premisses, so in the universe of Nature modifications or what we call things, together with their changes, flow from the one ontological principle, the divine substance. Leibniz, however, tries to combine mechanical causality with teleology. Each monad unfolds and develops according to an inner law of change, but the whole system of changes is directed, in virtue of the pre-established harmony, to the attainment of an end. Descartes excluded from natural philosophy or physics the consideration of final causes. But for Leibniz there is no need to choose between mechanical and final causality. They are really two aspects of one process.

The influence of mediaeval philosophy on the rationalist systems of the pre-Kantian era is sufficiently obvious. For instance, all three philosophers utilize the category of substance. At the same time the idea of substance undergoes equally obvious changes. With Descartes material substance is identified with geometrical extension, a theory which is foreign to mediaeval thought, while Leibniz tries to give an essentially dynamic interpretation to the concept of substance. Again, though the idea of God plays an integral part in the systems of all three thinkers, we can see, in the philosophies of Spinoza and Leibniz at any rate, a tendency to eliminate the idea of personal and voluntary creation. This is evidently the case with Spinoza. The divine substance expresses itself necessarily in its modifications, not, of course, by a necessity imposed from without (this is impossible, because there is no other substance), but by an inner necessity. Human freedom, therefore, goes by the board, together with the Christian concepts of sin, merit and so on. Leibniz, indeed, endeavoured to combine his idea of quasi-logical development of the world with the recognition of contingency and of human freedom. And he made distinctions with this end in view. But, as will be seen in due course, it is arguable that his efforts were not particularly successful. He attempted to 'rationalize' the mediaeval (or, more accurately, Christian) conception of the mystery of personal and voluntary creation, while retaining the fundamental idea; but the task which he set himself was no easy one. Descartes was, indeed, a believing Catholic, and Leibniz professed himself a Christian. But in continental rationalism as a whole we can see a tendency towards the speculative rationalization of Christian dogmas.[1] This tendency reached its climax in the philosophy of Hegel in the nineteenth century, though Hegel belongs, of course, to a different period and to a different climate of thought.

3. We have seen that the certainty of mathematics, its deductive method and its successful application in Renaissance science helped to provide the continental rationalists with a model of method and an ideal of procedure and purpose. But there was another side to Renaissance science besides its use of mathematics. For scientific progress was also felt to depend very largely on attention to empirical data and on the use of controlled experiment. Appeal to authority and to tradition was ousted in favour of experience, of reliance on factual data and on the empirical testing of hypotheses. And although we cannot account for the rise of British empiricism merely in terms of the conviction that scientific advance was based on actual observation of the empirical data, the development of the experimental method in the sciences naturally tended to stimulate and confirm the theory that all our knowledge is based on perception, on direct acquaintance with internal and external events. Indeed, 'The scientific insistence on going to the observable "facts" as a necessary basis for explanatory theory found its correlative and its theoretical justification in the empiricist thesis that our factual knowledge is ultimately based on

---

[1] This statement does not cover Spinoza, who was not a Christian. And it does not refer, of course, to those eighteenth-century writers who rejected Christian dogma. But these writers, though 'rationalists' in a modern sense of the term, were not speculative philosophers after the style of Descartes and Leibniz.

perception.'[1] We cannot obtain factual knowledge by *a priori* reasoning, by quasi-mathematical deduction from alleged innate ideas or principles, but only by experience and within the limits of experience. There is, of course, such a thing as *a priori* reasoning. We see it in pure mathematics. And by such reasoning we reach conclusions which are certain. But mathematical propositions do not give us factual information about the world; they state, as Hume put it, relations between ideas. For factual information about the world, indeed about reality in general, we have to turn to experience, to sense-perception and to introspection. And though such inductively-based knowledge enjoys varying degrees of probability, it is not and cannot be absolutely certain. If we wish for absolute certainty, we must confine ourselves to propositions which state something about the relations of ideas or the implications of the meanings of symbols, but which do not give us factual information about the world. If we wish for factual information about the world, we must content ourselves with probabilities, which is all that inductively-based generalizations can give us. A philosophical system which possesses absolute certainty and which at the same time would give us information about reality and be capable of indefinite extension through the deductive discovery of hitherto unknown factual truths is a will-o'-the-wisp.

True, this description of empiricism certainly will not fit all those who are customarily reckoned as empiricists. But it indicates the general tendency of this movement of thought. And the nature of empiricism is revealed most clearly in its historical development, since it is possible to regard this development as consisting, in large part at least, in a progressive application of the thesis, enunciated by Locke, that all our ideas come from experience, from sense-perception and from introspection.

In view of his insistence on the experimental basis of knowledge and on induction as contrasted with deduction, Francis Bacon can be called an empiricist. The appositeness of this name is not, however, so clear in the case of Hobbes. He maintained, indeed, that all our knowledge begins with sensation and can be traced back to sensation as its ultimate fount. And this entitles us to call him an empiricist. At the same time he was deeply influenced by the idea of mathematical method as a model of reasoning, and in this respect he stands closer to the continental rationalists than

[1] Vol. III, p. 290.

do other British philosophers of the early modern period. He was, however, a nominalist, and he did not think that we can in fact demonstrate causal relations. He certainly tried to extend the scope of Galileo's mechanics to cover all the subject-matter of philosophy; but it is more appropriate, I think, to class him with the empiricists than with the rationalists, if we have to choose between the two labels. And I have followed this procedure in the present volume, while at the same time I have attempted to point out some of the requisite qualifications.

The real father of classical British empiricism, however, was John Locke (1632–1704), whose declared aim was to inquire into the source, certainty and extent of human knowledge, and also into the grounds and degrees of belief, opinion and assent. In connection with the first problem, the source of our knowledge, he delivered a vigorous attack on the theory of innate ideas. He then attempted to show how all the ideas which we have can be explained on the hypothesis that they originate in sense-perception and in introspection or, as he put it, reflection. But though Locke asserted the ultimately experimental origin of all our ideas, he did not restrict knowledge to the immediate data of experience. On the contrary, there are complex ideas, built up out of simple ideas, which have objective references. Thus we have, for example, the idea of material substance, the idea of a substratum which supports primary qualities, such as extension, and those 'powers' which produce in the percipient subject ideas of colour, sound and so on. And Locke was convinced that there actually are particular material substances, even though we can never perceive them. Similarly, we have the complex idea of the causal relation; and Locke used the principle of causality to demonstrate the existence of God, of a being, that is to say, who is not the object of direct experience. In other words, Locke combined the empiricist thesis that all our ideas originate in experience with a modest metaphysics. And if there were no Berkeley and no Hume, we might be inclined to look on Locke's philosophy as a watered-down form of Scholasticism, with Cartesian elements thrown in, the whole being expressed in a sometimes confused and inconsistent manner. In point of fact, however, we not unnaturally tend to regard his philosophy as the point of departure for his empiricist successors.

Berkeley (1685–1753) attacked Locke's conception of material substance. He had, indeed, a particular motive for dwelling at length on this point. For he considered that belief in material substance was a fundamental element in materialism, which, as a devout Christian, he was intent on refuting. But he had, of course, other grounds for attacking Locke's thesis. There was the general empiricist ground or reason, namely, that material substance as defined by Locke is an unknowable substrate. We have, therefore, no clear idea of it, and we have no warrant for saying that it exists. A so-called material thing is simply what we perceive it to be. But nobody has perceived or can perceive an imperceptible substrate. Experience, then, gives us no ground for asserting its existence. But there were other reasons which arose out of Locke's unfortunate habit or common, though not invariable, practice of speaking as though it is ideas which we perceive directly, and not things. Starting with Locke's position in regard to secondary and primary qualities (which will be explained in the chapter on Locke), Berkeley argued that all of them, including the primary qualities, such as extension, figure and motion, are ideas. He then asked how ideas could possibly exist in or be supported by a material substance. If all that we perceive is ideas, these ideas must exist in minds. To say that they exist in an unknowable, material substrate is to make an unintelligible statement. The latter has no possible function to fulfil.

To say that Berkeley got rid of Locke's material substance is to mention only one aspect of his empiricism. And just as Locke's empiricism is only a part of his philosophy, so is Berkeley's empiricism only one aspect of his philosophy. For he went on to build up a speculative idealist metaphysic, for which the only realities are God, finite minds and the ideas of finite minds. Indeed, he used his empiricist conclusions as a foundation of a theistic metaphysic. And this attempt to erect a metaphysical philosophy on the basis of a phenomenalistic account of material things constitutes one of the chief points of interest in Berkeley's thought. But in giving a brief and necessarily inadequate sketch of the development of classical British empiricism it is sufficient to draw attention to his elimination of Locke's material substance. If we leave aside the theory of 'ideas', we can say that for Berkeley the so-called material thing or sensible object consists simply of phenomena, of those qualities which we perceive in it. And this, in Berkeley's opinion, is precisely what the man-in-the-street believes it to consist of. For he has never heard of, let alone perceived, any occult substance or substratum. In the eyes of the plain man the tree is simply that which we perceive it, or can perceive it, to be. And we perceive, and can perceive, only qualities.

Now, Berkeley's phenomenalistic analysis of material things was not extended to finite selves. In other words, though he eliminated material substance, he retained spiritual substance. Hume (1711–76), however, proceeded to eliminate spiritual substance as well. All our ideas are derived from impressions, the elementary data of experience. And in order to determine the objective reference of any complex idea, we have to ask, from what impressions is it derived. Now, there is no impression of a spiritual substance. If I look into myself, I perceive only a series of psychic events such as desires, feelings, thoughts. Nowhere do I perceive an underlying, permanent substance or soul. That we have some idea of a spiritual substance can be explained by reference to the working of mental association; but we have no ground for asserting that such a substance exists.

Analysis of the idea of spiritual substance, however, does not occupy so prominent a position in Hume's writings as his analysis of the causal relation. In accordance with his regular programme he asks from what impression or impressions is our idea of causality derived. And he answers that all that we observe is constant conjunction. When, for example, A is always followed by B, in such a way that when A is absent B does not occur and that when B occurs it is, as far as we can ascertain empirically, always preceded by A, we speak of A as the cause and of B as the effect. To be sure, the idea of necessary connection also belongs to our idea of causality. But we cannot point to any sense-impression from which it is derived. The idea can be explained with the help of the principle of association: it is, so to speak, a subjective contribution. We can inspect the objective relations between cause A and effect B as long as we like; we shall find nothing more than constant conjunction.

In this case we obviously cannot legitimately use the principle of causality to transcend experience in such a way as to extend our knowledge. We say that A is the cause of B because, so far as our experience goes, we find that the occurrence of A is always followed by the occurrence of B and that B never occurs when A has not previously occurred. But though we may believe that B has some cause, we cannot legitimately argue that A is this cause unless we observe A and B occurring in the relation which has just been described. We cannot argue, therefore, that phenomena are caused by substances which are not only never observed but also in principle unobservable. Nor can we argue, as in their different ways both Locke and Berkeley argued, to the existence of God. We can form a hypothesis if we like; but no causal argument in favour of God's existence can possibly give us any certain knowledge. For God transcends our experience. With Hume, therefore, the metaphysics of both Locke and Berkeley go overboard, and both minds and bodies are analysed in phenomenalistic terms. In fact we can be certain of very little, and scepticism may seem to result. But, as will be seen later, Hume answers that we cannot live and act in accordance with pure scepticism. Practical life rests on beliefs, such as belief in the uniformity of nature, which cannot be given any adequate rational justification. But this is no reason for renouncing these beliefs. In his study a man may be a sceptic, realizing how little is capable of proof; but when he turns from his academic reflections he has to act on the fundamental beliefs according to which all men act, whatever their philosophical views may be.

The aspect of classical British empiricism which first impresses itself on the mind is perhaps its negative aspect, namely, the progressive elimination of traditional metaphysics. But it is important to note the more positive aspects. For example, we can see the growth of the approach to philosophy which is now generally known as logical or linguistic analysis. Berkeley asks what it means to say of a material thing that it exists. And he answers that to say that a material thing exists is to say that it is perceived by a subject. Hume asks what it means to say that A is the cause of B, and he gives a phenomenalistic answer. Moreover, in the philosophy of Hume we can find all the main tenets of what is sometimes called 'logical empiricism'. That this is the case will be shown later. But it is worth while pointing out in advance that Hume is very much a living philosopher. True, he often expresses in psychological terms questions and answers which would be expressed in a different way even by those who accept him as being in some sense their 'master'. But this does not affect the fact that he is one of those philosophers whose thought is a living force in contemporary philosophy.

4. It is in the seventeenth rather than in the eighteenth century that we see the most vigorous manifestation of the impulse to systematic philosophical construction which owed so much to the

new scientific outlook. The succeeding century is not marked to the same extent by brilliant and bold metaphysical speculation, and in its last decades philosophy takes a new turn with the thought of Immanuel Kant.

If we leave out of account Francis Bacon, we can say that the seventeenth century is headed by two systems, that of Descartes on the Continent and that of Hobbes in England. From both the epistemological and the metaphysical points of view their philosophies are very different. But both men were influenced by the ideal of mathematical method, and both were systematizers on the grand scale. One can note that Hobbes, who had personal relations with Mersenne, a friend of Descartes, was acquainted with the latter's *Meditations* and wrote a series of objections against them, to which Descartes replied.

The philosophy of Hobbes excited a sharp reaction in England. In particular the so-called Cambridge Platonists, such as Cudworth (1617–88) and Henry More (1614–87), opposed his materialism and determinism and what they regarded as his atheism. They were also opposed to empiricism and are frequently called 'rationalists'. But though some of them were, indeed, influenced to a minor extent by Descartes, their rationalism sprang rather from other sources. They believed in fundamental speculative and ethical truths or principles which are not derived from experience but discerned immediately by reason, and which reflect the eternal divine truth. They were also concerned to show the reasonableness of Christianity. They can be called Christian Platonists, provided that the term 'Platonist' is understood in a wide sense. In histories of philosophy they are rarely accorded a prominent position. But it is as well to remember their existence if for no other reason than as a corrective to the not uncommon persuasion that British philosophy has been throughout empiricist in character, apart, of course, from the idealist interlude of the second half of the nineteenth and the first decades of the twentieth centuries. Empiricism is doubtless the distinguishing characteristic of English philosophy; but at the same time there is another, if less prominent, tradition, of which Cambridge Platonism in the seventeenth century forms one phase.

Cartesianism was far more influential on the Continent than was the system of Hobbes in England. At the same time it is a mistake to think that Cartesianism swept everything before it, even in France. A notable example of unfavourable reaction is seen in the case of Blaise Pascal (1623–62). Pascal, the Kierkegaard of the seventeenth century, was uncompromising in his opposition, not, of course, to mathematics (he was himself a mathematical genius), but to the spirit of Cartesianism, which he regarded as naturalistic in character. In the interests of Christian apologetics he emphasized on the one hand the weakness of man and on the other his need of faith, of submission to revelation and of supernatural grace.

We have already seen that Descartes left behind him a legacy in the form of the problem of interaction between mind and body, a problem which was discussed by the occasionalists. Among their names we sometimes find that of Malebranche (1638–1715). But though the latter can be called an occasionalist if we consider only one element of his thought, his philosophy went far beyond occasionalism. It was a metaphysical system of an original stamp which combined elements taken from Cartesianism with elements developed under Augustinian inspiration and which might have become a system of idealistic pantheism, had not Malebranche, who was an Oratorian priest, endeavoured to remain within the bounds of orthodoxy. As it is, his philosophy remains one of the most notable products of French thought. Incidentally, it exercised some influence on the mind of Bishop Berkeley in the eighteenth century.

In the seventeenth century we have, therefore, the systems of Hobbes, Descartes and Malebranche. But these philosophies are by no means the only notable achievements of the century. The year 1632 saw the births of two of the chief thinkers of the pre-Kantian period of modern philosophy, of Spinoza in Holland and of Locke in England. But their lives, as well as their philosophies, were very different. Spinoza was more or less a recluse, a man dominated by a vision of the one reality, the one divine and eternal substance, which manifests itself in those finite modifications which we call 'things'. This one substance he called God or Nature. Obviously, we have here an ambiguity. If we emphasize the second name, we have a naturalistic monism in which the God of Christianity and Judaism (Spinoza was himself a Jew) is eliminated. In the period under discussion Spinoza was frequently understood in this sense and was accordingly regarded and execrated as an atheist. Hence his influence was extremely limited, and he did not come into his own until the German romantic movement and the period of German post-Kantian idealism, when the term 'God' in the phrase 'God or Nature' was emphasized and Spinoza was depicted as a 'God-intoxicated man'. Locke, on the contrary, was by no means a recluse. A friend of scientists and philosophers, he moved on the fringe of the great world and held some government posts. His philosophy, as has already been remarked, followed a rather traditional pattern; he was much respected; and he influenced profoundly not only the subsequent development of British philosophy but also the philosophy of the French Enlightenment in the eighteenth century. Indeed, in the extent of Locke's influence we see an evident refutation of the notion that British and continental thought in the pre-Kantian era flowed in parallel channels without any intermingling of their waters.

In 1642, ten years after the birth of Locke, there was born another of the most influential figures in modern thought, Isaac Newton. He was not, of course, primarily a philosopher, as we understand the word today, and his great importance consists in the fact that he completed to all intents and purposes the classical scientific conception of the world which Galileo in particular had done so much to promote. But Newton laid more stress than had Galileo on empirical observation, induction and the place of probability in science. And for this reason his physics tended to undermine the Galilean-Cartesian ideal of *a priori* method and to encourage the empiricist approach in the field of philosophy. Thus he influenced the mind of Hume to a considerable extent. At the same time, though Newton was not primarily a philosopher, he did not hesitate to go beyond physics or 'experimental philosophy' and to indulge in metaphysical speculation. Indeed, the confident way in which he drew metaphysical conclusions from physical hypotheses was attacked by Berkeley who saw that the tenuous character of the connections between Newton's physics and his theological conclusions might make a (for Berkeley) unfortunate impression on men's minds. And in point of fact a number of French philosophers of the eighteenth century, while accepting Newton's general approach to physics, employed it in a non-theistic setting which was alien to the latter's mind. At the end of the eighteenth century Newton's physics exercised a powerful influence on the thought of Kant.

Though he lived until 1716, Leibniz can be considered the last of the great seventeenth-century speculative philosophers. He evidently had some regard for Spinoza, though he did not manifest

INTRODUCTION

33

this regard to the public. Further, he attempted to hang Spinoza, as it were, round the neck of Descartes, as though the former's system were a logical development of the latter's. In other words, he seems to have been at pains to make it clear that his own philosophy differed greatly from those of his predecessors or, more accurately, that it contained their good points while omitting the bad points in Cartesianism which led to its development into the system of Spinoza. However this may be, there can be no doubt that Leibniz remained faithful to the general spirit and inspiration of continental rationalism. He made a careful critical study of Locke's empiricism, which was eventually published as *New Essays Concerning the Human Understanding*.

Like Newton (and, indeed, like Descartes), Leibniz was an eminent mathematician, though he did not agree with Newton's theories about space and time; and he carried on a controversy about this subject with Samuel Clarke, one of the latter's disciples and admirers. But though Leibniz was a great mathematician, and though the influence of his mathematical studies upon his philosophy is clear enough, his mind was so many-sided that it is not surprising if a great variety of elements and lines of thought can be found in his diverse writings. For example, his conception of the world as a dynamic and progressively self-unfolding and developing system of active entities (monads) and of human history as moving towards an intelligible goal probably had some effect on the rise of the historical outlook. Again, through some aspects of his thought such as his interpretation of space and time as phenomenal, he prepared the way for Kant. If, however, one mentions the influence of Leibniz or his partial anticipation of a thesis maintained by a later thinker, this is not to deny that his system is interesting in itself.

5. The eighteenth century is known as the century of the Enlightenment (also as the Age of Reason). This term can hardly be defined. For though we speak of the philosophy of the Enlightenment, no one school or set of determinate philosophical theories is meant. The term indicates, however, an attitude and a prevalent disposition of mind and outlook, and these can be described in a general way.

Provided that the word 'rationalistic' is not understood as necessarily referring to rationalism in the sense explained in section two of this chapter, one can say that the general spirit of the Enlightenment was rationalistic in character. That is to say, the typical thinkers and writers of the period believed that the human reason was the apt and only instrument for solving problems connected with man and society. Just as Newton had interpreted Nature and had set the pattern for the free, rational and unprejudiced investigation of the physical world, so should man employ his reason for interpreting moral, religious, social and political life. It may be said, of course, that the ideal of using the reason to interpret human life was in no way alien to the mediaeval mind. And this is true. But the point is that the writers of the Enlightenment generally meant by reason a reason unhampered by belief in revelation, by submission to authority, by deference to established customs and institutions. In the religious sphere some explained away religion in a naturalistic manner; but even those who retained religious belief based it simply on reason, without reference to unquestionable divine revelation or to emotional or mystical experience. In the moral sphere the tendency was to separate morality from all metaphysical and theological premisses and in this sense to make it autonomous. In the social and political spheres too the characteristic thinkers of the Enlightenment endeavoured to discover a rational foundation for and justification of political society. Mention was made in the first section of this chapter of Hume's idea that a science of man was needed to complement the science of Nature. And this idea represents very well the spirit of the Enlightenment. For the Enlightenment does not represent a humanistic reaction against the new development in science or natural philosophy, which began with the scientific phase of the Renaissance and which culminated in the work of Newton. It represents rather the extension of the scientific outlook to man himself and a combination of humanism, which had been a characteristic of the first phase of the Renaissance, with this scientific outlook.

There were, indeed, considerable differences between the ideas of the various philosophers of the Enlightenment. Some believed in self-evident principles, the truth of which is immediately discerned by the unprejudiced reason. Others were empiricists. Some believed in God, others did not. Again, there were considerable differences of spirit between the phases of the Enlightenment in Britain, France and Germany. In France, for example, the characteristic thinkers of the period were bitterly opposed to the *ancien régime* and to the Church. In England, however, the Revolution had already taken place, and Catholicism, with its strict concept of revelation and its authoritarianism, counted for very little, being to all intents and purposes still a proscribed religion. Hence we would not expect to find among the British philosophers of the Enlightenment the same degree of hostility towards the Established Church or towards the civil powers that we can find among a number of their French contemporaries. Again, crudely materialistic interpretations of the human mind and of psychical processes were more characteristic of a certain section of French thinkers than of British thinkers of the time.

At the same time, in spite of all differences in spirit and in particular tenets, there was considerable interchange of ideas between the writers of France and England. Locke, for instance, exercised a very considerable influence on eighteenth-century thought in France. There existed in fact a kind of international and cosmopolitan-minded set of thinkers and writers who were united at any rate in their hostility, which showed itself in varying degrees according to circumstances, to ecclesiastical and political authoritarianism and to what they regarded as obscurantism and tyranny. And they looked on philosophy as an instrument of liberation, enlightenment and social and political progress. They were, in short, rationalists more or less in the modern sense, free-thinkers with a profound confidence in the power of reason to promote the betterment of man and of society and with a belief in the deleterious effects of ecclesiastical and political absolutism. Or, to put the matter another way, the liberal and humanitarian rationalists of the nineteenth century were the descendants of the characteristic thinkers of the Enlightenment.

The great systems of the seventeenth century helped, of course, to prepare the way for the Enlightenment. But in the eighteenth century we find not so much outstanding philosophers elaborating original and mutually incompatible metaphysical systems as a comparatively large number of writers with a belief in progress and a conviction that 'enlightenment', diffused through philosophical reflection, would secure in man's moral, social and political life a degree of progress worthy of an age which already possessed a scientific interpretation of Nature. The eighteenth-century philosophers in France were scarcely of the stature of Descartes. But their writings, easily understandable by educated people and sometimes superficial, were undeniably influential. They contributed to the coming of the French Revolution. And the philosophers of the Enlightenment in general exercised a lasting influence on the formation of the liberal mind and on the growth of a secularist outlook. One may have a favourable or an unfavourable view of the ideas of men such as Diderot and Voltaire; but one can hardly deny that, for good or ill, their ideas exercised a powerful influence.

In England, Locke's writings contributed to the philosophical current of thought which is known as deism. In his work on the *Reasonableness of Christianity* and elsewhere he insisted on reason as the judge of revelation, though he did not reject the idea of revelation. The deists, however, tended to reduce Christianity to natural religion. True, they differed considerably in their views about religion in general and Christianity in particular. But, while believing in God, they tended to reduce the Christian dogmas to truths which can be established by reason and to deny the unique and supernatural character of Christianity and God's miraculous intervention in the world. Among the deists were John Toland (1670–1722), Matthew Tindal (*c.* 1656–1733) and the Viscount Bolingbroke (1678–1751), who looked on Locke as his master and as superior to most other philosophers put together. Among the opponents of the deists were Samuel Clarke (1675–1729) and Bishop Butler (1692–1752), author of the famous work *The Analogy of Religion*.

In eighteenth-century philosophy in England we find also a strong interest in ethics. Characteristic of the time is the moral-sense theory, represented by Shaftesbury (1671–1713), Hutcheson (1694–1746), to a certain extent Butler, and Adam Smith (1723–90). As against Hobbes's interpretation of man as fundamentally egoistic they insisted on man's social nature. And they maintained that man possesses an inborn 'sense' or sentiment by which he discerns moral values and distinctions. David Hume had affiliations with this current of thought in that he found the basis of moral attitudes and distinctions in feeling rather than in reasoning or the intuition of eternal and self-evident principles. But at the same time he contributed to the growth of utilitarianism. In the case of several important virtues, for example, the feeling or sentiment of moral approbation is directed towards that which is socially useful. In France utilitarianism was represented by Claude Helvetius (1715–71), who did much to prepare the way for the utilitarian moral theories of Bentham, James and John Stuart Mill in the nineteenth century.

Though Locke was not the first to mention or discuss the

principle of the association of ideas, it was largely through his influence that the foundations of the associationist psychology were laid in the eighteenth century. In England David Hartley (1705–57) tried to explain man's mental life with the aid of the principle of association of ideas, combined with the theory that our ideas are faint copies of sensations. He also tried to explain man's moral convictions with the aid of the same principle. And, in general, those moralists who started by assuming that man seeks by nature simply his own interest, in particular his own pleasure, used the principle to show how it is possible for man to seek virtue for its own sake and to act altruistically. For example, if the practice of some virtue is experienced by me as conducing to my own interest or benefit, I can come by the operation of the principle of association to approve of and practise this virtue without any advertence to the advantage which such conduct brings me. The utilitarians of the nineteenth century made copious use of this principle in explaining how altruism is possible in spite of the supposed fact that man naturally seeks his own satisfaction and pleasure.

The two outstanding eighteenth-century philosophers in Great Britain were obviously Berkeley and Hume. But it has already been mentioned that though the former's philosophy can be regarded as constituting a stage in the development of empiricism, it was at the same time much more than this. For on an empiricist foundation Berkeley developed an idealist and spiritualist metaphysics, orientated towards the acceptance of Christianity. His philosophy thus stands apart not only from deism but also from the interpretations of man which have just been mentioned. For the implicit tendency of the associationist current of thought was towards materialism and to the denial of any spiritual soul in man, whereas for Berkeley there are, besides God, only finite spirits and their ideas. Hume, however, though it would be wrong to call him a materialist, represents much better the spirit of the Enlightenment, with his empiricism, scepticism, liberalism and freedom from all theological assumptions and preoccupations.

In the last half of the century a reaction against empiricism and in favour of rationalism made itself felt. It was represented, for example, by Richard Price (1723–91) and Thomas Reid (1710–96). The former insisted that reason, not emotion, is authoritative in morals. We enjoy intellectual intuition of objective moral distinctions. For Reid and his followers there are a number of self-evident principles, principles of 'common sense', which are the foundation of all reasoning and which neither admit of direct proof nor need it. Just as the materialism of Hobbes stimulated the reaction of the Cambridge Platonists, so the empiricism of Hume stimulated a reaction. Indeed, there is continuity between the Cambridge Platonists and the Scottish philosophers of common sense, headed by Reid. Both groups represent a tradition in British philosophy which is weaker and less conspicuous than empiricism, but which is there none the less.

The deist movement in England had its counterpart in France. Voltaire (1694–1778), for example, was not an atheist, even though the Lisbon earthquake of 1755, while not making him abandon all belief in God, caused him to modify his views about the relation of the world to God and about the nature of the divine activity. But atheism was represented by a considerable number of writers. The Baron d'Holbach (1725–89), for instance, was a pronounced atheist. Ignorance and fear led to belief in the gods, weakness worshipped them, credulity preserves them, tyranny uses religion for its own ends. La Mettrie (1709–51) was also an atheist, and he tried to improve on the assertion of Pierre Bayle (1647–1706) that a State of atheists is possible[1] by saying that it is desirable. Again, Diderot (1713–84), who was one of the editors of the *Encyclopédie*,[2] passed from deism to atheism. All these writers, both deists and atheists, were anti-clericals and hostile to Catholicism.

Locke endeavoured to explain the origin of our ideas on empiricist principles; but he did not reduce man's psychical life to sensation. Condillac (1715–80), however, who aimed at developing a consistent empiricism, tried to explain all mental life in terms of sensations, 'transformed' sensations and signs or symbols. His sensationalism, which was worked out in an elaborate manner, was influential in France; but for outspoken materialism we have to turn rather to other writers. Mention has already been made of La Mettrie's attempt in *Man a Machine* to extend Descartes' mechanistic interpretation of infra-human life and of the body to man as a totality. D'Holbach maintained that mind is an epiphenomenon of the brain, and Cabanis (1757–1808) summed up

---

[1] Bayle maintained that religion does not affect morality.
[2] This work, edited by Diderot and d'Alembert, was designed to give an account of the progress achieved in the different sciences and, by implication at least, to promote a secularist outlook.

his idea of man in the often quoted words, *Les nerfs—voilà tout l'homme*. According to him, the brain secretes thought as the liver secretes bile. Goethe later described the unpleasant impression made on him in his student days by d'Holbach's *Système de la nature*.

A materialist interpretation of man, however, by no means always involved a rejection of moral ideals and principles. Thus Diderot emphasized the ideal of self-sacrifice and demanded of man benevolence, pity and altruism. D'Holbach, too, made morality consist in altruism, in service of the common good. And in the utilitarian theory of Helvetius the concept of the greatest possible happiness of the greatest number played a fundamental part. This moral idealism was, of course, separated from theological presuppositions and assumptions. Instead it was closely connected with the idea of social and legal reform. According to Helvetius, for example, the rational control of man's environment and the making of good laws would lead people to seek the public advantage. And d'Holbach emphasized the need for social and political reorganization. With appropriate systems of legislation, supported by sensible sanctions, and of education, man would be induced by his pursuit of his own advantage to act virtuously, that is to say, in a manner useful to society.

It has been remarked that the characteristic writers of the French Enlightenment were opposed to political tyranny. But this must not be taken to mean that they were all convinced 'democrats'. Montesquieu (1689–1755), indeed, concerned himself with the problem of liberty, and as a result of his analysis of the British constitution he insisted on the separation of powers as a condition of liberty. That is to say, the legislative, executive and judicial powers should be independent in the sense that they should not be subject to the will either of one man or of one body of men, whether of a small body of nobles or of the people. Montesquieu was opposed to any form of absolutism. But Voltaire, although he too was influenced by his knowledge of British practice and thought, particularly the thought of Locke, looked to the enlightened despot to achieve the necessary reforms. Like Locke, he advocated within limits the principle of toleration; but he was not notably concerned with the establishment of a democracy. One of his charges against the Church, for example, was that it exercised a hampering power over the sovereign and prevented really strong government. To find an outstanding advocate of democracy in a literal sense we have to turn to

Rousseau (1712–78). In general, we find among the writers of the
French Enlightenment either an insistence on constitutionalism,
as with Montesquieu, or the hope for an enlightened ruler, as
with Voltaire. But in both cases the inspiration of and admiration for British political life is evident, though Voltaire was
more impressed by freedom of discussion than by representative
government.

Locke had maintained the doctrine of natural rights, that is to
say, the natural rights of individuals, which are not derived from
the State and cannot legitimately be abolished by the State. This
theory, which has its antecedents in mediaeval thought and which
was applied in the American Declaration of Independence, was
influential also on the Continent. Voltaire, for example, supposed
that there are self-evident moral principles and natural rights.
Indeed, in a good deal of eighteenth-century French philosophy
we can find the same sort of attempt to combine empiricism with
elements derived from 'rationalism' that we find in Locke himself.
With the utilitarians, however, another point of view comes to the
fore. In the writings of Helvetius, for instance, the greatest
happiness of the greatest number replaces as the standard of value
Locke's natural rights. But Helvetius does not appear to have
fully understood that this substitution implied the rejection of the
theory of natural rights. For if utility is the standard, rights are
themselves justified only by their utility. In England, however,
this was seen by Hume. Rights are founded on convention, on
general rules which experience has shown to be useful, not on self-
evident principles or on eternal truths.

Liberty in the economic sphere was demanded by the so-called
'physiocrats', Quesnay (1694–1774) and Turgot (1727–81). If
governments abstain from all avoidable interference in this sphere,
and if individuals are left free to pursue their interests, the public
advantage will inevitably be promoted. The reason for this is that
there are natural economic laws which produce prosperity when
nobody interferes with their operation. Here we have the policy
of economic *laissez-faire*. It reflects to some extent the liberalism
of Locke; but it is obviously based on a naïve belief in the harmony
between the operation of natural laws[1] and the attainment of the
greatest happiness of the greatest number.

We have noticed the dismal materialism expounded by some of

[1] Clearly, the term 'natural law', as used in this context, must be sharply
distinguished from the term when used in the context of a 'rationalist' system of
ethics.

the French philosophers of the eighteenth century. But, speaking generally, the thinkers of the period, including the materialists, manifested a strong belief in progress and in the dependence of progress on intellectual enlightenment. This belief received its classic expression in France in the *Esquisse d'un tableau historique des progrès de l'esprit humain* (1794) by Condorcet (1743–94). The scientific culture which began in the sixteenth century is destined to indefinite development.

The belief of the Encyclopaedists and others that progress consists in intellectual enlightenment and in the growth of civilization and that progress of this kind is inevitably accompanied by moral progress was sharply challenged by Rousseau. Associated for a time with Diderot and his circle, Rousseau subsequently broke with them and insisted on the virtues of the natural or uncivilized man, on the corruption of man by historic social institutions and by civilization in its actual development, and on the importance of emotion and of the heart in human life. But he is far better known for his great political work, *The Social Contract*. For the moment, however, it is sufficient to say that though Rousseau's starting-point is individualistic, in the sense that the State is justified in terms of a contract between individuals, the whole tendency of his work is to stress the concept of society as against the concept of the individual. Of all the political writings of the French Enlightenment Rousseau's book proved to be the most influential. And one reason for its influence on later thinkers was the fact that the author tended to leave behind the liberal individualism which was one of the characteristics of the philosophy of his period.

We have seen that the philosophy of the Enlightenment in France was inclined to be more extreme than eighteenth-century thought in England. Deism tended to give place to atheism, empiricism to become outspoken materialism. When, however, we turn to the Enlightenment (*Aufklärung*) in Germany, we find a rather different atmosphere.

Leibniz was the first great German philosopher, and the first phase of the Enlightenment in Germany consisted in a prolongation of his philosophy. His doctrine was systematized, not without some changes in its contents, let alone in its spirit, by Christian Wolff (1679–1754). Unlike most of the other well-known philosophers of the pre-Kantian period, Wolff was a university professor; and the textbooks which he published

enjoyed a great success. Among his followers were Bilfinger
(1693–1750), Knutzen (1713–51), whose lectures at Königsberg
were attended by Kant, and Baumgarten (1714–62).

The second phase of the German *Aufklärung* shows the influence
of the Enlightenment in France and England. If it is said that
this phase is typified by Frederick the Great (1712–86), this does
not mean, of course, that the king was himself a philosopher. But
he admired the thinkers of the French Enlightenment, and he
invited both Helvetius and Voltaire to Potsdam. He looked upon
himself as the embodiment of the enlightened monarch, and he
endeavoured to spread education and science in his territory. He
is therefore of some importance in the philosophical field, as being
one of the instruments by which the influence of the French
Enlightenment was introduced to Germany.

Deism found a German defender in Samuel Reimarus
(1694–1768). Moses Mendelssohn (1729–86), one of the 'popular
philosophers' (so called because they excluded subtleties from
philosophy and tried to reduce it to the capacity of the mediocre
mind), was also influenced by the Enlightenment. But much more
important was Gotthold Ephraim Lessing (1729–81), the principal
literary representative of the *Aufklärung*. Well known for his
saying that if God were to offer him truth with one hand and the
search for truth with the other he would choose the latter, he did
not think in point of fact that in metaphysics and theology at
least absolute truth is attainable or, indeed, that there is such a
thing. Reason alone must decide about the content of religion,
but the latter cannot be given a final expression. There is, as it
were, a continuous education of the human race by God, to which
we cannot put a full stop at any given moment in the form of
unquestionable propositions. As for morality, it is in itself
independent of metaphysics and theology. The human race
attains its majority, as it were, when it comes to understand this
fact and when man does his duty without regard to reward either
in this life or in the next. By this idea of progress towards understanding the autonomy of ethics as well as by his rationalistic
attitude towards Christian doctrine and towards Biblical exegesis
Lessing gives ample evidence of the influence of eighteenth-
century thought in France and England.

In the third phase of eighteenth-century philosophy in Germany[1]

---

[1] I am excluding, of course, the philosophy of Kant, which will be briefly
treated in the eighth section of this chapter.

a different attitude manifests itself. Indeed, it is rather misleading to include this phase under the heading of the Enlightenment; and those writers who do so are accustomed to speak of men like Hamann, Herder and Jacobi as 'overcoming' the spirit of the Enlightenment. But it is convenient to mention them here.

Johann Georg Hamann (1730–88) disliked the intellectualism of the Enlightenment and what he regarded as the illegitimate dichotomy between reason and sensibility. Indeed, language itself shows the unjustifiable character of this separation. For in the word we see the union of reason and sense. With Hamann we find the analytical and rationalist outlook giving way before a synthesizing and almost mystical attitude. He revived Bruno's idea of the *coincidentia oppositorum* or synthesis of opposites,[1] and his aim was to see in Nature and in history the self-revelation of God.

A like reaction against rationalism appears in the thought of Friedrich Heinrich Jacobi (1743–1819). Reason alone, which in its isolation is 'heathen', brings us either to a materialistic, deterministic and atheistic philosophy or to the scepticism of Hume. God is apprehended by faith rather than by reason, by the heart or by intuitive 'feeling' rather than by the coldly logical and analytic process of the intellect. Indeed, Jacobi is one of the leading representatives of the idea of religious sentiment or feeling.

Johann Gottfried Herder (1744–1803), who will be mentioned again in the section on the rise of the philosophy of history, shared with Hamann his dislike of the separation between reason and sensibility and also his interest in the philosophy of language. It is true that Herder is linked with the characteristic thinkers of the French Enlightenment by his belief in progress; but he envisaged progress in a different manner. Instead of being concerned simply with the progress of man towards the development of one type, the type of the free-thinker who becomes, as it were, more and more separated from the Transcendent and from Nature, he tried to see history as a whole. Each nation has its own history and line of development, prefigured in its natural endowments and in its relations to its natural environment. At the same time the different lines of development form one pattern, one great harmony; and the whole process of evolution is the manifestation or working-out of divine providence.

---

[1] This idea was borrowed by Bruno from Nicholas of Cusa. See vol. III, ch. XV and ch. XVI, section 6.

These thinkers had, of course, some connections with the Enlightenment. And in Herder's idea of history we can find an application of some of Leibniz's ideas, and also the influence of Montesquieu. At the same time the spirit of a man like Herder is markedly different from that of a man like Voltaire in France or of Reimarus in Germany. Indeed, in their reaction against the narrow rationalism of the eighteenth century and in their feeling for the unity of Nature and history these thinkers may be considered as representatives of a period of transition between the philosophy of the Enlightenment and the speculative idealism of the nineteenth century.

6. In the third volume of this *History*[1] an account was given of the political theories of men such as Machiavelli, Hooker, Bodin and Grotius. The first outstanding political philosophy of the period covered in the present volume is that of Thomas Hobbes. His chief political work, *Leviathan*, which was published in 1651, appears to be, when regarded superficially, a resolute defence of absolute monarchy. And it is quite true that Hobbes, who had a horror of anarchy and of civil war, emphasizes centralized power and the indivisibility of sovereignty. But his theory has fundamentally nothing to do with the notion of the divine right of kings or with the principle of legitimacy, and it could be used to support any strong *de facto* government, whether a monarchy or not. This was seen at the time by those who thought, though wrongly, that Hobbes had written the *Leviathan* to flatter Cromwell.

Hobbes begins with an extreme statement of individualism. In the so-called 'state of nature', the state which precedes, logically at least, the formation of political society, each individual strives after his self-preservation and the acquisition of power for the better attainment of this end; and there is no law in existence with reference to which his actions can be called unjust. This is the state of the war of every man against every man. It is a state of atomic individualism. Whether it existed as a historical reality or not is a secondary question: the main point is that if we think away political society and all that follows from its institution, we are left with a multiplicity of human beings, each of which seeks his own pleasure and self-preservation.

At the same time reason makes men aware of the fact that self-preservation can best be secured if they unite and substitute organized co-operation for the anarchy of the state of nature in

[1] Ch. XX.

which no man can feel safe from his fellows but in which life is attended by constant fear. Hobbes depicts men, therefore, as making a social covenant by which each man agrees to hand over to a sovereign his right of governing himself provided that every other member of the prospective society does the same. This covenant is obviously a fiction, a philosophical and rationalistic justification of society. But the point is that the constitution of political society and the erection of the sovereign take place together, by one act. It follows that if the sovereign loses his power, the society is dissolved. And this is precisely what happened, as Hobbes thought, during the civil war. The cementing bond of society is the sovereign. Hence if enlightened self-interest dictates the formation of political society, it also dictates the concentration of power in the hands of the sovereign. Any division of sovereignty was abhorrent to Hobbes, as tending towards social dissolution. He was not interested in monarchic absolutism as such; he was concerned with the cohesion of society. And if one presupposes an egoistic and individualistic interpretation of man, it follows that concentration of power in the hands of the sovereign is required to overcome the centrifugal forces which are always at work.

Perhaps the most significant feature of Hobbes's political theory is its naturalism. He does, indeed, speak of laws of nature or natural law, but he has not got in mind the mediaeval metaphysically based concept of the moral natural law. He means the laws of self-preservation and power. Moral distinctions come into being with the formation of the State, the establishment of rights and the institution of positive law. True, Hobbes does pay at any rate some lip-service to the idea of divine law; but his thoroughgoing Erastianism shows that to all intents and purposes the will of the sovereign, expressed in law, is the norm of morality. At the same time Hobbes is not concerned to expound a totalitarian doctrine in so far as this means that all life, including, for instance, economic life, should be actively directed and controlled by the State. His view is rather that the institution of the State and the concentration of indivisible sovereignty renders it possible for men to pursue their several ends in security and in a well-ordered manner. And though he speaks of the commonwealth as the mortal god, to whom, after the immortal God, we owe reverence, it is obvious that the State is for him a creation of enlightened self-interest. And if the sovereign loses his power to govern and can no longer protect his subjects, that is the end of his title to rule.

Locke also starts from an individualistic position and makes society depend on a compact or agreement. But his individualism is different from that of Hobbes. The state of nature is not by essence a state of war between each man and his fellows. And in the state of nature there are natural rights and duties which are antecedent to the State. Chief among these rights is the right of private property. Men form political society for the more secure enjoyment and regulation of these rights. As for government, this is instituted by society as a necessary device to preserve peace, defend society and protect rights and liberties; but its function is, or should be, confined to this preservation of rights and liberty. And one of the most effective checks to unbridled despotism is the division of powers, so that the legislative and executive powers are not vested simply in the hands of one man.

With Locke, then, as with Hobbes, the State is the creation of enlightened self-interest, though the former stands closer to the mediaeval philosophers inasmuch as he allows that man is by nature inclined to social life and even impelled to it. The general spirit, however, of Locke's theory is different from that of Hobbes. Behind the latter we can see the fear of civil war and anarchy; behind the former we can see a concern with the preservation and promotion of liberty. The stress which Locke lays on the separation between the legislative and executive powers reflects to some extent the struggle between parliament and monarch. The emphasis placed on the right to property is often said to reflect the outlook of the Whig landowners, the class to which Locke's patrons belonged. And there is some truth in this interpretation, though it should not be exaggerated. Locke certainly did not envisage a monopoly of power in the hands of the landowners. According to the philosopher's statement, he wrote to justify, or hoped that his political treatise would justify, the Revolution of 1688. And it was his liberal outlook, with his defence of natural rights, and, within limits, of the principle of toleration, which exercised most influence on the eighteenth century, particularly in America. The common-sense atmosphere of his philosophy and its appearance (sometimes deceptive) of simplicity doubtless helped to extend its influence.

Both Hobbes and Locke founded the State on a covenant or compact or contract. Hume, however, pointed out the absence of historical support for this theory. He also observed that if government is justified by consent of the governed, as Locke thought, it would be extremely difficult to justify the Revolution of 1688 and the title of William of Orange to rule in England. For the majority of the people were simply not asked for their opinions. In fact, it would be very difficult to justify any extant government. Political obligation cannot be derived from expressed consent; for we acknowledge this obligation even when there is no evidence at all of any compact or agreement. It is founded rather on a sense of self-interest. Through experience men come to feel what is for their interest and they act in certain ways without making any explicit agreements to do so. Political society and civic obedience can be justified on purely utilitarian grounds without the need of having recourse either to philosophical fictions like that of the social compact or to eternal and self-evident truths. If we wish to find a justification for political society and political obligation, we can find it in their utility, which is first known by a kind of feeling or sense of interest.

When we turn to Rousseau we find again the idea of a social contract. Political society rests ultimately upon a voluntary agreement whereby men agree to renounce the freedom of the state of nature for their own advantage and to attain freedom to live according to law. In the state of nature each individual possesses complete independence and sovereignty over himself; and when they join together to form society, the sovereignty which originally belonged to them as separate individuals belongs to them corporately. And this sovereignty is inalienable. The executive appointed by the people is simply the servant or practical instrument of the people.

This doctrine of popular sovereignty represents the democratic side of Rousseau's political theory. He himself came from Geneva, and he admired the vigorous and independent political life of the Swiss canton, which he contrasted with the sophisticated and artificial atmosphere of French civilization and with the monarchic constitution and oppressive ways of the *ancien régime*. Indeed, Rousseau's ideas about active popular government would be quite impracticable in anything but a Greek city-state or a small Swiss canton. At the same time his democratic ideas were influential in the movement which found expression in the French Revolution.

But though Rousseau's doctrine of the social contract falls into the general pattern of the political theory of the Enlightenment, he added a new feature to political philosophy which was of considerable importance. Like Hobbes and Locke before him, he envisaged individuals as agreeing together to form society. But once the social contract has taken place, a new body or organism comes into being which possesses a common life and a common will. This common or general will always tends to the preservation and welfare of the whole, and it is the rule or norm of law and of justice and injustice. This infallible general will is not the same thing as 'the will of all'. If the citizens meet together and vote, their individual wills are expressed in their votes, and if the votes are unanimous, we have the will of all. But individuals may have an incorrect notion of what is for the public advantage, whereas the general will is never mistaken. In other words, the community always wills what is for its good, but it may be deceived in its idea what is actually for its good.

The general will thus becomes, when considered in itself, something inarticulate: it needs interpretation, articulate expression. There can be little doubt that Rousseau himself thought of it as finding expression, in practice, in the expressed will of the majority. And if one has in mind a small Swiss canton in which it is possible for all the citizens to vote on important issues, either as individuals or as members of associations, it is natural to think in this way. But in a large State such direct reference to the people is impracticable, except perhaps on rare occasions by means of a referendum. And in such a State the tendency will be for a few men, or for one man, to claim to embody in their wills, or in his will, the general will which is immanent in the people. Thus we find Robespierre saying of the Jacobins that 'our will is the general will', while Napoleon seems to have regarded himself, on occasion at least, as the organ and embodiment of the Revolution.

We are thus faced with the odd situation of Rousseau, the enthusiastic democrat, starting with individualism, the freedom of the individual in the state of nature, and ending with a theory of the organic State in which the quasi-mystical general will is embodied either in the will of the majority or in the will of one or more leaders. We then have either the despotism of the majority or the despotism of the leader or group of leaders. To say this is not to say that Rousseau fully understood the trend of his own theory. But he originated a paradoxical idea of liberty. To be free is to act according to one's will and according to the law of which one is oneself the author. But the individual whose private will is at variance with the general will does not actually will what he 'really' wills. In being compelled, therefore, to submit to the expression of the general will which represents his own 'real' will, he is being forced to be free. The freedom of man in society can thus come to mean something very different from what is meant by freedom in the state of nature. And though Rousseau's political theory is akin to Locke's so far as the bare idea of a social contract is concerned, it looks forward at the same time to the philosophy of Hegel for whom the obedient citizen is truly free, since he obeys a law which is the expression of the universal, of the essential nature of the human spirit. It also looks forward to much later political developments which would have been abhorrent to Rousseau, as indeed to Hegel, but which could find in Rousseau's theory a theoretical justification.

7. It is not infrequently said that in the period of the Enlighten-ment a historical outlook was lacking. What is meant by this statement? Obviously, the statement does not mean that historio-graphy was not practised in the eighteenth century. At least, if this were the meaning of the statement, the statement would be false. To see this, we have only to think, for example, of Hume's *History of England*, of *The Decline and Fall of the Roman Empire* by Edward Gibbon (1737–94) and of the historical writings of Voltaire and Montesquieu. Nor should the statement be taken to mean that the eighteenth century was marked by no improve-ments in the writing of history. For example, there was a needed reaction against preoccupation with military, dynastic and diplomatic historiography. Emphasis was laid on cultural and intellectual factors, and attention was paid to the life of the people and to men's habits and customs. This emphasis is clear, for instance, in Voltaire's *Essai sur les mœurs*. Again, Montesquieu emphasized the influence of material conditions, such as climate, on the development of a people or nation and on its customs and laws.

At the same time the historiography of the eighteenth century suffered from serious defects. In the first place historians were, generally speaking, insufficiently critical of their sources and dis-inclined to carry out the work of historical research and of pains-taking evaluation of evidence and documents which is required for objective writing. True, one could hardly expect a man of the world who dabbled in many branches of philosophy and letters to

give himself to research of this kind. But the comparative absence
of the latter constituted a defect none the less.

In the second place the eighteenth-century historians were too
much inclined to use history as a means of proving a thesis and as
a source of moral lessons. Gibbon was concerned to show that the
victory of Christianity had been a victory of barbarism and
bigotry over enlightened civilization. Writers such as Voltaire
concentrated in a rather complacent fashion on the victory of
rationalism over what they regarded as the dead weight of
tradition and obscurantism. They assumed not only the theory
of progress but also the idea that progress consists in the advance
of rationalism, free-thinking and science. According to Bolingbroke in his *Letters on the Study and Use of History* (1752), history
is philosophy teaching us by examples how we ought to conduct
ourselves in the situations of public and private life. And when the
eighteenth-century historians emphasized the moral lessons of
history, they were thinking, of course, of a morality set free from
theological presuppositions, and connections. They were all
opposed to the theological interpretation of history which had
been given by Bossuet (1627–1704) in his *Discours sur l'histoire
universelle*. But it does not seem to have occurred to them that in
interpreting history in function of the Enlightenment, of the Age
of Reason, they were showing an analogous, if different, bias. It
would be a great mistake to imagine that because the writers of
the Enlightenment were free-thinkers and rationalists, they were
exempt from bias and from the tendency to subordinate historiography to moralistic and preconceived purposes. Ranke's call for
objectivity in the first half of the nineteenth century applies just
as much to the rationalist as to the theologically-minded historians.
If we attribute bias to Bossuet, we cannot declare Gibbon exempt.
The eighteenth-century historians were concerned not so much to
understand the mentality and outlook of the men of past ages as
to use what they knew, or thought they knew, of past eras to
prove a thesis or to derive moral lessons or conclusions unfavourable to religion, at least to supernatural religion. In particular,
the spirit of the Enlightenment was so sharply opposed to that of
the Middle Ages that the historians of the former period not only
failed to understand the mentality of the Middle Ages but also
made no real effort to do so. For them the use of the Middle Ages
was to serve as a foil to the Age of Reason. And this attitude is
one of the reasons why the Enlightenment is said to be lacking in

an historical spirit. As we have seen, this accusation does not mean, or at least should not be taken to mean, that no interesting developments in historiography took place. It indicates rather a lack of imaginative insight and a tendency to interpret past history according to the standards of the Age of Reason. Gibbon, for example, is the opposite of Bossuet so far as the content of his thesis is concerned; but the secularist and rationalist thesis was no less a thesis than the bishop's preconceived theological scheme.

If one admits, as one must, that historiography is more than mere chronicling and that it involves selection and interpretation, it becomes very difficult to draw a hard-and-fast line between historiography and philosophy of history. However, when we find historians interpreting history as the working-out of some kind of general plan or reducing historical development to the operation of certain universal laws, it is reasonable to begin speaking of philosophy of history. A man who endeavours to write, for instance, the objective history of a particular region would not normally, I think, be classed as a philosopher of history. We are not accustomed to speak of Hume or of Justus Möser (author of an Osnabrückische Geschichte, 1768) as philosophers of history. But when a man treats of universal history and either gives a finalistic interpretation of historical development or concerns himself with universally-operative laws, it is not improper to speak of him as a philosopher of history. Bossuet in the seventeenth century would count as one. And in the eighteenth century there are a number of notable examples.

The most eminent of these is doubtless John-Baptist Vico (1668–1744). Vico was a Christian, and he did not belong to the camp of those who rejected the theological interpretation of history represented by St. Augustine and Bossuet. At the same time in his work *Principi di una scienza nuova d'intorno alla commune natura delle nazioni* (*Principles of a New Science Concerning the Common Nature of Nations*) he left aside purely theological considerations to examine the natural laws governing historical development. There are two points which we can notice here about this New Science. In the first place Vico did not think in terms of a lineal progress or development of humanity as a whole, but in terms of a series of cyclic developments. That is to say, the laws which govern the movement of history are exemplified in the rise, progress, decline and fall of each particular people or nation. In the second place Vico characterized each successive phase in a cycle by its system of law. In the theocratic phase law is regarded as having divine origins and sanctions. This is the age of the gods. In the aristocratic phase law is in the hands of a few families (for example, in the hands of the patrician families in the Roman Republic). This is the age of heroes. In the phase of human government, the age of men, we have a rationalized system of law, in which there are equal rights for all citizens. In this scheme we can see an adumbration of Comte's three stages. But Vico was not a positivist philosopher; and further, as we have already seen, he retained the Greek idea of historical cycles, which was different from the nineteenth-century idea of human progress.

Montesquieu also concerned himself with law. In his *Esprit des lois* (1748) he set himself to examine the different systems of positive law. He tried to show that each is a system of laws which are linked by mutual relations, so that any given law involves a particular set of other laws and excludes another set. But why does one nation possess this system and another nation that system? By way of answer Montesquieu emphasized the part played by the form of government; but he also emphasized the influence of natural factors such as climate and geographical conditions as well as of acquired factors such as commercial relations and religious beliefs. Each people or nation will have its own constitution and system of law; but the practical problem is fundamentally the same for all, namely, that of developing the system of law which, given the relevant natural and historical conditions, will favour the greatest amount of liberty. It is at this point that the influence of the British constitution makes its mark on Montesquieu's thought. Liberty, he thought, is best assured by a separation of the legislative, executive and judicial powers.

With Condorcet we find a different conception of progress from that of Vico. As has already been remarked, in his *Esquisse d'un tableau historique des progrès de l'esprit humain* (1794) he envisages the indefinite progress of the human race. Before the sixteenth century we can distinguish a number of epochs, and we can find movements of retrogression, in particular the Middle Ages. But the Renaissance ushered in the beginning of a new scientific and moral culture to the development of which we can set no limits. Men's minds can, however, be limited by prejudice and narrow ideas, such as those fostered by religious dogma. Hence follows the importance of education, especially of scientific education.

In Germany, Lessing too proposed an optimistic theory of

historical progress. In his work *Die Erziehung des Menschenge-schlects* (1780) he depicted history as the progressive education of the human race. There are occasional retrogressions and stoppages on the path of progress, but even these enter into the general scheme and serve its realization through the centuries. As for religion, history is, indeed, the education of the human race by God. But there is no final and absolute form of religious belief. Rather is each religion a stage in the progressive 'revelation' of God.

In his work on language (*Ueber den Ursprung der Sprache*, 1772) Herder dealt with the natural origin of language and attacked the view that speech was originally communicated by God to man. In regard to religion he emphasized its natural character. It is closely allied with poetry and myth and is due originally to man's desire to explain phenomena. In developed religion, especially in Christianity, we see the growth and strength of the moral element; and this is why Christianity responds to the human being's moral needs and yearnings. In other words, Herder reacted strongly against the rationalistic criticism of and opposition to religion, especially Christianity, which was characteristic of the eighteenth century. He disliked the separation of the analytic and critical reason from man's other powers, and he showed a sense for human nature as a whole. In his *Ideen zur Philosophie der Geschichte der Menschheit* (*Ideas for the Philosophy of the History of Mankind*, 1784-91) he described history as a purely natural history of human powers, actions and propensities, modified by time and place. And he tried to trace man's development in connection with the character of his physical environment, proposing a theory of the origin of human culture. Theologically speaking, the histories of the different nations form a harmonious whole, the working out of divine providence.

It was only natural that in a period when thought centred round man himself, interest should have grown in the historical development of human culture. And in the eighteenth century we can see an attempt, or rather a series of attempts, to understand history by discovering some alternative principles of explanation to the theological principles of St. Augustine and Bossuet. But even those who believe that the construction of a philosophy of history is a profitable undertaking must admit that the philosophical historians of the eighteenth century were over-hasty in the development of their syntheses. Vico, for instance, based his

cyclic interpretation of history largely on a consideration of
Roman history. And none of them possessed a sufficiently wide
and accurate factual knowledge to warrant the construction of a
philosophy of history, even granting that such a thing is a legitimate enterprise. Indeed, some of the men of the French Enlightenment were inclined to despise and belittle the painstaking work
of a Muratori (1672–1750), who prepared a great collection of
sources for Italian history. At the same time we can see the growth
of a broad view of the development of human culture, considered
in relation to a variety of factors from the influence of climate to
the influence of religion. This is especially observable in the case
of Herder, who passes beyond the confines of the Enlightenment
when this term is understood in the narrow sense, particularly,
that is, with reference to French rationalism.

8. Mention has already been made of a number of philosophers
who died in the early years of the nineteenth century. But among
those who wrote in the closing decades of the eighteenth century
by far the greatest name is that of Immanuel Kant (1724–1804).
Whatever one may think of his philosophy, nobody would deny
his outstanding historical importance. Indeed, in certain respects
his thought marks a crisis in European philosophy, so that we can
speak of the pre-Kantian and the post-Kantian eras in modern
philosophy. If Descartes and Locke can be regarded as the
dominating figures in the thought of the seventeenth and
eighteenth centuries, that of the nineteenth century is dominated
by Kant. To speak in this way is, indeed, to be guilty of over-
simplification. To imagine that all the philosophers of the
nineteenth century were Kantians would be as erroneous as to
suppose that the philosophers of the eighteenth century were all
either Cartesians or followers of Locke. Yet just as Descartes'
influence on the development of continental rationalism and
Locke's influence on the development of British empiricism are
both beyond doubt, even though Spinoza and Leibniz on the
Continent and Berkeley and Hume in England were all original
thinkers, so is Kant's influence on nineteenth-century thought
undeniable, even though Hegel, for example, was a great thinker
of marked originality who cannot be classed as a 'Kantian'.
Indeed, Kant's attitude towards speculative metaphysics has
exercised a powerful influence ever since his time. And many
people today think that he successfully exposed its pretensions,
even though they may not be prepared to accept much of his

positive thought. It is true that to over-emphasize what I may call the negative or destructive influence of Kant is to give a one-sided view of his philosophy. But this does not alter the fact that in the eyes of many people he appears as the great debunker of speculative metaphysics.

Kant's intellectual life falls into two periods, the pre-critical and the critical periods. In the first he was under the influence of the Leibnizian-Wolffian tradition; in the second he worked out his own original point of view. His first great work, *The Critique of Pure Reason*, appeared in 1781. Kant was then fifty-seven years old; but he had already been engaged for some ten years or more in the elaboration of his own philosophy, and this is why he was able to publish in quick succession the works which have made his name famous. In 1783 appeared the *Prolegomena to Any Future Metaphysic*, in 1785 the *Fundamental Principles of the Metaphysic of Morals*, in 1788 the *Critique of Practical Reason*, in 1790 the *Critique of Judgment*, in 1793 *Religion within the Limits of Bare Reason*. The papers found in his study after his death and published posthumously show that he was working until the end on the reconsideration, reconstruction or completion of certain parts of his philosophical system.

It would be inappropriate to expound the philosophy of Kant in an introductory chapter. But something must be said about the problems which presented themselves to him and about his general line of thought.

Among Kant's works two are concerned with moral philosophy and one with religion. This fact is significant. For if we take a broad view of the matter, we can say that Kant's fundamental problem was not dissimilar to that of Descartes. He declared that there were for him two main objects of wonder and admiration, 'the starry heavens above and the moral law within'. On the one hand he was faced by the scientific conception of the world, with the physical universe of Copernicus, Kepler and Newton, as subject to mechanical causality and determined in its motions. On the other hand he was faced by the rational creature who can understand the physical world, set over against it, so to speak, as subject to object, who is conscious of moral obligation and of freedom, and who sees in the world the expression of rational purpose. How can these two aspects of reality be reconciled? How can we harmonize the physical world, the sphere of deter-minism, with the moral order, the sphere of freedom? It is not simply a matter of juxtaposing the two worlds, as though they were completely separate and independent. For they meet in man. Man is both an item in Nature, in the physical system, and a moral and free agent. The question is, therefore, how can the two points of view, the scientific and the moral, be harmonized without denying either of them. This, it seems to me, is Kant's fundamental problem. And it is as well to realize this from the outset. Otherwise the emphasis which is very naturally placed on the analytical and critical aspects of his thought may almost totally obscure the profound speculative motivation of his philosophy.

But though Kant's general problem was not unlike that of Descartes, a great deal of water had flowed under the bridge since the latter's time; and when we come to Kant's particular problems the change becomes evident. On the one hand he had before him the metaphysical systems of the great continental rationalists. Descartes had tried to put metaphysical philosophy on a scientific basis; but the emergence of conflicting systems and the failure to attain assured conclusions cast doubt on the validity of the aim of traditional metaphysics, the aim of extending our knowledge of reality, especially of reality as transcending the data of sense-experience. On the other hand Kant was faced by British empiricism, culminating in the philosophy of Hume. But pure empiricism, it seemed to him, was quite unable to justify or account for the success of Newtonian physics and the evident fact that it increased man's knowledge of the world. On Hume's principles an informative statement about the world would be no more than a statement of what has actually been experienced. For example, we have always found, as far as our experience goes, that on the occurrence of event A event B regularly follows. But the empiricism of Hume would give us no objective justification for the universal statement that whenever A occurs B must follow. In other words, pure empiricism cannot account for universal and necessary informative judgments (which Kant called synthetic *a priori* judgments). Yet the Newtonian physics presupposes the validity of such judgments. Both of the main lines of modern philosophy, therefore, seem to be defective. The rationalist metaphysics does not appear to provide any certain knowledge about the world. And this prompts us to ask whether metaphysical knowledge is, indeed, possible. Pure empiricism, however, is unable to justify a branch of study, namely, physical science, which certainly does increase our knowledge of the world. And this prompts us to ask what is missing in pure empiricism and how the universal, necessary and informative judgments of science are possible. How can we justify the assurance with which we make these judgments?

The problem or problems can be expressed in this way. On the one hand Kant saw that the metaphysicians[1] tended to confuse logical relations with causal relations and to imagine that one could produce by *a priori* reasoning a system which would give us true and certain information about reality. But it did not seem to him at all evident that, even if we avoid this confusion, we can obtain metaphysical knowledge, say about God, by employing the principle of causality. Hence we can profitably ask whether metaphysics is possible and, if so, in what sense it is possible. On the other hand, while agreeing with the empiricists that all our knowledge begins in some sense with experience, Kant saw that the Newtonian physics could not be justified on purely empiricist lines. For the Newtonian physics presupposed, in his opinion, the uniformity of Nature. And it was precisely the belief in the uniformity of Nature of which Hume could give no adequate theoretical justification, even though he tried to give a psychological account of the origin of the belief. The question arises, therefore, what is the theoretical justification of our belief if we once assume with the empiricists that all our knowledge begins with experience?

In answering this last question Kant proposes an original hypothesis. Even if all our knowledge begins with experience, it does not necessarily follow that it all arises from experience. For it may be the case (and Kant thought that it is in fact the case) that our experience comprises two elements, impressions which are given and the *a priori* forms and elements by which these impressions are synthesized. Kant does not mean to suggest that we have innate ideas, nor that the *a priori* elements in cognition are objects of knowledge antecedently to experience. What he is suggesting is that man, the experiencing and knowing subject, is so constituted that he necessarily (because he is what he is) synthesizes the ultimately given data or impressions in certain ways. In other words, the subject, man, is not simply the passive recipient of impressions: he actively (and unconsciously) synthesizes the raw data, so to speak, imposing on them the *a priori*

[1] This applies to the pre-Kantian continental rationalists, not to a mediaeval philosopher such as Aquinas. Kant's knowledge of mediaeval philosophy, however, was extremely meagre.

forms and categories by which the world of our experience is built
up. The world of experience, the phenomenal world or reality as
it appears to us, is not simply our construction, a dream as it were;
nor is it simply something given; it is the result of an application
of *a priori* forms and categories to what is given.

What is the advantage of such an hypothesis? It can be illustrated in this way. Appearances are the same both for the man
who accepts the Copernican hypothesis that the earth revolves
round the sun and for the man who does not accept it or knows
nothing of it. As far as appearances go, both men see the sun
rising in the east and setting in the west. But the Copernican
hypothesis accounts for facts which cannot be accounted for on
the geocentric hypothesis. Similarly, the world appears in the
same way to the man who recognizes no *a priori* element in knowledge as it appears to the man who does recognize such an element.
But on the hypothesis that there is such an element we can explain
what pure empiricism cannot explain. If we assume, for example,
that by the very fact that our minds are what they are we synthesize data according to the causal relation, Nature will always
appear to us as governed by causal laws. In other words, we are
assured of the uniformity of Nature. Nature means Nature as
appearing; it cannot mean anything else. And given the subjective constants in human cognition, there must be corresponding
constants in phenomenal reality. If, for instance, we necessarily
apply *a priori* forms of space and time to raw sense-data (of which
we are not directly conscious), Nature must always appear to us
as spatio-temporal.

I do not propose to enter into any detailed account of Kant's
a priori conditions of experience. The appropriate place to do
this will be in the relevant chapters in the sixth volume. But
there is one important point which must be noted because it
bears directly on Kant's problem about the possibility of metaphysics.

The function, Kant asserts, of the *a priori* conditions of experience is to synthesize the manifold of sense-impressions. And what
we know with their aid is phenomenal reality. We cannot, therefore, legitimately use a subjective category of the understanding
to transcend experience. We cannot, for instance, legitimately
employ the concept of causality to transcend phenomena by using
a causal argument to prove the existence of God. Nor can we ever
know metaphenomenal reality, if we are talking about certain

theoretical knowledge. Yet this is precisely what the meta-physicians have attempted to do. They have tried to extend our theoretical or scientific knowledge to reality as it is in itself; and they have used categories having validity only within the phenomenal world to transcend phenomena. Such attempts were foredoomed to failure. And Kant tries to show that metaphysical arguments of the traditional type lead to insoluble antinomies. It is no matter for wonder, therefore, if metaphysics makes no progress comparable to that of physical science.

The only 'scientific' metaphysics which there can be is the metaphysics of knowledge, the analysis of the *a priori* elements in human experience. And the greater part of Kant's work consists in an attempt to perform this task of analysis. In *The Critique of Pure Reason* he attempts to analyse the *a priori* elements which govern the formation of our synthetic *a priori* judgments. In the *Critique of Practical Reason* he investigates the *a priori* element in the moral judgment. In the *Critique of Judgment* he sets out to analyse the *a priori* elements governing our aesthetic and teleological judgments.

But though Kant ruled out what he regarded as classical metaphysics, he was far from showing indifference towards the principal themes treated by the metaphysicians. These themes were for him freedom, immortality and· God. And he endeavoured to reinstate on a different basis what he had excluded from the province of theoretical and scientific knowledge.

Kant starts from the fact of the awareness or consciousness of moral obligation. And he tries to show that moral obligation presupposes freedom. If I ought, I can. Further, the moral law commands perfect conformity with itself, perfect virtue. But this is an ideal for the attainment of which, Kant assumes, endless duration is required. Hence immortality, in the sense of never-ending progress towards the ideal, is a 'postulate' of the moral law. Again, though morality does not mean acting with a view to one's happiness, morality should produce happiness. But the proportioning of happiness to virtue requires the idea of a Being who can and will effect the connection. The idea of God is thus a 'postulate' of the moral law. We cannot prove, in the way that some metaphysicians sought to prove, that man is free, that his soul is immortal and that there exists a transcendent God. But we are conscious of moral obligation; and freedom, immortality and God are 'postulates' of the moral law. It is a matter of practical faith, that is to say, of a faith involved in committing oneself to moral activity.

This doctrine of 'postulates' is sometimes interpreted either as a cheap pragmatism or as a conventional concession to the prejudices of the orthodox. But I think that Kant himself took the matter much more seriously. He regarded man as a kind of mixed being. As part of the natural order, he is subject to mechanical causality like any other natural object. But he is also a moral being who is conscious of obligation. And to recognize obligation is to recognize that the moral law has a claim upon one which one is free to fulfil or reject.[1] Moreover, to recognize a moral order is to recognize implicitly that moral activity is not doomed to frustration and that ultimately human existence 'makes sense'. But it cannot make sense without immortality and God. We cannot prove freedom, immortality and God's existence scientifically. For these ideas have no place in science. Nor can we prove them by the arguments of traditional metaphysics. For these arguments are invalid. But if a man recognizes moral obligation at all, he is implicitly asserting a moral order which in turn implies the immortality of the soul and the existence of God. It is not a case of strict logical implication, so that we can produce a series of watertight proofs. Rather is it a case of discovering and affirming by faith that view of reality which alone gives full meaning and value to the consciousness of moral obligation mediated by conscience.

Kant leaves us, therefore, with what one may call perhaps a bifurcated reality. On the one hand there is the world of Newtonian science, a world governed by necessary causal laws. This is the phenomenal world, not in the sense that it is mere illusion, but in the sense that it presupposes the operation of those subjective conditions of experience which determine the ways in which things appear to us. On the other hand there is the supersensuous world of the free human spirit and of God. According to Kant, we cannot give any strict theoretical proof that there is such a supersensuous world. At the same time we have no adequate reason for asserting that the material world, governed by mechanical causality, is the only world. And if our interpretation of the world as a mechanical system depends on the operation of

---

[1] The moral law, for Kant, is promulgated by the practical reason. In a sense which will be explained in the appropriate place man gives the law to himself. But obligation is without meaning except in relation to a being which is free to obey or disobey the law.

subjective conditions of experience, of sense-experience, that is to say, we have even less reason for making this assertion than we should have in any case. Moreover, the moral life, especially the consciousness of obligation, opens up a sphere of reality which the moral man affirms by faith as a postulate or demand of the moral law.

This is not the place to subject Kant's philosophy to critical discussion. I wish instead to remark that what I have called Kant's 'bifurcation' represents a dilemma of the modern mind. We have seen that the new scientific conception of the world threatened to monopolize man's view of reality as a whole. Descartes in the seventeenth century endeavoured to combine the affirmation of spiritual reality with an acceptance of the world of mechanical causality. But he believed that he could show conclusively that, for example, there exists an infinite and transcendent God. Kant, in the closing decades of the eighteenth century, refused to allow that such truths are capable of being proved in the ways in which Descartes and Leibniz had thought that they could be proved. At the same time he felt strongly that the world of Newtonian physics was not coterminous with reality. He therefore relegated the affirmation of supersensuous reality to the sphere of 'faith', trying to justify this by reference to the moral consciousness. Now, there are people today who regard science as the only means of extending our factual *knowledge*, though at the same time they feel that the world as presented by science is not the only reality and that it in some way points beyond itself. For them the system of Kant possesses a certain contemporaneity, even if, as developed in his works, it cannot stand up to criticism. There is, that is to say, some similarity between their situation and that in which Kant found himself. I say 'some similarity' because the setting of the problem has changed very much since the time of Kant. On the one hand there have been changes in scientific theory. On the other hand philosophy has developed in a variety of ways. Yet it is arguable that the basic situation remains the same.

To end the present chapter with a consideration of Kant's philosophy is, I think, appropriate. Brought up in a diluted version of continental rationalism, he was awoken from his dogmatic slumbers, as he put it, by David Hume. At the same time, though he rejected the claims of the continental metaphysicians to increase our knowledge of reality, he was also convinced

of the insufficiency of pure empiricism. We can say, therefore, that in his thought the influence of continental rationalism
and British empiricism combined to give rise to a new and
original system. It must be added, however, that Kant put a full
stop neither to metaphysics nor to empiricism. Yet he made a
difference to both. Metaphysics in the nineteenth century was not
the same as it had been in the seventeenth and eighteenth centuries. And though British empiricism in the nineteenth century
was more or less unaffected by Kant, the neo-empiricism of the
twentieth century has consciously tried to deal metaphysics a far
more decisive blow than was delivered by Kant who, when all is
said and done, was himself something of a metaphysician.

CHAPTER II

DESCARTES (1)

Life and works[1]—*Descartes' aim—His idea of method—The theory of innate ideas—Methodic doubt.*

1. RENÉ DESCARTES was born on March 31st, 1596, in Touraine, being the third child of a councillor of the parliament of Brittany. In 1604 his father sent him to the college of La Flèche which had been founded by Henry IV and was directed by the Fathers of the Society of Jesus. Descartes remained at the college until 1612, the last few years being given to the study of logic, philosophy and mathematics. He tells us[2] of his extreme desire to acquire knowledge, and it is clear that he was an ardent student and a gifted pupil. 'I did not feel that I was esteemed inferior to my fellow-students, although there were amongst them some destined to fill the places of our masters.'[3] When we remember that Descartes later subjected traditional learning to strong adverse criticism and that even as a schoolboy he became so dissatisfied with a great part of what he had been taught (mathematics excepted) that on leaving the college he quitted for a time the pursuit of learning, we may be tempted to draw the conclusion that he felt resentment towards his masters and contempt for their system of education. But this was far from being the case. He spoke of the Jesuits of La Flèche with affection and respect, and he regarded their system of education as greatly superior to that provided in most other pedagogical institutions. It is clear from his writings that he considered that he had been given the best education available within the framework of tradition. Yet on looking back he came to the conclusion that the traditional learning, in some of its branches at least, was not based on any solid foundation. Thus he remarks sarcastically that 'philosophy teaches us to speak with an appearance of truth about all things and causes us to be

---

[1] In the references to the writings of Descartes the following abbreviations have been used. *D.M.* stands for the *Discourse on Method*, *R.D.* for the *Rules for the Direction of the Mind*, *M.* for the *Meditations*, *P.P.* for the *Principles of Philosophy*, *S.T.* for the *Search after Truth*, *P.S.* for the *Passions of the Soul*, *O.* and *R.O.* for *Objections* and *Replies to Objections* respectively. The letters *A.T.* refer to the edition of the works of Descartes by Charles Adam and Paul Tannery; Paris, 13 vols., 1897–1913.
[2] *D.M.*, 1; *A.T.*, VI, 3.   [3] *D.M.*, 1; *A.T.*, VI, 5.

admired by the less learned', and that though it has been cultivated
for centuries by the best minds 'no single thing is to be found in it
which is not matter of dispute and which in consequence is not
dubious'.[1] Mathematics, indeed, delighted him because of its
certainty and clarity, 'but I did not yet understand its true
use'.[2]

After leaving La Flèche, Descartes amused himself for a short
while, but he soon resolved to study and to learn from the book of
the world, as he put it, seeking a knowledge which would be useful
for life. He accordingly attached himself to the army of Prince
Maurice of Nassau. This may appear to have been a somewhat
odd move to make. But Descartes did not accept pay as a soldier,
and he combined his new profession with mathematical studies.
He wrote a number of papers and notes, including a treatise on
music, the *Compendium musicae*, which was published after his
death.

In 1619 Descartes left the service of Maurice of Nassau and went
to Germany, where he witnessed the coronation of the Emperor
Ferdinand at Frankfurt. Joining the army of Maximilian of
Bavaria, he was stationed at Neuberg on the Danube; and it was
at this time that in secluded reflection he began to lay the foundations of his philosophy. On November 10th, 1619, he had three
consecutive dreams which convinced him that his mission was to
seek truth by reason, and he made a vow to make a pilgrimage to
the shrine of Our Lady at Loreto in Italy. Further military service
in Bohemia and Hungary and travel in Silesia, northern Germany
and the Netherlands, followed by a visit to his father at Rennes,
prevented him from fulfilling this vow for the time being. But in
1623 he made his way to Italy and visited Loreto before proceeding to Rome.

For a few years Descartes resided at Paris, where he enjoyed the
friendship of men like Mersenne, a fellow-pupil of La Flèche, and
the encouragement of Cardinal de Bérulle. But he found life at
Paris too distracting, and in 1628 he retired to Holland, where he
remained until 1649, apart from visits to France in 1644, 1647
and 1648.

The publication of his *Traité du monde* was suspended because
of the condemnation of Galileo, and the work was not published
until 1677. But in 1637 Descartes published in French his *Discourse on the Method of rightly conducting the Reason and seeking*

---

[1] *D.M.*, 1; *A.T.*, vi, 6 and 8.   [2] *D.M.*, 1; *A.T.*, vi, 7.

for Truth in the Sciences, together with essays on meteors, dioptrics and geometry. The *Rules for the Direction of the Mind* had apparently been written in 1628, though it was published posthumously. In 1641 appeared the *Meditations on First Philosophy* in a Latin version. This was accompanied by six sets of objections or criticisms submitted by various theologians and philosophers and by Descartes' answers to these objections. The first set consists of objections by Caterus, a Dutch theologian, the second of criticisms by a group of theologians and philosophers, the third, fourth and fifth of objections by Hobbes, Arnauld and Gassendi respectively, and the sixth of criticisms by a second group of theologians and philosophers. In 1642 another edition of the *Meditations* was published which contained in addition a seventh set of objections by the Jesuit Bourdin, together with Descartes' replies and his letter to Father Dinet, also a Jesuit, who had been one of the philosopher's instructors at La Flèche and for whom he had a warm regard. A French translation of the *Meditations* was published in 1647 and a second French edition, containing also the seven sets of objections, in 1661. The French translation had been made by the Duc de Luynes, not by Descartes, but the first edition of it had been seen and partly revised by the philosopher.

The *Principles of Philosophy* was published in Latin in 1644. It was translated into French by the Abbé Claude Picot, and this translation, after having been read by Descartes, was published in 1647, being prefaced by a letter from the author to the translator in which the plan of the work is explained. The treatise entitled *The Passions of the Soul* (1649) was written in French and published, more, it appears, owing to the entreaties of friends than to the author's own desire, shortly before Descartes' death. In addition we possess an unfinished dialogue, *The Search after Truth by the Light of Nature*, a Latin translation of which appeared in 1701, and Latin *Notes directed against a Certain Programme*, a reply written by Descartes to a manifesto about the nature of the mind, which had been composed by Regius or Le Roy of Utrecht, first a friend and later an opponent of the philosopher. Finally, the works of Descartes contain a mass of correspondence which is of considerable value for the elucidation of his thought.

In September 1649 Descartes left Holland for Sweden in response to the pressing invitation of Queen Christina who wished to be instructed in his philosophy. The rigours of the Swedish winter, however, coupled with the queen's practice of expecting

Descartes, who was accustomed to lie for a long time in bed, engaged in reflection, to come to her library at five in the morning, were too much for the poor man, and he was not strong enough to withstand an attack of fever which developed at the end of January 1650. And on February 11th he died.

Descartes was a man of moderation and of a kindly disposition. For example, he is known to have been generous to his servants and attendants and solicitous for their welfare, and they in turn were much attached to their master. He possessed some close friends like Mersenne, but he found that a retired and quiet life was essential for his work, and he never married. As for his religious convictions, he always professed himself a Catholic and he died piously in that faith. There has indeed been some controversy about the sincerity of his protestations of Catholic belief. But in my opinion doubts about his sincerity are founded either on some totally inadequate factual ground, such as his act of timidity or of prudence in suspending publication of the *Traité du monde*, or on the *a priori* assumption that a philosopher who consciously and deliberately set out to construct a new philosophical system could not have really believed in Catholic dogmas. For the most part Descartes avoided discussion of purely theological matters. His point of view was that the road to heaven is as open to the ignorant as to the learned and that revealed mysteries transcend the comprehension of the human mind. He occupied himself, therefore, with problems which in his opinion could be solved by reason alone. He was a philosopher and a mathematician,[1] not a theologian; and he acted accordingly. We cannot legitimately conclude that his personal religious beliefs were not what he said they were.

2. The fundamental aim of Descartes was, obviously enough, to attain philosophical truth by the use of reason. 'I wished to give myself entirely to the search after truth.'[2] But what he was seeking was not to discover a multiplicity of isolated truths but to develop a system of true propositions, in which nothing would be presupposed which was not self-evident and indubitable. There would then be an organic connection between all the parts of the system, and the whole edifice would rest on a sure foundation. It would thus be impervious to the corroding and destructive effect of scepticism.

[1] Descartes was the real founder of analytic or co-ordinate geometry. At least, his *Géométrie* (1637) was the first work on the subject to be published.
[2] *D.M.*, 4; *A.T.*, VI, 31.

What did Descartes understand by philosophy? 'Philosophy means the study of wisdom, and by wisdom we understand not only prudence in affairs but also a perfect knowledge of all things which man can know both for the conduct of his life and for the conservation of his health and the invention of all the arts.'[1] Under the general heading of philosophy, therefore, Descartes included not only metaphysics but also physics or natural philosophy, the latter standing to the former as trunk to roots. And the branches issuing from this trunk are the other sciences, the three principal ones being medicine, mechanics and morals. By morals 'I mean the highest and most perfect moral science which, presupposing a complete knowledge of the other sciences, is the last degree of wisdom.'[2]

It is not surprising that from time to time Descartes insisted on the practical value of philosophy. The civilization of any nation, he says, is proportionate to the superiority of its philosophy, and 'a State can have no greater good than the possession of true philosophy'.[3] Again, he speaks of 'opening to each one the road by which he can find in himself, and without borrowing from any other, the whole knowledge which is essential to him for the direction of his life'.[4] This practical value of philosophy is seen most clearly in the part which comes last in the order of development, especially in ethics. For 'just as it is not from the roots or the trunks of trees that one gathers the fruit but only from the extremities of their branches, so the main use of philosophy is dependent on those of its parts which we cannot learn until the end'.[5] In theory, therefore, Descartes laid great stress on ethics. But he never elaborated a systematic moral science in accordance with his plan; and his name is associated with an idea of method and with metaphysics rather than with ethics.

Now, it is undeniable that in one sense at least Descartes consciously and deliberately broke with the past. First of all he was determined to start again from the beginning, as it were, without trusting to the authority of any previous philosophy. He charged the Aristotelians not only with relying on Aristotle's authority but also with failing to understand him properly and with pretending to find in his writings solutions to problems 'of which he says nothing and of which he possibly had not thought at all'.[6] Descartes was resolved to rely on his own reason, not on authority.

[1] *P.P.*, Prefatory Letter; *A.T.*, IX B, 2.   [2] *P.P.*, Prefatory Letter; *A.T.*, IX B, 14.
[3] *P.P.*, Prefatory Letter; *A.T.*, IX B, 3.   [4] *S.T.*; *A.T.*, X, 496.
[5] *P.P.*, Prefatory Letter; *A.T.*, IX B, 15.   [6] *D.M.*, 6; *A.T.*, VI, 70.

Secondly, he was resolved to avoid that confusion of the clear and evident with what is conjectural or at best only probable of which he accused the Scholastics. For him there was only one kind of knowledge worthy of the name, certain knowledge. Thirdly, Descartes was determined to attain and work with clear and distinct ideas and not, as he accused the Scholastics of sometimes doing, to use terms without any clear meaning or possibly without any meaning at all. For instance, 'when they [the Scholastics] distinguish substance from extension or quantity, either they mean nothing by the word substance or they simply form in their minds a confused idea of incorporeal substance which they falsely attribute to corporeal substance'.[1] For confused ideas Descartes would substitute clear and distinct ideas.

Descartes, indeed, attached little value to historical learning or to book-learning in general. And in view of this fact it is not surprising that his strictures on Aristotelianism and Scholasticism were based on the impression made on him by a decadent Aristotelianism and by what may be called a textbook Scholasticism rather than on any profound study of the great thinkers of the Greek and mediaeval periods. When, for example, he accuses the Scholastics of appealing to authority, he neglects the fact that Aquinas himself had roundly declared that appeal to authority is the weakest of all arguments in philosophy. But such considerations leave Descartes' general attitude towards previous and contemporary philosophy unaltered. At the time when he hoped to get his *Principles of Philosophy* adopted as a philosophical textbook by the Jesuits, whom he regarded as supreme in the educational sphere, he diminished to some extent his attacks on Scholasticism and renounced the frontal attack which he had threatened. But his point of view remained the same, namely, that a clear break must be made with the past.

This does not mean, however, that Descartes was intent on rejecting all that other philosophers had held to be true. He did not take it for granted that all the propositions enunciated by previous philosophers were false. Some of them at least might very well be true. At the same time they should be rediscovered, in the sense that their truth should be proved in an orderly way by proceeding systematically from basic and indubitable to derived propositions. Descartes wished to find and apply the right method in the search for truth, a method which would enable him

[1] *P.P.*, II, 9; *A.T.*, IX B, 68.

to demonstrate truths in a rational and systematic order, irrespect-
ive of whether these truths had been previously acknowledged or
not. His primary aim was not so much to produce a novel
philosophy, as far as content was concerned, as to produce a
certain and well-ordered philosophy. And his chief enemy was
scepticism rather than Scholasticism. If, therefore, he set himself
systematically to doubt all that could possibly be doubted as a
preliminary to the establishment of certain knowledge, he did not
assume from the outset that none of the propositions which he
doubted would turn out later to be certainly true. 'I argued to
myself that there was no plausibility in the claim of any private
individual to reform a State by altering everything and by over-
turning it throughout, in order to set it right again. Nor, again,
is it probable that the whole body of the sciences, or the order of
teaching established by the Schools, should be reformed. But as
regards all the opinions which up to this time I had embraced, I
thought that I could not do better than endeavour once for all to
sweep them completely away, so that they might later on be
replaced either by others which were better or by the same when
I had made them conform to a rational scheme.'[1] Further reference will be made later to the Cartesian method of doubt; but it is
as well to notice the last sentence in this quotation.

If, therefore, Descartes were faced with the assertion that some
of his philosophical views were either similar to those which had
been held by other philosophers or that they were in some way
indebted to the latter, he could reply that this was a point of
minor importance. For he never pretended to be the first man to
discover philosophical propositions which were true. What he did
claim was that he had developed a method of demonstrating truths
according to the order demanded by the exigencies of reason itself.

In the quotation given above Descartes refers to making truths
conform to a rational scheme. His ideal of philosophy was that
of an organically connected system of scientifically established
truths, that is to say, of truths so ordered that the mind passes
from fundamental self-evident truths to other evident truths
implied by the former. This ideal was suggested in large part by
mathematics. Both in the *Rules* and in the *Discourse* he speaks
explicitly about the influence exercised by mathematics on his
mind. Thus in the latter work[2] he tells us that in his earlier days
he had studied mathematics, geometrical analysis and algebra,

---

[1] *D.M.*, 2; *A.T.*, vi, 13–14.   [2] *D.M.*, 2; *A.T.*, vi, 17.

that he was impressed by the clarity and certainty of these sciences when compared with other branches of study, and that it is necessary to investigate the peculiar characteristics of the mathematical method, which give it its superiority, with a view to applying this method in other branches of science. But this presupposes, of course, that all sciences are similar in the sense that the method which is applicable in mathematics is applicable elsewhere. And this is, indeed, what Descartes thought. All the sciences taken together 'are identical with human wisdom which always remains one and the same, however applied to different subjects'.[1] There is only one kind of knowledge, certain and evident knowledge. And ultimately there is only one science, though it possesses interconnected branches. Hence there can be only one scientific method.

This notion that all sciences are ultimately one science or, rather, organically connected branches of one science, which is identified with human wisdom or understanding, constitutes, of course, a major assumption. But the full proof of its validity, Descartes might say, cannot be given in advance. It is only by employing the right method in building up a unified body of science, an orderly system of the sciences, capable of indefinite progressive development, that we can manifest its validity at all.

It is to be noted that Descartes' theory that all the sciences are ultimately one science and that there is one universal scientific method separates him at once from the Aristotelians. The latter believed that the different subject-matters of different sciences demand different methods. For example, we cannot apply in ethics the method which is appropriate in mathematics; for the difference of subject-matter excludes any such assimilation of ethics to mathematics. But this is a point of view which is expressly attacked by Descartes. He recognized, indeed, a distinction between the sciences, which depended entirely on the mind's cognitive activity, and the arts (such as harp-playing), which depend on the exercise and disposition of the body. We can say perhaps that he admitted a distinction between science and skill, between knowing that and knowing how. But there is only one kind of science; and it does not become differentiated into diverse types through differences of subject-matter. Descartes thus turned his back on the Aristotelian and Scholastic idea of different types of sciences, with their different methods of

[1] *R.D.*, 1; *A.T.*, x, 360

procedure, and substituted instead the idea of one universal science and of one universal method. He was doubtless encouraged to do this by his success in showing that geometrical propositions can be proved by arithmetical means. Aristotle, who asserted that geometry and arithmetic constitute distinct sciences, had denied that geometrical propositions can be proved arithmetically.[1]

Descartes' ideal aim, therefore, was to construct this comprehensive scientific philosophy. In metaphysics, the roots of the tree according to his analogy, he starts with the intuitively apprehended existence of the finite self and proceeds to establish the criterion of truth, the existence of God and the existence of the material world. Physics, the trunk of the tree, depends on metaphysics, in the sense at least that physics cannot be considered an organic part of science until the ultimate principles of physics have been shown to follow from metaphysical principles. And the practical sciences, the branches of the tree, will be truly sciences when their organic dependence on physics or natural philosophy has been made clear. Descartes did not, indeed, pretend to realize this aim in its entirety; but he thought that he had made a start and that he had pointed out the way to the complete fulfilment of his purpose.

Now, what has been said hitherto may have given the impression that Descartes was concerned simply with the systematic arrangement and proof of truths which had already been enunciated. But this would be an erroneous impression. For he also believed that the use of the appropriate method would enable the philosopher to discover hitherto unknown truths. He did not say that Scholastic logic is worthless, but in his view it 'serves better for explaining to others those things which one knows . . . than in learning what is new'.[2] Its use is primarily didactic. Descartes' own logic, he says, is not, like that of the Schools, 'a dialectic which teaches how to make the things which we know understood by others or even to repeat, without forming any judgment on them, many words respecting those things which we do not know': rather is it 'the logic which teaches us how best to direct our reason in order to discover those truths of which we are ignorant'.[3]

Something further will be said in the next section about this claim that the new 'logic' enables us to discover hitherto unknown

---

[1] *Anal. Post.*, 1, 7.   [2] *D.M.*, 2; *A.T.*, vi, 17.
[3] *P.P.*, Prefatory Letter; *A.T.*, ix B, 13-14.

truths. But we may note here the problem to which the claim
gives rise. Let us suppose that mathematical method means the
deduction from self-evident principles of propositions which are
logically implied by these principles. Now, if we wish to claim
that we can deduce factual truths about the world in this way,
we shall have to assimilate the causal relation to the relation of
logical implication. We can then maintain that the truths of
physics, for example, can be deduced *a priori*. But if we assimilate
causality to logical implication, we shall be driven in the end to
adopt a monistic system, such as that of Spinoza, in which finite
things are, as it were, logical consequences of an ultimate ontological principle. Metaphysics and logic will merge with one another
And if we claim that the truths of physics can be deduced *a priori*,
experiment will play no integral part in the development of physics.
That is to say, the true conclusions of the physicist will not
depend on experimental verification. The part played by experiment will be at most a means of showing people that the conclusions reached by *a priori* deduction, independently of all
experiment, are in fact true. But, as will be seen later, Descartes
did not begin in metaphysics with the ontological principle which
is prior in the order of being. He did not begin, as Spinoza did,
with God, but with the finite self. Nor does his method, as
exemplified in the *Meditations*, bear any very close resemblances
to that of the mathematician. As for physics, Descartes did not
in fact deny the rôle of experiment. The problem facing Descartes,
therefore, was to reconcile his actual procedure with his ideal
picture of a universal science and of a universal quasi-mathematical method. But he never gave any satisfactory solution to
this problem. Nor, indeed, does he appear to have seen clearly the
discrepancies between his ideal of assimilating all sciences to
mathematics and his actual procedures. This is one reason, of
course, why the assertion that Spinozism is a logical development
of Cartesianism has considerable plausibility. At the same time
Descartes' philosophy consists in what he actually did when he
philosophized rather than in what he might have done or perhaps
ought to have done, had he fully developed the pan-mathematical
aspect of his ideal. And if we once admit this, we must add that
he should have revised his ideal of science and of scientific method
in the light of the procedures which he considered appropriate
when dealing with concrete philosophical problems.

3. What is the Cartesian method? Descartes tells us that 'by

method I understand (a set of) certain and easy rules such that anyone who observes them exactly will never take anything false to be true and, without any waste of mental effort but by increasing his knowledge step by step, will arrive at a true under- standing of all those things which do not surpass his capacity'.[1] We are told, therefore, that method consists in a set of rules. But Descartes does not mean to imply that there is a technique which can be applied in such a way that the natural capacities of the human mind are irrelevant. On the contrary, the rules are rules for employing rightly the natural capacities and operations of the mind. And Descartes points out that unless the mind were already able to employ its fundamental operations, it would be unable to understand even the simplest precepts or rules of the matter.[2] If left to itself, the mind is infallible. That is to say, if it uses its natural light and capacities, without the disturbing influence of other factors, with regard to matters which do not surpass its capacity of understanding, it will not err. If this were not the case, no technique could supply for the mind's own radical deficiency. But we may allow ourselves to be deflected from the true path of rational reflection by factors such as prejudice, passion, the influence of education, impatience and the over-hasty desire to attain results; and then the mind becomes blinded, as it were, and does not employ its natural operations correctly. Hence a set of rules is of great utility, even though these rules presuppose the mind's natural capacities and operations.

What are these fundamental operations of the mind? They are two, namely, intuition and deduction; 'two mental operations by which we are able, entirely without any fear of illusion, to arrive at the knowledge of things'.[3] The former is described as being 'not the fluctuating assurance of the senses nor the fallacious judgment which results from the arbitrary composition of the imagination, but the conception which arises so readily and distinctly in an unclouded and attentive mind that we are wholly freed from doubt concerning the object of our understanding. Or, what comes to the same thing, intuition is the conception, without doubt, of an unclouded and attentive mind, which springs from the light of reason alone.'[4] By intuition, therefore, is meant a purely intellectual activity, an intellectual seeing or vision which is so clear and distinct that it leaves no room for doubt.

---

[1] *R.D.*, 4; *A.T.*, x, 371-2.   [2] *R.D.*, 4; *A.T.*, x, 372.
[3] *R.D.*, 3; *A.T.*, x, 368.   [4] *Ibid.*

Deduction is described as 'all necessary inference from other facts which are known with certainty'.[1] It is true that intuition is required even in deductive reasoning. For we must see the truth of each proposition clearly and distinctly before we proceed to the next step. At the same time deduction is distinguishable from intuition by the fact that to the former, though not to the latter, there belongs 'a certain movement or succession'.[2]

Descartes does what he can to reduce deduction to intuition. In the case, for instance, of propositions which are deduced immediately from first principles we can say that their truth is known now by intuition and now by deduction, according to the point of view which we adopt. 'But the first principles themselves are given by intuition alone while the remote conclusions, on the contrary, are furnished only by deduction.'[3] In long processes of deductive reasoning the certitude of deduction depends in some degree upon the validity of memory; and this introduces another factor. So Descartes suggests that by frequently going over the process we can reduce the part played by memory until we approximate at least to an intuitive grasp of the truth of the remote conclusions as evidently implied by the first principles. All the same, though Descartes subordinates deduction to intuition in this way, he continues to speak of them as two mental operations.

Intuition and deduction are spoken of as 'two methods which are the most certain routes to knowledge'.[4] But though they are the ways to attain certain knowledge, they are not 'the method' of which Descartes speaks in the definition quoted at the beginning of this section. For intuition and deduction are not rules. The method consists rather in rules for employing aright these two mental operations. And it is said to consist above all in order. That is to say, we must observe the rules of orderly thinking. These rules are given in the *Rules for the Direction of the Mind* and in the *Discourse on Method*. In the latter work the first of four precepts enumerated is 'to accept nothing as true which I did not clearly recognize to be so: that is to say, carefully to avoid precipitation and prejudices in judgments, and to accept in them nothing more than what was presented to my mind so clearly and distinctly that I could have no occasion to doubt it'.[5] Observance of this precept involves the use of methodic doubt. That is to say, we must systematically subject to doubt all the opinions which we already possess, in order that we may discover what is indubitable and what can therefore serve as a foundation for the edifice of science. As I shall return to this subject in the fifth section of this chapter, I say no more about it here.

In the fifth of the *Rules for the Direction of the Mind* Descartes gives a summary of his method. 'Method consists wholly in the ordering and disposing (literally, in the order and disposition) of those objects to which the attention of the mind must be directed if we are to discover any truth. We shall observe this method exactly if we reduce involved and obscure propositions step by step to those which are simpler, and if we then start with the intuitive apprehension of the simplest propositions and try by retracing our path through the same steps to ascend to the knowledge of all the others.'[1] The meaning of this rule is not immediately evident. But the order thus described has two aspects; and these must now be briefly explained.

The first part of the method is that we should reduce involved and obscure propositions step by step to those which are simpler. And this injunction is generally said to correspond to the second precept of the *Discourse on Method*. 'The second (precept) was to divide up each of the difficulties which I was to examine into as many parts as possible and as seemed requisite.'[2] This is the method which Descartes later calls the method of analysis or resolution. It can hardly be said that he always used the term 'analysis' in precisely the same sense; but, as here described, it consists in breaking down, as it were, the multiple data of knowledge into their simplest elements or element. Descartes was certainly influenced in his conception of method by mathematics. But he considered that Euclidean geometry, for example, has a serious drawback, namely, that the axioms and first principles are not 'justified'. That is to say, the geometer does not show how his first principles are reached. The method of analysis or resolution, however, 'justifies' the first principles of a science by making it clear in a systematic manner how they are reached and why they are asserted. In this sense analysis is a logic of discovery. And Descartes was convinced that he had followed the way of analysis in his *Meditations*, by resolving the multiple data of knowledge into the primary existential proposition, *Cogito, ergo sum*, and by showing how the basic truths of metaphysics are discovered in their proper order. In his replies to the second set of *Objections* he

---

[1] *R.D.*, 5; *A.T.*, x, 379.　　　　[2] *D.M.*, 2; *A.T.*, vi, 18.

remarks that 'analysis shows the true way by which a thing was methodically discovered and derived, as it were, *a priori*, so that if the reader cares to follow it and to give sufficient attention to everything, he understands the matter no less perfectly and makes it as much his own as though he himself had discovered it. . . . But I have used in my *Meditations* only analysis, which seems to me to be the best and truest method of teaching.'[1]

The second part of the method summarized in the fifth Rule says that we should 'start with the intuitive apprehension of the simplest propositions and try by retracing our path through the same steps to ascend to the knowledge of all the others'. This is what Descartes later calls synthesis or the method of composition. In synthesis we start with the intuitively perceived first principles or most simple propositions (which are arrived at last in analysis) and proceed to deduce in an orderly way, making sure that no step is omitted and that each succeeding proposition really does follow from the preceding one. This is the method employed by the Euclidean geometers. According to Descartes, whereas analysis is the method of discovery, synthesis is the method best suited for demonstrating what is already known; and it is the method employed in the *Principles of Philosophy*.

In his replies to the second set of *Objections* Descartes asserts that 'there are two things which I distinguish in the geometrical mode of writing, namely, the order and the method of proof. The order consists merely in putting forward first those things which should be known without the aid of what comes subsequently and in arranging all other matters so that their proof depends on what precedes them. I certainly tried to follow this order as accurately as possible in my *Meditations*. . . .'[2] He then goes on to divide the method of proof into analysis and synthesis and to say, as already quoted, that in the *Meditations* he used only analysis.

Now, according to Descartes, analysis enables us to arrive at the intuition of 'simple natures'. And the question arises, what he meant by this term. Perhaps this can best be shown by employing one of his own examples. A body has extension and figure. And it cannot be said to be literally compounded of corporeal nature, extension and figure, 'since these elements have never existed in isolation from each other. But relatively to our understanding we call it a compound constructed out of these three

---

[1] *R.O.*, 2; *A.T.*, IX, 121–2, cf. VII, 155–6.
[2] *R.O.*, 2; *A.T.*, IX, 121, cf. VII, 155.

natures.'[1] We can analyse body into these natures; but we cannot, for instance, analyse figure into further elements. Simple natures are thus the ultimate elements at which the process of analysis arrives and which are known in clear and distinct ideas.

Figure, extension, motion and so on are said to form a group of material simple natures, in the sense that they are found only in bodies. But there is also a group of 'intellectual' or spiritual simple natures, such as willing, thinking and doubting. Further, there is a group of simple natures which are common to spiritual and material things, such as existence, unity and duration. And Descartes includes in this group what we call 'common notions', which connect together other simple natures and on which the validity of inference or deduction depends. One of the examples which he gives is 'things which are the same as a third thing are the same as one another'.

Those 'simple natures' are the ultimate elements at which analysis arrives so long as it keeps within the sphere of clear and distinct ideas. (One might proceed further, but only at the cost of falling into mental confusion.) And they are the ultimate materials, as it were, or starting-points of deductive inference. That Descartes also speaks of 'simple propositions' is not surprising when one considers that deduction is deduction of propositions from propositions. But it is not immediately evident how Descartes can think himself justified in speaking about simple natures as propositions. Nor can it well be claimed that Descartes proceeded to explain his meaning in a clear and unambiguous manner. For if he had done so, we should presumably not be confronted with the divergent interpretations which we find in the commentaries. We might perhaps explain the matter in terms of the distinction between the act of intuition and the act of judgment. We intuit the simple nature, but we affirm its simplicity and its distinctness from other simple natures in the proposition. But Descartes can scarcely mean to imply that simple natures are without relations. As we have seen, he mentions figure as an example of a simple nature; but in discussing the twelfth Rule he says that figure is conjoined with extension (another simple nature) because we cannot conceive figure without extension. Nor does the simplicity of the act of intuition necessarily mean that the object of the intuition does not comprise two elements which are necessarily connected, provided, of course, that the apprehension

[1] *R.D.*, 12; *A.T.*, x, 418.

of the connection is immediate. For if it were not immediate, that is, if there were movement or succession, we should have a case of deduction. However, perhaps the natural way of understanding Descartes is this. We intuit first of all propositions. When in his explanation of the third Rule he gives examples of intuition, he mentions in fact only propositions. 'Thus each individual can perceive by intellectual intuition that he exists, that he thinks, that a triangle is bounded by three lines only, a sphere by a single surface, and so on.'[1] It is from such propositions that simple natures like existence are disengaged by a kind of abstraction. But when we judge of their simplicity, this judgment takes the form of a proposition. And there remain necessary connections of 'conjunction' or discrimination between simple natures, which are themselves affirmed by propositions.

Now, simple natures, some commentators have argued, remain in the ideal order. Whether we prefer to call them concepts or essences, they are abstracted from the existential order and become like mathematical objects, such as the perfect lines and circles of the geometer. Hence we can no more deduce from them existential conclusions than we can conclude from a mathematical proposition about the triangle that there are any existent triangles. Yet in his *Meditations* Descartes lays down an existential proposition, *Cogito, ergo sum*, as the fundamental principle and proceeds on this basis to prove the existence of God. We must say, therefore, that he turns his back on his own method.

It is perhaps arguable that Descartes, in order to be consistent, should have prescinded from the existential order. But, obviously enough, he did not wish to produce a metaphysics with no existential reference or one whose existential reference was in doubt. And to say that his introduction of existential propositions does not square with his mathematical method is to exaggerate the rôle of mathematics in the Cartesian idea of method. It was Descartes' conviction that in mathematics we can see the clearest example available of the orderly use of intuition and deduction; but this does not mean that he intended to assimilate metaphysics to mathematics in the sense of confining the former to the ideal order. And, as we have seen, in the *Rules for the Direction of the Mind* he gives as an instance of what he means by intuition a man's intuitive knowledge of the fact that he exists.[2] In the *Meditations* he proposes as questions or problems for treatment

---

[1] *R.D.*, 3; *A.T.*, x, 368.   [2] *Ibid.*

the existence of God and the immortality of the soul. Having subjected to doubt all that can be doubted, he arrives at the 'simple' and indubitable proposition, *Cogito, ergo sum*. He then proceeds to analyse the nature of the self whose existence is affirmed, after which, as a kind of prolongation of the original intuition, he proceeds to establish the existence of God. But already in the *Rules* he had given as an example of a necessary proposition which many people erroneously think to be contingent, 'I exist, therefore God exists.'[1] And the general line of argument of the *Meditations* is presented in the fourth part of the *Discourse of Method*. Hence, even if it is disputable whether all the features of Descartes' global idea of method fit well together, and even if there is much that is obscure or ambiguous, it appears that the method actually employed in the *Meditations* is not alien from this global idea.

It is worth adding that in a letter to Clerselier, Descartes points out that the word 'principle' can be understood in different senses. It may signify an abstract principle such as the statement that it is impossible for the same thing to be and not to be at the same time. And from a principle like this we cannot deduce the existence of anything. Or it may be used to signify, for instance, the proposition affirming one's existence. And from this principle we can deduce the existence of God and of creatures other than oneself. 'It may be that there is no one principle to which all things can be reduced; and the manner in which one reduces other propositions to this, that it is impossible for the same thing to exist and not to exist at the same time, is superfluous and of no use. On the other hand it is of great utility if one begins to assure oneself of the existence of God, and then of that of all creatures, by the consideration of one's own existence.'[2] There is no question of deducing existential propositions from abstract logical or mathematical propositions.

Another point to notice is that in the *Meditations*, where he follows what he calls the analytic method of proof, Descartes is concerned with the *ordo cognoscendi*, the order of discovery, not with the *ordo essendi*, the order of being. In the latter order God is prior; ontologically prior, that is to say. But in the order of discovery one's own existence is prior. I know intuitively that I exist, and by inspection or analysis of the intuitive material expressed in the proposition *Cogito, ergo sum*, I can discover first

[1] *R.D.*, 12; *A.T.*, X, 422.   [2] *A.T.*, IV, 445.

that God exists and afterwards that material things exist corresponding to my clear and distinct ideas of them.

When we turn to physics, we find Descartes speaking as though physics could be deduced from metaphysics. But we have to make a distinction between our knowledge of the laws which would govern any material world which God might choose to create and our knowledge of the existence of the material things which He has created. We can arrive by analysis at simple natures such as extension and motion. And from these one can deduce the general laws which govern any material world; that is to say, one can deduce the most general laws of physics or natural philosophy. In this sense physics depends on metaphysics. In the *Discourse on Method* Descartes summarizes the contents of the *Traité du monde* and remarks that 'I pointed out what are the laws of nature, and, without resting my reasons on any other principle than the infinite perfections of God, I tried to demonstrate all those of which one could have any doubt, and to show that even if God had created other worlds He could not have created any in which these laws would fail to be observed.'[1] But that there actually is a world in which these laws are exemplified is known with certainty, as will be seen later on, only because the divine veracity guarantees the objectivity of our clear and distinct ideas of material things.

This deductive interpretation of physics gives rise to the question whether or not experiment has any part to play in the Cartesian method. And this question is rendered all the more acute by Descartes' contention that his logic enables us to discover truths hitherto unknown. The question concerns his theory, not his practice. For that he actually performed experimental work is a historical fact.[2] We are faced with two sets of texts. On the one hand he speaks scornfully of philosophers who 'neglect experience and imagine that truth will spring from their brain like Minerva from the head of Jupiter',[3] and writes to the Princess Elizabeth that he would not dare to undertake the task of explaining the development of the human system, 'being short of the requisite experimental evidence'.[4] On the other hand we find him writing to Mersenne in 1638 that 'my physics is nothing else but geometry',[5] and in 1640 that he would consider himself entirely ignorant of

---

[1] *D.M.*, 5; *A.T.*, VI, 43.
[2] Descartes practised dissection and was interested in the practical study of anatomy. He also made some experiments in physics.
[3] *R.D.*, 5; *A.T.*, X, 380.   [4] *A.T.*, V, 112.   [5] *Ibid.*, II, 268.

physics if he were 'only able to explain how things might be and were unable to demonstrate that they could not be otherwise',[1] since he has reduced physics to the laws of mathematics. This does not, however, prevent his also writing to Mersenne in 1638 that to demand geometrical demonstrations of matters which depend on physics is to demand the impossible.[2] It is, indeed, clear that Descartes attributed some sort of rôle to experience and experiment. But it is not so clear what that rôle was.

In the first place, Descartes did not think that we can deduce *a priori* the existence of particular physical things. That there is such a thing as a magnet, for example, is known by experience. But to ascertain the true nature of the magnet it is necessary to apply the Cartesian method. First of all, of course, the philosopher must 'collect' the observations with which sense-experience provides him. For these are the empirical data which he is going to investigate, and they are presupposed by the method. Then he will try to 'deduce (by analysis, that is to say) the character of that inter-mixture of simple natures which is necessary to produce all those effects which he has seen to take place in connection with the magnet. This achieved, he can boldly assert that he has discovered the real nature of the magnet in so far as human intelligence and the given experimental observations can supply him with this knowledge.'[3] The philosopher can then reverse the process, starting with the simple natures and deducing the effects. These should, of course, be consistent with the effects which are actually observed. And experience or experiment can tell us whether they are consistent.

In the second place, Descartes makes a distinction between the primary and more general effects and the more particular effects which can be deduced from principles or 'first causes'. The former can, he thinks, be deduced without great difficulty. But there is an infinity of particular effects which might be deduced from the same first principles. How, therefore, are we to distinguish between the effects which actually take place and those which might follow but do not, because God has willed otherwise? We can do this only by empirical observation and experiment. 'When I wished to descend to those (effects) which were more particular, so many objects of various kinds presented themselves to me that I did not think that it was possible for the human mind to distinguish the forms or species of bodies which are on the earth from an infinitude

---

[1] *A.T.*, iii, 39.   [2] *Ibid.*, ii, 141.   [3] *R.D.*, 12; *A.T.*, x, 427.

of others which might have been so if it had been the will of
God to place them there, or consequently to apply them to our use,
if it were not that we arrive at the causes by the effects and avail
ourselves of many particular experiments.'[1] Descartes seems here
to be speaking of the different kinds of things which might have
been created, given the ultimate principles or simple natures. But
he also says that 'I observed hardly any particular effect as to
which I could not recognize that it might be deduced from the
principles in different ways.'[2] And he concludes, 'I do not know
any other plan than again to try to find experiments of such a
nature that their result is not the same if it has to be explained in
one way as it would be if explained in another.'[3]

Descartes' 'pan-mathematicism' is thus not absolute: he does
not refuse to allow any rôle to experience and experiment in
physics. At the same time it is noticeable that the part which he
assigns to verificatory experiment is to supply for the limitations
of the human mind. In other words, although he does in fact give
experiment a part to play in the development of our scientific
knowledge of the world, and although he recognizes that we cannot
in fact discover new particular truths in physics without the aid
of sense-experience, his ideal remains that of pure deduction. He
can speak scornfully of natural philosophers who disdain any
appeal to experience because he recognizes that we cannot in fact
dispense with it. But he is far from being an empiricist. The ideal
of assimilating physics to mathematics remains always before his
eyes; and his general attitude is far removed from that of Francis
Bacon. It may be somewhat misleading to speak of Descartes'
'pan-mathematicism'; but the use of the term none the less
draws attention to the general line of his thought and helps to
differentiate his conception of natural philosophy from that
of Bacon.

It is perhaps over-optimistic to say that Descartes' theory of
innate ideas sheds further light on the nature of the function which
he attributes to experiment in scientific method. For the theory
is itself not free from obscurity. However, it is relevant to any
discussion of the experimental element in Cartesian method. And
in the next section I propose to say something about the theory.

4. Descartes speaks of discovering the first principles or first
causes of everything which is or which can be in the world without
'deriving them from any other source than certain germs of truth

[1] *D.M.*, 6; *A.T.*, vi, 64.　　[2] *D.M.*, 6; *A.T.*, vi, 64-5.　　[3] *D.M.*, 6; *A.T.*, vi, 65.

which exist naturally in our souls'.[1] Again, he declares that 'we shall without difficulty set aside all the prejudices of the senses and in this respect rely upon our understanding alone by reflecting carefully on the ideas implanted therein by nature'.[2] Passages of this sort inevitably suggest that according to Descartes we can construct metaphysics and physics by logical deduction from a number of innate ideas implanted in the mind by 'nature' or, as we afterwards learn, by God. All clear and distinct ideas are innate. And all scientific knowledge is knowledge of or by means of innate ideas.

Regius objected that the mind has no need of innate ideas or axioms. The faculty of thinking is quite sufficient to explain its processes. To this Descartes replied that 'I never wrote or concluded that the mind required innate ideas which were in some way different from its faculty of thinking.'[3] We are accustomed to say that certain diseases are innate in certain families, not because 'the babes of these families suffer from these diseases in their mother's womb, but because they are born with a certain disposition or propensity for contracting them'.[4] In other words, we have a faculty of thinking, and this faculty, owing to its innate constitution, conceives things in certain ways. Descartes mentions the general 'notion' that 'things which are equal to the same thing are equal to one another' and challenges his opponent to show how this notion can be derived from corporeal movements, when the latter are particular, the former universal.[5] Elsewhere he mentions other common notions or 'eternal truths' (for example, *ex nihilo nihil fit*) which have their seat in the mind.[6]

Statements of this sort tend to suggest that for Descartes innate ideas are *a priori* forms of thought which are not really distinct from the faculty of thinking. Axioms such as those mentioned above are not present in the mind as objects of thought from the beginning; but they are virtually present in the sense that by reason of its innate constitution the mind thinks in these ways. Descartes' theory would thus constitute to some extent an anticipation of Kant's theory of the *a priori*, with the important difference that Descartes does not say, and indeed does not believe, that the *a priori* forms of thought are applicable only within the field of sense-experience.

[1] *D.M.*, 6; *A.T.*, VI, 64. [2] *P.P.*, 2, 3; *A.T.*, VIII, 42, cf. IX B, 65.
[3] *Notes Against a Programme*, 12; *A.T.*, VIII B, 357.
[4] *Notes Against a Programme*, 12; *A.T.*, VIII B, 358.
[5] *Notes Against a Programme*, 12; *A.T.*, VIII B, 359. [6] *P.P.*, 1, 49. *A.T.*, VIII, 23-4.

Yet it is clear that Descartes does not restrict innate ideas to forms of thought or moulds of conception. For he speaks of all clear and distinct ideas as innate. The idea of God, for example, is said to be innate. Such ideas are not, indeed, innate in the sense that they are present in the baby's mind as fully-fledged ideas. But the mind produces them, as it were, out of its own potentialities on the occasion of experience of some sort. It does not derive them from sense-experience. As has already been remarked, Descartes was no empiricist. But sense-experience can furnish the occasion on which these ideas are formed. The latter, clear and distinct ideas, are quite different from the 'adventitious' ideas, the confused ideas which are caused by sense-experience, and from 'factitious' ideas, the constructions of the imagination. They are instances of the mind's actualization of its inner potentialities. It can hardly be claimed, I think, that Descartes provided a clear, positive account of the nature and genesis of innate ideas. But it is at least evident that he distinguished between 'adventitious', 'factitious' and clear and distinct ideas, and that he considered ideas of this third class to be virtually innate, implanted in the mind by nature or, more properly, by God.

This theory of innate ideas is obviously relevant to Descartes' conception not only of metaphysics but also of physics. Our clear and distinct ideas of simple natures are innate. So is our knowledge of the universal and certain principles and laws of physics. They cannot be derived from sense-experience, for this gives us particulars, not the universal. What, then, is the rôle of experience? As we have seen, it furnishes the occasions on which the mind recognizes those ideas which it draws, as it were, out of its own potentialities. Further, it is by means of experience that we are aware that there are external objects corresponding to our ideas. 'In our ideas there is nothing which is not innate in the mind or faculty of thinking, except only those circumstances which point to experience; the fact, for example, that we judge that this or that idea, which we now have present to our thought, is to be referred to a certain external thing, not because these external things transmitted the ideas themselves to the mind through the organs of sense, but because they transmitted something which gave it the occasion to form these ideas, by means of an innate faculty, at this time rather than at another.'[1]

What becomes, then, of Descartes' remarks about the need for

---

[1] *Notes Against a Programme*, 13; A.T., VIII B, 358–9.

experiments in physics? The answer has already been given in the last section. Verificatory experiment plays a part in physics because of the limitations of the human mind. A deductive system remains the ideal. And empirical hypotheses cannot be said to provide us with real scientific knowledge.

5. Allusion has already been made to Descartes' use of methodic doubt. As a preliminary to the search for absolute certainty he thought that it was necessary to doubt all that could be doubted and to treat provisionally as false all that could be doubted. 'Because I wished to give myself entirely to the search after truth, I thought that it was necessary for me to adopt an apparently opposite course and to reject as absolutely false everything concerning which I could imagine the least ground of doubt, in order to see whether afterwards there remained anything in my beliefs which was entirely certain.'[1]

The doubt recommended and practised by Descartes is universal in the sense that it is applied universally to all that can be doubted; that is, to every proposition about whose truth doubt is possible. It is methodic in the sense that it is practised not for the sake of doubting but as a preliminary stage in the attainment of certainty and in sifting the true from the false, the certain from the probable, the indubitable from the doubtful. It is thus also provisional not only in the sense that it is a preliminary stage in the attainment of certainty but also in the sense that Descartes does not necessarily aim at substituting new propositions for those in which he formerly believed. For it may be found later that one or more propositions which were formerly only opinions, accepted, for example, on the authority of past writers or of teachers, are intrinsically certain on purely rational grounds. The doubt is also theoretical in the sense that we should not make use of it in conduct. For in conduct it frequently happens that we are obliged to follow opinions which are only probable. In other words, what Descartes proposes to do is to re-think philosophy from the start. And to do this it is necessary to examine all his opinions systematically in the hope of finding a certain and secure foundation on which to build. But all this is a matter of theoretical reflection. He does not propose, for example, to live as though there were no moral law until he has deduced a code of ethics which will satisfy all the requirements of the Cartesian method.

How far can doubt be extended? In the first place I can doubt

[1] *D.M.*, 4; *A.T.*, VI, 31.

all that I have learned through the senses. 'I have sometimes experienced that these senses were deceptive, and it is wiser not to trust entirely to anything by which we have once been deceived.'[1] It may be objected that though I am sometimes deceived about the nature of very distant or very small objects of sense, there are very many instances of sense-perception in which it would be extravagant to imagine that I am or can be subject to deception. For example, how can I be deceived in thinking that this object is my body? All the same, it is conceivable that 'we are asleep and that all these particulars, for example that we open our eyes, shake our head, extend our hands, or even perhaps that we have such hands, are not true'.[2] In fine, it may be, to use the title of a play by Calderón, that 'life is a dream' and that all which appears to us to be substantial and real is not so in fact.

This doubt does not, however, affect the propositions of mathematics. 'For whether I am awake or asleep two and three always make five, and the square can never have more than four sides, and it does not seem possible that truths so clear and apparent can be suspected of any uncertainty.'[3] I have sometimes been deceived in my judgments about the objects of the senses, and it is therefore not altogether unnatural to envisage the possibility of my being always deceived, since the hypothesis has a partial basis in experience. But I see very clearly that two and three added together make five, and I have never met with any contrary instance. At first sight, therefore, it appears that I cannot be deceived in such matters. There is ground for doubting 'adventitious ideas' which are derived through the senses; but there seems to be no ground at all for doubting propositions the truth of which I see very clearly and distinctly like the truths of mathematics. Empirical propositions, one might say, are doubtful, but analytic propositions are surely indubitable.

Yet it is possible, given a metaphysical hypothesis, to doubt even the propositions of mathematics. For I can suppose that 'some evil genius, no less powerful than deceitful, has employed his whole energies in deceiving me'.[4] In other words, by a voluntary effort I can envisage the possibility of my having been so constituted that I am deceived even in thinking that those propositions are true which inevitably appear to me to be certain. Descartes did not think, of course, that the hypothesis mentioned

[1] M., I; A.T., vii, 18, cf. ix, 14.　　[3] M., I; A.T., vii, 19, cf. ix, 15.
[2] M., I; A.T., vii, 20, cf. ix, 16.　　[4] M., I; A.T., vii, 22, cf. ix, 17.

is a probable hypothesis or that there is positive ground for doubting the truths of mathematics. But he was searching for absolute certainty, and in his opinion a necessary first stage was to doubt all that could be doubted, even though the possibility of doubting might rest on a fictitious hypothesis. Only by this sifting of supposed truths to the very limit could he hope to arrive at a fundamental truth, doubt of which would prove to be impossible.

Hence Descartes was willing to set aside as doubtful or to treat provisionally as false not only all propositions concerning the existence and nature of material things but also the principles and demonstrations of those mathematical sciences which had appeared to him to be models of clarity and certainty. In this sense, as has already been remarked, his doubt was universal, not, as we shall see, that he found it possible in fact to doubt every truth without exception, but in the sense that no proposition, however evident its truth might appear to be, was to be excepted from the test.

There has been a certain amount of controversy about the question whether Descartes' doubt was 'real' or not. But it is rather difficult, I think, to give a simple answer to this question. Obviously, if Descartes proposed to doubt or to treat provisionally as false all that could be doubted, he had to have some reason for doubting a proposition before he could doubt it. For if he could find no reason at all, the proposition in question would be indubitable, and he would have already found what he was looking for, namely, a truth which was absolutely certain and could not be doubted. And if there was a reason for doubting, the doubt would presumably be 'real' to the extent that the reason was real. But it is not easy to gather from the writings of Descartes a clear and precise account of the way in which he regarded the reasons which he offered for doubting the truth of different propositions. Doubts concerning the proposition that material things are in themselves precisely what they appear to our senses to be were for him amply justified. Believing that things are not in themselves coloured, for example, he naturally thought that our adventitious ideas of things as coloured are not trustworthy. As for propositions like 'the entire testimony of the senses must be rejected' or 'material things are only mental images' (that is, there are no extramentally existent material things corresponding to our clear ideas of them), Descartes was well aware that we cannot in practice believe or act on such assumptions. 'We must note the distinction emphasized by me in various passages between the practical activities of our life and an inquiry into truth; for when it is a case of regulating our life it would assuredly be stupid not to trust the senses. . . . It was for this reason that somewhere I announced that no one in his sound mind seriously doubted about such matters.'[1] On the other hand, even though we cannot have any real feeling of doubt in our practical lives about the objective existence of material things, we can prove the proposition asserting that they exist only after God's existence has been proved. And certain knowledge of God's existence depends on knowledge of my existence as a thinking subject. From the point of view of our acquisition of metaphysical knowledge we can doubt the existence of material things, even if we have to introduce the hypothesis of the 'evil genius' in order to be able to do so. At the same time the introduction of this hypothesis makes the doubt 'hyperbolical' to use Descartes' word in the sixth *Meditation*.[2] And his remark in the same *Meditation*, 'being still ignorant or rather supposing myself to be ignorant of the author of my being',[3] helps to underline the fact that the hypothesis of the 'evil genius' is an admittedly voluntary and deliberate fiction.

While I certainly would not care to affirm that what Descartes says in the *Discourse on Method* and in the *Meditations* always lends support to this interpretation, his general point of view, as represented in his replies to criticism and in his *Notes Against a Programme*, is that doubt about the existence of God or about the distinction between sleep and waking is equivalent to a deliberate abstaining from asserting and making use within the framework of his philosophical system of the propositions that God exists and that material things exist until they have been proved according to the order demanded by the *ratio cognoscendi*. Thus in the *Notes Against a Programme* Descartes asserts, 'I proposed, at the beginning of my *Meditations*, to regard as doubtful all the doctrines which did not owe their original discovery to me, but had been for long denounced by the sceptics. What could be more unjust than to attribute to a writer opinions which he states only to the end that he may refute them? What more foolish than to imagine that, at least for the time being, while these false opinions are being propounded previous to their refutation, the author commits himself to them. . . ? Is there anyone obtuse enough to think

---

[1] R.O., 5; A.T., VII, 350–1.   [2] A.T., VII, 89, cf. IX, 71.
[3] A.T., VII, 77, cf. IX, 61.

that the man who compiled such a book was ignorant, so long as he was writing its first pages, of what he had undertaken to prove in the following?'[1] Descartes pleads, therefore, that his mode of procedure no more implies that he doubted God's existence before he formulated the proofs that God exists than the fact that any other writer undertakes to prove this proposition implies previous real doubt about its truth. But it is true, of course, that Descartes enjoined systematic doubt of all that could be doubted, whereas philosophers like Aquinas and Scotus had not done so. The relevant question is, indeed, in what precise sense this doubt is to be understood. And it does not seem to me that Descartes provides any very clear and consistent analysis of the meaning which he attaches to the term. All we can do is to try to interpret what he says in the *Discourse on Method*, the *Meditations* and the *Principles of Philosophy* in the light of his answers to questions and hostile criticism.

[1] *A.T.*, VIII B, 367.

CHAPTER III

DESCARTES (2)

Cogito, ergo sum—*Thinking and the thinker—The criterion of truth—The existence of God—The accusation of a vicious circle—The explanation of error—The certainty of mathematics—The ontological argument for God's existence.*

1. As we have seen, Descartes employed methodic doubt with a view to discovering whether there was any indubitable truth. And whoever knows anything at all about his philosophy knows that he found this truth in the affirmation *Cogito, ergo sum,* 'I think, therefore I am.'

However much I doubt, I must exist: otherwise I could not doubt. In the very act of doubting my existence is manifest. I may be deceived when I judge that material things exist which correspond to my ideas of them. And if I employ the metaphysical hypothesis of an 'evil genius' who has so made me that I am deceived all along the line, I can conceive, though admittedly with difficulty, the possibility that I am deceived in thinking that the propositions of mathematics are certainly true. But however far I extend the application of doubt, I cannot extend it to my own existence. For in the very act of doubting my existence is revealed. Here we have a privileged truth which is immune from the corroding influence not only of the natural doubt which I may feel concerning judgments about material things but also of the 'hyperbolical' doubt which is rendered possible by the fictitious hypothesis of the *malin génie.* If I am deceived, I must exist to be deceived: if I am dreaming, I must exist to dream.

This point had been made already centuries before by St. Augustine.[1] And we might perhaps expect Descartes to follow Augustine in expressing his fundamental existential truth in the form, *Si fallor, sum,* 'If I am deceived, I exist.' But doubting is a form of thinking. 'By the word *thought* I understand all that of which we are conscious as operating in us.'[2] And though the

---

[1] *De libero arbitrio*, 2, 3, 7. St. Augustine, however, did not attempt to construct a philosophy systematically on this basis. His *Si fallor, sum* is an example of an indubitable truth which refutes scepticism; but it does not play in Augustine's philosophy the fundamental rôle which is played by the *Cogito, ergo sum* in the system of Descartes. [2] *P.P.*, 1, 9; *A.T.*, VIII, 7, cf. IX B, 28.

absolute certainty of my existence becomes most manifest to me in the act of doubting,[1] Descartes, while drawing attention to the *Si fallor, sum*, prefers to formulate his truth in the non-hypothetical form, *Cogito, ergo sum*.

Obviously, this certainty of my own existence obtains only when I am thinking, when I am conscious. 'I am, I exist, that is certain. But how often? Just when I think; for it might possibly be the case that if I ceased entirely to think, I should likewise cease altogether to exist.'[2] 'If I had only ceased from thinking, even if all the rest of what I had ever imagined had really existed, I should have no reason for thinking that I had existed.'[3] From the fact that I exist when I think and while I think, I cannot conclude without more ado that I exist when I am not thinking. 'I am, I exist, is necessarily true each time that I pronounce it or that I mentally conceive it.'[4] Although if I ceased to think I obviously could not assert my existence, I cannot possibly conceive my non-existence here and now; for to conceive is to exist.

Now, Descartes speaks of 'this proposition *I think, therefore I am*'.[5] And the proposition is obviously expressed in an inferential form. But he had already said that 'each individual can mentally have an intuition of the fact that he exists and that he thinks'.[6] The question arises, therefore, whether according to Descartes I infer or intuit my existence.

The answer to this question is given as follows. 'He who says, *I think, hence I am or exist*, does not deduce existence from thought by a syllogism, but by a simple act of mental vision, he recognizes it as if it were a thing which is known through itself (*per se*). This is evident from the fact that if it were deduced syllogistically, the major premise, that *everything which thinks is or exists*, would have to be known previously; but it has been learned rather from the individual's experience—that unless he exists he cannot think. For our mind is so constituted by nature that general propositions are formed out of the knowledge of particulars.'[7] It is true that in the *Principles of Philosophy* Descartes says that 'I did not deny that we must first of all know what is knowledge, what is existence, what is certainty and that in order to think we must be, and such

---

[1] For example, 'We cannot doubt our existence without existing while we doubt' (*P.P.*, 1, 7; *A.T.*, IX B, 27, cf. VIII, 7). Again, 'I doubt, therefore I am; or, which is the same thing, I think, therefore I am' (*S.T.*; *A.T.*, x, 523).
[2] *M.*, 2; *A.T.*, VII, 27, cf. IX, 21.   [3] *D.M.*, 4; *A.T.*, VI, 32–3.
[4] *M.*, 2; *A.T.*, VII, 25.   [5] *P.P.*, 1, 10; *A.T.*, VIII, 8, cf. IX B, 19.
[6] *R.D.*, 3; *A.T.*, x, 368.   [7] *R.O.*, 2, 3; *A.T.*, VII, 140–1, cf. IX, 110–11.

like.'[1] But while admitting to Burman that he had said this in the *Principles* he explains that the priority of the major premiss, 'whatever thinks, is', is implicit, not explicit. 'For I attend only to what I experience within myself, namely, *I think, therefore I am*, and I do not give attention to that general notion, *whatever thinks, is*.'[2] Descartes may not express himself either with perfect clarity or with perfect consistency. But his general position is this. I intuit in my own case the necessary connection between my thinking and my existing. That is to say, I intuit in a concrete case the impossibility of my thinking without my existing. And I express this intuition in the proposition *Cogito, ergo sum*. Logically speaking, this proposition presupposes a general premiss. But this does not mean that I first think of a general premiss and then draw a particular conclusion. On the contrary, my explicit knowledge of the general premiss follows my intuition of the objective and necessary connection between my thinking and my existing.[3] Or perhaps we can say that it is concomitant with the intuition, in the sense that it is discovered as latent in or intrinsically implied by the intuition.

What, however, is meant by 'think' in the proposition *Cogito, ergo sum?* 'By the word *thought* I understand all that of which we are conscious as operating in us. And that is why not only understanding, willing and imagining but also feeling are here the same thing as thought.'[4] But the meaning of this passage must be clearly understood. Otherwise it may appear that Descartes is involved in inconsistency by including under *thought* imagining and feeling when at the same time he is 'feigning' that all material things are non-existent. What he means is that even if I neither felt nor perceived nor imagined any real existent object, either part of my body or external to my body, it would none the less be true that I appear to myself to imagine and perceive and feel, and consequently that I have these experiences so far as they are conscious mental processes. 'It is at least quite certain that it seems to me that I see light, that I hear noise, and that I feel heat. This cannot be false; this is, properly speaking, what is in me called feeling; and used precisely in this sense it is no other thing

---

[1] *P.P.*, I, 10; *A.T.*, VIII, 8, cf. IX B, 29.   [2] *A.T.*, V, 147.
[3] According to Descartes, knowledge of what existence, certainty and knowledge are and of the proposition that in order to think we must be is innate knowledge (*R.O.*, 6, 1; *A.T.*, VII, 422, cf. IX, 225). But it must be remembered that innate ideas are for him virtually innate.
[4] *P.P.*, I, 9; *A.T.*, VIII, 7, cf. IX B, 28.

than thinking.'[1] In his reply to the fifth set of objections Descartes points out that 'from the fact that I think that I walk I can very well infer the existence of the mind which so thinks, but not that of the body which walks'.[2] I can dream that I am walking, and I must exist to dream; but it does not follow that I am actually walking. Similarly, he argues, if I think that I perceive the sun or smell a rose I must exist; and this would hold good even if there were no real sun and no objective rose.

The *Cogito, ergo sum* is therefore the indubitable truth on which Descartes proposes to found his philosophy. 'I came to the conclusion that I could accept it without scruple as the first principle of the philosophy for which I was seeking.'[3] 'This conclusion, *I think, therefore I am*, is the first and most certain of all which occur to one who philosophizes in an orderly way.'[4] It is the first and most certain existential judgment. Descartes does not propose to build his philosophy on an abstract logical principle. In spite of anything which some critics may have said, his concern is not simply with essences or with possibilities: he is concerned with the existing reality, and his primary principle is an existential proposition. But we have to remember that when Descartes says that this proposition is the first and most certain, he is thinking of the *ordo cognoscendi*. This is why he says that it is the first and most certain of all which occur to a man who philosophizes in an orderly way. He does not mean to imply, for example, that our existence is more firmly grounded than God's existence as far as the *ordo essendi* is concerned. He means simply that in the *ordo cognoscendi* or *ordo inveniendi* the *Cogito, ergo sum* is fundamental since it cannot be doubted. It is obviously possible to doubt whether God exists; for there are in fact people who doubt this. But it is not possible to doubt my own existence, since the proposition 'I doubt whether I exist' is self-contradictory. I could not doubt unless I existed, at any rate during the period of doubt. I can, of course, utter the words, 'I doubt whether I exist', but in uttering them I cannot help affirming my own existence. This is really Descartes' point.

2. But when I affirm my own existence, what is it precisely that I affirm as existing? It must be remembered that I have already 'feigned' that no extramental thing exists. By making the hypothesis of the evil genius I have been able to doubt, at least

[1] *M.*, 2; *A.T.*, VII, 29, cf. IX, 23.   [2] *R.O.*, 2, 1; *A.T.*, VII, 352.
[3] *D.M.*, 4; *A.T.*, VI, 32.   [4] *P.P.*, 1, 7; *A.T.*, VIII, 7, cf. IX B 27.

with a 'hyperbolical' doubt, whether the things which I seem to perceive and to feel really exist. And this hyperbolical doubt has been applied even to the existence of my own body. Now, the *Cogito, ergo sum* is affirmed even in the presence of this hyperbolical doubt. The point is that even given the hypothesis of the evil genius and all the consequences which flow from it I cannot doubt my own existence without affirming it. But inasmuch as this hypothesis is presupposed I cannot, when I affirm my own existence, be affirming the existence of my body or of anything distinct from my thinking. Hence, says Descartes, when I affirm my own existence in the *Cogito, ergo sum* I am affirming the existence of myself as something which thinks, and nothing more. 'But what then am I? A thing which thinks. What is a thing which thinks? It is a thing which doubts, understands, affirms, denies, wills, refuses, and which also imagines and feels.'[1]

It has been brought as an objection against Descartes that he here makes a real distinction between soul or mind or consciousness and body and that he has no right to make such a distinction at this stage, since he has not proved that no corporeal thing can think or that thinking is an essentially spiritual process. And it is true, of course, that by applying hyperbolical doubt to the existence of the body and by then declaring that even in the face of this hyperbolical doubt I cannot deny the existence of myself as a thinking thing, Descartes implies that this thinking thing, which is called 'myself', is not the body. But he insists that in the second *Meditation* he did not assume that no corporeal thing can think: all he intended to assert was that the I whose existence I assert in the *Cogito, ergo sum* is a thinking thing. And to state that I am a thinking thing is not the same as to state that soul and body are ontologically distinct, the one being immaterial, the other material. In other words, the first assertion must be understood from an epistemological point of view. If I think away the body and then assert my own existence I assert the existence of myself as a thinking thing, as a subject; but I do not necessarily state anything about the ontological relation between mind and body. As far as the actual point reached is concerned, we can say that whether a corporeal thing can think or not, the thinking is there, and it is of this thinking that I affirm the existence as an indubitable fact. This is why in his replies to objections Descartes insists that his doctrine about the precise relation between mind

[1] *M.*, 2; *A.T.* VII, 28, cf. IX, 22.

and body is established at a later stage, namely, in the sixth
Meditation and not in the second. 'But besides this you here ask
how I prove that a body cannot think. Pardon me if I reply that
I have not yet given ground for the raising of the question; for I
first treat of it in the sixth *Meditation*.'[1] Similarly, in the reply
to the third set of *Objections* Descartes remarks: 'A thing which
thinks, he says, may be something corporeal; and the opposite of
this has been assumed, not proved. But in fact I did not assume
the opposite, neither did I use it as a basis for my argument; I left
it wholly undetermined until *Meditation VI* in which its proof is
given.'[2] In the reply to the fourth set of *Objections* he admits that
if he had been looking only for ordinary or 'vulgar' certitude he
might, already in the second *Meditation*, have drawn from the
conceivability of thinking without reference to the body the conclusion that mind and body are really distinct. 'But, since one of
those hyperbolical doubts adduced in the first *Meditation* went so
far as to prevent me from being sure of this very fact, that things
are in their true nature exactly as we perceive them to be, so long
as I supposed that I had no knowledge of the author of my being,
all that I have said about God and about truth in the third, fourth
and fifth *Meditations* serves to further the conclusion as to the real
distinction between mind and body, which is finally completed in
the sixth *Meditation*.'[3] Finally, in reply to the seventh set of
Objections, Descartes asserts that 'I deny that I ever presupposed
in any way that the mind was incorporeal. I finally proved this
in the sixth *Meditation*.'[4] It can hardly be repeated too often
that Descartes proceeds in the *Meditations* according to the *ordo
cognoscendi* or *inveniendi* in a methodical and systematic manner,
and that he does not wish to be interpreted as asserting more at
any given stage of his reflections than is required at the moment.

There is another objection to which allusion must be made here.
Descartes, it is said, had no right to assume that thinking requires
a thinker. Thinking, or rather thoughts, constitute a datum; but
the 'I' is not a datum. Similarly, he had no justification for
asserting that I am 'a thing which thinks'. What he did was to
assume uncritically the Scholastic notion of substance when this
doctrine ought really to have been subjected to the test of doubt.

It seems to me to be true that Descartes assumes that thinking
requires a thinker. In the *Discourse on Method*, after pointing out

[1] *R.O.*, 2, 1; *A.T.*, VII, 131, cf. IX, 104.
[2] *R.O.*, 3, 2; *A.T.*, VII, 175, cf. IX, 136.
[3] *R.O.*, 4, 1; *A.T.*, VII, 226, cf. IX, 175–6.   [4] *R.O.*, 7, 5; *A.T.*, VII, 492.

that to doubt or to be deceived I must exist and that if I ceased
from thinking I should have no reason for saying that I existed,
he remarks: 'From that I knew that I was a substance the whole
nature of which is to think, and that for its existence there is no
need of any place, nor does it depend on any material thing.'[1]
Here he certainly assumes the doctrine of substance. It may be
objected, of course, that it is illegitimate to press what is said in
the *Discourse on Method*. In this work he talks, for example, as
though the real ontological distinction between soul and body
were known immediately on the establishment of the *Cogito, ergo
sum*, whereas in the replies to objections he draws attention to the
fact that he treats of this distinction in the sixth, and not in the
second, *Meditation*. And if we are going to accept this reply in
regard to the precise nature of the distinction between soul and
body and refrain from pressing what is said in the *Discourse*, we
ought also to refrain from giving too much weight to what is said
in the same work about knowing myself as 'a substance the whole
essence or nature of which is to think'. However, in the second
Meditation Descartes seems to assume that thinking requires a
thinker, and in his replies to the third set of *Objections* he simply
asserts that 'it is certain that no thought can exist apart from a
thing which thinks, no activity, no accident can be without a
substance in which to exist'.[2]

The charge against Descartes that he assumed a doctrine of
substance seems, therefore, to be justified. It is true that critics
who bring this charge are sometimes phenomenalists, who think
that Descartes was misled by grammatical forms into making
the false assumption that thinking requires a thinker. But it is
not necessary to be a phenomenalist in order to admit the validity
of the charge. For the point seems to me to be, not that Descartes
was wrong in saying that thinking requires a thinker, but that the
exigencies of his method required that this proposition should be
submitted to doubt and not assumed.

It is, however, to be remarked that both in the *Meditations* and
in the *Principles of Philosophy* Descartes treats of substance after
proving the existence of God. And it might be said, therefore, that
the assertion of the doctrine of substance as an ontological doctrine
is not simply assumed, but that it is established only when
Descartes has proved the existence of God as guarantor of the
validity of all our clear and distinct ideas. As far as regards the

[1] *D.M.*, 4; *A.T.*, VI, 33.   [2] *R.O.*, 3, 2; *A.T.*, VII, 175–6, cf. IX, 136.

oning.

Cogito, ergo sum, Descartes was convinced, it may be said, that after thinking away all that can be doubted I apprehend, not simply a thinking or a thought, which is uncritically attributed to a thinker as substance, but rather a thinking I or ego. I apprehend not merely a 'thinking' but 'me thinking'. He may be right or wrong in believing that he, or any other individual, does apprehend this immediately as an indubitable datum, but, whether right or wrong, he would not be in the position of assuming uncritically a doctrine of substance.

In any case it seems true to say that for Descartes what is apprehended in the *Cogito, ergo sum* is simply the I which is left when everything other than 'thinking' has been thought away. It is, of course, a concrete existing I which is apprehended, and not a transcendental ego; but it is not the I of ordinary discourse, that is to say, for example, the M. Descartes who speaks with his friends and who is listened to and observed by them. If the ego of the *Cogito, ergo sum* is contrasted with Fichte's transcendental ego, one can doubtless talk about it as the 'empirical' ego; but the fact remains that it is not precisely the I of the sentence, 'I went for a walk in the park this afternoon.'

3. Having discovered an indubitable truth, *Cogito, ergo sum*, Descartes inquires 'what is required in a proposition for it to be true and certain. For since I had just discovered one which I knew to be such, I thought that I ought also to know in what this certainty consisted.'[1] In other words, by examining a proposition which is recognized to be true and certain, he hopes to find a general criterion of certainty. And he comes to the conclusion that there is nothing in the proposition, *I think, therefore I am*, which assures him of its truth except that he sees very clearly and distinctly what is affirmed. Hence, 'I came to the conclusion that I might assume as a general rule that the things which we conceive very clearly and distinctly are all true.'[2] Similarly, 'it seems to me that I can establish as a general rule that all things which I perceive (in the French version, conceive) very clearly and very distinctly are true'.[3]

What is meant by clear and distinct perception? In the *Principles of Philosophy*[4] Descartes tells us that 'I call that clear which is present and apparent to an attentive mind, in the same way as we assert that we see objects clearly when, being present

[1] *D.M.*, 4; *A.T.*, VI, 33.
[2] *Ibid.*
[3] *M.*, 3; *A.T.*, VII, 35, cf. IX, 27.
[4] I, 45-6; *A.T.*, VIII, 22, cf. IX B, 44.

to the beholding eye, they operate upon it with sufficient strength. But the distinct is that which is so precise and different from all other objects that it contains within itself nothing but what is clear.' We have to distinguish between clarity and distinctness. A severe pain, for example, may be very clearly perceived, but it may be confused by the sufferer with the false judgment which he makes about its nature. 'In this way perception can be clear without being distinct, though it cannot be distinct without being also clear.' This criterion of truth was doubtless suggested to Descartes by mathematics. A true mathematical proposition imposes itself, as it were, on the mind: when it is seen clearly and distinctly, the mind cannot help assenting to it. Similarly, I affirm the proposition, *I think, therefore I am,* not because I apply some extrinsic criterion of truth, but simply because I see clearly and distinctly that so it is.

Now, it might seem that having discovered this criterion of truth Descartes could go on to apply it without more ado. But the matter, he thinks, is not so simple as it appears. In the first place, 'there is some difficulty in ascertaining which are those (things) that we distinctly perceive'.[1] In the second place, 'perhaps a God might have endowed me with such a nature that I may have been deceived even concerning things which seemed to me most manifest. . . . I am constrained to admit that it is easy for Him, if He wishes it, to cause me to err, even in matters in which I believe myself to have the best evidence.'[2] True, in view of the fact that I have no reason to believe that there is a deceiving God, and indeed in view of the fact that I have not yet satisfied myself that there is a God at all, the reason for doubting the validity of the criterion is 'very slight and, so to speak, metaphysical'.[3] But none the less it has to be taken into account. And this means that I must prove the existence of a God who is not a deceiver.

If Descartes is prepared to entertain a hyperbolical doubt about the truth of propositions which are seen clearly and distinctly, it may at first sight appear that this doubt should be extended even to the proposition, *I think, therefore I am.* But this is certainly not the case. And the reason why it is not the case is obvious enough from what has already been said. I might have been so constituted that I am deceived when a mathematical proposition, for example, seems to me so clear that I cannot help accepting it as true; but I cannot be so constituted that I am

---

[1] *D.M.,* 4; *A.T.,* VI, 33.   [2] *M.,* 3; *A.T.,* VII, 36, cf. IX, 28.   [3] *Ibid.*

deceived in thinking that I exist. For I cannot be deceived unless
I exist. The *Cogito, ergo sum*, provided it is taken in the sense of
affirming my existence while I think, eludes all doubt, even hyperbolical doubt. It occupies a privileged position, since it is the
necessary condition of all thought, all doubt and all deception.

4. It is necessary, therefore, to prove the existence of a God
who is not a deceiver if I am to be assured that I am not deceived
in accepting as true those propositions which I perceive very
clearly and distinctly. Further, it is necessary to prove God's
existence without reference to the external world considered as a
really existent object of sensation and thought. For if one of the
functions of the proof is to dissipate my hyperbolical doubt about
the real existence of things distinct from my thinking, I should
obviously be involved in a vicious circle, were I to base my proof
on the assumption that there is a really existent extramental
world corresponding to my ideas of it. Descartes is thus debarred
by the exigencies of his method from utilizing the type of proof
which had been given by St. Thomas. He has to prove God's
existence from within, so to speak.

In the third *Meditation* Descartes begins by examining the ideas
which he has in his mind. Considered only as subjective modifications or 'modes of thought', they are alike. But if they are considered in their representative character, according to content,
they differ very much from one another, some containing more
'objective reality' than others. Now, all these ideas are in some
way caused. And 'it is manifest by the natural light that there
must be at least as much reality in the efficient and total cause as
in its effect. . . . That which is more perfect, that is to say, which
has more reality within itself, cannot proceed from the less
perfect.'[1]

Some ideas, like my adventitious ideas of colours, tactile
qualities, and so on, might have been produced by myself. As for
ideas like substance and duration, these might have been derived
from the idea which I have of myself. It is, indeed, not so easy to
see how this can be so in the case of ideas like extension and
motion, given that 'I' am only a thinking thing. 'But because they
are merely certain modes of substance and because I myself am
also a substance, it would seem that they might be contained in
me eminently.'[2]

The question is, therefore, whether the idea of God could have

[1] *M.*, 3; *A.T.*, VII, 40–1, cf. IX, 32.   [2] *M.*, 3; *A.T.*, VII, 45, cf. IX, 35.

been produced by myself. What is this idea? 'By the name God I understand a substance which is infinite, independent, all-knowing, all-powerful and by which I myself and everything else, if anything else exists, have been created.'[1] And if I examine these attributes or characteristics I shall see that the ideas of them cannot have been produced by myself. Inasmuch as I am substance, I can form the idea of substance; but at the same time I should not, as a finite substance, possess the idea of infinite substance unless it proceeded from an existing infinite substance. It may be said that I can perfectly well form for myself the idea of the infinite by a negation of finitude. But, according to Descartes, my idea of the infinite is not a merely negative idea; for I see clearly that there is more reality in infinite than in finite substance. Indeed, in some way the idea of the infinite must be prior to that of the finite. For how could I recognize my finitude and limitations except by comparing myself with the idea of an infinite and perfect being? Moreover, although I do not comprehend the nature of the infinite, my idea of it is sufficiently clear and distinct to convince me that it contains more reality than any other idea and that it cannot be a mere mental construction of my own. It may be objected that all the perfections which I attribute to God may be in me potentially. After all, I am conscious that my knowledge increases. And possibly it might increase to infinitude. But in reality this objection is fallacious. For the possession of potentiality and the ability to increase in perfection are imperfections if we compare them with the idea which we have of the actual infinite perfection of God. 'The objective being of an idea cannot be produced by something which exists potentially . . . but only by a being which is formal or actual.'[2]

This argument can, however, be supplemented by a somewhat different line of reasoning. I can ask whether I, who possess the idea of an infinite and perfect being, can exist if this being does not exist. Is it possible that I derive my existence from myself, from my parents or from some other source less perfect than God?

If I were myself the author of my being, 'I should have bestowed on myself every perfection of which I possessed any idea and would thus be God.'[3] Descartes argues that if I were cause of my own existence I would be the cause of the idea of the perfect which is present in my mind, and in order to be this I should have

[1] *M.*, 3; *A.T.*, vii, 45, cf. ix, 35–6.   [2] *M.*, 3; *A.T.*, vii, 47, cf. ix, 37–8.
[3] *M.*, 3; *A.T.*, vii, 48, cf. ix, 38.

to be the perfect being, God Himself. He argues, too, that it is not necessary to bring in the notion of the beginning of my existence in the past. For 'in order to be conserved in each moment in which it endures, a substance has need of the same power and action as would be required to produce and create it anew if it did not yet exist; so that the light of nature shows us clearly that the distinction between creation and conservation is solely a distinction of reason'.[1] I can ask myself, therefore, whether I possess the power of making myself, who now am, exist also in the future. If I had this power, I should be conscious of it. 'But I am conscious of nothing of the kind, and by this I know clearly that I depend on some being different from myself.'[2]

But this Being which is different from myself cannot be something less than God. There must be at least as much reality in the cause as in the effect. And it follows, therefore, that the being on which I depend must either be God or possess the idea of God. But if it is a being less than God, though possessing the idea of God, we can raise a further question about the existence of this being. And ultimately, to avoid an infinite regress, we must arrive at the affirmation of God's existence. 'It is perfectly clear that in this there can be no regress to infinity, since what is in question is not so much the cause which formerly created me as that which conserves me at the present time.'[3]

In so far as the second line of argument is peculiar to Descartes and cannot be reduced simply to some form of the traditional causal proof of God's existence, its special characteristic is the use made in it of the idea of God as the infinite perfect being. And it shares this feature with the first line of argument. The latter, it is true, proceeds simply from the idea of God to the affirmation of God's existence, whereas the second argument affirms God not only as cause of the idea of the perfect but also as cause of myself, the being which has the idea. And so the second argument adds something to the first. But they both involve consideration of the idea of God as the infinite perfect being, and Descartes claims that 'the great advantage in proving the existence of God in this way by the idea of Him is that we recognize at the same time what He is in so far as the weakness of our nature permits. For when we reflect on the idea of Him which is implanted in us, we perceive that He is eternal, omniscient, omnipotent . . . and that

---

[1] M., 3; A.T., VII, 49, cf. IX, 39.   [2] Ibid.
[3] M., 3; A.T., VII, 50, cf. IX, 40.

in fine He has in Himself all that in which we can clearly recognize any infinite perfection or good that is not limited by some imperfection.'[1]

It is clear, therefore, that for Descartes the idea of the perfect is a privileged idea. It is an idea which must not only be caused by an external cause but also resemble the being of which it is an idea in the way that a copy resembles a model. Our idea of the perfect and infinite being is, indeed, admittedly inadequate to the reality in the sense that we cannot comprehend God; but it is none the less clear and distinct. And it is a privileged idea in the sense that its presence forces us to transcend ourselves, by affirming that it is produced by an external cause, and at the same time to recognize its objectively representative character. Other ideas, according to Descartes, might have been produced by us. In the case of some ideas it may be highly improbable that they are mental fictions, but it is at least conceivable, even if only barely conceivable. But reflection convinces us that this is inconceivable in the case of the idea of the perfect.

Many of us will probably feel very doubtful whether it is as clear and certain that the idea of the infinitely perfect being is inexplicable as a mental construction of our own. And some critics would probably wish to go further and maintain that there is really no such idea at all, even though we use the phrase 'infinite perfect being'. But Descartes at any rate was firmly convinced not only of the tenability but also of the necessity of his thesis. According to him, the idea is a positive idea, that is, an idea with a positive content which is relatively clear and distinct; it cannot have been derived from sense-perception; it is not a mental fiction, variable at will; 'and consequently the only alternative is that it is innate in me, just as the idea of myself is innate in me'.[2] This idea is in fact the image and likeness of God in me; it is 'like the mark of the workman imprinted on his work',[3] placed in me by God when He created me.

Now, reference has already been made to the *Notes Against a Programme* where Descartes denies that by postulating innate ideas he meant to assert that these ideas are *actual* or that they are some kind of species (in the Scholastic sense, meaning accidental modifications of the intellect) distinct from the faculty of thought. He never intended to imply that infants in the womb

[1] *P.P.*, 1, 22; *A.T.*, VIII, 13, cf. IX B, 35.
[2] *M.*, 3; *A.T.*, VII, 51, cf. IX, 41.   [3] *Ibid*.

have an actual notion of God, but only that there is in us by nature an innate potentiality whereby we know God. And this statement seems to imply a Leibnizian conception of innate ideas, namely, that we are capable of forming the idea of God from within. That is to say, without any reference to the external world the self-conscious subject can form within himself the idea of God. In so far as innate ideas are contrasted with ideas derived from sense-perception we can say that the idea of God is innate in the sense that it is produced by a natural and inborn capacity of the mind, being thus potentially rather than actually innate. In the third *Meditation* Descartes speaks of my knowledge of myself as a thing 'which incessantly aspires after something which is better and greater than myself'.[1] And this suggests that the potentially innate idea of God is made actual under the impulse of an inborn orientation of the finite human being to its author and creator, this orientation being manifested in an aspiration towards an object more perfect than the self. And it would be natural to see in this view some connection with the Augustinian tradition with which Descartes had some acquaintance through his relation with the Oratory of Cardinal de Bérulle.

It is, however, difficult to see how the interpretation of the innateness of the idea of God can be reconciled with other statements by Descartes. For we have already seen that in the third *Meditation* he asks, 'how would it be possible that I should know that I doubt and desire, that is to say, that something is lacking to me, and that I am not quite perfect, unless I had within me some idea of a being more perfect than myself, in comparison with which I recognize the deficiencies of my nature?'[2] And he expressly states that 'the notion of the infinite is in some way earlier than the notion of the finite—to wit, the notion of God before that of myself'.[3] This passage clearly suggests that it is not that I form the idea of the infinite and perfect being because I am conscious of my imperfection and lack and of my aspiration to the perfect, but rather that I am conscious of my imperfection only because I already possess the idea of the perfect. It may be true that we cannot conclude from this that the idea of God is actually innate; but at least it seems to be stated that the idea of the perfect and infinite being, even if it is only potentially 'innate', is produced as an actual idea before the idea of the self. And in this case it seems to follow that Descartes changes his position between the

[1] *A.T.*, VII, 51, cf. IX, 41.   [2] *A.T.*, VII, 45-6, cf. IX, 36.   [3] *Ibid.*

second and third *Meditations*. The primacy of the *Cogito, ergo sum* gives place to the primacy of the idea of the perfect.

It can, of course, be said that the *Cogito, ergo sum* is a proposition or judgment, whereas the idea of the perfect is not. And Descartes has never denied that the *Cogito, ergo sum* presupposes some ideas. It presupposes, for example, some idea of the self. It may also, therefore, presuppose the idea of the perfect, without the primacy of the *Cogito, ergo sum* as the fundamental existential judgment being thereby impaired. For even if the idea of the perfect precedes this judgment, the affirmation of God's existence does not.

But one would have also, I think, to make some distinction between the *Cogito, ergo sum* of the second *Meditation* and that of the third. In the first case we have an inadequate and abstract idea of the self and affirmation of the self's existence. In the second case we have a less inadequate idea of the self, that is, of the self as possessing the idea of the perfect. And the starting-point of the argument is not the bare *Cogito, ergo sum*, considered without reference to the idea of God, but the *Cogito, ergo sum* considered as the affirmation of the existence of a being possessing the idea of the perfect and conscious of its own imperfections, finitude and limitation in the light of this idea. The datum is therefore not the bare self but the self as having within it the representative likeness of the infinite perfect being.

The aim of these remarks is not to suggest that Descartes' arguments for the existence of God can be rendered impervious to criticism. For example, he may escape from the charge that he postulates actual innate ideas by explaining in the *Notes Against a Programme* that innate ideas in his sense of the term are ideas 'which come from no other source than our faculty of thinking and are accordingly, together with this faculty, innate in us, that is, always existing in us potentially. For existence in any faculty is not actual but merely potential existence, since the very word "faculty" designates nothing more or less than a potentiality.'[1] But it is obviously open to anyone to maintain that the idea of God is not innate even in this sense. At the same time we have to try to discover what Descartes really means before we can profitably criticize what he says. To point out inconsistencies is easy enough; but behind the inconsistencies is a point of view which he is trying to express. And his point of view does not seem to involve

[1] *A.T.*, VIII B, 361.

a substitution in the third *Meditation* of the primacy of the idea of the perfect for the primacy of the *Cogito, ergo sum* implied in the second *Meditation.* It is rather that a more adequate understanding of the 'I', the existence of which is affirmed in the *Cogito, ergo sum*, reveals that it is a thinking self which possesses the idea of the perfect. And this is the foundation of the argument for God's existence. 'The whole strength of the argument which I have here made use of to prove the existence of God consists in this, that I recognize that it is not possible that my nature should be what it is, and indeed that I should have in myself the idea of a God, if God did not truly exist.'[1]

5. In the *Meditations* Descartes concludes from the two foregoing proofs of God's existence that God is not a deceiver. For God, the supremely perfect being, liable to no error or defect, exists. And 'from this it is manifest that He cannot be a deceiver, since the light of nature teaches us that fraud and deception necessarily proceed from some defect'.[2] Since God is perfect, He cannot have deceived. Hence those propositions which I see very clearly and distinctly must be true. It is certainty about God's existence which enables me to apply universally and confidently the criterion of truth which was suggested by reflection on the privileged proposition, *I think, therefore I am.*

But before we go any further we have to consider the question whether in proving God's existence Descartes is not involved in a vicious circle by using the very criterion which is to be guaranteed by the conclusion of the proof. The question is simple enough. Descartes has to prove God's existence before he can assure himself that it is legitimate to make use of the criterion of clarity and distinctness outside the *Cogito, ergo sum.* But can he, and does he, prove God's existence without making use of this criterion? If he makes use of it, he proves God's existence by means of the very criterion which is established as a criterion only when God's existence has been proved.

It may seem that the question should be raised only when Descartes' other argument for God's existence, namely, the so-called ontological argument, has been outlined. But I do not think that this is so. It is, indeed, true that in the *Principles of Philosophy* the ontological argument is given before the others. But in the *Meditations*, where Descartes is especially concerned with the *ordo cognoscendi* or *ordo inveniendi*, he does not give the

---

[1] *M.*, 3; *A.T.*, VII, 51–2. cf. IX, 41.   [2] *M.*, 3; *A.T.*, VII, 52. cf. IX, 41.

ontological argument until the fifth *Meditation*, when he has
already established his criterion of certain truth. Hence the use
of the criterion in this particular argument would not involve him
in a vicious circle. And I think, therefore, that it is best to restrict
the discussion of the accusation that he is guilty of a vicious circle
to the two arguments given in the third *Meditation*.

This accusation was clearly expressed by Arnauld in the fourth
set of *Objections*. 'The only remaining scruple I have is an uncertainty as to how a circular reasoning is to be avoided in saying:
the only secure reason we have for believing that what we clearly
and distinctly perceive is true, is the fact that God exists. But
we can be sure that God exists, only because we clearly and evidently perceive it. Therefore prior to being certain that God exists,
we should be certain that whatever we clearly and evidently
perceive is true.'[1]

Various ways of rescuing Descartes from the vicious circle have
been proposed, but Descartes himself tried to meet the objection
by making a distinction between what we perceive clearly and
distinctly here and now and what we remember to have perceived
clearly and distinctly on a former occasion. In answer to Arnauld
he remarks that 'we are sure that God exists because we have
attended to the proofs which established this fact; but afterwards
it is enough for us to remember that we have perceived something
clearly, in order to be sure that it is true. But this would not
suffice, unless we knew that God existed and that He did not
deceive us.'[2] And he refers to the replies already given to the
second set of *Objections*, where he made the following declaration.
'When I said that we could know nothing with certainty unless
we were first aware that God existed, I announced in express
terms that I referred only to the science apprehending such conclusions as can recur in memory without attending further to the
proofs which led me to make them.'[3]

Descartes is quite right in saying that he had made this distinction. For he had done so towards the end of the fifth *Meditation*.
He there said, for example, that 'when I consider the nature of a
triangle, I who have some little knowledge of the principles of
geometry recognize quite clearly that the three angles are equal
to two right angles, and it is not possible for me not to believe
this so long as I apply my mind to its demonstration; but so soon

---

[1] *A.T.*, VII, 214, cf. IX, 166.   [2] *R.O.*, 4, 2; *A.T.*, VII, 246, cf. IX, 190.
[3] *R.O.*, 2, 3; *A.T.*, VII, 140, cf. IX, 110.

as I abstain from attending to the proof, although I still recollect having clearly comprehended it, it may easily occur that I come to doubt its truth, if I am ignorant of there being a God. For I can persuade myself of being so constituted by nature that I can easily deceive myself even in these matters which I believe myself to apprehend with the greatest evidence and clarity. . . .'[1]

We are not told in this passage that the divine veracity guarantees the absolute and universal validity of memory. Nor, indeed, did Descartes think that it does. In the *Interview with Burman* he remarks that 'everyone must experience for himself whether he has a good memory or not. And if he has doubts on this score, he should make use of written notes or something of the kind to help him.'[2] What the divine veracity guarantees is that I am not deceived in thinking that those propositions are true which I remember having perceived clearly and distinctly. It does not guarantee, for example, that my recollection of what was said in some conversation is correct.

The question arises, therefore, whether Descartes' proofs of the existence of God, as given in the third *Meditation*, involve the use of certain axioms or principles. One has only to read them to see that this is the case. And if these principles are employed in the proofs because their validity has been previously seen with clarity and distinctness, it is difficult to see how a vicious circle is to be avoided. For it is only at the conclusion of the proofs when God's existence has been demonstrated, that we are assured that those propositions are true which we remember to have seen clearly and distinctly.

Obviously, Descartes has to show that the employment of memory is not essential for proving God's existence. He might say that the proof is not so much a deduction or movement of the mind from one step to another, the validity of the first step being remembered when the second is taken, as a viewing of the datum, namely the existence of myself as possessing the idea of the perfect, which gradually increases in adequacy until the relation of the self to God is explicitly recognized. It would also have to be maintained that the principles or axioms which appear to be presupposed by the proofs are not seen on a former occasion and then later employed because one remembers that one has seen their validity but seen here and now in a concrete case, so that the total

---

[1] *M.*, 5; *A.T.*, VII, 69–70, cf. IX, 55.
[2] *Entretien avec Burman*, edit. Ch. Adam, pp. 8–9.

viewing of the datum includes the perception of the principles or axioms in a concrete application. And this is in fact what Descartes appears to imply in the *Interview with Burman*. When accused of involving himself in a vicious circle by proving God's existence with the help of axioms, the validity of which is not yet certain, he answers that the author of the third *Meditation* is not subject to any deception in regard to the axioms, because his attention is fixed on them. 'As long as he does this, he is certain that he is not deceived, and he is compelled to give his assent to them.'[1] In answer to the retort that one cannot conceive more than one thing at a time, Descartes replies that this is simply not true.

It can hardly be claimed, however, that this reply meets all objections. As we have seen, Descartes pressed doubt to the point of 'hyperbolical' doubt by means of the fictitious hypothesis of the evil genius. Although the *Cogito, ergo sum* is impervious to all doubt whatsoever, since we can say *Dubito, ergo sum*, Descartes appears to say that we can envisage at least the bare possibility of our being deceived in regard to the truth of any other proposition which we perceive clearly and distinctly here and now. True, he does not always speak in this way; but this is what the hypothesis of the evil genius seems to imply.[2] And the question then arises whether his solution of the problem of the vicious circle enables him to remove this hyperbolical doubt. For even if in proving God's existence I do not employ my memory but perceive the truth of axioms by attending to them here and now, it seems that this perception is subject to hyperbolical doubt until I have proved the existence of a God who is not a deceiver. But how can I ever be assured of the truth of this conclusion if the latter rests on axioms or principles which are themselves subject to doubt until the conclusion has been proved? If the validity of the conclusion, the proposition affirming God's existence, is to be used to assure myself of the validity of the principles on which the conclusion rests, I appear to be involved in a vicious circle.

---

[1] *Entretien avec Burman*, edit. Ch. Adam, p. 9.

[2] Some historians have interpreted Descartes as drawing a distinction between knowing a thing in a simple act of mental vision and knowing it with perfect science. Thus the atheist would know that the three angles of a triangle are equal to two right angles, but he would not know it with perfect science until he was assured of God's existence. And Descartes does, indeed, say that though the atheist can know clearly that the three angles of a triangle are equal to two right angles, 'such knowledge on his part cannot constitute true science' (*R.O.*, 2, 3; *A.T.*, VII, 140-1, cf. IX, 110-11). But the reason he gives for stating that such knowledge cannot constitute true science is that 'no knowledge which can be rendered doubtful should be called science' (*Ibid.*).

To answer this difficulty, Descartes would have to explain hyperbolical doubt as affecting only the memory of having seen propositions clearly and distinctly. In other words, he ought to make his theory of hyperbolical doubt agree more clearly with his reply to Arnauld than he appears to have done. He could then escape the charge of being involved in a vicious circle, provided that the use of memory is not essential to the proofs of God's existence. Or he would have to show that the clear and distinct perception of the axioms which he himself admits to be involved in the proofs is itself involved in the basic and privileged intuition which is expressed in the *Cogito, ergo sum.*

There are doubtless further difficulties which could be raised. Suppose, for example, that I am now pursuing a line of reasoning in mathematics which involves reliance on memory. Or suppose that I am simply making use of mathematical propositions which I recollect having perceived clearly and distinctly on a previous occasion. What is my guarantee that I can rely confidently on my memory? Memory of the fact that I once proved God's existence? Or must I recall to mind an actual proof of God's existence? In the fifth *Meditation* Descartes says that even when I do not recollect the reasons which led me to affirm that God exists, that He is not a deceiver and that consequently all that I perceive clearly and distinctly is true, I still have a true and certain knowledge of this last proposition. For, provided that I recollect having perceived its truth clearly and distinctly in the past, 'no contrary reason can be brought forward which could ever cause me to doubt of its truth'.[1] Assurance of the existence of God removes hyperbolical doubt, and so I can dismiss any suggestions which proceed from such doubt. It may be questioned, however, whether this answer of Descartes meets all the difficulties which arise out of his various ways of speaking.

The Cartesian system could, of course, be so amended that the vicious circle, real or apparent, would disappear. For example, if Descartes had used the divine veracity simply to assure himself that material things exist corresponding to our ideas of them, Arnauld's accusation would have been deprived of its foundation. We might wish to criticize the representative theory of perception which would seem to be presupposed, but there would be no vicious circle. For Descartes does not presuppose the existence of material things when proving God's existence. For this reason it may be a

[1] *M.*, 5; *A.T.*, VII, 70, cf. IX, 55-6.

mistake to attach too much importance to the problem of the vicious circle; and it may appear that I have devoted a disproportionate amount of space to the subject. At the same time when we are considering a philosopher who aims at developing a closely knit system in which each step follows logically from the previous step and in which no presuppositions are made which are illegitimate from the methodological point of view, it is a matter of some importance to examine whether or not he has achieved his aims. And the proofs of God's existence provide an obvious case in which this is at least questionable. However, if Descartes can successfully maintain that the proofs do not necessarily involve the employment of memory and that the perception of any axioms involved in the proofs is somehow included in the basic and privileged intuition, he can free himself from Arnauld's charge. Unfortunately Descartes does not develop his position in an unambiguous and thoroughly consistent manner. And this, of course, is the reason why historians can give somewhat divergent accounts of his position.

6. If, however, we once assume that we have proved the existence and veracity of God, the problem of truth undergoes a change. The question is now, not how I can be sure that I have attained certainty outside the *Cogito, ergo sum*, but rather how error is to be explained. If God has created me, I cannot attribute error either to my understanding as such or to my will as such. To make error necessary would be to make God responsible for it. And I have already ascertained that God is not a deceiver.

'Whence then come my errors? They come from the sole fact that since the will is much wider in its range and compass than the understanding, I do not restrain it (the will) within the same bounds but extend it also to things which I do not understand. And as the will is of itself indifferent to these, it easily turns aside from the true and the good, and so I am deceived and sin.'[1] Provided only that I refrain from making a judgment about something which I do not see clearly and distinctly, I shall not fall into error. But while 'the perception of the understanding extends only to the few objects which present themselves to it and is always very limited, the will, on the other hand, may in some measure be said to be infinite . . . so that we easily extend it beyond that which we apprehend clearly. And when we do this there is no wonder if it happens that we are deceived.'[2] The will goes out

---

[1] *M.*, 4; *A.T.*, VII, 58, cf. IX, 46.   [2] *P.P.*, I, 35; *A.T.*, VIII, 18, cf. IX B, 40.

to things which the individual does not yet possess, even to things which the intellect does not understand. Hence we are easily led to judge about what we do not clearly understand. This is not the fault of God; for error is not rendered necessary by the will's 'infinity'. 'It is in the misuse of the free will that the privation which constitutes the characteristic nature of error is met with', that is, the privation is found in an act 'in so far as it proceeds from me', not 'in the faculty which I have received from God, nor even in the act in so far as it depends on Him'.[1]

7. Having satisfied himself that he cannot fall into error provided that he restricts his judgments to what he perceives clearly and distinctly, Descartes goes on to justify our belief in the certainty of pure mathematics. Like other thinkers before him, such as Plato and St. Augustine, he is struck by the fact that we discover rather than invent the properties of, for instance, a triangle. In pure mathematics we have a progressive insight into eternal essence or natures and their interrelations; and the truth of mathematical propositions, so far from being dependent on our free choice, imposes itself upon the mind because we see it clearly and distinctly. So we[2] can take it that we cannot be deceived when we assert mathematical propositions which we deduce from propositions which have been clearly and distinctly seen.

8. One might expect that after having ascertained the certain truth of two existential judgments (namely, the *Cogito, ergo sum* and the proposition affirming God's existence) and of all judgments of the ideal order which are clearly and distinctly perceived, Descartes would immediately go on to consider what we are entitled to assert about the existence and nature of material things. In point of fact, however, he proceeds to expound the ontological argument for God's existence. And the connection of this theme with the foregoing is the following reflection. If 'all which I know clearly and distinctly as pertaining to this object really does belong to it, may I not derive from this an argument demonstrating the existence of God?'[3] I know, for example, that all the properties which I clearly and distinctly perceive to belong to the essence of a triangle really do belong to it. Can I demonstrate the existence of God by considering the perfections contained in the idea of God?

[1] *M.*, 4; *A.T.*, VII, 60, cf. IX, 47–8.
[2] It would be more accurate to say 'I', since Descartes has not yet proved the existence of a plurality of selves.
[3] *M.*, 5; *A.T.*, VII, 65, cf. IX, 52.

Descartes answers that this is possible. For existence is itself one of the perfections of God and belongs to the divine essence. It is true, of course, that I can conceive a rectilinear triangle without ascribing existence to it, though I am forced to admit that the sum of its angles amounts to two right angles. And the explanation of this is simple enough. Existence is not an essential perfection of the idea of a triangle. And from the fact that I cannot conceive a rectilinear triangle the angles of which do not amount to two right angles it follows only that if there is any existent rectilinear triangle its angles equal two right angles; but it does not necessarily follow that there is any existent rectilinear triangle. The divine essence, however, being supreme perfection, comprises existence, which is itself a perfection. Hence I cannot conceive God except as existing. That is to say, I cannot understand the idea of God, which expresses His essence, and at the same time deny His existence. The necessity of conceiving God as existence is thus a necessity in the object itself, in the divine essence, and it is useless to object that my thought does not impose necessity on things. 'It is not within my power to think of God without existence (that is, of a supremely perfect being devoid of a supreme perfection), though it is in my power to imagine a horse either with wings or without wings.'[1] The idea of God is thus on this count also a privileged idea; it occupies a unique status. 'I cannot conceive anything but God Himself to whose essence existence[2] pertains.'[3]

We shall encounter this argument again, in the revised form in which Leibniz defended it and in connection with Kant's adverse criticism of it. But it may be worth while to make the following points here with reference to Descartes' assessment of its value.

In the first place Descartes refused to admit that the ontological argument can be reduced to a mere matter of verbal definition. Thus in his reply to the first set of *Objections* he denies that he intended to say merely that when it is understood what the meaning of the word 'God' is, it is understood that God exists in fact as well as an idea of our minds. 'Here there is a manifest error in the form of the argument; for the only conclusion to be drawn is—hence, when we understand what the word "God" means, we understand that it means that God exists in fact as well

---

[1] *M.*, 5; *A.T.*, VII, 67, cf. IX, 53.
[2] The French version adds the words 'with necessity'.
[3] *M.*, 5; *A.T.*, VII, 68, cf. IX, 54.

as in the mind. But because a word implies something, this is no reason for its being true. My argument, however, was of the following kind. That which we clearly and distinctly understand to belong to the true and immutable nature of anything, its essence or form, can be truly affirmed of that thing. But after we have with sufficient accuracy investigated the nature of God, we clearly and distinctly understand that to exist belongs to His true and immutable nature. Therefore we can with truth affirm of God that He exists.'[1] Descartes thus believes that we have a positive insight into the divine nature or essence. Without this supposition the ontological argument cannot, indeed, stand; yet it constitutes one of the major difficulties in accepting the argument as valid. Leibniz saw this, and attempted to cope with the difficulty.[2]

The second point which I wish to mention has already been alluded to in passing. As we have seen, Descartes does not expound the ontological argument until the fifth *Meditation*, when he has already proved the existence of God and established that all that we perceive clearly and distinctly is true. And this implies that the argument, while elucidating a truth about God, namely, that He exists necessarily or in virtue of His essence, is of no avail for the atheist who is not already certain that whatever he clearly and distinctly perceives is true. And the atheist cannot know this last fact until he knows that God exists. Hence it would appear that the real proofs of God's existence offered by Descartes are those contained in the third *Meditation* and that the function of the ontological argument is simply to elucidate a truth about God. On the other hand, even in the fifth *Meditation* (in the French version) Descartes speaks of the ontological argument as 'demonstrating the existence of God'.[3] And towards the end of the *Meditation* he seems to say that we can draw from it the conclusion that all that we see clearly and distinctly is true; a conclusion which would imply that the argument is a perfectly valid proof of God's existence, independently of the other proofs already given. Moreover, in the *Principles of Philosophy*,[4] he gives the ontological argument first and clearly says that it is a demonstration of God's existence. The question arises, therefore, whether we have two incompatible assessments of the ontological argument or whether some explanation of Descartes' procedure can be found

---

[1] *R.O.*, i; *A.T.*, vii, 115–16, cf. ix, 91.
[2] Another difficulty, discussed by Kant, concerns the belief that existence can properly be called a perfection.
[3] *A.T.*, ix, 52.
[4] i, 14; *A.T.*, viii, 10, cf. ix b, 31.

which will harmonize the two apparently different ways of speaking.

It does not seem to me that Descartes' different ways of speaking can be rendered perfectly consistent. At the same time a general line of harmonization can be found if we bear in mind his distinction between the *ordo inveniendi*, the order of discovery or the order in which a philosopher investigates his subject analytically, and the *ordo docendi*, the order of teaching or systematic exposition of truths already discovered.[1] In the order of discovery, as far as explicit knowledge is concerned, we know our own imperfection before the divine perfection. Hence the order of discovery seems to demand an *a posteriori* proof of God's existence; and this is given in the third *Meditation*. The ontological argument is reserved till later, when it is introduced to elucidate a truth about God, in dependence on the then already established principle that whatever we see clearly and distinctly is true. According to the order of teaching, however, so far as it represents the *ordo essendi* or order of being, the infinite perfection of God is prior to our imperfection; and so in the *Principles of Philosophy* Descartes starts with the ontological argument which is based on the infinite perfection of God. By doing this he appears to neglect his own doctrine that the existence of God must be proved before we can extend the use of the criterion of clarity and distinctness beyond the *Cogito, ergo sum*. But if, as seems to be the case, he looked on the proofs contained in the third *Meditation* as a prolongation and deepening of the original intuition expressed in the *Cogito, ergo sum*, it may be that he regarded the ontological argument in the same light.

It is possible that Descartes' treatment of our knowledge of God's existence combines, without sufficient discrimination, two attitudes or points of view. There is first the 'rationalist' point of view, according to which the arguments are really inferential processes. And if they are regarded in this light, Descartes did well to separate the ontological argument from the *a posteriori* proofs of the third *Meditation*, though at the same time the problem of the vicious circle in regard to the latter becomes acute. And there is secondly the 'Augustinian' point of view. One does not really know oneself, the self whose existence is affirmed in the *Cogito, ergo sum*, unless it is known as one term of the total relationship, self-God. What is required is not so much a process of

---

[1] Cf. *Entretien avec Burman, A.T.*, v, 153; edit. Ch. Adam, pp. 27–9.

inferential argument as a prolonged and ever more profound viewing of the datum. We know the self as imperfect only because we have an implicit awareness of God in the innate idea of the perfect. And one function of the ontological argument is to show by penetration of the idea of the perfect, which is part of the original datum, that God does not exist simply in relation to us but that He exists necessarily and eternally in virtue of His essence.

CHAPTER IV

DESCARTES (3)

*The existence of bodies—Substances and their principal attri-
butes—The relation between mind and body.*

1. So far we are assured of the truth of only two existential
propositions, 'I exist' and 'God exists'. But we also know that all
the things which we apprehend clearly and distinctly belong to
the realm of possibility. That is to say, they can be created by
God, even if we do not yet know whether they have been so
created. It is therefore sufficient, says Descartes, that we (or,
more accurately, I) should be able to apprehend one thing clearly
and distinctly apart from another to be assured that the two are
really different and that the one can be created without the other.

Now, on the one hand I see that nothing belongs to my essence,
as affirmed in the *Cogito, ergo sum*, except that I am a thinking
and unextended thing, while on the other hand I have a clear and
distinct idea of body as an extended and unthinking thing. And
it follows that 'this I (that is to say, my soul by which I am what
I am) is entirely and absolutely distinct from my body, and can
exist without it'.[1]

In this case, of course, my existence as a thinking thing does not
of itself prove the existence of my body, let alone of other bodies.
But I find in myself certain faculties and activities, such as the
power of changing position and of local motion in general, which
clearly imply the existence of corporeal or extended substance,
the body.[2] For in the clear and distinct perception of such
activities extension is in some way included, whereas thinking or
intellection is not. Further, sense-perception involves a certain
passivity, in the sense that I receive impressions of 'ideas' and that
it does not depend simply and solely on myself what impressions
I receive. This faculty of sense-perception does not presuppose
thought, and it must exist in some substance other than myself
considered as an essentially thinking and unextended thing. Again,
inasmuch as I receive impressions, sometimes against my will, I

---

[1] *M.*, 6; *A.T.*, VII, 78, cf. IX, 62.
[2] It should be noted how Descartes assumes that faculties and activities must
be the faculties and activities of substances.

am inevitably inclined to believe that they come to me from
bodies other than my own. And because God, who is no deceiver,
has given me 'a very great inclination to believe that they
(impressions or 'ideas' of sense) are conveyed to me by corporeal
objects, I do not see how He could be defended from the accusation of deceit if these ideas were produced by causes other than
corporeal objects. Hence we must allow that corporeal objects
exist.'[1] Perhaps they are not exactly what sense-perception
suggests that they are; but at any rate they must exist as external
objects in respect of all that we clearly and distinctly perceive in
them.

Descartes deals rather summarily with the existence of bodies.
Moreover, neither in the *Meditations* nor in the *Principles of
Philosophy* does he treat specifically the problem of our knowledge
of the existence of other minds. But his general argument is that
we receive impressions and 'ideas' and that as God has implanted
in us a natural inclination to attribute them to the activity of
external material causes, the latter must exist. For God would be
a deceiver, were He to give us this natural inclination and yet at
the same time to produce these impressions directly and immediately by His own activity. And Descartes, if called upon,
would doubtless produce an analogous argument, with an appeal
to the divine veracity, to existence, the existence of other minds.

We can dismiss, therefore, that form of hyperbolical doubt
which formerly suggested to us that life might be a dream and that
no corporeal things exist corresponding to our ideas of them. 'I
ought to set aside all the doubts of these past days as hyperbolical
and ridiculous, particularly that very general uncertainty respecting sleep, which I could not distinguish from the waking state. . . .'[2]
And being thus assured of the existence of both mind and body,
we can proceed to inquire more closely into the nature of each
and into the relationship between the two.

2. Descartes defined substance as 'an existent thing which
requires nothing but itself in order to exist'.[3] But this definition,
if understood in a strict and literal sense, applies to God alone.
'To speak truth, nothing but God answers to this description, as
being that which is absolutely self-sustaining; for we perceive that
there is no created thing which can exist without being sustained
by His power.'[4] But Descartes did not draw the Spinozistic

[1] *M.*, 6; *A.T.*, VII, 78–80, cf. IX, 63.   [2] *M.*, 6; *A.T.*, VII, 89, cf. IX, 71.
[3] *P.P.*, I, 51; *A.T.*, VIII, 24, cf. IX B, 47.   [4] *Ibid.*

conclusion that there is only one substance, God, and that all
creatures are simply modifications of this one substance. He concluded instead that the word 'substance' cannot be predicated in
a univocal sense of God and of other beings. He thus proceeds
in the opposite way, so to speak, to that in which the Scholastics
proceeded. For while the latter applied the word 'substance' first
to natural things, the objects of experience, and then in an
analogical sense to God, Descartes applies the word primarily to
God and then secondarily, and analogically, to creatures. This
procedure is in accordance with his professed intention of going
from cause to effect rather than the other way round. And though
he was by no means a pantheist himself we can, of course, detect
in his manner of proceeding a preliminary stage in the development of the Spinozistic conception of substance. But to say this
is not to suggest that Descartes would have approved of this
conception.

However, if we leave God out of account and think only of
substance in its application to creatures, we can say that there are
two kinds of substances and that the word is predicated in a
univocal sense of these two classes of things. 'Created substances,
however, whether corporeal or thinking, may be conceived under
this common concept; for they are things which need only the
concurrence of God in order to exist.'[1]

Now, what we perceive are not substances as such but rather
attributes of substances. And inasmuch as these attributes are
rooted in different substances and manifest the latter, they give
us knowledge of substances. But not all attributes are on an equal
footing. For 'there is always one principal property of substance
which constitutes its nature and essence, and on which all the
others depend'.[2] The idea of substance as that which needs
nothing else (save, in the case of created things, the divine activity
of conservation) is a common notion, and it will not serve to
differentiate one kind of substance from another. We can do this
only by considering the attributes, properties and qualities of substances. On this point the Scholastics would have agreed. But
Descartes went on to assign to each kind of substance a principal
attribute which he proceeded to identify to all intents and purposes with the substance itself. For his way of determining what
is the principal attribute of a given type of substance is to ask what

[1] *P.P.*, I, 52; *A.T.*, VIII, 25, cf. IX B, 47.
[2] *P.P.*, I, 53; *A.T.*, VIII, 25, cf. IX B, 48.

it is' that we perceive clearly and distinctly as an indispensable attribute of the thing, so that all other attributes, properties and qualities are seen to presuppose it and depend upon it. And the conclusion seems to be that we cannot distinguish between the substance and its principal attribute. They are to all intents and purposes identical. As will be noted later, this point of view involved him in certain theological difficulties.

We have already seen that for Descartes the principal attribute of spiritual substance is thinking. And he was prepared to maintain that spiritual substance is in some sense always thinking. Thus he tells Arnauld that 'I have no doubt that the mind begins to think at the same time that it is infused into the body of an infant, and that it is at the same time conscious of its own thought, though afterwards it does not remember it, because the specific forms[1] of these thoughts do not live in the memory.'[2] So again he asks Gassendi: 'But why should it (the soul or mind) not always think, when it is a thinking substance? Why is it strange that we do not remember the thoughts it has had when in the womb or in a stupor, when we do not even remember most of those which we know we have had when grown up, in good health, and awake?'[3] And, indeed, if the essence of the soul is to think, it must obviously either always think, even when at first sight it does not do so, or cease to exist when not thinking. Descartes' conclusion follows from his premises. Whether the premises are true or not, is another question.

What, then, is the principal attribute of corporeal substance? It must be extension. We cannot conceive figure or action, for example, without extension; but we can conceive extension without figure or action. 'Thus extension in length, breadth and depth constitutes the nature of corporeal substance.'[4] Here we have the geometrical conception of corporeal substance, considered apart from motion and energy.

These principal attributes are inseparable from the substances of which they are attributes. But there are also modifications which are separable, not in the sense that they can exist apart from the substances of which they are modifications, but in the sense that the substances can exist without those particular modifications. For example, though thinking is essential to the mind, the latter has different thoughts successively. And though

[1] Cf. the Scholastic term *species* as used for a mental modification or idea.
   R.O., 4, 2; *A.T.*, VII, 240, cf. IX, 190.   [3] *R.O.*, 5, 2, 4; *A.T.*, VII, 356–7.
[4] *P.P.*, I, 53; *A.T.*, VIII, 25, cf. IX, B, 48.

a thought cannot exist apart from the mind, the latter can exist without this or that particular thought. Similarly, though extension is essential to corporeal substance, a particular quantity or shape is not. The size and figure of a body can vary. And these variable modifications of the attributes of thought and extension are called by Descartes 'modes'. He does, indeed, say that 'when we here speak of modes we mean nothing more than what are elsewhere termed attributes or qualities'.[1] But he proceeds to distinguish his uses of these terms and adds that because in God there is no change we should not ascribe to Him modes or qualities but only attributes. And when we consider thought and extension as 'modes' of substances we are thinking of them as modifiable in diverse ways. In practice, therefore, the word 'mode' should be restricted to the variable modifications of created substances.[2]

3. The natural conclusion to draw from the foregoing is that the human being consists of two separate substances and that the relation of mind to body is analogous to that of the pilot in the ship. In Scholastic Aristotelianism the human being was depicted as a unity, soul standing to body as form to matter. The soul, moreover, was not reduced to mind: it was regarded as the principle of biological, sensitive and intellectual life. And in Thomism at least it was depicted as giving existence to the body, in the sense of making the body what it is, a human body. Clearly, this view of the soul facilitated insistence on the unity of the human being. Soul and body together form one complete substance. But on Descartes' principles it would appear to be very difficult to maintain that there is any intrinsic relationship between the two factors. For if Descartes begins by saying that I am a substance the whole nature of which is to think, and if the body does not think and is not included in my clear and distinct idea of myself as a thinking thing, it would seem to follow that the body does not belong to my essence or nature. And in this case I am a soul lodged in a body. True, if I can move my body and direct some of its activities, there is at least this relationship between the two that the soul stands to the body as mover to moved and the body to the soul as instrument to agent. And if this is so, the analogy of the relationship between a captain or a pilot and his ship is not inapt. It is, therefore, easy to understand

---

[1] *P.P.*, I, 56; *A.T.*, VIII, 26, cf. IX B, 49.

[2] Descartes remarks that there are in created substances invariable attributes 'like existence and duration in the existing and enduring thing' (*P.P.*, I, 56; *A.T.*, VIII, 26, cf. IX B, 49). These should not be called modes.

Arnauld's remark in the fourth set of *Objections* that the theory of my clearly and distinctly perceiving myself to be merely a thinking being leads to the conclusion that 'nothing corporeal belongs to the essence of man, who is hence entirely spirit, while his body is merely the vehicle of spirit; whence follows the definition of man as a spirit which makes use of a body'.[1]

In point of fact, however, Descartes had already stated in the sixth *Meditation* that the self is not lodged in the body as a pilot in a ship. There must be, he says, some truth in all things which nature teaches us. For nature in general means either God or the order of things created by God, while nature in particular means the complexus of things which He has given us. And God, as we have seen, is no deceiver. If, therefore, nature teaches me that I have a body which is affected by pain and which feels hunger and thirst, I cannot doubt that there is some truth in all this. But 'nature also teaches me by these sensations of pain, hunger, thirst, etc., that I am not only lodged in my body as a pilot in a vessel, but that I am very closely united to it, and, so to speak, so intermingled with it that I seem to compose with it one whole. For if this were not the case, when my body is hurt, I, who am merely a thinking being, should not feel pain, for I should perceive this wound by the understanding only, just as the sailor perceives by sight when something is damaged in his vessel.'[2]

Descartes appears to be in a difficult position. On the one hand, his application of the criterion of clarity and distinctness leads him to emphasize the real distinction between soul and body and even to represent each of them as being a complete substance. On the other hand, he does not want to accept the conclusion which appears to follow, namely, that the soul is simply lodged in a body which it uses as a kind of extrinsic vehicle or instrument. And he did not reject this conclusion simply to avoid criticism on theological grounds. For he was aware of empirical data which militate against the truth of the conclusion. He was aware, in other words, that the soul is influenced by the body and the body by the soul and that they must in some sense constitute a unity. He was not prepared to deny the facts of interaction, and, as is well known, he tried to ascertain the point of interaction. 'In order to understand all these things more perfectly we must know that the soul is really joined to the whole body, and that we cannot, properly speaking, say that it exists in any one of its parts

[1] *A.T.*, VII, 203, cf. IX, 158.   [2] *M.*, 6; *A.T.*, VII, 81, cf. IX, 64.

to the exclusion of the others, because it is one and in some manner indivisible. . . . (But) it is likewise necessary to know that although the soul is joined to the whole body, there is yet a certain part in which it exercises its functions more particularly than in all the others; and it is usually believed that this part is the brain, or possibly the heart. . . . But, in examining the matter with care, it seems as though I have clearly ascertained that the part of the body in which the soul exercises its functions immediately is in no way the heart, nor the whole of the brain, but merely the most inward of all its parts, to wit, a certain very small gland which is situated in the middle of its substance and which is so suspended above the duct whereby the animal spirits[1] in its anterior cavities have communication with those in the posterior that the slightest movements which take place in it alter very greatly the course of these spirits; and reciprocally that the smallest changes which occur in the course of the spirits may do much to change the movements of this gland.'[2] Localization of the point of interaction does not, indeed, solve the problems arising in connection with the relationship between an immaterial soul and a material body; and from one point of view it seems to underline the distinction between soul and body. However, it is clear that Descartes had no intention of denying interaction.

This combination of two lines of thought, namely that of emphasizing the distinction between soul and body and that of accepting and trying to explain interaction and the total unity of man, is reflected in Descartes' reply to Arnauld. If soul and body are said to be incomplete substances 'because they cannot exist by themselves . . . I confess that it seems to me to be a contradiction for them to be substances. . . . Taken alone, they are complete (substances). And I know that thinking substance is a complete thing no less than that which is extended.'[3] Here Descartes says that soul and body are complete substances, underlining the distinction between them. At the same time 'it is true that in another sense they can be called incomplete substances; that is, in a sense which allows that in so far as they are substances they have no lack of completeness, and which merely asserts that

[1] The 'animal spirits' here referred to are 'the most animated and subtle portions of the blood' which enter into the cavities of the brain. They are material bodies 'of extreme minuteness', which 'move very quickly like the particles of the flame which issues from a torch'; and they are conducted into the nerves and muscles 'by means of which they move the body in all the different ways in which it can be moved' (P.S., 1, 10; A.T., XI, 334–5).
[2] P.S., 1, 30–1; A.T., XI, 351–2.   [3] R.O., 4, 1; A.T., VII, 222, cf. IX, 173.

in so far as they referred to some other substance, in unison with which they form a single self-subsistent thing. . . . Mind and body are incomplete substances viewed in relation to the man who is the unity which they form together.'[1]

In view of this unsatisfactory position of uneasy balance it is understandable that a Cartesian like Geulincx maintained a theory of occasionalism according to which there is no real causal interaction between soul and body. On the occasion of an act of my will, for example, God moves the arm. Indeed, Descartes had himself given grounds for the development of such a theory. For example, in the *Notes Against a Programme* he speaks of external objects transmitting to the mind through the organs of sense, not ideas themselves, but 'something which gave the mind occasion to form these ideas, by means of an innate faculty, at this time rather than at another'.[2] A passage like this inevitably suggests the picture of two series of events, ideas in the mental series and movements in the corporeal series, the latter being the occasion on which the former are produced by the mind itself. And inasmuch as Descartes stressed the constant conserving activity of God in the world, this conservation being interpreted as an ever-renewed creation, one might draw the conclusion that God is the only direct causal agent. I do not mean to suggest that Descartes himself asserted a theory of occasionalism; for, as we have seen, he maintained that interaction takes place. But his treatment of the subject understandably led to the assertion of an occasionalist theory, offered partly as an explanation of what 'interaction' really means, by those who maintained Descartes' general position with regard to the nature and status of mind.

[1] *Ibid.*   [2] *A.T.*, VIII B, 359.

CHAPTER V

DESCARTES (4)

The qualities of bodies—Descartes and the dogma of transub-stantiation—Space and place—Motion—Duration and time—The origin of motion—The laws of motion—The divine activity in the world—Living bodies.

1. WE have seen that according to Descartes the principal attri-bute of corporeal substance is extension, 'thus extension[1] in length, breadth and depth constitutes the nature of corporeal substance'.[2] We can allow, therefore, that size and figure are objective natural phenomena. For they are modes or variable modifications of extension. But what is to be said about qualities like colour, sound and taste, the so-called 'secondary qualities'? Do they exist objectively in corporeal substances or not?

Descartes' answer to this question resembles that already given by Galileo.[3] These qualities are nothing in external things 'but the various dispositions of these objects which have the power of moving our nerves in various ways'.[4] Light, colour, smell, taste, sound and the tactile qualities 'are nothing more, as far as is known to us, than certain dispositions of objects consisting of magnitude, figure and motion'.[5] Thus the secondary qualities exist in us as sentient subjects rather than in external things. The latter, extended things in motion, cause in us the sensations of colour, sound and so on. This is what Descartes meant when he said at an earlier stage of his inquiry that corporeal things might not turn out to be precisely what they seem to be. We read, for example: 'Hence we must allow that corporeal things exist. How-ever, they are perhaps not exactly what we perceive by the senses, because this apprehension by the senses is in many instances very obscure and confused.'[6] Extension is what we perceive clearly and distinctly to belong to the essence or nature of corporeal substance. But our ideas of colours and sounds are not clear and distinct.

---

[1] 'By extension we understand whatever has length, breadth and depth, not inquiring whether it is a real body or merely space' (*R.D.*, 14; *A.T.*, x, 442). This is the preliminary idea of extension.

[2] *P.P.*, 1, 53; *A.T.*, VIII, 25, cf. IX B, 48.   [3] See vol. III, p. 287.

[4] *P.P.*, 4, 198; *A.T.*, VIII, 322–3, cf. IX B, 317.

[5] *P.P.*, 4, 199; *A.T.*, VIII, 323, cf. IX B, 318.

[6] *M.*, 6; *A.T.*, VII, 80, cf. IX, 63.

The natural conclusion would seem to be that our ideas of colours, sounds and so on are not innate ideas but adventitious ideas, coming from outside, caused, that is to say, by external corporeal things. Descartes held that there are in bodies imperceptible particles, though they are not, like Democritus' atoms, indivisible.[1] And this naturally suggests that in his opinion these particles in motion cause a stimulation of the sense-organs which leads to the perception of colours, sounds and other secondary qualities. Arnauld certainly understood him in this sense. 'M. Descartes recognizes no sense-qualities, but only certain motions of the minute bodies which surround us, by means of which we perceive the different impressions to which we afterwards give the names of colour, savour and odour.'[2] And in his reply Descartes asserts that what stimulates the senses is the 'superficies which forms the boundary of the dimensions of the perceived body', because 'no sense is stimulated otherwise than by contact' and 'contact takes place only at the surface'.[3] He then goes on to say that by surface we must not understand only the external figure of bodies as felt by the fingers. For there are in bodies minute particles which are imperceptible, and the surface of a body is the superficies which immediately surrounds its separate particles.

In the *Notes Against a Programme*, however, Descartes asserts that 'nothing reaches our mind from external objects through the organs of sense beyond certain corporeal movements', and he draws the conclusion that 'the ideas of pain, colour, sound and the like (must) be innate'.[4] Hence, if the ideas of secondary qualities are innate, they can hardly be at the same time adventitious. Corporeal movements stimulate the senses, and on the occasion of these movements the mind produces its ideas of colours and so on. In this sense they are innate. Indeed, in the *Notes Against a Programme* Descartes says that all ideas are innate, even the ideas of corporeal movements themselves. For we do not conceive them in the precise form in which they exist. We must distinguish, therefore, between the corporeal movements and the ideas of them which we form on the occasion of our being stimulated by them.

This theory implies, of course, a representative theory of perception. What is perceived is in the mind, though it represents what is outside the mind. And this theory gives rise to obvious

---

[1] *P.P.*, 4, 201–2; *A.T.*, VIII, 324–5, cf. IX B, 319–20.
[2] Fourth set of *Objections*; *A.T.*, VII, 217, cf. IX, 169.
[3] *R.O.*, 4; *A.T.*, VII, 249, cf. IX, 192.
[4] *A.T.*, VIII B, 359.

problems. But, quite apart from this point, the distinction between innate, adventitious and factitious ideas appears to break down if it turns out that all ideas are innate. It appears that Descartes first intended to restrict innate ideas to clear and distinct ideas, distinguishing them from ideas which are adventitious and confused, but that he later came to think that all ideas are innate, in which case, of course, not all innate ideas are clear and distinct. And there is evidently a link between these different ways of speaking about ideas and the different ways in which he speaks about the relation between soul and body. For if there can be real relations of efficient causality between body and mind, there can be adventitious ideas whereas on an occasionalistic hypothesis all ideas must be innate, in Descartes' sense of the word 'innate'.

However, if we neglect Descartes' different ways of speaking and select only one aspect of his thought, we can say that he geometrized bodies, in the sense that he reduced them, as they exist in themselves, to extension, figure and size. This interpretation should not be pressed, it is true; but his tendency is to introduce a bifurcation between the world of the physicist, who can neglect all qualities like colour except in so far as they can be reduced to the movements of particles, and the world of ordinary sense-perception. The key to truth is purely rational intuition. We cannot say simply that perception is delusive; but it must submit itself to the final judgment of pure intelligence. The mathematical spirit is here paramount in Descartes' thought.

2. At this point I wish to mention briefly a theological difficulty in which Descartes was involved through his theory of corporeal substance. The difficulty, to which a vague, passing allusion was made in the last chapter, concerns the dogma of transubstantiation. According to the dogmatic decrees of the Council of Trent, at the consecration in the Mass the substance of the bread and wine are changed into the Body and Blood of Christ, while the accidents[1] of the bread and wine remain. But if, as Descartes held, extension is identical with corporeal substance, and if qualities are subjective, it seems to follow that there are no real accidents which can remain after the conversion of the substance.

Arnauld raises this point in the fourth set of *Objections* in the section headed, 'Matters likely to cause difficulty to theologians.' 'It is an article of our faith,' says Arnauld, 'that the substance of

---

[1] The word actually used is *species*, not *accidentia*.

the bread passes out of the bread of the Eucharist, and that only
its accidents remain. Now these are extension, figure, colour,
odour, savour and the other sensible qualities. But M. Descartes
recognizes no sense-qualities, but only certain motions of the
minute bodies which surround us, by means of which we perceive
the different impressions to which we afterwards give the names
of colour, savour and the like. Hence there remain figure, extension and mobility. But M. Descartes denies that these powers can
be comprehended apart from the substance in which they inhere
and hence that they can exist apart from it.'[1]

In his reply to Arnauld Descartes observes that the Council of
Trent employs the word *species*, not the word *accidens*, and he
understands *species* as meaning 'semblance'. The semblance or
appearances of bread and wine remain after the consecration. Now,
species can only mean what is required for acting on the senses.
And that which stimulates the senses is the superficies of a body,
that is, 'the limit which is conceived to lie between the particles
of a body and the bodies that surround it, a boundary which has
absolutely none but a modal reality'.[2] Further, as the substance
of the bread is changed into another substance in such a way that
the second substance 'is entirely contained within the same limits
as those within which the other substances previously were, or in
precisely the same place as that in which the bread and wine
previously existed, or rather (since these boundaries are continually moving) in that in which they would exist if they were
present, it necessarily follows that the new substance would act
on our senses in entirely the same way as that in which the bread
and wine would act, if no transubstantiation had occurred.'[3]

So far as possible Descartes avoided theological controversy.
'For the extension of Jesus Christ in this holy sacrament, I have
not explained it, because I was not obliged to do so, and because
I abstain as far as I can from questions of theology.'[4] But he did
so in another letter.[5] However, since Arnauld raised the question,
Descartes felt obliged to attempt to reconcile his theory of modes
with the dogma of transubstantiation, or rather to show how the
dogma could be satisfactorily maintained and explained, given a
theory of modes which he looked on as being certainly true. But
though he did not deny the dogma (if he had, the problem of
reconciling his theory with it would obviously not have arisen),

[1] *A.T.*, VII, 217–18, cf. IX, 169.   [2] *R.O.*, 4; *A.T.*, VII, 250–1, cf. IX, 193.
[3] *R.O.*, 4; *A.T.*, VII, 251, cf. IX, 193–4.
[4] Letter to Père Mesland; *A.T.*, IV, 119.   [5] *A.T.*, IV, 162–70.

his explanation of its implications in the light of his own theory of modes has not satisfied Catholic theologians. For though it is perfectly true that the Council of Trent used the word *species* and not the word *accidens*, it is clear enough that *species* was taken and intended in the sense of *accidens* and not merely in the very broad sense of 'appearance'. Descartes' attitude is clear enough. 'If I may here speak the truth freely and without offence, I avow that I venture to hope that a time will some day come when the doctrine that postulates the existence of real accidents will be banished by theologians as being foreign to rational thought, incomprehensible and causing uncertainty in the faith, and that mine will be accepted in its place as being certain and indubitable.'[1] His hope has not been fulfilled.

It may be noted that quite apart from its theological connections and repercussions Descartes' discussion of this matter makes it clear that although he talked about 'substances' and 'modes' it is a mistake to understand these terms as implying acceptance of the Scholastic theory of substances and accidents. 'Substance' really means for him what one clearly and distinctly perceives to be the fundamental attribute of a thing, while the substitution of the word 'mode' for 'accident' helps to indicate his disbelief in real accidents which, though only through divine power, can exist in separation from the substance of which they were accidents.

Perhaps it is worth adding that though the dogma of transubstantiation is understood by Catholic theologians as implying the existence of real accidents, it is not taken as necessarily implying that material things are, for example, coloured in a formal sense. In other words, the dogma cannot be used to settle the problem of secondary qualities.

3. If the nature or essence of corporeal substance consists in extension, what account is to be given of space? Descartes' answer is that 'space or internal place and the corporeal substance which is contained in it are different only in the way in which they are conceived by us'.[2] If we think away from a body, a stone, for example, all that is not essential to its nature as a body, we are left with extension in length, breadth and depth; 'and this is comprised in our idea of space, not only of that which is full of body, but also of that which is called a vacuum'.[3] All the same, there

---

[1] *R.O.*, 4; *A.T.*, VII, 255, cf. IX, 197.
[2] *P.P.*, 2, 10; *A.T.*, VIII, 45; cf. IX B, 68.
[3] *P.P.*, 2, 11; *A.T.*, VIII, 46, cf. IX B, 69.

is a difference in our ways of conceiving corporeal substance and space. For when we think of space, we think, for example, of the extension actually filled by a stone as capable of being filled by other bodies when the stone has been removed. We think, in other words, not of extension as forming the substance of a particular body but of extension in general.

As for place, 'the words place and space signify nothing different from the body which is said to be in a place'.[1] The place of a body is not another body. There is, however, this difference between the terms place and space, that the former indicates situation; that is, situation in regard to other bodies. We often say, Descartes remarks, that one thing has taken the place of another thing, even though the former does not possess the same size or shape as the latter and does not occupy, therefore, the same space. And when we speak of a change of place in this way we are thinking of the situation of a body with reference to other bodies. 'If we say that a thing is in a particular place, we simply mean that it is situated in a certain manner in reference to certain other things.'[2] And it is important to observe that there is no such thing as absolute place; that is to say, that there are no immovable points of reference. If a man is crossing a river in a boat and if he sits still the whole time, he can be said to retain the same place if we are thinking of his situation or position with reference to the boat, though we can also say that his place changes if we are thinking of his situation with reference to the banks of the river. And 'if at length we are persuaded that there are no points in the universe which are really immovable, as will presently be shown to be probable, we shall conclude that there is nothing which has a permanent place except in so far as it is fixed by our thought'.[3] Place is relative.

We have seen that there is no real distinction between space or internal place and the extension which forms the essence of corporeal substances. From this it follows that there can be no empty space, no vacuum, in the strict sense. Because a pitcher is made to hold water, we say that it is empty when there is no water in it; but it contains air. An absolutely empty space, containing no body at all, is impossible. 'And therefore, if it is asked what would happen if God removed all the body contained in a vessel without permitting its place to be occupied by another

---

[1] *P.P.*, 2, 13; *A.T.*, VIII, 47, cf. IX B, 69–70.
[2] *P.P.*, 2, 14; *A.T.*, VIII, 48, cf. IX B, 71.
[3] *P.P.*, 2, 13; *A.T.*, VIII, 47, cf. IX B, 70.

body, we shall answer that the sides of the vessel will thereby come into immediate contiguity with one another.'[1] There could be no distance between them, for distance is a mode of extension, and without extended substance there can be no extension.

Other conclusions are also drawn by Descartes from his doctrine that extension is the essence of corporeal substance. First, there can be no atoms in the strict sense. For any particle of matter must be extended, and if it is extended it is in principle divisible, even though we have no means of dividing it physically. There can be atoms only in a relative sense, relative, that is, to our power to divide. Secondly, the world is indefinitely extended in the sense that it cannot have definable limits. For if we conceive limits, we conceive space beyond the limits; but empty space is not conceivable. Thirdly, the heavens and the earth must be formed of the same matter, if corporeal substance and extension are fundamentally the same. The old theory that the heavenly bodies are composed of a special kind of matter is excluded. Finally, there cannot be a plurality of worlds. On the one hand, the matter whose nature is extended substance fills all imaginable spaces, while on the other we cannot conceive any other kind of matter.

4. The geometrical conception of body as extension gives us by itself a static universe. But obviously motion is a fact, and its nature has to be considered. We need consider, however, only local motion, since Descartes states that he can conceive no other kind.

In common parlance, motion is 'the action by which any body passes from one place to another'.[2] And we can say of a given body that it is in motion and not in motion at the same time, according to the points of reference which we adopt. A man on a moving ship is in motion with reference to the shore which he is leaving, but he can be at the same time at rest with reference to the parts of the ship.

Properly speaking, however, motion is 'the transference of one part of matter or of one body from the vicinity of those bodies which are in immediate contact with it, and which we regard as being in repose, into the vicinity of others'.[3] In this definition the terms 'part of matter' and 'body' must be understood as meaning all that is transported, even though it is composed of many parts

[1] P.P., 2, 18; A.T., VIII, 50, cf. IX B, 73.
[2] P.P., 2, 24; A.T., VIII, 53, cf. IX B, 75.
[3] P.P., 2, 25; A.T., VIII, 53, cf. IX B, 76.

which have their own motion. And the word 'transportation' must be understood as indicating that motion is in the material body, not in the agent which moves it. Motion and rest are simply different modes of a body. Further, the definition of motion as the transportation of a body from the vicinity of others implies that a moving thing can have only one motion; whereas if the word 'place' had been used, we could have ascribed several movements to the same body, since place can be understood in relation to different points of reference. Finally, in the definition the words 'and which we regard as in repose' delimit the meaning of the words 'those bodies which are in immediate contact with it'.

5. The concept of time is connected with that of motion. But we must make a distinction between time and duration. The latter, is a mode of a thing in so far as it is considered as continuing to exist.[1] Time, however, which is described (and here Descartes employs Aristotelian language) as the measure of movement, is distinct from duration in a general sense. 'But in order to comprehend the duration of all things under the same measure, we usually compare their duration with the duration of the greatest and most regular motions, which are those that create years and days, and these we term time. Hence this adds nothing to the notion of duration, taken generally, but a mode of thinking.'[2] Hence Descartes can say that time is only a mode of thinking or, as the French version of the *Principles of Philosophy* explains, 'only a mode of thinking this duration'.[3] Things have duration or endure, but we can think of this duration by means of a comparison, and then we have the concept of time, which is a common measure of different durations.

6. We have, then, in the material world corporeal substance, considered as extension, and motion. Now, as has already been remarked, if we consider the geometrical conception of corporeal substance by itself, we arrive at the idea of a static world. For the idea of extension does not of itself imply the concept of motion. Therefore motion necessarily appears as something added to corporeal substance. And, indeed, motion is for Descartes a mode of corporeal substance. Thus we have to inquire into the origin of motion. And at this point Descartes introduces the idea of God and of the divine agency. For God is the first cause of motion in the world. Moreover, He conserves an equal quantity of motion

---

[1] *P.P.*, 1, 56; *A.T.*, VIII, 26, cf. IX B, 49.
[2] *P.P.*, 1, 57; *A.T.*, VIII, 27, cf. IX B, 49-50.   [3] *Ibid.*

in the universe, so that though there is transference of motion the total quantity remains the same. 'It seems to me that it is evident that it is none other than God who by His omnipotence has created matter with the movement and repose of its parts, and who conserves now in the universe, by His ordinary concurrence, as much movement and repose as He put there in creating it. For although movement is only a mode in the matter which is moved, matter nevertheless preserves a certain quantity of it which never increases or diminishes, though in some of its parts there is sometimes more and sometimes less. . . .'[1] God, we may say, created the world with a certain amount of energy, and the total quantity of energy in the world remains the same, though it is constantly being transferred from one body to the other.

We may note in passing that Descartes tries to deduce the conservation of the quantity of movement from metaphysical premises, that is to say, from consideration of the divine perfections. 'We know also that it is a perfection in God, not only that He is immovable in His nature, but also that He acts in a manner which He never changes. So besides the changes that we see in the world and those in which we believe because God has revealed them, and that we know to take place or to have taken place in nature without any change on the part of the Creator, we ought not to postulate any others in His works, from fear of attributing inconstancy to Him. From this it follows that, since He has moved in different ways the parts of matter when He created them, and since He preserves all (the parts) in the same fashion and with the same laws which He has made them observe at their creation, He conserves incessantly in this matter an equal quantity of movement.'[2]

7. Descartes also speaks as though the fundamental laws of motion can be deduced from metaphysical premises. 'From the fact that God is in no way subject to change and that He acts always in the same manner we can arrive at the knowledge of certain rules which I call the laws of nature.'[3] In the Latin version we read, 'And from this same immutability of God certain rules or laws of nature can be known. . . .'[4] This idea is, of course, in accordance with Descartes' view, to which allusion was made in the second chapter, that physics is dependent on metaphysics in

---

[1] *P.P.*, 2, 36; *A.T.*, VIII, 61, cf. IX B, 83.
[2] *P.P.*, 2, 36; *A.T.*, VIII, 61–2, cf. IX B, 84.
[3] *P.P.*, 2, 37; *A.T.*, IX B, 84.
[4] *A.T.*, VIII, 62.

the sense that the fundamental principles of physics follow from metaphysical premisses.

The first law is that each thing, so far as it depends on itself, continues always in the same state of rest or motion and never changes except through the agency of some other thing. No body which is at rest ever begins to move of itself, and no body which is in motion ever stops moving of itself. The truth of this proposition can be seen exemplified in the behaviour of projectiles. If a ball is thrown into the air, why does it continue to move after it has left the hand of the thrower? The reason is that in accordance with the laws of nature 'all bodies which are in motion continue to move until their movement is stopped by some other bodies'.[1] In the case of the ball the resistance of the air gradually diminishes the speed of the ball's motion. The Aristotelian theory of 'violent' motion and the fourteenth-century theory of impetus are alike discarded.[2]

The second law is that every moving body tends to continue its movement in a straight line. If it describes a circular path, this is due to its encountering other bodies. And every body which moves in this way is constantly tending to recede from the centre of the circle which it describes. Descartes first gives a metaphysical reason for this behaviour. 'This rule, like the preceding, depends on the fact that God is immovable and that He conserves movement in matter by a very simple operation. . . .'[3] But he then proceeds to cite some empirical confirmation of the law.

'The third law which I observe in nature is that if a body which is moving and which encounters another body has less force for continuing to move in a straight line than the other body has for resisting it, it loses its direction without losing anything of its movement; and that if it has more force, it moves the other body along with itself and loses as much of its movement as it gives to the other.'[4] Again Descartes tries to prove the law by referring both to the divine immutability and constancy in action and to empirical confirmation. It can hardly be claimed, however, that the connections which Descartes asserts between the divine immutability and constancy on the one hand and his laws of motion on the other provide much support for the view that the fundamental laws of physics can be deduced from metaphysics.

[1] *P.P.*, 2, 38; *A.T.*, viii, 63, cf. ix b, 85.
[2] See vol. iii, pp. 157–60.
[3] *P.P.*, 2, 39; *A.T.*, viii, 63, cf. ix b, 86.
[4] *P.P.*, 2, 40; *A.T.*, viii, 65, cf. ix b, 86–7.

8. All this suggests a deistic conception of the world. The picture which naturally occurs to the mind is that of God creating the world as a system of bodies in motion and then leaving it to carry on by itself. And this is, indeed, the picture which suggested itself to Pascal who remarks in the *Pensées*:[1] 'I cannot forgive Descartes. He would have liked, in the whole of his philosophy, to be able to by-pass God. But he could not help making Him give a shove to set the world in motion; after that he has nothing further to do with God.' But Pascal's criticism is exaggerated, as I propose to show.

We have seen that Descartes insisted on the necessity of divine conservation in order that the created universe should continue to exist. And this conservation was asserted to be equivalent to a perpetual re-creation. Now, this theory is in turn closely connected with his theory of the discontinuity of motion and time. 'All the course of my life can be divided into an infinite number of parts, none of which is in any way dependent on the other; and thus from the fact that I was in existence a short time ago it does not follow that I must be in existence now, unless some cause at this instant, so to speak, produces me anew, that is to say, conserves me. It is as a matter of fact perfectly clear and evident to all those who consider with attention the nature of time, that in order to be conserved in each moment in which it endures a substance has need of the same power and action as would be necessary to produce and create it anew, supposing that it did not yet exist. So the light of nature shows us clearly that the distinction between creation and conservation is only a distinction of reason.'[2] Time is discontinuous. In the *Principles of Philosophy*,[3] Descartes says that time or the duration of things is 'of such a kind that its parts do not depend one upon the other and never co-exist', and in a letter to Chanut he says that 'all the moments of its (the world's) duration are independent the one from the other'.[4] Therefore, all the moments of duration being independent, the moments of my existence are discrete and independent. Hence the necessity of constant re-creation.

But Descartes did not imagine that in point of fact there is no continuity in the life of the self or that the latter really consists of a multitude of discrete selves without any common identity. Nor did he think that there is no continuity in motion and time. What

---

[1] p. 77.   [2] *M.*, 3; *A.T.*, IX, 39, cf. VII, 49.
[3] I, 21; *A.T.*, VIII, 13, cf. IX B, 34.   [4] *A.T.*, V, 53.

he thought was that God supplies the continuity by His never-ceasing creative activity. And this suggests a very different picture of the world from the deistic conception alluded to above. The order of Nature and the sequences which Descartes attributes to natural laws are seen to depend on the unceasing creative activity of God. Just as it is not simply the beginning of my existence, but also my continued existence and the continuity of my self, which depend on the divine activity, so both the continued existence of material things and the continuity of motion depend on the same cause. The universe is seen to depend in every positive aspect and at every moment on God.

9. So far we have considered the nature of the self as a thing which thinks and the nature of corporeal substance, which is extension. But nothing has been said specifically about living bodies, and it is necessary to inquire how Descartes regarded them. The scope of this question is clearly delimited by what has already been said. For there are only two kinds of created substance, spiritual and corporeal. The question is, therefore, to which class living bodies belong. Furthermore, the answer to the question is obvious from the start. For since living bodies can hardly be ascribed to the class of spiritual substances, they must belong to the class of corporeal substances. And if the essence of corporeal substances is extension, the essence of living bodies must be extension. And our task is that of inquiry into the implications of this position.

In the first place Descartes insists that there is no good reason for attributing reason to animals. And he appeals especially to the absence of any good evidence in favour of saying that animals talk intelligently or can do so. Some animals, it is true, have organs which enable them to utter words. Parrots, for example, can talk, in the sense that they can utter words. But there is no evidence that they talk intelligently; that is, that they think of what they are saying, that they understand the meanings of the words which they utter, or that they can invent signs to express thoughts. Animals give signs of their feelings, it is true, but the evidence goes to show that this is an automatic, and not an intelligent, process. Human beings, on the other hand, even the most stupid, can arrange words to express thoughts, and dumb people can learn or invent other conventional signs to express thoughts. 'And this does not show merely that the brutes have less reason than men, but that they have none at all, since it is

clear that very little is required in order to be able to talk.'[1]
Many animals, it is true, exhibit more dexterity in certain types
of action than human beings do; but this does not prove that they
are endowed with minds. If it did, their superior dexterity would
show a superiority in mind, and then it would be impossible to
explain their incapacity for language. Their dexterity 'shows
rather that they have no reason at all, and that it is nature which
acts in them according to the disposition of their organs, just as
a clock, which is only composed of wheels and weights, is able to
tell the hours and measure the time more correctly than we do
with all our wisdom'.[2]

Animals, therefore, have no reason or mind. On this point the
Scholastics would have agreed. But Descartes draws the conclusion
that animals are machines or automata, thus excluding the
Aristotelian-Scholastic theory of the presence in animals of
sensitive 'souls'.[3] If animals have no minds in the sense in which
human beings have minds, they cannot be anything else but
matter in motion. When Arnauld objected that the behaviour of
animals cannot be explained without the idea of 'soul' (distinct
from the body, but not incorruptible), Descartes replied that 'all
the actions of brutes resemble only those of ours which occur
without the aid of the mind. Hence we are driven to conclude
that we can recognize no principle of motion in them beyond the
disposition of their organs and the continual discharge of the
animal spirits which are produced by the beat of the heart as it
rarefies the blood.'[4] In a letter of reply to Henry More, dated
February 5th, 1649, Descartes does, indeed, assert that 'I do not
deprive any animal of life', meaning that he does not refuse to
describe animals as living things; but the reason which he gives is
that he makes life consist 'only in the warmth of the heart'.[5]
Again, 'I do not refuse them feeling inasmuch as it depends on the
organs of the body.'[6] We are inclined to think that animal life
is more than merely material processes because we observe in
them some actions analogous to our own; and since we attribute
the movements of our own bodies to our minds, we are naturally
inclined to attribute the movements of animals to some vital
principle. But investigation shows that animal behaviour can be
exhaustively described without the introduction of any mind or of
any unobservable vital principle.

[1] *D.M.*, 5; *A.T.*, vi, 58.   [2] *D.M.*, 5; *A.T.*, vi, 59.
[3] Descartes also rejected, of course. the idea of a 'vegetative soul' or principle
in plants.   [4] *R.O.*, 4, 1; *A.T.*, vii, 230, cf. ix, 178–9.   [5] *A.T.*, v, 278.   [6] *Ibid.*

Descartes is therefore prepared to say that animals are machines or automata. He is also prepared to say the same thing about the human body. A great many physical processes continue without the intervention of mind: respiration, digestion, the circulation of the blood, all these proceed automatically. True, we can deliberately walk, for example; but the mind does not move the limbs immediately; it influences the animal spirits at the pineal gland, and what it does is not to create new movement or energy, but rather to alter its direction or to apply movement originally created by God. Hence the human body is like a machine which can work to a great extent automatically, though its energy can be applied in different ways by the workman. 'The body of a living man differs from that of a dead man just as does a watch or other automaton (that is, a machine which moves of itself), when it is wound up and contains in itself the corporeal principle of those movements for which it is designed along with all that is requisite for its action, from the same watch or other machine when it is broken and when the principle of its movement ceases to act.'[1]

We can look at Descartes' theory of animals from two points of view. From the humanistic point of view, it is an exaltation of man or a reassertion of the unique position of man against those who would reduce the difference between man and brute to one of degree only. And this is not an interpretation which has simply been invented by historians; for Descartes himself provides the ground for it. For example, in the *Discourse on Method* he observes that 'next to the error of those who deny God . . . there is none which is more effectual in leading feeble spirits from the straight path of virtue than to imagine that the soul of the brute is of the same nature as our own, and that in consequence after this life we have nothing to fear or to hope for any more than the flies and the ants. As a matter of fact, when one comes to know how greatly they differ, we understand much better the reasons which go to prove that our soul is of its nature entirely independent of the body, and in consequence that it is not liable to die with it.'[2] And writing to the Marquis of Newcastle,[3] he alludes to Montaigne and Charron, the former of whom compared man disadvantageously with the animals, while the latter, by saying that the wise differ from the common man as much as the common man does from the beasts, implied that men and animals differ only in degree, without there being any radical difference.

[1] *P.S.*, 1, 6; *A.T.*, xi, 330–1.   [2] *D.M.*, 5; *A.T.*, vi, 59.   [3] *A.T.*, iv, 573–5.

On the other hand, Descartes' interpretation of animals as machines, however crude it may be, is in accordance with the original separation he makes between the two worlds of spirit and matter. It represents or foreshadows the attempt to reduce the sciences to physics, and in physics, he says, he does not accept or desire any other principles than those of geometry or abstract mathematics.[1] The whole material world can be treated as a mechanical system, and there is no need for introducing or considering any but efficient causes. Final causality is a theological conception, and, however true it may be, it has no place in physics. Explanation by means of final causes, of 'souls', of occult vital principles and of substantial forms does nothing to promote the advance of physical science. And the same principles of explanation which are employed in regard to inanimate bodies must be applied also in the case of living bodies.

[1] *P.P.*, 2, 64; *A.T.*, VIII, 78–9, cf. IX B, 101–2.

CHAPTER VI

DESCARTES (5)

*Man's awareness of freedom—Freedom and God—Provisional
ethics and moral science—The passions and their control—The
nature of the good—Comments on Descartes' ethical ideas—
General remarks about Descartes.*

1. MAN'S possession of free will, or more strictly my possession
of free will, is a primary datum, in the sense that my awareness of
it is logically prior to the *Cogito, ergo sum.* For it is precisely the
possession of freedom which permits me to indulge in hyperbolical
doubt. I have a natural inclination to believe in the existence of
material things and in the demonstrations of mathematics, and to
doubt these things, especially the latter, effort or deliberate choice
is needed. Thus 'whoever turns out to have created us, and even
if he should prove to be all-powerful and deceitful, we still experience a freedom through which we can abstain from accepting as
true and indisputable those things of which we have not certain
knowledge, and thus prevent our ever being deceived'.[1]

That we possess this freedom is, indeed, self-evident. 'We had
before a very clear proof of this; for at the same time as we tried
to doubt all things and even supposed that He who created us
employed His unlimited powers in deceiving us in every way, we
perceived in ourselves a liberty such that we were able to abstain
from believing what was not perfectly certain and indubitable.
But that of which we could not doubt at such a time is as self-
evident and clear as anything which we can ever know.'[2] The
capacity to apply methodic doubt presupposes freedom. Indeed,
awareness of freedom or liberty is an 'innate idea'.

This power of acting freely is man's greatest perfection, and by
using it 'we are in a special way masters of our actions and thereby
merit praise or blame'.[3] Indeed, the universal practice of praising
and blaming ourselves and others for actions shows the self-
evident character of human freedom. We all perceive naturally
that man is free.

[1] *P.P.*, I, 6; *A.T.*, VIII, 6, cf. IX B, 27.
[2] *P.P.*, I, 39; *A.T.*, VIII, 19–20, cf. IX B, 41.
[3] *P.P.*, I, 37; *A.T.*, VIII, 18, cf. IX B, 40.

2. We are certain, therefore, of man's possession of freedom, and this certainty is logically prior to certainty about God's existence. But once God's existence has been proved, it becomes necessary to re-examine human freedom in the light of what we know about God. For we know that God not only knows from eternity all that is or will be but also pre-ordains it. And the question arises, therefore, how human freedom can be reconciled with divine pre-ordination.

In the *Principles of Philosophy* Descartes avoids offering any positive solution to this problem. And this avoidance is in accord with his explicit resolution to steer clear of theological controversy. We are certain of two things. In the first place we are certain of our freedom. In the second place we may come to recognize clearly and distinctly that God is omnipotent and that He pre-ordains all events. But it does not follow that we can comprehend how it is that divine pre-ordination leaves man's free acts undetermined. To deny freedom because of divine pre-ordination would be absurd. 'For it would be absurd to doubt what we comprehend and experience within ourselves just because we do not comprehend a matter which from its nature we know to be incomprehensible.'[1] The wisest course is to acknowledge that the solution of the problem transcends the power of our understanding. 'We shall have no trouble at all if we recollect that our thought is finite, and that the omnipotence of God, whereby He has not only known from all eternity that which is or can be but also willed and pre-ordained it, is infinite.'[2]

In point of fact, however, Descartes did not content himself with this position. For he gave his opinions on theological issues connected with human freedom. What is more, he spoke in different ways at different times. For example, he went so far as to express his opinion in a controversy between Dutch Protestants, saying that he agreed with the followers of Gomar rather than with the Arminians. This was equivalent to saying that he preferred a strict doctrine of predestination. And as he dragged in the Jesuits, expressing his disagreement with them,[3] it would appear that he preferred Jansenism to Molinism. The Jansenists taught that divine grace is irresistible, and the only freedom which they really admitted was equivalent to spontaneity. An act may be done without any sense of constraint, but it is none the less

[1] *P.P.*, 1, 41; *A.T.*, VIII, 20, cf. IX B, 42.   [2] *Ibid.*
[3] *Entretien avec Burman*, edit. Ch. Adam, p. 81.

determined by the attraction of 'delectation', earthly or heavenly.
The Molinists held that it is the free co-operation of the will which
renders grace efficacious, and that man's liberty of indifference
is not impaired or destroyed by divine foreknowledge. That
Descartes should show some sympathy with the Jansenists is not
surprising when one recalls his statement that 'in order that I
should be free, it is not necessary that I should be indifferent in
the choice of one or the other of two contraries. Rather, the more
I lean towards the one, whether I see clearly that the good and the
true are to be found in it, or whether God so disposes my inward
thought, the more freely do I choose and embrace it. Without
a doubt, both divine grace and natural knowledge, far from
diminishing my liberty, rather increase and strengthen it. Hence
this indifference which I feel when I am not swayed by any reason
to one side rather than the other is the lowest grade of liberty and
reveals a lack of knowledge rather than a perfection of the will.'[1]
It is true that if Descartes intended to explain what the partisans
of liberty of indifference meant by it, he misrepresented their
meaning. For he seems to understand by it a state of indifference
brought about by lack of knowledge, whereas they meant by it an
ability to choose either of two contraries even when the requisite
conditions for intelligent choice, including knowledge, are present.
At the same time he certainly thought that the more the will is
directed to the objectively preferable choice, whether by grace
or by natural knowledge, the greater our freedom; and he seems
to imply that ability to make another choice does not belong
essentially to true liberty. Thus he states in a letter to Mersenne
that 'I move the more freely towards an object in proportion
to the number of the reasons which compel me; for it is certain
that my will is then set in motion with greater ease and
spontaneity.'[2]

But in his correspondence with the Princess Elizabeth of
Bohemia Descartes speaks in a rather different way, adopting a
position more akin to that of the Jesuits. Thus he presents us
with an analogy. Two men, who are well known to be enemies,
are ordered by the king to be at a certain place at a certain time.
The king is perfectly aware that a fight will ensue; and we must
say that he wills it, even though it would infringe his own decrees.
But though he foresees and wills the fight, he in no way determines
the wills of the two men. Their action is due to their own choice.

[1] *M.*, 4; *A.T.*, VII, 57–8.   [2] *A.T.*, III, 381–2.

So God foresees and 'pre-ordains' all human actions, but He does not determine the human will. In other words, God foresees a man's free act because he is going to perform it; but he is not going to perform it because God foresees it.

The fact of the matter seems to be that when dealing with the theological issues of the free-will controversy Descartes adopted more or less impromptu solutions without any real attempt to render them consistent.[1] What he was really interested in was the problem of error. He wished to stress man's freedom not to assent to a proposition when there is any room for doubt and at the same time to allow for inevitable assent when the truth of a proposition is perceived with certainty. We embrace or reject error freely. Therefore God is not responsible. But truth clearly perceived imposes itself on the mind like a divine illumination.

3. Human freedom being presupposed, we can inquire into Descartes' moral doctrine. In the *Discourse on Method*,[2] before embarking on the application of his method of doubt, he proposes for himself a provisional ethic. Thus he resolves to obey the laws and customs of his country, to be firm and resolute in his actions and to follow faithfully even dubious opinions (opinions which have not yet been established beyond doubt) when his mind has once been made up about them. He resolves also to try always to conquer himself rather than fortune and to alter his desires rather than to try to change the order of the world. Finally he resolves to spend his whole life in cultivating his reason and in making as much progress as possible in the pursuit of truth.

Obviously, these maxims or resolutions constitute a rough-and-ready personal programme; they are far removed from 'the highest and most perfect moral science which, presupposing a complete knowledge of the other sciences, is the last degree of wisdom'.[3] But Descartes never worked out this perfect moral science. He doubtless did not feel that he was in a position to do so. In any case, whatever the reasons for it may have been, the Cartesian ethic is missing from the system, although according to the programme laid down it should have formed its crown.

Nevertheless Descartes did write something on ethical themes and on subjects relevant to ethics. And we can profitably consider first of all what he has to say on the passions, in so far as this concerns moral philosophy.

---

[1] *La liberté chez Descartes et la théologie* by E. Gilson may profitably be consulted. Cf. Bibliography.

[2] 3; *A.T.*, VI, 22–8. [3] *P.P.*, Prefatory Letter; *A.T.*, IX B, 14.

4. Descartes' analysis of the passions involves the theory of interaction. That is to say, he holds that passion is excited or caused in the soul by the body. 'What in the soul is a passion is in the body, commonly speaking, an action.'[1] In the general sense of the word 'passions' and perceptions are the same. 'We may usually term one's passions all those kinds of perception or forms of knowledge which are found in us, because it is often not our soul which makes them what they are, and because it always receives them from the things which are represented by them.'[2] But if understood in a narrower sense, and it is in this sense that the word 'passions' is taken in what follows, 'we may define them generally as the perceptions, feelings or emotions of the soul which we relate specially to it and which are caused, maintained and fortified by some movement of the spirits'.[3] In explanation of this rather obscure definition Descartes makes the following points. The passions can be called perceptions when this word is used to signify all the thoughts which are not actions of the soul. (Thus clear and distinct perceptions are actions of the soul.) We can call them feelings because they are received into the soul. And we can, with greater accuracy, call them emotions because of all the thoughts which the soul can have it is the emotions which are most prone to agitate and disturb it. The clause 'which we relate specially to it (the soul)' is inserted to exclude feelings like scents, sounds and colours, which we relate to external things, and those like hunger, thirst and pain, which we relate to our own bodies. Mention of the causal activity of 'the spirits' is inserted to exclude those desires which are caused by the soul itself. The passions, therefore, are emotions of the soul which are caused by the body; and they must, of course, be distinguished from the perception that we have of these passions. The emotion of fear and the clear perception of the fear and its nature are not the same thing.

The passions, says Descartes, 'are all good in their nature';[4] but they can be misused, and they can be allowed to grow to excess. We have, therefore, to control them. But the passions 'depend absolutely on the actions which govern and direct them, and they can be altered only indirectly by the soul'.[5] That is to say, the passions depend on and are excited by physiological conditions: they are all caused by some movement of the animal

[1] P.S., 1, 2; A.T., XI, 328.   [2] P.S., 1, 17; A.T., XI, 342.
[3] P.S., 1, 27; A.T., XI, 349.   [4] P.S., 3, 211; A.T., XI, 485.
[5] P.S., 1, 41; A.T., XI, 359.

spirits. And the natural conclusion, therefore, would be that to control them we ought to change the physical causes which produce them rather than try to expel them directly without doing anything to alter their causes. For while the causes remain, the commotion of the soul remains, and in this case the most that we can do is 'not to yield to its effects and to restrain many of the movements to which it disposes the body. For example, if anger causes us to lift our hand to strike, the will can usually hold it back; if fear incites our legs to flee, the will can arrest them, and so on in other similar cases.'[1] But though we would perhaps naturally interpret the indirect control of the passions as altering, so far as we can, the physical conditions which produce them, Descartes gives us a rather different interpretation. For he says that we can control the passions indirectly 'by the representation of things which are usually united to the passions which we desire to have, and which are contrary to those which we desire to set aside. Thus in order to excite courage in oneself and remove fear, it is not sufficient to have the will to do so, but we must also apply ourselves to consider the reasons, the objects or the examples which persuade us that the peril is not great. . . .'[2] This interpretation, however, is not a rejection of the first interpretation suggested: it is rather a device which we have to adopt when we cannot easily change directly the external causes of a passion.

5. But because the passions 'can bring us to any kind of action only by the intervention of the desire which they excite, it is this desire especially which we should be careful to regulate, and it is in this that the principal use of morality consists'.[3] The question arises, therefore, when is desire good and when is it bad? And Descartes' answer is that desire is good when it follows from true knowledge and bad when it is founded on some error. But what is the knowledge which renders a desire good? Descartes does not seem to speak very clearly. He tells us, indeed, that 'the error which we most ordinarily commit in respect to desires is that of not sufficiently distinguishing the things which depend on us from those which do not so depend'.[4] But to know that something depends on our free will and is not simply an event which happens to us and which we have to bear as best we may does not necessarily render the desire for this thing a good desire. However,

---

[1] P.S., 1, 46; A.T., XI, 364.　　[2] P.S., 1, 45; A.T., XI, 362–3.
[3] P.S., 2, 144; A.T., XI, 436.　　[4] Ibid.

Descartes is, of course, aware of this, and he adds that we have 'to try to know very clearly and to consider with attention the goodness of that which is to be desired'.[1] Presumably he means that a first condition of moral choice is to distinguish what lies in our power from what is not subject to our control. Events of the latter type are ordained by Providence, and we have to submit to them. But, then, having ascertained what lies within our own power, we have to discriminate between what is good and what is bad. And following after virtue consists in performing those actions which we have judged to be the best.[2]

In a letter of 1645 to the Princess Elizabeth, Descartes amplifies the subjects somewhat while commenting on Seneca's *De vita beata*. To be in the possession of beatitude, to live in beatitude, 'is nothing else but to have one's spirit perfectly content and satisfied'.[3] What are the things which confer on us this supreme contentment? They are of two kinds. The first depend on ourselves, namely virtue and wisdom. The second, like honour, riches and health, do not depend (not entirely at least) on ourselves. But though perfect contentment demands the presence of both classes of goods, we are concerned strictly only with the first class, namely, with things which depend on ourselves and which can consequently be obtained by all.

In order to attain beatitude in this restricted sense, there are three rules to be observed. According to Descartes, they are the rules already given in the *Discourse on Method*; but actually he changes the first rule, substituting knowledge for provisional maxims. The first rule is to make every effort to know what one ought to do and what one ought not to do in all the occurrences of life. The second is to have a firm and constant resolution to carry out all the dictates of reason without being turned aside by passion or appetite. 'And it is firmness in this resolution which I think should be taken as virtue.'[4] The third rule is to consider that all the goods which one does not possess are outside the scope of one's power, and to accustom oneself not to desire them; 'for there is nothing but desire and regret . . . which can prevent us from being content'.[5]

However, it is not every desire which is incompatible with beatitude, but only those which are accompanied by impatience or sadness. 'Also it is not necessary that our reason should never

---

[1] *P.S.*, 2, 144; *A.T.*, XI, 437.   [2] *P.S.*, 2, 144 and 148; *A.T.*, XI, 436 and 442.
[3] *A.T.*, IV, 264.   [4] *A.T.*, IV, 265.   [5] *A.T.*, IV, 266.

be mistaken. It is sufficient that our conscience bear witness to us that we have never wanted in resolution and virtue to carry out all the things which we have judged the best. And so virtue alone is sufficient to render us content in this life.'[1]

Obviously, we are not told very much more by these observations about the content of morality, about, that is to say, the concrete dictates of reason. But Descartes held that before a scientific ethic could be elaborated it was first of all necessary to establish the science of human nature; and he did not pretend to have done this. Hence he did not feel that he was in a position to work out the scientific ethic which the programme of his system demanded. However, in another of his letters to the Princess Elizabeth on ethical topics he says that he will drop Seneca and give his own opinions; and he proceeds to say two things are required for right moral judgment, first, knowledge of truth and, secondly, the habit of remembering and assenting to this knowledge on all occasions which require it. And this knowledge involves knowledge of God; 'for this teaches us to receive in good part all that happens to us, as being expressly sent to us by God'.[2] Secondly, it is necessary to know the nature of the soul, as self-subsistent, independent of the body, nobler than the latter, and immortal. Thirdly, we should realize the extent of the universe and not imagine a finite world made expressly for our convenience. Fourthly, each one should consider that he forms part of a greater whole, the universe, and, more particularly, of a certain State, society and family, and that he ought to prefer the interests of the whole. And there are other things the knowledge of which is desirable; the nature of the passions, for example, the character of the ethical code of our own society, and so on. Generally speaking, as Descartes says in other letters, the supreme good 'consists in the exercise of virtue or (which is the same) in the possession of all the perfections the acquisition of which depends on our free will, and in the satisfaction of mind which follows this acquisition'.[3] And 'the true use of our reason for the conduct of life consists only in examining and considering without passion the value of all the perfections, both of body and mind, which can be acquired by our industry, in order that, being ordinarily obliged to deprive ourselves of some to have others, we may always choose the best. . . .'[4]

6. It is scarcely worth while following any further the rather

---

[1] *A.T.*, IV, 266-7.   [2] *A.T.*, IV, 291.   [3] *A.T.*, IV, 305.   [4] *A.T.*, IV, 286-7.

haphazard remarks made by Descartes to the Princess Elizabeth. But there are several points to be noticed.

In the first place it is clear that Descartes accepted the traditional theory that the end of human life is 'beatitude'. But whereas for a mediaeval thinker like Aquinas beatitude, perfect beatitude at least, meant the vision of God in heaven, for Descartes it meant a tranquillity or contentment of soul obtainable in this life by one's own efforts. I do not mean to suggest that Descartes denied that man has a supernatural destiny which cannot be attained without grace or that beatitude in the fullest sense is the beatitude of heaven. What I want to draw attention to is simply the fact that he prescinds from purely theological themes and from revelation and sketches, since one cannot use the word 'develops', a natural ethic, a purely philosophical moral theory. In the moral theory of the historic Aquinas, however, there is no such clear-cut abstracting from revealed doctrines.[1]

In the second place one can hardly fail to notice the influence on Descartes' reflections of the writings and ideas of ancient moralists, in particular of the Stoics. It is true that he begins *The Passions of the Soul* with a customary derogatory allusion to the ancients, but this does not mean, of course, that he was not influenced by them; and mention has been made of his use of Seneca in the letters to the Princess Elizabeth. Indeed, the notion of virtue as the end of life, the stress on self-control in face of the passions, and the emphasis on bearing patiently, as expressions of divine providence, all the events which happen to us and which do not lie under our control, represent eminently Stoic ideas. Descartes was not simply a Stoic, of course. For one thing, he attached more value to external goods than did the Stoics; and in this respect he stands closer to Aristotle than to the Stoics. But one whole line of thought in his ethical theory, namely, the line of thought represented by his emphasis on the self-sufficiency of the virtuous man and by his constantly repeated distinction between things which lie in our power and those which do not, is unmistakably Stoic in inspiration and flavour.[2]

Thirdly, attention must be drawn to the intellectualist tendency in Descartes' ethical thought. In a letter written to Père Mesland

[1] I say 'historic Aquinas' to make it clear that I am alluding to Aquinas himself rather than to the sort of ethical theory which is often presented by Thomists and in which no explicit reference is made to revealed doctrines.
[2] On this subject see F. Strowski: *Pascal et son temps*, I, 113-20. Cf. Bibliography.

in 1644 he says that if we see clearly that something is evil 'it
would be impossible for us to sin during the time that we see it in
this way. That is why they say, *Omnis peccans est ignorans.*'[1]
And passages of this sort would seem to imply acceptance of the
Socratic notion that virtue is knowledge and vice ignorance. But
though it does indeed appear to have been Descartes' settled
conviction that we cannot see *clearly* that something is evil and
yet choose it, this 'seeing clearly' has to be understood in a somewhat restricted sense. Descartes agreed with the Scholastics that
nobody chooses evil precisely as such; a man can choose what is
evil only because he represents it to himself as being in some
respect a good. If he saw clearly here and now the evil of an evil
action, discerning that it is evil and why it is evil, he could not
choose it; for the will is set towards the good. But though he may
remember having heard that an action is evil or having himself
seen on a former occasion that it is evil, this does not prevent him
from attending here and now to the aspects of the action under
which it appears to him as desirable and good. And so he can
choose to perform it. Again, we must distinguish between seeing
a good with genuine clarity and seeing it with only apparent
clarity. If we saw the good with genuine clarity in the moment of
choice, we should inevitably choose it. But the influence of the
passions may divert our attention; and 'we are always free to
prevent ourselves from pursuing a good which is clearly known to
us, or from admitting an evident truth, provided only that we
think that it is a good to bear witness to our free will by doing so'.[2]

In general one can say that Descartes holds not only that we
always choose what is or appears to be good and that we cannot
choose evil precisely as such, but also that if we at the moment
of choice saw with genuine and complete clarity that a particular
good was good in an unqualified manner, we should inevitably
choose it. But in point of fact our knowledge is not so complete
that it can exclude the influence of the passions. The intellectualist
thesis remains, therefore, an abstract thesis. It asserts how
people would behave if certain conditions were fufilled which are
not in fact fulfilled.

Finally, although in the remarks which he actually makes about
ethical subjects Descartes emphasizes the virtue of resignation,
this does not mean that his developed ethical science, if he
had ever developed one, would have been simply an ethic of

[1] *A.T.*, IV, 117.   [2] *Letter to Mersenne*; *A.T.*, III, 379.

resignation. A perfect ethical system demands a previous complete knowledge of the other sciences, including physiology and medicine. And he doubtless thought that, given this complete scientific knowledge, man could then work out the moral conditions for the practical exercise and application of this knowledge. For the latter would give man a thorough understanding not only of scientific law and of what was not subject to man's free will but also of what lay in his power. And once man possessed a complete understanding of what lay in his power, he could then evolve an adequate theory about the way in which his free will should be exercised in the concrete. And in this way he would elaborate a dynamic ethic or an ethic of action, and not simply an ethic of resignation.

7. Nobody, I think, would wish to question the truth of the statement that Descartes is the most important French philosopher. His influence has been felt throughout the whole course of French philosophy. For example, one of the main characteristics of this philosophy has been a close alliance between philosophical reflection and the sciences. And though the more recent French thinkers have not followed his example of attempting to work out a complete, deductive system, they have recognized their place in a tradition which goes back to the inspiration of Descartes. Thus Bergson refers to the close alliance between philosophy and mathematics in the thought of Descartes and draws attention to the fact that in the nineteenth century men such as Comte, Cournot and Renouvier came to philosophy through mathematics, one of them, Henri Poincaré, being a mathematician of genius.[1] Again, Descartes' preoccupation with clear and distinct ideas, fortified by his use of comparatively simple language, has been reflected in the clarity of French philosophical writing when considered as a whole. To be sure, certain French thinkers have adopted an obscure style and diction mainly under foreign influence; but, by and large, the philosophers of France have continued the Cartesian tradition in the matter of clarity and in the avoidance of obscure jargon.

The clarity of Descartes is, indeed, somewhat deceptive. For it is not by any means always an easy matter to interpret his meaning. And it can hardly be claimed that he is always consistent. Yet there certainly is a sense in which it is true to say that Descartes is, and that Hegel, for instance, is not, a clear writer.

---

[1] 'La philosophie française', p. 251 (in *La Revue de Paris*, May–June 1915).

This fact being presupposed, some philosophers have tried to find in Descartes a deeper meaning, a profound tendency of his thought, which possesses a permanent value independent of the Cartesian system as a whole. Thus in his *History of Philosophy* Hegel salutes Descartes as the real originator of modern philosophy, whose chief merit is to have started from thought without presuppositions. For Hegel Cartesianism is certainly inadequate. For one thing, Descartes, while starting with thought or consciousness, does not deduce the contents of consciousness from thought or reason itself, but accepts them empirically. Again, the ego of Descartes is only the empirical ego. In other words, Cartesianism forms only a stage in the development of philosophy towards absolute idealism. But it is a stage of great importance; for in starting with consciousness or thought Descartes brought about a revolution in philosophy.

Edmund Husserl interpreted the importance of Descartes in a rather different way. For him Descartes' *Meditations* represent a turning-point in the history of philosophical method. The latter aimed at a unification of the sciences, and he saw the necessity of a subjectivist starting-point. Philosophy must start with the meditations of the self-reflecting ego. And Descartes begins by 'bracketing' the existence of the material world and by treating the self as body and material things as phenomena in relation to a subject, the conscious ego. To this extent Descartes can be considered as a forerunner of modern phenomenology. But he did not understand the significance of his own procedure. He saw the necessity of questioning the 'natural' interpretation of experience and of freeing himself from all presuppositions; but instead of treating the ego as pure consciousness and exploring the field of 'transcendental subjectivity', the field of essences as phenomena for a pure subject, he interpreted the ego as a thinking substance and proceeded to develop a realist philosophy with the help of the principle of causality.

Thus while Hegel looked on the philosophy of Descartes as a stage in the development of absolute idealism and Husserl regarded it as an anticipation of phenomenology, both men laid stress on 'subjectivity' as the Cartesian point of departure. M. Jean-Paul Sartre does the same, though within the framework, of course, of a philosophy which is different from that either of Hegel or of Husserl. In his lecture, 'Existentialism and Humanism', Sartre remarks that the starting-point for philosophy must be the subjectivity of the individual, and that the primal truth is *I think, therefore I am*, which is the absolute truth of consciousness as it attains to itself. But he then goes on to argue that in the 'I think' I am conscious of myself in the presence of the other. The existence of others is discovered in the *Cogito* itself, so that we find ourselves at once in a world of inter-subjectivity. And it is worth remarking that the existentialists in general, while starting with the free individual subject, depict the consciousness of the subject as consciousness of the self in a world and in the presence of the other. Hence, though their starting-point has some affinity with that of Descartes, they do not involve themselves in the business of proving the existence of the external world as something not already given within the consciousness of the self. In other words, they do not start with the self-enclosed ego.

Hegel, Husserl and Sartre are, of course, simply three examples of the use made of Cartesianism by later thinkers. Many other examples could be given. One might cite, for instance, Maine de Biran's substitution of *Volo, ergo sum* for Descartes' *Cogito, ergo sum*. But all these thinkers have this in common, that they interpret the inner significance and permanent value of Cartesianism in function of a philosophy which was not that of Descartes. I do not say this by way of criticism. Hegel, Husserl and Sartre are all philosophers. Reference has, indeed, been made to Hegel's *History of Philosophy*. But this work forms an integral part of the Hegelian system: it is not a work of purely historical exegesis. And a philosopher certainly enjoys the right of deciding according to his own point of view what is living and what is dead in the philosophy of Descartes. At the same time, if Descartes is interpreted as an absolute idealist or as a phenomenologist or as an existentialist or, with La Mettrie, as a materialist who took the wrong path and failed to recognize the 'real' significance and the 'true' exigencies and direction of his thought, one runs the risk of failing to see him in his historical perspective. Descartes certainly tried to ground his philosophy in 'subjectivity' if one means by this that he tried to found his system on the *Cogito, ergo sum*. And it is perfectly true that this was an innovation of importance, and that when one looks back from a later stage of philosophical development one can see connections between this innovation and later idealism. But though there are what may be called idealist elements in Cartesianism, it would be most misleading to describe the latter as an idealist system. For Descartes grounded his philosophy on an existential proposition, and he was concerned to establish an objective interpretation of reality which he did not regard as reducible to the activity of consciousness. Again, if one emphasizes simply the connection between Descartes' mechanistic account of material reality and the mechanistic materialism which appeared in the eighteenth-century French Enlightenment, one obscures the fact that he sought to reconcile the 'geometric' view of the world with a belief in God, in the divine activity and in the spirituality of the human soul. Yet this is one of the most important aspects of his philosophy when we consider it in its historical setting.

In a sense Descartes' philosophy was an intensely personal enterprise. The autobiographical parts of the *Discourse on Method* show this clearly enough. He was animated, not by a merely superficial intellectual curiosity, but by a passion for the attainment of certainty. And he considered that the possession of a true system of philosophy was of importance for human life. But that for which he sought was objective certainty, self-evident truth and demonstrated truth. Descartes' insistence on 'subjectivity' (to use a later term) as the point of departure must not be confused with subjectivism. The attainment of something analogous to the objective, impersonal truth of mathematics remained his goal. In this sense he aspired to transcend tradition. That is to say, he aspired to establish the true philosophy which would rest on pure reason and not on past tradition, and which would be free from the limitations of space and time. The fact that we can discern in it the influence of tradition and of contemporary conditions is not, of course, a matter for astonishment. On the contrary, it would be astonishing if we could find no such influence. But the fact that Cartesianism is to a large extent dated does not deprive him of his claim to be considered the father of modern philosophy in the pre-Kantian period.

CHAPTER VII

PASCAL

Life and spirit of Pascal—The geometrical method, its scope and limits—'The heart'—Pascal's method in apologetics—The wretchedness and the greatness of man—The wager-argument —Pascal as a philosopher.

1. IN turning from Descartes to Pascal we are confronted by a man of very different stamp of mind. Both men were, indeed, mathematicians, and both were Catholics; but whereas the former was primarily a philosopher the latter was primarily an apologist. Descartes, it is true, can be considered to a certain extent as a religious apologist in the sense at least that he was aware of the religious and moral significance of his thought; but it is natural to think of him first and foremost as a systematic philosopher, intent on unfolding the 'order of reasons' and elaborating an organically connected and rationally established coherent body of philosophical truth capable of indefinite development. Though he was not a rationalist if by this word we mean a man who rejects the ideas of divine revelation and of the supernatural, he represents rationalism in the sense that he devoted himself to the pursuit of truth as attainable by the philosophical and scientific reflection of the human mind. He was a Catholic philosopher in the sense that he was a philosopher who was a Catholic; but he was not a Catholic philosopher in the sense that he was primarily concerned with defending the truths of faith. Pascal, however, was concerned with showing how the Christian revelation solves the problems which arise out of the human situation. In so far as he devoted himself to drawing attention to and exhibiting these problems he might perhaps be called an 'existentialist' philosopher, if we wished to use this term in a wide and perhaps rather misleading sense. But in so far as he was concerned with insisting that the answers to these problems, to the extent that the answers are available, are provided by Christian revelation and life he would probably be better classed as a Christian apologist than as a philosopher. We can understand at least how it is that while some writers see in him one of the greatest of French philosophers, others refuse to call him a philosopher. Henri Bergson and Victor Delbos, for

example, placed him side by side with Descartes, as the two chief French representatives of different lines of thought, and Jacques Chevalier sees in him a great philosopher precisely because he concerned himself with 'the questions that a man puts to himself face to face with death'.[1] Renouvier, on the other hand, considered Pascal too personal a thinker to merit the title of philosopher, and Émile Bréhier roundly declares that 'Pascal n'est pas un philosophe: c'est un savant et un apologiste de la religion catholique.'[2] These judgments are obviously partly dependent on personal decisions as to what constitutes philosophy and a philosopher. But at the same time they serve to emphasize the difference between Pascal and Descartes, a difference of which Pascal was indeed conscious. Indeed, in certain well-known aphorisms he explicitly rejected 'philosophy', meaning by this the sort of thing which Descartes attempted to do or which Pascal interpreted him as trying to do. In his opinion the great rationalist was too much occupied with the material world and too little concerned with the 'one thing necessary', to which a genuine love of wisdom would direct a man's attention.

Blaise Pascal was born in 1623, his father being the king's elected representative, the president of the Cour des Aides, at Clermont in the Auvergne. Biographers have dwelt on the influence of his early environment, the stark, rugged scenery of the Auvergne, on his character. He was educated by his father who in 1631 moved to Paris, and from childhood he displayed signs of outstanding intelligence and mental power. Whether the story of his rediscovery of geometry for himself at a time when his father was teaching him Greek and Latin is true or false, his interest in and ability for mathematics and physics were shown at an early date, and in 1639 he wrote an essay on conic sections, which was printed in the following year. Later he invented an adding-machine or mechanical computer, inspired by a desire to help his father in the assessment of taxes when he was occupying a Government post at Rouen. There followed the important series of experiments to prove the truth of Torricelli's experimental discovery of the vacuum, and these in turn provided the basis for the enunciation of fundamental principles in hydrostatics. Further, towards the end of his short life, when he was preoccupied with theological and religious problems, he laid the foundations of the infinitesimal

---

[1] *Pascal*, p. 14.
[2] *Histoire de la Philosophie*, Tome II, 1re partie, 1942, p. 129.

calculus, the integral calculus and the calculus of probabilities. It is therefore not exactly true to say that Pascal's asceticism diverted him from all 'this-worldly' activity and frustrated his mathematical genius as some critics have stated.

In 1654 Pascal underwent the spiritual experience recorded in his *Memorial*, an experience which gave him a fresh realization of the personal God and of the place of Christ in his life. And from this time his life bore a profoundly religious stamp. But this does not mean that we can justifiably divide it into two successive and separated phases, the scientific and the religious. For in abandoning himself to God he did not renounce all scientific and mathematical interests as 'worldly'; rather did he come to look on his scientific activities in a new light, as part of his service of God. If he subordinated mathematics to morals and natural morality to supernatural charity, he was simply embracing the point of view of any convinced Christian.

But though his 'conversion' did not produce in Pascal a complete renunciation of his scientific and mathematical interests, it certainly turned his mind towards theological themes. In 1652 his sister Jacqueline became a member of the community of Port Royal, the stronghold of Mère Angélique; and after his experience of 1654 Pascal formed intimate contacts with the Port Royal circle, the members of which were partisans of Jansenius, bishop of Ypres and author of the famous *Augustinus*. A number of propositions taken from this work had been condemned by the Holy See in May 1653; and the line taken by Arnauld and other partisans of Jansenius who belonged to the Port Royal circle was to accept the condemnation but to deny that the propositions were to be found in the writings of Jansenius in the sense in which they had been declared to be heretical. This attitude was regarded by Rome as equivalent to a dishonest evasion and was itself subjected to censure. But as far as Pascal is concerned he never committed himself to any sectarian or party standpoint, whether to that of Jansenius himself or to the milder views propagated by some of the associates of Port Royal. He declared that he did not belong to Port Royal but to the Catholic Church, and there is no adequate reason for questioning his sincerity. It is a mistake, therefore, to speak of him as a Jansenist if the term is used in a strict sense, namely, to indicate one who accepted and defended the condemned propositions. If at one time he tended towards the position represented by these propositions, he worked himself free of it. At the same time he was to a certain extent in sympathy with the Jansenists. He over-emphasized as they did, the corruption of human nature after the Fall and the powerlessness of man to become or to do anything pleasing to God without divine grace, even though he avoided the Jansenist denial of the part played by free will in accepting or rejecting grace. What attracted him to the Jansenists of Port Royal was not so much this or that specific tenet as the general attitude of Christian 'integralism' and refusal of compromise with the spirit of the world. In a society impregnated by deistic humanism and by rationalist scepticism and free thought he considered that it was above all the ideas of human corruption and of the necessity and power of divine grace which should be emphasized and that the highest Christian ideals should be maintained in their purity without any compromise or attempt to accommodate them to human weakness. And it was in this spirit that he wrote the celebrated *Lettres provinciales* (1655-7), which were condemned by the Congregation of the Index in 1657.

These letters are best known for the attack contained in them on the moral theology of the Jesuits. Pascal regarded the casuistry (the application of moral principles to particular cases) of the moral theologians as evidence of moral laxity and as an unjustifiable attempt to make Christianity easier for the more or less worldly-minded. In his writings on the subject he selects for mention and condemnation extreme cases of moral accommodation from certain authors, and he tends to confuse casuistry itself with the abuse of it. Furthermore, he tends to attribute to moral theologians unworthy motives which were certainly absent from their minds. The *Lettres provinciales*, in fine, show a lack of balanced judgment and a failure to distinguish between the fundamental and valid principles of moral theology and the abuse of casuistry. However, the main underlying issue is clear enough. The Jesuits believed that in the contemporary world the humanistic side of Christianity should be stressed and that when the ideals of the Christian life are applied to individual cases, there is no call to assert an obligation when there is good reason for thinking that there is no such obligation. Their motive was not that of extending their own dominion over consciences but that of including as many as possible in the ranks of practising Christian believers. Pascal, on the other hand, tended to look on humanism as equivalent to paganism, and any tempering of the wind to the shorn lamb he regarded as an intolerable tampering with the purity of the

Christian ideal. For good measure he accused the Jesuits of hypocrisy. In one sense he got the better of the dispute. For he was a brilliant writer, whereas his opponents did not produce any answer which was capable of having an effect equal to the *Lettres provinciales*. But in the long run Pascal was defeated. For moral theology and casuistry had a long history and process of development before them.

From soon after the time of his conversion Pascal seems to have formed the idea of composing an apology for the Christian religion with a view to converting the free-thinkers and sceptics of his time, as well as Catholics who did not live up to the precepts of Christ. But this project was never completed, and at his death in 1662 he left behind him only a sketch of the work, consisting mainly of aphorisms and notes, though there are some more extended passages. The collection of these thoughts is known as the *Pensées*[1] of Pascal.

2. Descartes tended to believe in one sovereign method of universal applicability, the mathematical method. And in his eyes the ideal attitude or spirit was that of the mathematician. It is true that these two statements are in some respects exaggerated and that they stand in need of qualification, as has already been indicated in the chapters on the Cartesian philosophy. But there can be little doubt, I think, that they represent the general impression which the writings of Descartes leave on the mind. Furthermore, they represent the idea which Pascal had of Descartes. And the former profoundly disagreed with the great rationalist's exaltation of the mathematical method and of the mathematical spirit. It is therefore somewhat surprising to find Pascal included in some histories of philosophy among the disciples of Descartes. The man who could make the comment, 'Descartes useless and uncertain',[2] can hardly be reckoned as an ardent Cartesian.

To say this, however, is not to say that Pascal despised the mathematical method or that he ever renounced his own mathematical and scientific achievements. Within its own limited field of application the geometrical method[3] of definition and orderly

---

[1] In references to this work I have used the letter *P* as an abbreviation. Page numbers are given according to the edition by Léon Brunschvicg (1914).

[2] *P.*, 2, 78, p. 361.

[3] Pascal used the word 'geometry' as a generic term, including under it mechanics, arithmetic and geometry in a narrower sense (*De l'esprit géométrique*, p. 173).

demonstration is supreme. 'An infallible method is sought by all. Logicians make profession of arriving at it, but the geometers alone attain it, and outside their science and what imitates it there are no true demonstrations.'[1] An ideal mathematical or geometrical method would indeed involve defining all terms and proving all propositions;[2] but this ideal method is beyond us. 'For that which surpasses geometry surpasses us.'[3] It does not follow, however, that geometry is uncertain. According to Pascal the geometer cannot define terms such as space, time, movement, number and equality; but the reason for this is that when the word 'time', for example, is pronounced the minds of all are directed towards the same object. The reference of the term would not be made clearer by any attempted definition. And as for our incapacity to prove all propositions, we must bear in mind the fact that basic propositions or principles are intuited. They cannot be demonstrated, but they are none the less evident. It is this fact which rescues mathematics from the corroding influence of Pyrrhonism or scepticism. It is true that 'reason', the analytic and deductive operation of the mind, comes up against the indefinable and the indemonstratable; and it follows that 'reason' alone cannot justify mathematics as a science which yields certitude. But 'the heart (that is, immediate perception or intuition) perceives that there are three dimensions in space, and that numbers are infinite. . . . We intuit principles and conclude to propositions; and all this with certitude, although by different ways. And it is as useless and ridiculous for the reason to demand of the heart proofs of its first principles before it (reason) is willing to assent to them as it would be for the heart to demand of the reason our intuition of all the propositions which the latter

---

[1] *De l'art de persuader*, p. 194.

[2] It should be noted that when Pascal speaks here of definitions, he means 'the giving of names to things which one has clearly designated in terms perfectly known; and I am speaking only of this sort of definition' (*De l'esprit géométrique*, p. 166). He can therefore say that geometrical definitions are conventional or arbitrary and not subject to contradiction or dispute. In other words, he is speaking of the use of conventional symbols to designate things, and not of propositions which give or purport to give the nature of things. If one says that time is the movement of a created thing, the statement is a definition if it is equivalent to a decision to use the word 'time' in this sense. One is free to use it in this sense if one chooses, provided that one does not also use the same word to designate something else. But if one means to say that time, considered as an 'object', that is, time as known by all, is the same as the movement of a created thing, this statement is not a definition but a proposition, and it is subject to dispute or contradiction. A proposition needs to be proved unless it is self-evident; and then it is an axiom or principle. (Cf. *De l'esprit géométrique*, pp. 170–1.)

[3] *De l'esprit géométrique*, p. 165.

demonstrated before it is ready to accept them.'[1] The evidence which attaches to principles is sufficient to qualify them for performing the function which they are required to perform.

It is worth while drawing attention in passing to Pascal's remarks, quoted above, that while logicians claim to have arrived at an infallible method, the geometers alone have in fact done so. Elsewhere he suggests that 'logic has perhaps borrowed the rules of geometry without understanding their force'.[2] The ideal rational method is the mathematical method, not that of Aristotelian and Scholastic logic. On this point Pascal sides with Descartes and accepts with him the common revolt against and depreciation of the logic of the Schools. It must be added, with regard to the general relation of logic to mathematics, that Leibniz later took the opposite view. For him mathematical logic was a particular form taken by general logic.

But though Pascal was a 'Cartesian' to the extent that he asserted the supremacy of the mathematical method within the field of deduction and demonstration, he by no means shared Descartes' convictions concerning the extent of its applicability and usefulness. We cannot, for example, develop the natural sciences in a purely *a priori* manner. We must recognize the probable character of our hypotheses. And in establishing empirical facts experience, or rather the experimental method, must be our guide. Authority is the source of our theological knowledge; for the mysteries of faith surpass the reach of the human reason. But this is not the case with regard to our mathematical and scientific knowledge. The secrets of nature are indeed hidden; but experience and experiment gradually increase our knowledge of them. Experiences 'are the sole principles of physics'.[3] It follows that our knowledge is limited by our experience. 'When we say that the diamond is the hardest of all bodies, we mean of all bodies with which we are acquainted, and we cannot and ought not to include those of bodies of which we are entirely ignorant.'[4] 'For in all matters in which proof consists in experiences and not in demonstrations one cannot make any universal assertion save by general enumeration of all the parts and of all the different cases.'[5] With regard to the existence or possibility of a void or vacuum, it is experience alone which can decide whether there is or can be a vacuum or not. Authority is not

---

[1] *P.*, 4. 282, p. 460.
[2] *De l'art de persuader*, p. 194.
[3] *Fragment d'un traité du vide*, p. 78.
[4] *Ibid.*, p. 82.
[5] *Ibid.*

sufficient to solve the problem. Nor can the question be decided by *a priori* mathematical demonstration.

The geometrical method is also inefficacious in the metaphysical field. Take, for example, the problem of God. Pascal seems at first sight to contradict himself. On the one hand he asserts that 'we know, then, the existence and the nature of the finite, because we are finite and extended like it. We know the existence of the infinite and are ignorant of its nature, because while like us it has extension, unlike us it has no limits. But we know neither the existence nor the nature of God; for He has neither extension nor limits. By faith, however, we know His existence, and by glory (by the *lumen gloriae*, Pascal means) we shall know His nature.'[1] Again, 'Let us speak now according to our natural light. If there is a God, He is infinitely incomprehensible; for, possessing neither parts nor limits, He has no relation with us. We are therefore incapable of knowing either what He is or whether He is.'[2] Here Pascal seems to say clearly that the natural reason is incapable of proving God's existence and that faith alone can assure us of this truth. On the other hand, there are passages in which he appears to admit that there are or may be valid philosophical proofs of God's existence. And at first sight it may appear that a contradiction is involved. The explanation, however, is simple enough. In the first place, 'the metaphysical proofs of God are so remote from men's reasoning and so complicated that they have little effect. And even when they serve for some people, they do so only during the moment these people see the demonstration. An hour later they are afraid that they may have been deceived.'[3] Again, while proofs based on the marvels of nature may serve to draw the attention of believers to the work of God, they are of no service to atheists. On the contrary, to attempt to convince atheists by an argument based on the movement of the heavenly bodies is to 'give them reason for thinking that the proofs of our religion are very weak; and I see by reason and by experience that nothing is more calculated to excite in them this contempt'.[4] In other words, if the object of proving God's existence is to convince agnostics and atheists, the abstract metaphysical proofs are no use, while physical arguments are worse than useless. Reasoning of both types is inefficacious.

But Pascal had a profounder reason for rejecting the traditional proofs of God's existence. The knowledge of God which he had in

[1] *P.*, 3, 233, p. 436.   [2] *Ibid.*   [3] *P.*, 7, 543, p. 570.   [4] *P.*, 4, 242, p. 446.

mind was the knowledge of God as revealed in Christ, mediator and redeemer, a knowledge which is the response to man's intimate consciousness of his own misery. But a purely philosophical knowledge of God involves knowledge neither of man's need for redemption nor of Christ the redeemer. It can coexist with pride and with ignorance of God as man's supreme good and final end. The Christian religion 'teaches man these two truths together, that there is a God, for whom men have a capacity, and that there is a corruption in nature, which renders them unworthy of Him. It is equally important for men to know both these points; and it is equally dangerous for man to know God without knowing his own misery and to know his own misery without knowing the redeemer who can heal him. Knowledge of one of these truths by itself produces either the pride of the philosophers who have known God but not their misery or the despair of the atheists who know their own misery without (knowing the) redeemer.'[1] In other words, philosophical proofs of God's existence are not only insufficient to convince 'hardened atheists'[2] but also 'useless and sterile'[3] inasmuch as the knowledge attained would be knowledge of God without Christ. It would be deism: and deism is not Christianity. 'The God of the Christians is not a God who is simply the author of geometrical truths and of the order of the elements; this is the concept of the pagans and of the epicureans. . . . All those who seek God apart from Jesus Christ and who stop at nature either find no light to satisfy them or arrive at forming for themselves a way of knowing God and of serving Him without a mediator; and thereby they fall either into atheism or into deism, which are two things which the Christian religion almost equally abhors.'[4]

As Pascal is concerned simply with knowledge of God as the supernatural end of man, with God as revealed in Christ, mediator and redeemer, he excludes natural religion and philosophical theism to all intents and purposes. It is clear enough that the use of the geometrical method will not lead man to knowledge of God in this sense. Pascal doubtless exaggerates the distinction between the God of the philosophers and 'the God of Abraham, Isaac and Jacob'; but he leaves us in no doubt about the meaning he attaches to 'knowledge of God'. And his attitude towards Descartes is thus understandable. 'I cannot forgive Descartes. He would have liked to have been able to by-pass God in the whole

[1] *P.*, 8. 556, p. 580.　　　[2] *Ibid.*, 9, 581.　　　[3] *Ibid.*　　　[4] *Ibid.*

of his philosophy. But he could not help making God give a shove to set the world in motion; and after that he has no more to do with God.'[1] I do not mean to suggest that Pascal was just to Descartes; for I do not think that he was. But his attitude is understandable. In his view Descartes' philosophy omitted the *unum necessarium*. This is one reason for the maxim: 'To write against those who devote too much study to the sciences. Descartes.'[2] We can understand too how Pascal could write to Fermat, the great French mathematician, that in his opinion geometry is *le plus haut exercice de l'esprit and le plus beau métier du monde* but that at the same time it is so 'useless' that 'I make little difference between a man who is only a geometer and an able artisan.'[3]

If philosophy is unable to establish the existence of God, at least if it is unable to establish the existence in the only sense in which it is worth while doing so, it is also incapable of revealing to man where lies true happiness. 'The Stoics say: "Retreat within yourselves; it is there that you will find your repose." And this is not true. The others say: "Go outside yourselves: seek happiness in diversions." And this is not true. . . . Happiness is neither outside us nor within us, it is in God, both outside and within us.'[4] Instinct prompts us to seek happiness outside ourselves; and external things draw us, even if we do not realize it. 'And so it is useless for the philosophers to say: "Retreat within yourselves; you will find your good there"; people do not believe them. And those who believe them are the emptiest and most foolish.'[5]

Further, being unable to discover and agree about the true end of man the philosophers have also been unable to discover and agree about the moral law. True, there are natural laws; but the corruption of human nature prevents us from obtaining a clear view of them. And even if we knew clearly by philosophical reflection what true justice is, for example, we should be unable to practise it without divine grace. 'The nature of self-love and of this human ego is to love only itself and to consider only itself.'[6] And in point of fact 'larceny, incest, murder of children and of parents, all have had their place among virtuous actions'.[7] 'Three degrees of latitude reverse the whole of jurisprudence, a meridian, decides about truth. . . . A pleasing justice which is bounded by a

[1] *P.*, 2, 77, pp. 360–1. [2] *P.*, 2, 76, p. 360. [3] *P.*, p. 229. [4] *P.*, 7, 465, p. 546.
[5] *P.*, 7, 464, p. 546. [6] *P.*, 2, 100, pp. 375–6. [7] *P.*, 5, 294, p. 466.

river! Truth this side of the Pyrenees, error beyond.'[1] Man, left
to himself, is blind and corrupted. And the philosophers have
been unable to remedy this state of affairs. Some of them, such
as the Stoics, have indeed provided the world with elevated
discourses; but their virtue was infected and corrupted by
pride.

It is no matter of astonishment, therefore, if Pascal declares
that 'we do not think that the whole of philosophy is worth an
hour's labour',[2] and that 'to mock at philosophy is to philosophize
truly'.[3] By 'philosophy' he means primarily natural philosophy
and science, the knowledge of external things, which he depreciates
in comparison with the science of man. But the point is that
reason alone is unable to establish the science of man. For without
the light of the Christian religion man is incomprehensible to himself. Reason has its own sphere, mathematics and the natural
sciences or natural philosophy; but the truths which it is really
important for man to know, his nature and his supernatural
destiny, these cannot be discovered by the philosopher or the
scientist. 'I had passed a long time in the study of the abstract
sciences; and the scant communication which one can have in
them (that is, the comparative fewness of the people with whom
one shares these studies and with whom one can 'communicate')
had disgusted me. When I began the study of man, I saw that
these abstract sciences are not proper to man. . . .'[4]

When Pascal depreciates 'reason', he is using the term in a
narrow sense, to mean the abstract, analytic and deductive
operation of the mind as it is found in 'geometry'. He is not, of
course, depreciating the use of reason in a wide sense. His outline
of a Christian apology is obviously a work of the mind. For the
matter of that, his criticism of reason in the narrow sense is,
whether we agree with it or not, a reasoned criticism. To put the
matter briefly, Pascal wishes to make two points. First, mathematical method and scientific method are not the only means by
which we come to know truth. Secondly, mathematical and
scientific truths are not those which it is most important for man
to know. From neither of these propositions does it follow that
reasoning in general or the use of the mind is to be condemned.

3. It is as well to remember this when we are considering what
Pascal has to say about 'the heart'. For if we interpret his polemic
against 'reason' as a polemic against the mind and against all

[1] P., 5, 294, p. 465.   [2] P., 2, 79, p. 361.   [3] P., 1, 4, p. 321.   [4] P., 21, 44, p. 399.

thought, we shall be inclined to interpret 'the heart' in an exclusively emotional sense. But in distinguishing between heart and reason it was not Pascal's intention to suggest that human beings should abandon the use of their mind and hand themselves over to the dominion of their emotions. The famous statement, 'the heart has its reasons which the reason does not understand',[1] does indeed appear to imply an antithesis between mind and heart, intellectual activity and emotion. But we have already seen that according to Pascal it is by 'the heart' that we know the first principles from which the reason derives other propositions. And it is obvious enough that heart cannot here mean simply emotion. It is necessary, therefore, to ask what Pascal did mean by the term.

It can hardly be said that Pascal uses the term *le cœur* in any one clearly defined sense. Sometimes it appears to be used as synonymous with 'the will'. And when it is used in this sense it does not designate a kind of knowledge or an immediate instrument of knowing, but rather the movement of desire and interest which directs the attention of the intellect to some object. 'The will is one of the principal organs of belief; not that it forms belief, but because things are true or false according to the aspect under which one sees them. The will, which takes pleasure in one (aspect) rather than another, turns away the mind from considering the qualities of those things which it does not wish to see. And so the mind, following the will, stops to contemplate the aspect which the will loves.'[2] At other times *le cœur* designates a kind of knowledge or an instrument of knowing. And this is Pascal's characteristic use of the term. It is exemplified in his statement that we apprehend first principles by 'the heart'. 'We know truth not only by the reason but also by the heart. It is in this second way that we know the first principles.'[3] Pascal also makes use of the terms 'nature' and 'instinct'. 'Nature confounds the Pyrrhonists, and reason confounds the dogmatics.'[4] 'Instinct and reason, characteristics of two natures.'[5] 'Heart, instinct, principles.'[6]

It is clear that even when 'the heart' is used to designate a way of knowing or an instrument of knowledge the term bears different shades of meaning in different contexts. When Pascal says that principles are felt by the heart, he is obviously talking about

[1] *P.*, 4, 277, p. 458.   [2] *P.*, 2, 99, p. 375.   [3] *P.*, 4, 282, p. 459.
[4] *P.*, 7, 434, p. 531.   [5] *P.*, 6, 344, p. 487.   [6] *P.*, 4, 281, p. 459.

intuition. And in the case of the first principles of geometry there can hardly be question of loving the principles. But when he asserts that 'it is the heart which feels (perceives) God, and not the reason',[1] he is thinking of a loving apprehension of God, apprehension which is open to those who have no knowledge of metaphysical arguments for God's existence or even of historical and empirical arguments in favour of Christianity. He does not refer to mere emotion, but rather to the loving apprehension of God which is found in the sincere Christian believer. And this is itself the effect of God in the soul, it is a supernatural faith in-formed by love or charity, which belongs to 'the order of charity or love' rather than to 'the order of the mind (*l'esprit*)'. Again, it is by 'the heart' or 'instinct' that we know that waking life is not a dream. A man may be unable to prove by demonstrative argument that waking life is not a dream, but it does not follow that he does not *know* the difference between waking life and the dream-state. He knows it by 'the heart'. Here the term 'heart' refers to instinctive, immediate, unreasoned apprehension of a truth. And Pascal's point is that we can have certitude (in his opinion legitimate certitude) even when the reason is unable to prove that of which we have certitude. For 'reason' is not the only way in which we come to know truth; and it is mere prejudice and pride on the part of the rationalists if they think that it is.

Pascal, as is evident, did not develop a technical vocabulary in which the function and meaning of each word is clearly defined. Sometimes the function of a term is that of suggesting meaning rather than of stating it. Thus words like 'heart', 'instinct' and 'feeling' suggest immediacy, spontaneity and directness. On the level of common sense we have, for example, a spontaneous and immediate apprehension or awareness of the reality of the external world; and the resulting conviction or certitude is legitimate, even though it is unsupported by rational proofs. On the level of 'geometry' we have an immediate awareness of principles; and even though these principles cannot be demonstrated our certi-tude is legitimate and lies at the foundation of deductive reason-ing. On the level of the moral life there is a spontaneous and direct apprehension of values, though this apprehension can be obscured or corrupted. And on the level of the religious life the devout believer possesses a loving apprehension of God which is immune from the attacks of scepticism. In general, 'the heart' is a kind

[1] *P.*, 4, 278, p. 458.

of intellectual instinct, rooted in the inmost nature of the soul.

4. If we wish to talk about Pascal's method, we have to mention both heart and reason. It is a mistake to think that he wished to substitute feeling for reason or to deny, for example, the relevance of reasoned argument to the apprehension of religious truth. In mathematics deduction and demonstration would be deprived of certainty, were it not for the immediate apprehension of evident first principles. But without the work of the discursive and deductive reason there would be no mathematics. Again, though the simple and devout Christian possesses legitimate certitude through his loving apprehension of God, this certitude is a personal matter; and it by no means follows that arguments in favour of the Christian religion are not required. We cannot satisfy sceptics and agnostics by appealing to the simple and devout Christian's interior appropriation of the truth. And Pascal himself projected an apology for Christianity, that is to say, a reasoned defence of the Christian religion. The arguments to which he appealed were based on empirical and historical facts, the presence of the Christian faith as an empirical fact, miracles, prophecy and so on; but the arguments were reasoned arguments. In Pascal's opinion we cannot prove the truth of Christianity by 'geometry', by *a priori* deductive reasoning. We have to turn to empirical data and show how their convergence points infallibly to the truth of Christianity. But the process of exhibiting this convergence is the work of the mind.

It is, indeed, necessary to emphasize this fact, because Pascal's aphorisms about feeling may easily give a wrong impression. At the same time the concept of 'the heart' has an important part to play even in his reasoned defence of the Christian religion. For while the heart does not, indeed, supply the proofs, it discerns the significance of the facts cited in the proofs, and it discerns too the significance of the convergence of probabilities. Of two men who listen to the arguments and understand the words one may see the cumulative force of the arguments while the other does not. If all the arguments have been mentioned, the difference between the two men is not that the one has heard an argument which the other has not: it is rather that the one has an intuitive grasp of the force and significance of the converging arguments, which is lacking to the other. In the development of an apologetic, therefore, it is essential to display the arguments in the most persuasive form, not in order to persuade people to embrace a conclusion repugnant to the mind, but in order to facilitate the working of 'the heart'.

5. Any prolonged exposition and discussion of Pascal's apology for Christianity would be out of place in a history of philosophy. At the same time the reader of a chapter on Pascal will legitimately expect to find some indication of the line taken. And we can hardly understand his general outlook without some reference to his defence for Christianity.

Pascal sets out first to show the 'misery of man without God', that is to say, 'that nature is corrupted'.[1] In comparison with the realm of nature, what is man? 'A nothing in comparison with the infinite, a whole with regard to nothing, a mean between nothing and everything. Infinitely removed from understanding either extreme, the end of all things and their beginning are alike invincibly hidden from him in impenetrable mystery. He is equally incapable of seeing either the nothingness from which he was taken or the infinite in which he is enveloped.'[2] Man can know neither the infinitely great nor the infinitely small. Nor can he have a complete knowledge even of those things which fall between either extreme. For all things are bound together in mutual relations, and a complete knowledge of any part demands knowledge of the whole. His intellectual capacity is limited, and he is also liable to be led astray by the senses and the imagination. Further, he takes custom for natural law; and in social life he mistakes the rule of power for the rule of justice. He is dominated by self-love, and this inclination to self-interest blinds his eyes to true justice and is the origin of disorder in social and political life. Again, man is riddled with contradictions, and he is a riddle to himself. He can be satisfied with nothing less than the infinite, but in point of fact he finds no complete satisfaction.

In his picture of the misery or wretchedness of man, Pascal draws on the writings of the Pyrrhonists or sceptics, and up to a certain point he sides with Montaigne and Charron. Montaigne, he said, is invaluable for confounding the pride of those who attribute too much to human nature and who ignore man's corruption and weakness. But we have to remember that what Pascal wishes to show is the wretchedness of man 'without God'. His aim is not to promote scepticism and disillusionment for their own sakes, still less despair, but by showing what man is without

[1] *P.*, 2, 60, p. 342.   [2] *P.*, 2, 72, p. 350.

God to facilitate favourable dispositions for considering the claims of the Christian religion. Pascal was very conscious of the powerlessness of mere argument to convince those who lacked the requisite dispositions.

But there is another aspect of man to be considered, his 'greatness'. And his greatness can be inferred even from his wretchedness. 'The greatness of man is so evident that it can be inferred even from his wretchedness. For that which is nature in animals we call wretchedness in man. And by this we recognize that his nature being now like that of the animals, he is fallen from a better nature which formerly was his. For who is unhappy at not being a king, except a deposed king?'[1] Even man's excesses reveal his craving for the infinite. And his power of recognizing his wretchedness is itself a sign of his greatness. 'Man knows that he is wretched. He is wretched, then, because he is wretched; but he is great, because he knows it.'[2] Further, 'thought constitutes the greatness of man'.[3] 'Man is only a reed, the frailest thing in nature; but he is a thinking reed. It is not required that the whole universe should arm itself to crush him; a breath of wind, a drop of water is sufficient to destroy him. But were the universe to crush him, man would still be nobler than that which slays him. For he knows that he dies and that the universe has the better of him. But the universe knows nothing of this.'[4] 'Spatially, the universe encompasses and engulfs me like a point. But by thought I encompass the universe.'[5] Man is filled with an insatiable desire for happiness, and this desire is a source of unhappiness. But 'the infinite gulf can be filled only by an infinite and changeless object, that is by God Himself'.[6] So here again man's wretchedness reveals his greatness, his capacity for God.

We are faced, therefore, by contraries; man's wretchedness and man's greatness. And we must hold together these contraries in our thought. For it is precisely the simultaneous presence of these contraries which constitute the problem. 'What a chimera then is man! How strange and monstrous! A chaos, a subject of contradictions, a prodigy. Judge of all things, yet a stupid earthworm; depository of truth, yet a cesspool of uncertainty and error; the glory and the refuse of the universe. Who will unravel this tangle?'[7] The philosophers cannot do so. The Pyrrhonists

[1] P., 6, 409, p. 512. [2] P., 6, 416, p. 515. [3] P., 6, 346, p. 488.
[4] P., 6, 347, p. 488. [5] P., 6, 348, p. 488. [6] P., 7, 425, p. 519.
[7] P., 7, 434, p. 531.

make man nothing, while others make of him a god; man is both great and wretched at the same time.

If man cannot solve the problem which arises out of his own nature, let him hear God. But where is the voice of God to be found? Not in the pagan religions, which lack authority and proof and which authorize vice. In the Jewish religion? Here we have an explanation of man's wretchedness in the scriptural account of the Fall. But the Old Testament looks beyond itself, and its prophecies are fulfilled in Christ, who provides the remedy which is not provided by Judaism. Here we have the mediator and redeemer, foretold by the prophets and proving His authority by miracles and the sublimity of His doctrine. 'The knowledge of God without that of our wretchedness produces pride. The knowledge of our wretchedness without the knowledge of God produces despair. The knowledge of Jesus Christ forms the middle point; for there we find both God and our wretchedness.'[1]

6. In the *Pensées*[2] there occurs the famous wager-argument. Its significance and purpose are not immediately clear, and a number of different interpretations have been offered by commentators. It seems, however, to be sufficiently evident that Pascal did not develop this argument as a proof of God's existence. Nor did he intend it as a substitute for proofs of Christianity. It appears to be addressed to a particular class of persons, namely, to those who are not yet convinced of the truth of the Christian religion, though they are also unconvinced by the arguments of sceptics and atheists, and who consequently remain in a state of suspended judgment. Pascal wishes to show people who find themselves in this state of mind that to believe is to their advantage and happiness, and that if it depended entirely on their own wills belief would be the only reasonable course of action. But it does not follow that he demands of them faith simply as an outcome of the wager-argument. What he seems to have in mind is rather the preparation of their minds and the production of dispositions favourable to belief, dispositions which are hindered by the passions and by attachment to things of this world. He is speaking to them *selon les lumières naturelles*, according to their natural lights or to common sense; but he did not consider that belief is simply a matter of a self-interested wager, of a betting on an objective uncertainty because, if it were true, it would be to one's advantage to have staked in favour of it. If he had thought this,

---

[1] *P*., 7. 527, p. 567.   [2] 3. 233, pp. 434–42.

it would be impossible to explain either his projected reasoned defence of Christianity or his conviction that it is God Himself who imparts the light of faith.

Either God exists or there is no God. The sceptic blames the Christian because he chooses a definite solution to the problem although reason cannot show which solution is true. 'I shall blame them for having made, not this choice, but a choice . . . the right course is not to wager.' 'Yes,' says Pascal, 'but you must wager. It does not depend on your will; you are already embarked on the affair.' In other words, to remain indifferent or to suspend judgment is itself to make a choice; it is to choose against God. And if, therefore, a man cannot help choosing one way or the other, he should consider where his interest lies. What is involved? A man's reason and his will, his knowledge and his happiness. His reason is not harmed more by choosing one way than by choosing the other way; for choose he must. As for happiness, it is obviously advantageous, and therefore reasonable, to wager for God. 'If you win, you win all; if you lose, you lose nothing.' 'There is here an infinity of an infinitely happy life to gain, one chance of gain against a finite number of chances of loss; and what you stake is finite.' Now, the finite is as nothing in comparison with the infinite. There is no need, therefore, for further deliberation.

It may be said that wagering for God means risking what is certain for what is uncertain. To risk a finite good for a certain infinite good is clearly advantageous; but the certainty of loss balances the possibility of gain when there is question of abandoning a certain finite good for an uncertain infinite good. In such a case it is better to retain what one actually and certainly possesses than to abandon it for an infinite good when one does not even know that there is an infinite good which could possibly be gained. But to this Pascal answers that every gambler stakes a certainty to gain an uncertainty, and he does this 'without sinning against reason'. Moreover, even though the man who wagers for God abandons some pleasures, he will acquire others, and he will win true virtue. 'At each step you take in this path, you will see such a certitude of gain and such a nothingness in what you hazard that you will recognize at the end that you have wagered for something which is certain and infinite and for which you have given nothing.' The prime requisite is to wager, to begin, not by piling up arguments for God's existence, but by lessening one's passions and following the behaviour of those who believe. In other words, though a man cannot give himself faith, there is a great deal that he can do by way of preparing himself, and if he does this, God will give him the faith which he seeks.

Pascal's words do indeed sometimes imply that religion lacks rational support. 'If one should do nothing except for what is certain, one ought to do nothing for religion. For it is not certain.'[1] But he argues that we are constantly running risks for the uncertain, in war, in commerce, in journeys. Moreover, nothing in human life is absolutely certain. It is not certain that we shall see tomorrow; but nobody thinks it irrational to act on the probability of his being alive the next day. 'And there is more certitude in religion than there is in our living till tomorrow.'[2] It is only reasonable to search for the truth; for if we die without adoring God, we are lost. 'But,' you will say, 'if He had willed that I should adore Him, He would have left me signs of His will.' 'So He has done, but you neglect them. Search for them: it is worth the trouble.'[3] 'I tell you that you would soon have faith, if you abandoned pleasure. It is for you to begin. If I could, I would give you faith, but I cannot do it. . . . You, however, can well abandon pleasure and find out whether what I say is true.'[4] The whole wager-argument is obviously an *argumentum ad hominem*, a device to move the sceptic to abandon his attitude of indifference and to do what he can to put himself in that condition in which faith becomes a real possibility. In spite of the way in which he sometimes expresses himself, Pascal does not intend to deny that there are signs of the truth of the Christian religion which in their convergence amount to an evident proof. But a man cannot, in his opinion, read those signs aright or grasp the force of their convergence unless he first abandons the state of indifference and makes serious efforts to conquer himself. Hence the wager-argument.

7. It is obvious that Pascal wrote as a convinced Christian. He did not seek to convert men to 'theism' but to Christianity. And he was profoundly conscious of the need for certain moral dispositions before conversion could be a practicable possibility. It is certainly possible to select and emphasize statements in which he plays down the work of reason to an exaggerated extent. Hence the accusations of fideism and immanentism which have been brought against him. But if we take a broad view and remember

[1] *P.*, 3, 234, p. 442. [2] *Ibid.* [3] *P.*, 3, 236, p. 443. [4] *P.*, 3, 241, p. 444.

that his main concern is to bring men to the point at which God Himself can operate and that it is Christian faith and not philosophical theism which he has in mind, we must acknowledge, I think, that his originality and genius as an apologist shows itself precisely in his concern with the moral preparation for faith. The value of his general attitude as an apologist for Christianity far outweighs in importance and perennial validity those aspects of his thought which are considered to be questionable or censurable by the Catholic theologian. It is a pity to miss the wood for the trees, and not to appreciate Pascal's importance and influence in the history of Christian apologetics.

But if Pascal was eminent as mathematician and scientist on the one hand and as a Christian apologist on the other, have we to conclude that he was not a philosopher? The answer depends, of course, on what we understand by a philosopher. If we understand by a philosopher a man who sets out to create a system by the use of reason alone, a system which is supposed to represent reality as a whole, then we certainly cannot call Pascal a philosopher. For he believed that problems arise which reason, unaided by faith, cannot solve. And he also believed that there are mysteries which transcend the comprehension of the mind even when it is enlightened by faith. The notion of an omnicompetent human reason was abhorrent to him. But, as we have seen, he had a reasoned view of the different modes and methods of human knowledge and of the different 'orders', the order of the flesh, the order of the mind or of science, and the order of charity. Even though he did not develop these ideas and distinctions in a technical view, we have here theories in epistemology and in the philosophy of values. His analysis of man can obviously be called a philosophy of man, even if it is a philosophy which to a great extent raises problems that are not soluble without reference to revelation. And in the course of this philosophy of man a good many ideas appear which are relevant to, for example, ethical and political analysis.

The word 'analysis' certainly has an application with regard to Pascal's thought. For example, it is not unreasonable to speak of him as analysing the different senses of the word 'knows' and as showing that its restriction to mathematical knowledge and what 'imitates' it is unjustified by ordinary usage. The ordinary man would certainly say that he 'knows' that the external world exists and that waking life is not a dream. And if one says that he does not 'really' know this, one is tacitly identifying knowledge with the sort of knowledge that pertains to the restricted sphere of mathematics.

Yet it would be as misleading to describe Pascal as a philosophical analyst as it would be to describe him as a systematic metaphysician. Can we describe him as an existentialist thinker, as some would do? Certainly, he is concerned with the existent human being and with his possibilities, above all with his possibility of choosing himself or of not choosing himself before God, to use existentialist language. But to use the term 'existentialist' with its modern connotations is also rather misleading, though it would be less misleading perhaps than 'analyst' or 'metaphysician'. In any case he is an 'existentialist' thinker because he is a religious thinker, a thinker who is primarily interested in the relation between man and God and in the lived appropriation of this relation. Pascal is not, like Descartes, a Christian thinker simply in the sense that he is a thinker who is a Christian: he is a Christian thinker in the sense that his Christianity is the inspiration of his thought and unifies his outlook on the world and man. If he is a philosopher, therefore, he is a religious philosopher, more specifically a Christian philosopher. He is a Christian philosopher of his age, in the sense that he addresses himself to his contemporaries and speaks a language which they can understand But this is not to say, of course, that his ideas have no lasting stimulative value. And perhaps this is the chief legacy of Pascal, that he left in his fragmentary writings a fertile source of stimulus and of inspiration for further development. Not all, indeed, feel this stimulus; and some find him repugnant. Others rank him with Descartes, as one of the two greatest of French philosophers, and feel for him the profoundest admiration. Possibly the former do him less and the latter more than justice.

CHAPTER VIII

CARTESIANISM

The spread of Cartesianism—Geulincx and the problem of inter-action.

1. CARTESIANISM spread and found defenders first of all in Holland, which had been Descartes' home for a considerable period. Thus Henri Regnier (1593–1639), who occupied the chair of philosophy at the academy, and from 1636 at the University of Utrecht, was a disciple of Descartes. So also, though only for a time, was Regnier's successor at Utrecht, Henricus Regius or Henri Le Roy (1598–1679). After espousing the cause of Descartes and defending him against the theologian Voëtius he later abandoned Cartesianism and wrote the manifesto which occasioned Descartes' *Notes Against a Programme*. Jean de Raey, author of *Clavis philosophiae naturalis* (1654), and Adrian Heereboord, author of *Parallelismus aristotelicae et cartesianae philosophiae* (1643), also taught at Leyden. Of greater importance was Christopher Wittich (1625–87), who tried to show the conformity between Cartesianism and orthodox Christianity and who attacked Spinoza. In 1688 he published a volume of *Annotations and Meditations* and in 1690 his *Antispinoza*. Geulincx will be considered separately.

In Germany the influence of Cartesianism was comparatively slight. Among German Cartesians one can indeed mention John Clauberg (1622–65), author of a *Metaphysica de Ente sive Ontosophia*; but he taught in Holland, at Herborn and Duisberg. Another German was Balthasar Bekker (1634–98), author of a work entitled *De philosophia cartesiana admonitio candida*. He distinguished himself by attacking the persecution of witches, maintaining that magic is nonsense because the spiritual cannot act upon the material.

In England Anthony Legrand or Antoine Le Grand, a Frenchman from Douai, published *Institutiones philosophicae* (1672 and 1678) and endeavoured to introduce Cartesianism into Oxford. He found a strong opponent in Samuel Parker, bishop of Oxford, in whose eyes Descartes was as much an infidel as Thomas Hobbes. But, quite apart from theological opposition, Cartesianism made little headway in the country. That is to say, his philosophy (in the modern sense of the term) made little headway, though his physics was widely accepted. Nor did Cartesianism have very much success in Italy, partly no doubt because the works of Descartes were placed on the Index of prohibited books in 1663 with the proviso *donec corrigantur*.[1] Michel Angelo Fardella (1650–1718) and Cardinal Gerdil (1718–1802) are generally classified under the heading of Italian Cartesians; but they were more influenced by Malebranche.

In Holland the influence of Descartes was felt mainly by university professors and lecturers, who issued manuals of Cartesian philosophy and endeavoured to defend the latter against attacks by theologians. In France, however, Cartesianism enjoyed a popular vogue, becoming the fashionable philosophy. Pierre-Sylvain Régis (1632–1707) did much to popularize it in general society by the lectures which he delivered in various centres, including Paris; and Jacques Rohault (1620–75), a physicist, endeavoured to substitute a science according to the mind of Descartes for the Aristotelian physics. (His *Traité de physique* was influential at Cambridge until it was discredited by Newton's *Principia*.) Louis de la Forge published in 1666 a *Traité de l'âme humaine, de ses facultés et fonctions et de son union avec le corps suivant les principes de R. Descartes*; and in the same year there appeared the *Discernement de l'âme et du corps* of Géraud de Cordemoy. A number of Oratorians saw in the 'spiritualist' side of Descartes' philosophy an affinity with St. Augustine and accorded their favour to Cartesianism. And though there was a very great difference between the spirit of Cartesianism and that of Jansenism, as may be seen from the writings of Pascal, several important Jansenists were influenced by Descartes. Thus Antoine Arnauld (1612–94), author of the fourth set of *Objections*, and Pierre Nicole (1625–95) utilized Cartesian ideas in the composition of *L'art de penser* (1662), the so-called 'logic of Port Royal'. The Jesuits, however, whose favour Descartes had constantly striven to secure, were generally hostile to the new philosophy.

In spite of what one may call the social success of Cartesianism in France, there was a considerable amount of official opposition. The placing of Descartes' works on the Roman Index in 1663 has already been mentioned. Ten years later the Parliament of Paris

---

[1] Nobody having taken it upon himself to 'correct' the works of Descartes, they remain on the Index to this day. The proviso *donec corrigantur* referred to points which had theological implications with regard, for example, to the dogma of transubstantiation.

was about to issue a decree against the teaching of Cartesianism
when it was prevented by the publication of *Arrêt burlesque* by
Boileau, who made fun of the opposition to reason as represented
by the philosophy of Descartes.[1] However, in 1675 the University
of Angers took steps to stop the teaching of the new philosophy,
and in 1677 the University of Caen adopted a similar course.
Pascal attacked Descartes' system as being deistic in character,
while Gassendi[2], the reviver of Epicurean atomism, criticized it
from an empiricist standpoint. Pierre Daniel Huet (1630–1721),
bishop of Avranches, in his *Censura philosophiae Cartesianae* and
other writings, maintained that scepticism could be overcome only
by religious faith, not by Cartesian rationalism.

Early in the eighteenth century Descartes' writings had already
become more or less official textbooks in philosophy in universities. And the influence of his philosophy had penetrated
ecclesiastical seminaries in spite of official prohibition and dis-
couragement. But by that time Cartesianism in the strict sense
had become a spent force. As one of the chief sources of the
development of metaphysics on the Continent before Kant,
Cartesianism is, of course, of great and lasting importance. But
in the eighteenth century other philosophies attracted the interests
and attention which in the seventeenth century had been given
to that of Descartes.

2. It has been remarked with truth that Cartesianism did not
receive quite the sort of development which the philosopher would
have desired. He considered that the metaphysical foundations
had been well and truly laid and he hoped that others would apply
his method in a fruitful way in the sciences. But apart from one
or two writers such as Rohault the Cartesians themselves hardly
fulfilled these expectations: they were more concerned with the
metaphysical and epistemological aspects of Cartesianism. And
one of the problems to which attention was particularly devoted
was the problem of the relation between soul and body. Descartes
did not deny interaction between soul and body; but though he
asserted it as a fact he did little to explain how it can take place.
His attempt to identify the point of interaction did not solve the
problem which arises out of his philosophy. For if man is to all
intents and purposes divided into two substances, a spiritual
mind and an extended body, the problem of explaining how

---

[1] Boileau's aesthetic theories were influenced by Cartesianism.
[2] For Gassendi, see vol. III, pp. 263–4.

interaction can take place becomes acute, and the problem is not answered satisfactorily by asserting that it does in fact take place and by trying to identify the site of interaction.

One way of treating this problem would be to admit the fact of interaction, as Descartes did, and then to revise the theories which led to difficulty in explaining how it can take place. But this would mean abandoning one of the chief characteristics of Cartesianism. And the Cartesians who devoted their attention to the problem chose to retain Descartes' dualistic position and to deny that interaction does in fact take place. This heroic way of disposing of the problem was adumbrated by Louis de la Forge and Géraud de Cordemoy; but it is associated above all with the names of Geulincx and Malebranche.

Arnold Geulincx (1625–69) was a professor at Louvain; but in 1658 he had to abandon his chair for reasons which are not very clear. He went to Leyden and there became a Calvinist. After a time he obtained a lectureship in the university. Some of his writings he published himself; but the more important appeared posthumously. Among these are the Γνῶθι σεαυτόν sive Ethica, Physica vera, Metaphysica vera et ad mentem peripateticam and Annotata in Principia philosophiae R. Cartesii.

According to Geulincx it is an evident principle that in all true activity the agent must know that he acts and how he acts. From this it clearly follows that a material thing cannot be a true causal agent producing effects either in another material thing or in a spiritual substance. For since a material thing lacks consciousness it cannot know that it acts and how it acts. It also follows that I, as a spiritual ego, do not really produce either in my own body or in other bodies those effects which my natural way of thinking, accepted by Aristotle as a criterion, leads me to suppose that I produce. For I do not know how these effects are produced. I am a spectator of the production of changes and movements in my body, but I am not the actor, the real causal agent, in spite of my interior acts of will. For I do not know the connection between my acts of will and the subsequent movements in my body. Similarly, I am aware of the production of sensations and perceptions in my field of consciousness; but it is not my body, or any external material thing, which truly produces these effects.

But if interaction is thus denied, how are we going to explain the fact that volitions are followed by movements in the body and that changes in the body are followed by sensations and perceptions in consciousness? The explanation is that my act of will is an occasional cause; that is, an occasion on which God produces a change or movement in the body. Similarly, a physical event in my body is an occasion on which God produces a psychical event in my consciousness. Body and soul are like two clocks, neither of which acts on the other but which keep perfect time because God constantly synchronizes their movements. At least this is the analogy to which Geulincx seems to incline, though certain passages suggest rather the analogy, which was later used by Leibniz, of two clocks which have been so constructed in the first instance that they always remain in perfect agreement.

This theory of 'occasionalism', if it is accepted at all, must obviously be applied more widely than in the particular context of the relation between soul and body. For it follows from the principles on which the theory rests that no human ego acts on any other human ego or on any body and that no body acts on any other body or on any mind or ego. One might perhaps conclude simply that the causal relation is nothing but regular sequence; but the conclusion which Geulincx drew was the theory, already asserted by Louis de la Forge, that God is the only real cause. And once one has drawn this conclusion one must inevitably tend in the direction of Spinozism. If my successive ideas are caused in me by God and I am simply a spectator of effects which God produces in me, and if all changes and movements in the corporeal world are effected by God, it is not a very long step to the conclusion that minds and bodies are both modes of God. I do not mean to say that Geulincx actually took the further step to Spinozism; but he came near to doing so. And his ethical ideas bear a resemblance to those of Spinoza. We are only spectators: we can change nothing. Therefore we should cultivate a true contempt of the finite and a thorough-going resignation to God and the divinely-caused order of things, restraining our desires and following the path of humility and obedience which reason dictates.

The theory of occasionalism is subject, of course, to the criticism that if true causal activity is defined as activity in which the agent knows both that he acts and how he produces the effect the theory may follow, but that the definition is arbitrary and by no means self-evident. However, if the principle and the theory are accepted, a possible further step, as suggested above, is an approach to

Spinozism. At the same time it is possible to attempt to incorporate the theory into a non-Spinozistic religious metaphysics. And this is what Malebranche tried to do. But since Malebranche was an original philosopher of considerable influence in his own right, it does not seem appropriate to include a brief consideration of his thought in a chapter on Cartesianism, especially if this means giving undue prominence to one particular feature of his philosophy. Hence I accord him separate treatment.

CHAPTER IX

MALEBRANCHE

Life and writings[1]—*The senses, the imagination, the understanding; avoidance of error and attainment of truth—God as the only true cause—Human liberty—The vision of eternal truths in God—Empirical knowledge of the soul—Knowledge of other minds and of the existence of bodies—God's existence and attributes—Malebranche in relation to Spinoza, Descartes and Berkeley—The influence of Malebranche.*

1. NICOLAS MALEBRANCHE was born at Paris in 1638. He studied philosophy at the college of La Marche, where he felt little attraction for the Aristotelianism which he was taught, and theology at the Sorbonne. In 1660 he joined the Oratorians and was ordained priest in 1664. It was in this year that he came upon a posthumous work of Descartes, the *Traité de l'homme*, which had been published by Louis de la Forge; and he conceived a great admiration for its author with whose philosophy he had no previous first-hand acquaintance. He therefore set himself to study the works of Descartes whom he never ceased to regard as a master in philosophy. It is perhaps worth noting that the treatise which had first attracted his attention was really a work on physiology, and also that Malebranche took pains to increase his knowledge of mathematics with a view to a better understanding of Descartes' philosophy. As far as his interest in mathematics and science went, Malebranche can be said to have entered into the Cartesian spirit.

At the same time Malebranche shared the strong inclination of the Oratorian Fathers to the thought of St. Augustine and, in general, to the Platonic-Augustinian tradition. And this combination of Cartesianism with the Augustinian inspiration was characteristic of his philosophy. In his eyes and in the eyes of those who shared his outlook this combination was not a forced combination of incompatibles; for the Paris Oratorians had always seen in the 'spiritualist' side of Descartes' philosophy an affinity with the thought of St. Augustine. But it meant, of course, that

---

[1] In the references to the writings of Malebranche the following abbreviations have been used. *R.V.* stands for *De la recherche de la vérité*, and *E.M.* for *Entretiens sur la métaphysique.*

Malebranche's outlook was definitely that of a Christian philosopher who made no rigid separation between theology and philosophy and who was intent on interpreting the world and human
experience in the light of his Christian faith. He was a Cartesian
in the sense that in his opinion the philosophy of Descartes was
true in the main as far as it went, and he certainly considered that
this philosophy was superior to Aristotelianism as an instrument
in interpreting experience and reality. But he did not think that
Cartesianism was an adequate and self-sufficing intellectual
instrument, and his metaphysic is markedly theocentric in character. He was certainly not the man to censure the philosophy of
Descartes in the way that Pascal did or to belittle the constructive
power of reason; but he was definitely a Christian thinker rather
than a philosopher who happened to be a Christian. In some
respects at least he gives the impression of being a thinker of the
Augustinian tradition who has accepted the seventeenth-century
science and mathematics and who sees in the Cartesian philosophy
an instrument for the construction of a new synthesis. In other
words he was an original thinker, and to label him either as a
'Cartesian' or as an 'Augustinian' is to give a misleading impression.
He was both; but the synthesis was a construction of Malebranche's
mind, not a mere artificial juxtaposition of heterogeneous
elements. It must be added, however, that though Malebranche
regularly represents his philosophy as a synthesis of St. Augustine
and Descartes and decries the Scholastics, the influence of
mediaeval Scholasticism on his thought was much greater than he
realized.

In his work *De la recherche de la vérité* (1674-5) Malebranche
investigates the causes of deception and error and discusses the
right method of arriving at truth. This was followed by *Éclair-
cissements sur la recherche de la vérité* (1678). The *Traité de la
nature et de la grâce* (1680) concerns such themes as the application
of the theory of occasionalism in the supernatural order and the
reconciliation of human liberty with the efficacity of divine grace.
The title of *Méditations Chrétiennes* (1683) speaks for itself. In
the *Traité de morale* (1684) Malebranche sets out to show that
there is only one true morality, the Christian morality, and that
other moral systems, such as Stoicism, do not satisfy the criteria
of true morality. The *Entretiens sur la métaphysique* (1688)
summarizes the author's system, whereas the *Traité de la communication des mouvements* (1692) is purely scientific in character.

In the *Traité de l'amour de Dieu* (1697) Malebranche discusses Fénelon's theory of the pure love of God in a way which was found highly acceptable by Bossuet. In the *Entretien d'un philosophe chrétien avec un philosophe chinois* (1708) he treats of matters connected with the existence and nature of God, and in *Réflexions sur la prémotion physique* (1715) he replies to the Jansenistically coloured work by Boursier, *L'action de Dieu sur les créatures ou de la prémotion physique* (1713).

Malebranche's literary life was accompanied by a good deal of polemics. Arnauld in particular became a determined adversary, attacking both Malebranche's philosophical ideas and his theories about grace. Indeed, he denounced Malebranche at Rome; and though the latter defended his views, his *Traité de la nature et de la grâce* was placed on the Index at the end of 1689. Fénelon also wrote against him. And his last work before his death in 1715 was, as we have seen, a reply to Boursier.

2. 'Error is the cause of men's wretchedness. It is the bad principle which has produced the evil in the world. It is error which has produced and maintained in our soul all the evils that afflict us, and we cannot hope for solid and true happiness save by striving seriously to avoid it.'[1] Error is not necessary to man: whatever the sceptics may say, he is capable of attaining truth. And a general rule can be established at once, namely, that 'we should never give a complete assent save to things that we see evidently'.[2] True, with regard to the revealed mysteries of faith it is our duty to submit to authority, but authority has no place in philosophy. If Descartes is to be preferred to Aristotle, this is not because he is Descartes but because of the evident character of the true propositions which he asserts: 'To be a faithful Christian one must believe blindly; but to be a philosopher one must see evidently.'[3] A distinction must indeed be made between necessary truths, such as are found in mathematics, metaphysics and 'even in a great part of physics and ethics'[4] and contingent truths, such as historical propositions. And we must remember that in morals, politics, medicine and all the practical sciences we have to content ourselves with probability, not because certainty is unattainable but because we have to act and cannot wait for the attainment of certainty. But this does not alter the fact that if we refrain from giving complete assent to any proposition the truth of which is not evident, we shall not err. For to assent to a probable truth as

---

[1] *R.V.*, I, I.   [2] *R.V.*, I, 3.   [3] *Ibid.*   [4] *Ibid.*

probably true is not to give complete assent and does not involve us in error.

However, even though error is not necessary to man but depends on the use of our free will, it is an empirical fact that we do fall into error. And in examining the causes of error we can best begin by considering the senses; for sensation is one of the three kinds of human 'perception', the other two being the imagination and the pure understanding.

'It is not our senses which deceive us; it is our will which deceives us by its precipitate judgments.'[1] Malebranche means that we do not use our free wills to restrain ourselves from making precipitate judgments about external things, from judging, that is to say, that the relation of things to us is a sure indication of the nature of things in themselves. 'When one feels warmth, one is in no way deceived by believing that one feels it. . . . But one is deceived if one judges that the warmth which one feels is outside the soul which feels it.'[2] Malebranche followed Descartes in denying the objectivity of the secondary qualities. These qualities, as objects of consciousness, are psychic modifications, not objective qualities of things in themselves. If we follow our natural inclination to suppose that they are objective qualities of things in themselves, we fall into error; but we are capable of restraining ourselves from making these precipitate judgments. Similarly, our sense-perception of primary qualities is no adequate indication of what things are in themselves. To take a simple illustration, 'the moon appears to our sight to be much larger than the greatest stars, and yet we have no doubt that it is incomparably smaller'.[3] Again, apparent movement and repose, swiftness and slowness, are all relative to us. In fine, we ought 'never to judge by the senses of what things are in themselves, but only of the relation which they have to our bodies'.[4]

Malebranche begins by accepting the Cartesian distinction between two kinds of substances, spiritual and unextended substance and material substance or extension, which is capable of receiving different shapes and of being moved.[5] And from the identification of material or corporeal substance with extension he draws the same conclusion as Descartes about qualities. But this is not to say that in his examination of sense-perception Malebranche simply repeats Descartes. He examines the matter at

[1] *R.V.*, I, 5.   [2] *Ibid.*   [3] *R.V.*, I, 6.
[4] *R.V.*, I, 5.   [5] *R.V.*, I, I.

length and makes careful distinctions. For example, he asserts[1] that in sensation there are four different elements to be distinguished: the action of the object (the movement of particles, for instance), the changes in the sense-organs, the nerves and the brain, the sensation or perception in the soul, and the judgment which the soul makes. And here we must further distinguish between the natural or automatic judgment, which inevitably accompanies sensation, and the free judgment, which we can, even if with difficulty, abstain from making. As these different elements are found together and take place as though instantaneously, we tend to confuse them and not to see that the sensation as a psychic event is in the soul and neither in one's own body nor in any other. Malebranche's final conclusion is that our senses are 'very faithful and exact in instructing us about the relations which all the bodies that surround us have with our body, but that they are incapable of telling us what these bodies are in themselves. To make a good use of them, we must use them only to conserve health and life. . . . Let us understand well that our senses have been given us for the conservation of our body. . . .'[2]

In his view of the physiological process involved in sensation Malebranche followed Descartes. That is to say, he thought of the nerves as minute channels or funnels through which pass the 'animal spirits'. When an external object acts on the sense-organ the peripheral surface of the nerves is set in motion and the animal spirits transmit this impression to the brain. There then takes place the psychic element in sensation, which belongs to the soul alone. During the physiological process, however, 'traces' are imprinted on the brain by the animal-spirits, and these 'traces' may be more or less profound. If, therefore, the animal-spirits are set in motion by some other cause than the presence of an external object acting on a sense-organ, these 'traces' are affected and a psychic image results. A man may will the production or reproduction of images, and on the act of will there follows a movement of the animal spirits, and when the traces imprinted on the fibres of the brain are affected images result. But movements of the animal spirits may take place because of some other cause than an act of the will, and then images are produced involuntarily. It is interesting to note also that Malebranche gives a mechanistic explanation of the association of images. If I see several things

[1] *R.V.*, I, 10.   [2] *R.V.*, I, 20.

associated together, there results a linkage between the corresponding traces in the brain and the excitation of one member of
the set of traces is linked with the excitation of the other members.
'If, for example, a man finds himself at some public ceremony,
and if he notes all the circumstances and all the principal per-
sonages assisting at it, the time, the place, the day and all the
other particulars, it is sufficient to recall the place, or even some
less remarkable circumstance of the ceremony, to represent to
himself all the others.'[1] And this association or linkage is of far-
reaching importance. 'The mutual linkage of traces, and consequently of ideas, is not only the foundation of all figures of rhetoric,
but also of an infinity of other things of greater importance in
morals, politics and, in general, in all the sciences which have some
relation to man.'[2] Furthermore, 'there are in our brains traces
which are linked naturally one with another and also with certain
emotions, because this is necessary for the conservation of life. . . .
For example, the trace of a great height which one sees below one
and over which one is in danger of falling, or the trace of some large
body which is ready to fall on us and crush us is naturally linked
with the trace which represents death, and with an emotion of the
spirits which disposes us to flight and to the desire of flight. This
linkage never changes, because it is necessary that it should be
always the same; and it consists in a disposition of the fibres of the
brain which we have from our birth.'[3] Memory is also explained
in terms of impressions on the fibres of the brain and habit with
reference to the passage of the animal spirits through channels
where they no longer find any resistance.

Imagination is thus parallel to sensation, in the sense that it is
the faculty of producing or reproducing images of material things
in the absence of those things; that is to say, when we are not actually
perceiving the things in question. Accordingly, the same sort of
remarks that were made about error with regard to sensation can
be made about error in connection with the imagination. If we
judge that images of material things represent things as they are
in themselves rather than things in relation to us, our judgment
is erroneous. But imagination can, of course, be the source or
occasion of additional error. The products of the imagination are
generally weaker than actual sensations, and we generally recognize them for what they are. But sometimes they are vivid and
possess the same force as sensations from the psychological point

[1] *R.V.*, 2, 1, 5.   [2] *Ibid.*   [3] *Ibid.*

of view, and then we may judge that the objects imagined are physically present when in actual fact they are not.

Under the general heading of imagination, however, Malebranche includes a great deal more than the mere reproduction of images in the ordinary sense. We have seen that he includes a study of memory; and this affords him the occasion for writing at length against scholars, historians and commentators who are more concerned with memory-work than with the 'pure understanding'. Of this type are all those who devote prolonged attention to examining what, for example, Aristotle held about immortality and who give little or no time to examining whether the human soul is in fact immortal. Worse still are those who imagine that Aristotle, or anyone else, is an authority in philosophical questions. 'In matters of theology we ought to love antiquity because we ought to love the truth, and truth is found in antiquity. . . . But in matters of philosophy we ought on the contrary to love novelty for the same reason, namely, that we ought always to love the truth and search for it. All the same, reason does not wish us to believe these new philosophers on their word any more than the ancient philosophers. Reason wishes us to examine their thoughts with attention and to accept them only when we cannot any longer doubt them. . . .'[1] Malebranche thus tries to combine open-mindedness and 'modernity' in philosophy with a loyal acceptance of the Catholic doctrine of Tradition, namely, that the writings and consent of the Fathers is a witness to theological truth.

In the third part of his treatise on the imagination Malebranche treats of 'the contagious communication of strong imaginations; I mean of the power which certain minds possess of involving others in their errors'.[2] The brains of some people receive very profound 'traces' from unimportant or comparatively unimportant objects. And though this is no fault in itself, it becomes a source of error if the imagination is allowed to dominate. For example, those with strong imaginations may be able to impress others and disseminate their ideas. Tertullian was of these. 'The respect which he had for the visions of Montanus and for his prophetesses is an incontestable proof of his weakness of judgment. This fire, these transports, these enthusiasms for trifling matters visibly mark a disorder of the imagination. How many irregular movements in his hyperboles and in his metaphors!

_____
[1] *R.V.*, 2, 2, 5.   [2] *R.V.*, 2, 3, 1.

How many pompous and splendid arguments which prove only by
their sensible brilliance, and which persuade only by stunning and
dazzling the mind!'[1] Montaigne was another writer whose words
have effect through the power of his imagination rather than
through the cogency of his arguments.

'The errors of the senses and of the imagination come from the
nature and constitution of the body, and they are discovered by
considering the soul's dependence on the body. But the errors of
the pure understanding can be discovered only by considering the
nature of the mind itself and of the ideas which are necessary for
its understanding of objects.'[2] What is meant by the term 'pure
understanding'? Malebranche tells us that he here means the
mind's faculty of knowing external objects without forming
corporeal images of them in the brain.[3] Now, the mind is finite
and limited. And if this fact is not borne in mind errors result.
For example, heresy is due to men's unwillingness to recognize this
fact and to believe what they do not comprehend. Again, some
do not pursue a right method in their thought. They apply themselves immediately to investigating hidden truths which cannot
be known unless other truths are known previously, and they do
not distinguish clearly between what is evident and what is
probable. Aristotle was a great sinner in this respect. The mathematicians, however, especially those who have used algebra and
the analytic method practised by Vieta and Descartes, have
proceeded in the right way. The capacity and scope of the mind
cannot literally be increased: 'the soul of man is, so to speak, a
determinate quantity or portion of thought which has limits
beyond which it cannot pass'.[4] But this does not mean that the
mind cannot perform its functions more or less well. And mathematics is the best means of training the mind to start with clear
and distinct ideas and to proceed in an orderly way. Arithmetic
and algebra, 'these two sciences are the foundation of all the
others, and they give the true means of acquiring all the exact
sciences, because one cannot make better use of the mind's capacity
than by arithmetic, and above all by algebra'.[5]

Malebranche proceeds to lay down some rules which should be
observed in the search for truth. The principal general rule is that
we ought to reason only on those matters about which we have
clear ideas and that we ought always to begin with the simplest

[1] *R.V.*, 2, 3, 3.   [2] *R.V.*, 3, 1, 1.   [3] *Ibid.*
[4] *R.V.*, 6, 1, 5   [5] *Ibid.*

and easiest things.[1] It is clear that, as far as concerns method, Malebranche follows the ideal of Descartes. We should base our search for truth on the perception of clear and distinct ideas and proceed in an orderly way, analogous to the order observed by mathematicians. For example, 'to consider the properties of extension, we ought to begin, as M. Descartes has done, with the simplest relations and pass from the simpler to the more complicated, not only because this method is natural and helps the mind in its operations, but also because since God always acts with order and by the simplest means, this way of examining our ideas and their relations will make us know His works better'.[2] Descartes is the hero, and Aristotle is the villain. Like other 'modern' philosophers of the period Malebranche obviously means Aristotelians when he talks about Aristotle and his misdoings. Of the historical significance of Aristotle and of his achievements in his own time they had little appreciation: it was Aristotle as represented by 'Aristotelianism' and as an authority to which they primarily objected. And Malebranche is careful to add that he is not endeavouring to substitute the authority of Descartes for that of Aristotle.

3. Mention has been made in the foregoing section of external objects exciting the sense-organs, of the animal spirits causing traces in the fibres of the brain and of images and ideas resulting from or caused by this physiological process. Similarly, mention has been made of the soul willing the movement of the animal spirits and thus exciting the imagination or moving the members of the body, as the case may be. But to speak in this way is to use ordinary language which does not accurately represent Malebranche's theory. For he accepted the Cartesian dichotomy between spirit and matter, thought and extension; and he drew the conclusion that neither can act directly on the other. He speaks, indeed, of 'the soul' (*l'âme*), but this term does not mean soul in the Aristotelian sense; it means the mind (*l'esprit*). And although he speaks of the soul's dependence on the body and of the close union between them, his theory is that mind and body are two things between which there is correspondence but not interaction. The mind thinks, but it does not, properly speaking, move the body. And the body is a machine adapted indeed by God to the soul, but not 'informed' by it according to the Aristotelian sense of the term. True, he traces at length the

---

[1] *R.V.*, 6, 2, 1.　　　[2] *R.V.*, 6, 2, 4.

correspondence between physical and psychic events, between, for example, modifications in the brain and modifications in the soul. But what he has in mind is psycho-physical parallelism rather than interaction. 'It seems to me quite certain that the will of spiritual beings is incapable of moving the smallest body which there is in the world. For it is evident that there is no necessary connection between our will, for example, to move our arm and the arm's movement. It is true that it moves when we will, and that we are thus the natural cause of the movement of our arm. But *natural* causes are not at all true causes, they are only *occasional* causes, which act only by the power and efficacy of God's will, as I have just explained.'[1]

Malebranche does not deny, therefore, that I am in some sense the natural cause of the movement of my arm. But the term 'natural cause' means here 'occasional cause'. How could my volition be anything else than an occasional cause? I certainly do not know how I move my arm, if I move it. 'There is no man who knows what he must do to move one of his fingers by means of the animal spirits. How then could men move their arms? These things appear to me to be evident and also, it seems to me, to all those who are willing to think, though they may be perhaps incomprehensible to all those who are only willing to sense.'[2] Here Malebranche assumes the very questionable assumption of Geulincx, that a true causal agent knows that he acts and how he acts. Moreover, that I should be the true cause of my arm's movement is a contradictory notion. 'A true cause is a cause between which and its effect the mind perceives a necessary connection. It is thus that I understand the term.'[3] To be a true cause is to be a creative agent, and no human agent can create. Nor can God communicate this power to a human being. Hence we must conclude that God moves my arm on the occasion of my willing that the arm should be moved.

God, therefore, is the one and only true cause. 'From all eternity God has willed, and He will continue eternally to will— or, to speak more precisely, God wills without cessation, but without change, succession or necessity, all that will take place in the course of time.'[4] But if God wills the creation and conservation of a chair, for example, He must will that it should be in one place rather than another at any given time. 'Therefore there is a contradiction in saying that one body can move another. I say even

[1] *R.V.*, 6, 2, 3.   [2] *Ibid.*   [3] *Ibid.*   [4] *E.M.*, 7, 9.

there is a contradiction in saying that you can move your arm-chair.... No power can transport it where God does not transport it or place it where God does not place it....'[1] Certainly, there is a natural order in the sense that God has willed, for example, that *A* should always be followed by *B*, and this order is constantly preserved because God has willed that it should be preserved. To all outward appearance, therefore, it seems that *A* causes *B*. But metaphysical reflection shows that *A* is simply an occasional cause. The fact that on the occurrence of event *A* God always causes event *B* does not show that *A* is a true cause of *B*. It is simply the occasion, according to the scheme of divine providence, of God's activity in producing *B*.

Here we have a curious combination of an empiricist analysis of causality with a metaphysical theory. As far as the connection between *A* and *B* is concerned, we can discover no more than a relation of regular sequence. But for Malebranche this does not mean that causality in general is nothing more than regular sequence. It means that natural causes are not true causes and that the only true cause is a supernatural agent, God. And this general principle must obviously hold good with regard to the relation between soul and body in man. There is parallelism but not interaction. And from this Malebranche draws the con-clusion that 'our soul is not at all united to our body in the way that common opinion supposes that it is. The soul is united immediately and directly to God alone.'[2]

4. If God is the one true cause, it may appear that human freedom must be denied, on the ground that God is the cause even of our acts of will. But Malebranche did not deny human freedom and responsibility, and some brief explanation must be given of the way in which he reconciled the assertion of human freedom with the attribution to God alone of all true causal efficacy.

Malebranche liked to find parallels and analogies between the material world and the spiritual world as also between the natural and supernatural orders. In the material world, the sphere of bodies, we find movement, and the corresponding factor in the spiritual world is inclination. 'Now, it seems to me that the inclinations of spirits are to the spiritual world that which move-ment is to the material world.'[3] If our nature had not been corrupted by the Fall, we should have been immediately aware

---

[1] *E.M.*, 7, 10.   [2] *E.M.*, 7, 15.   [3] *R.V.*, 4, 1.

of the fundamental inclination in our souls. As things are, however, we have to arrive at this knowledge by reflection and argument. Now, God has no other final end in all His operations than Himself. As creator He certainly wills the conservation and good of the beings which He has created, but 'God wills His glory as His principal end and (He wills also) the conservation of creatures, but for His glory'.[1] And the fundamental inclinations of creatures must correspond to the will and intentions of the creator. Accordingly, God has implanted in spiritual creatures a fundamental inclination towards Himself. This takes the form of an inclination towards the good in general and is the reason why we can never be satisfied with any finite good or set of finite goods. We encounter finite goods, and in virtue of our fundamental inclination to the good in general we desire and love them, above all those which have a close relation to the conservation of our being and the acquisition of happiness. For to say that we have an inclination towards the good in general and to say that we are naturally inclined towards the acquisition of happiness is ultimately the same thing. But no finite good can satisfy the inclination towards the good in general, and we cannot find happiness apart from God. We must acknowledge, therefore, that our wills are fundamentally orientated towards God, even if, through the blindness and disorders consequent on the Fall, we are not immediately conscious of this movement towards God.

Now, if God has implanted in the will an ineradicable inclination towards the good in general, an inclination which can be satisfied only by the supreme and infinite good, namely, God Himself, it is obvious that we are not ourselves the causes of this inclination and interior movement. It is a necessary inclination, not subject to our free control. Furthermore, 'our inclinations towards particular goods, which (inclinations) are common to all men, although they are not equally strong in all men, such as our inclination to the conservation of our being and of the being of those with whom we are united by nature, are also impressions of the will of God in us. For I call indifferently "natural inclinations" all the impressions of the author of nature which are common to all spirits.'[2] These inclinations too are natural and necessary.

What, therefore, is left for free will? Or, rather, what can free will mean, once given these premises? 'By the word *will* I intend to designate here the impression or the natural movement which

[1] *R.V.*, 4, 1.   [2] *Ibid*.

carries us towards the indeterminate good, the good in general. And by the word *freedom* I understand nothing else but the power which the spirit possesses of diverting this impression towards the objects which please us, and thus to bring it about that our natural inclinations terminate in some particular object.'[1] The movement towards the good in general or the universal good is irresistible; and this movement is in point of fact a movement or inclination towards God, 'Who alone is the general good, because He alone comprises in Himself all goods.'[2] But we are free with regard to particular finite goods. This can be illustrated by the example chosen by Malebranche.[3] A man represents to himself some dignity as a good. Immediately his will is drawn to it; that is to say, his movement towards the universal good moves him towards this particular object, the dignity, because his mind has represented it to him as a good. But as a matter of fact this dignity is not the universal good. Nor is the mind capable of seeing it clearly and distinctly as the universal good ('for the mind never sees clearly what is not the case'). Therefore the movement towards the universal good cannot be fully arrested, as it were, by this particular good. The will is naturally impelled beyond this particular good, and the man does not love the dignity necessarily or invincibly. He remains free. 'Now, his freedom consists in this that, not being fully convinced that this dignity comprises all the good which he is capable of loving, he can suspend his judgment and his love. Further, in virtue of the union which he has with the universal being or that which comprises all good, he can think of other things and consequently love other goods. . . .'[4] In other words, if I once apprehend or think of something as good, my will goes out towards it. But at the same time I am capable of refusing my consent to this movement or impulse in so far as it is directed towards this particular finite good.

In order to understand Malebranche's theory of liberty more clearly, it is helpful to remember that according to him the Fall resulted in the change of 'union' of soul with body into 'dependence' of soul on body. Before the Fall Adam possessed a preternatural power of suspending the operation of the laws of parallelism; but after the Fall the chain of physical events which results in 'traces' in the principal part of the brain is necessarily followed by the appearance of psychic events in the soul. According, therefore, to the necessary operation of the laws of parallelism,

[1] *R.V.*, 1, 1, 2.   [2] *Ibid.*   [3] *Ibid.*   [4] *Ibid.*

whenever a corporeal thing 'causes' traces in the brain, movements of the soul result. And in this sense the soul is subject to the body. Man, therefore, who after the Fall has no longer a clear consciousness of God, is drawn towards sensible things. 'The soul, after sin (original sin) has become, as it were, corporeal by inclination. Its love for sensible things constantly diminishes its union with or relation to intelligible things.'[1] And all sin comes ultimately from this subservience to the flesh. At the same time the reason is still a participation of the divine reason, and the will is still naturally drawn towards the universal good, God. Although, therefore, man is drawn towards finite goods, especially corporeal sources of pleasure, he is capable of seeing that no finite good is the universal good and of refusing his consent to the inclination or love of it. Nobody is captivated by a finite good except by his own choice.

5. The will is, therefore, an active power. This activity is, indeed, immanent, in the sense that though I can will or not will a finite good, my will cannot of itself produce an external effect. External effects are produced by God on the occasion of acts of will. None the less, the will is an active, and not a purely passive, power. The mind or pure understanding, however, is a passive power or faculty. It does not produce ideas: it receives them. The question arises, therefore, from what source does it receive them. How do ideas of things distinct from ourselves come to our minds?

These ideas cannot come from the bodies which they represent. Nor can they be produced by the soul itself. For their production by man himself would postulate a power which he does not possess, namely, that of creation. Nor can we suppose that God has placed in the soul from the beginning a complete stock of innate ideas. The only reasonable explanation of our ideas, according to Malebranche, is that 'we see all things in God'.[2] This celebrated theory of vision in God, for which Malebranche claimed the authority of St. Augustine, is one of the characteristic features of the former's philosophy.

God has in Himself 'the ideas of all the things which He has created; for otherwise He could not have produced them'.[3] Further, He is present to us in so intimate a manner that 'one can say that He is the place of spirits, in the same way spaces are in a sense the place of bodies'.[4] It follows, therefore, according to

[1] *R.V.*, 1, 13, 4.   [2] *R.V.*, 3, 2, 6.   [3] *Ibid.*   [4] *Ibid.*

Malebranche, that the mind can see in God the works of God, provided that He wills to reveal to it the ideas which represent them. And that God does so will can be shown by various arguments. For example, as we can desire to see all beings, sometimes one and sometimes another, 'it is certain that all beings are present to our mind; and it seems that they cannot all be present to our mind unless God is present to it, that is to say, He who comprises all things within the simplicity of His being'.[1] 'I do not think that we can well explain the way in which the mind knows a diversity of abstract and general truths otherwise than by the presence of Him who can illuminate the mind in an infinity of ways'.[2] Further, ideas act on our minds, illuminating them and rendering them happy or unhappy. But it is God alone who can change the modifications of our minds. 'It must be, then, that all our ideas are in the efficacious substance of the divinity, which alone is intelligible or capable of illuminating us, because it alone can affect our intelligences.'[3]

This does not mean, Malebranche remarks, that we see the essence of God. 'The essence of God is His absolute being, and minds do not at all see the divine substance taken absolutely, but only as relative to creatures or as participable by them.'[4] Malebranche thus tries to avoid the accusation that he is attributing the beatific vision, reserved for souls in heaven, to all men without distinction, and that he is naturalizing it. But it seems to me to be extremely difficult to see how the distinction between seeing the divine essence in itself and seeing the divine essence as externally imitable in creatures is of much real use for this purpose.

However, supposing that we do see our ideas in God, what is it that we see? What are these ideas? In the first place we see the so-called eternal truths. To be more precise, we see the ideas of these truths. A truth such as the proposition 'twice two is four' cannot be identified with God. 'So we do not say that we see God in seeing the truths, as St. Augustine says, but in seeing the *ideas* of these truths. For the ideas are real; but the equality between the ideas, which is the truth, is not real. . . . When one says that twice two makes four, the ideas of the numbers are real, but the equality which exists between them is only a relation. Thus according to our opinion we see God when we see eternal truths; not that these truths are God, but because the ideas on which

[1] *R.V.*, 3, 2, 6.   [2] *Ibid.*   [3] *Ibid.*   [4] *Ibid.*

these truths depend are in God. And perhaps even St. Augustine understood the matter in this way.'[1]

In the second place 'we believe also that one knows changing and corruptible things in God, although St. Augustine talks only of immutable and incorruptible things'.[2] But this statement of Malebranche may easily be misunderstood. In our knowledge of material things we can distinguish between the sensational element and the pure idea. The former is, indeed, caused by God but it is not seen in God. 'For God certainly knows sensible things, but He does not perceive them.'[3] The sensational element does not represent the thing as it is in itself. In itself it is extension; and it is this that we see in God as a pure idea. Does this mean that we see in God separate ideas of individual material things? No, we see in God only the pure idea of intelligible extension, which is the archetype of the material world. 'It is clear that matter is nothing else but extension';[4] for in our clear and distinct idea of matter we can discern only extension. And matter or body must have its archetype in God. This does not mean, of course, that God is material and extended: it means that there is in Him the pure idea of extension. And in this archetypal idea are contained ideally the possible relations which are exemplified concretely in the material world. 'When you contemplate intelligible extension, you see as yet only the archetype of the material world which we inhabit and that of an infinity of other possible worlds. In truth you then see the divine substance. For it is this alone which is visible, or which can illumine the mind. But you do not see the divine substance in itself or according to what it is. You see it only according to the relation which it has to material creatures, according as it is participable by them or according as it is representative of them. Consequently it is not, properly speaking, God whom you see, but only the matter which He can produce.'[5]

In the third place 'we believe finally that all minds see the eternal moral laws as well as other things in God, but in a somewhat different way'.[6] We see the eternal truths, for example, in virtue of the union which our minds have with the Word of God. But the moral order is known in virtue of the movement or inclination towards God which we receive constantly from the divine will. It is because of this natural and ever-present inclination that we know that 'we should love good and shun evil, that

[1] R.V., 3, 2, 6.   [2] Ibid.   [3] Ibid.
[4] R.V., 3, 2, 8, 2.   [5] E.M., 2, 2.   [6] R.V., 3, 2, 6.

we should love justice more than all riches, that it is better to
obey God than to command men, and an infinity of other natural
laws'.[1] For the knowledge of our fundamental orientation towards God as our final end comprises the knowledge of the natural
moral law. We have only to examine the implications of this
orientation to become aware of the law and of its obligatory
character.

6. According to Malebranche, therefore, the vision in God
which we possess comprises knowledge of the eternal truths, of
intelligible extension as the archetype of the material world and,
though in a different sense, of the natural moral law. But 'it is
not the same with the soul. We do not know it by its idea; we do
not at all see it in God; we know it only by *consciousness*.'[2] But
this does not mean that we have a clear vision of the soul itself;
'we know of our soul only what we perceive to take place in us'.[3]
If we had never experienced pain and so on, we should be ignorant
whether the soul is capable of having such modifications. That it
can have these modifications is known only experientially. If,
however, we knew the soul by the idea of it in God, we should be
capable of knowing *a priori* all the properties and modifications
of which it is capable, just as we can know *a priori* the properties
of extension. This is not to say that we are ignorant of the soul's
existence and of its nature as a thinking being. Indeed, the
knowledge which we have of it is sufficient to enable us to prove
the soul's spirituality and immortality. At the same time it must
be admitted that 'we do not possess as perfect a knowledge of the
nature of the soul as that which we possess of the nature of
bodies'.[4]

This is not perhaps the view which we would naturally expect
from Malebranche. But he gives a reason for it in terms of his own
analysis of our knowledge of material things. 'The knowledge
which we have of our soul by consciousness is imperfect, it is true,
but it is in no way false. The knowledge, on the contrary, which
we have of bodies by feeling or consciousness, if one can call
"consciousness" the feeling of that which takes place in our body,
is not only imperfect but false. It was therefore necessary for us
to have an idea of bodies to correct the feelings which we have
with regard to them. But we have no need of an idea of our souls,
since the consciousness which we have of them does not at all
involve us in error. In order not to be deceived in our knowledge

[1] *R.V.*, 3, 2, 6.   [2] *R.V.*, 3, 2, 7, 4.   [3] *Ibid.*   [4] *Ibid.*

of the soul it is sufficient that we do not confuse it with the body; and we can avoid this confusion by the use of reason.'[1] There was no need, then, for us to have a vision of the soul in God analogous to our vision of intelligible extension in God.

7. What, then, of our knowledge of other men and of the pure intelligences or angels? 'It is clear that we know them only by conjecture.'[2] We do not know the souls of other men in themselves, nor by means of their ideas in God. And as they are different from ourselves, we cannot know them by consciousness. 'We conjecture that the souls of other men are of like kind to ours.'[3] True, we know with certainty some facts about other souls. We know, for example, that every soul seeks for happiness. 'But I know it with evidence and certitude because it is God who informs me.'[4] What I know with certainty of other souls or minds is known by revelation. But when I draw conclusions about other people from my knowledge of myself I am often wrong. 'Thus the knowledge which we have of other men is extremely subject to error, if we judge of them by the feelings (perceptions) which we have our ourselves.'[5]

It is evident that Malebranche must make an analogous statement about our knowledge of the existence of other bodies. On the one hand sensations do not represent bodies as they are in themselves. And in any case the psychic events which follow on the chain of physical stimuli are caused by God, so that there is no absolutely compelling proof that they are in fact occasioned by the presence of external bodies, unless, indeed, we first assume the whole order of occasional causality. And this involves assuming the existence of bodies. On the other hand the idea of intelligible extension which we see in God does not of itself assure us of the existence of any bodies at all. For it is the infinite archetype of all possible bodies. Hence it would appear that Malebranche must have recourse to revelation as the source of certain knowledge that bodies do in fact exist. And so he does. 'There are three kinds of beings of which we have some knowledge, and to which we can have some relation: God, or the infinitely perfect being, who is the principle and cause of all things; spirits, which we know only by the interior feeling that we have of our nature; bodies, of whose existence we are assured by the revelation of it which we possess.'[6]

[1] R.V., 3, 2, 7, 4. [2] R.V., 3, 2, 7, 5. [3] Ibid.
[4] Ibid. [5] Ibid. [6] E.M., 6, 3.

The existence of bodies cannot be demonstrated, says Male-branche. It is rather the impossibility of a demonstration which can be demonstrated. For there is no necessary connection between the existence of bodies and the cause of their existence, namely, God. We know of their existence through revelation. But here we must distinguish between natural and supernatural revelation. Suppose that I prick my finger with a needle and feel pain. 'This feeling of pain that we have is a kind of revelation.'[1] It is not that the pain is truly caused by the prick: it is caused by God on the occasion of the prick. But in view of God's establish-ment of a regular order of occasional causality His causing the pain is an intimation or a kind of 'natural revelation' of the existence of bodies. The argument, however, does not of itself produce absolute certainty. Not that it is in itself defective; but we can have doubts about it, since in our present state we are able, for example, to conclude in some particular case that a psychic event is caused on the occasion of the presence and 'activity' of a body when this is not really true. Hence, if we desire greater certainty about the existence of bodies, we must have resource to supernatural revelation. The Scriptures make it abundantly clear that bodies do in fact exist. 'To deliver you entirely from your speculative doubt, faith furnishes us a demonstration which it is impossible to resist.'[2] In practice, however, 'natural revelation' suffices. 'For I am quite certain that you had no need of all that I have just said to you in order to assure yourself that you are in the company of Theodorus.'[3]

8. To be assured of the existence of bodies, therefore, we need to know that God exists. But how do we know this? Male-branche's principal argument is an adaptation of the so-called 'ontological argument' of St. Anselm, as used by Descartes. We have the idea of the infinite. But no finite thing represents or can represent the infinite. We cannot form for ourselves the idea of the infinite by adding to the finite. Rather do we conceive the finite by limiting the idea of the infinite. This idea of the infinite, that is to say of infinite being, is thus no mere mental construction of ours: it is something given, the attestation or effect of God's presence. In it we discern existence as necessarily included.' 'One can see a circle, a house, a sun, without its existing. For every-thing which is finite can be seen in the infinite, which comprises the intelligible ideas of finite things. But the infinite can be seen

only in itself. For no finite thing can represent the infinite. If one thinks of God, He must exist. Other beings, although known, may not exist. One can see their essence without their existence, their idea without them. But one cannot see the essence of the infinite without its existence, the idea of being without being. For being has no idea to represent it. There is no archetype which contains all its intelligible reality. It is its own archetype, and it comprises in itself the archetype of all beings.'[1] In having the idea of the infinite, therefore, we see God. 'I am certain that I see the infinite. Therefore the infinite exists, because I see it, and because I cannot see it except in itself.'[2] True, my perception of the infinite is limited, inasmuch as my mind is limited; but that which I perceive is infinite. 'Thus you see very well that this proposition, "there is a God", is by itself the clearest of all propositions which affirm the existence of anything, and that it is even as certain as the proposition, "I think, therefore I am."'[3]

The idea of God is thus the idea of the infinite, and the idea of the infinite is the idea of infinitely perfect being. 'You define God as He has defined Himself when speaking to Moses, *God is He who is. . . .* Being without restriction, in a word Being, this is the idea of God.'[4] And this meaning of the word 'God' gives us the key to knowledge of the divine attributes, so far as such knowledge is possible for us. 'It is clear that this word *God* being only an abbreviation for "infinitely perfect being" there is a contradiction in saying that we can be deceived if we attribute to God simply what we see clearly as pertaining to the infinite perfect being.'[5] We are justified in predicating of God any perfection which we see to be a true perfection and one which is not necessarily limited or mixed with imperfection. 'God, or the infinitely perfect being, is then, independent (of all causes) and immutable. He is also omnipotent, eternal, necessary, omnipresent. . . .'[6] That an infinite perfection surpasses our comprehension is no valid reason against attributing it to God. Men naturally tend to humanize God, to form anthropomorphic conceptions of Him; and some like to strip Him of all incomprehensible attributes.[7] But we must acknowledge, for example, that 'God is neither good nor merciful nor patient according to the vulgar notions (of these attributes). Those attributes as ordinarily conceived are unworthy of the infinitely perfect being. But God possesses these qualities in the

[1] *E.M.*, 2, 5. [2] *E.M.*, 8, 1. [3] *E.M.*, 2, 5. [4] *E.M.*, 2, 4.
[5] *E.M.*, 8, 1. [6] *E.M.*, 8, 3. [7] *E.M.*, 8, 9.

sense that reason tells us and the scripture, which cannot be contradicted, makes us believe.'[1] And we must recognize that God possesses all the perfections which pertain to the infinitely perfect being, even if we cannot comprehend them. God, for example, knows all things in Himself; but we cannot comprehend the divine knowledge.

Malebranche insists on freedom as a divine attribute. God necessarily loves that which is supremely and infinitely lovable, His own substance, the infinite good. And this infinite good is sufficient, if one may so speak, to satisfy the divine will. If, therefore, God creates finite things, He does so, indeed, out of goodness and love, but not from necessity. For creatures cannot add to the infinite anything which it lacks. God created the world freely, and He conserves it freely. 'The will to create the world contains no element of necessity, although, like other immanent operations, it is eternal and immutable.'[2]

But how can the divine freedom be reconciled with the divine immutability? Does not freedom suggest mutability, the power to act otherwise than one does act? Malebranche answers that God willed eternally to create the world. Indeed, as there is no past or future in God, there is one eternal creative act. And this act is immutable. At the same time God willed eternally but freely to create the world. If we once suppose the free decision to create and conserve the world, we can rely, as it were, on a stable order. God does not change His decrees. This does not mean that no miracle is possible. But God's eternal choice of this world and of this order comprised also the choice of those events which we call miracles. The fact, however, that God decreed from eternity the creation of the world and that this decree is immutable is not incompatible with the freedom of this decree. 'From all eternity God has willed, and He will continue eternally to will—or, to speak more exactly, God wills without cessation, but without change, without succession, without necessity—all that He will do in the course of time. The act of His eternal decree, although simple and immutable, is necessary only because it is. It cannot not be, because it is. But it is only because God wills it.'[3] The divine decrees are necessary only 'by supposition', on the supposition, that is to say, that God has made them; and He made them freely. 'At present you are seated. Can you be standing up? You can, absolutely speaking; but, according to the supposition (that you are sitting), you cannot. . . . (So God) wills to make decrees and establish simple and general laws to govern the world in a manner consonant with His attributes. But, these decrees once supposed, they cannot be changed. Not that they are necessary, absolutely speaking; but they are necessary by supposition. . . . (God) is immutable; this is one of the perfections of His nature. Nevertheless He is perfectly free in all that He does externally. He cannot change, because what He wills He wills without succession, by a simple and invariable act. But He can not will it, because He wills freely what He actually wills.'[1]

9. On this subject of divine freedom and on the problem of reconciling the divine freedom with the divine immutability Malebranche adds nothing to what the mediaeval theologians and philosophers had already said. He certainly contributes nothing new to the solution of the problem. However the fact that he repeats his predecessors is perhaps worth noting in view of his frequent polemics against the 'Aristotelians', even though, as a Catholic theologian, he could not say anything very different from what he did say. But his insistence on the divine freedom has this greater importance, that it illustrates the difference between him and Spinoza. The fact that Malebranche makes God the only true cause, coupled with the fact that he places infinite 'intelligible extension' in God, has led some historians to regard him as a link between Descartes and Spinoza. And this point of view is certainly understandable. At the same time the fact that He insists on the divine freedom shows clearly enough that he was a theist and not a pantheist.

As for Descartes, we have had occasion to note Malebranche's admiration for his great predecessor. Descartes inspired his admiration for mathematics and his conception of the right method to pursue in the search for truth. Several important theories defended by Malebranche were obviously Cartesian in origin; for example, the analysis of matter as extension. Further, the problem created by the Cartesian dualism of thought and extension provided the starting-point for Malebranche's doctrine of occasional causality. And, in general, the latter's devotion to the ideal of clear and distinct ideas and of indubitable evidence analogous to that obtained in mathematics was clearly the fruit of the Cartesian spirit.

Yet in spite of the undoubted influence of Descartes on his

[1] *E.M.*, 8, 2.

thought Malebranche's philosophy has a rather different flavour from that of Cartesianism. Perhaps the difference can be illustrated in this way. The bent of Descartes' mind was towards the discovery of new scientific truths by the aid of the correct method. He hoped that others would prolong his own reflections in fruitful deduction and scientific investigation. Hence, although the notion of God was essential to his system, his philosophy can hardly be called theocentric. It made room, it is true, for the mysteries of faith, but its dynamic impulse, so to speak, is towards the building-up of the sciences, a fact which is not altered by Descartes' faulty notion of scientific method. The philosophy of Malebranche on the contrary is evidently theocentric in character. The doctrines of God as the universal and only true cause and of our vision in God illustrate this character. For Malebranche false ideas of causality are intimately linked with false notions of the divine. The theory of occasional causality and a true idea of God go together. And when we recognize this, we are able to see the world in a true perspective, namely, as dependent at every moment on the infinite Godhead, not simply for existence but also for activity. And if we once recognize this utter dependence of creatures on the transcendent-immanent God, the only source of all being and activity, we shall be all the more ready to listen to the divine revelation, even though this revelation comprises incomprehensible mysteries. The mind is passive, receiving ideas, and it is folly to turn the ideas which we receive against the word of Him from whom we receive them.

Perhaps one may draw the following analogy between Malebranche and Berkeley. The latter in the eighteenth century accepted the principles of empiricism as laid down by Locke and drew some radical conclusions which Locke himself had not drawn; for example, that there is no such thing as material substance. Berkeley can therefore be depicted as carrying the development of empiricism a stage further than his predecessor. At the same time he propounded a thoroughly theocentric philosophy, and he based this metaphysical system, partly at least, on an application of empirical principles. Hence it would not be unreasonable to speak of Berkeley as using empiricism in the service of a theocentric philosophy. Similarly, Malebranche, at an earlier date, accepted many of the principles laid down by Descartes, and he drew conclusions which the latter had not himself drawn; for example, that there is no real interaction between soul and body.

In this sense he can be depicted as having developed Cartesianism. At the same time he used Cartesian principles and the conclusions which he drew from them in the service of a thoroughly theo-centric system with peculiarities of its own. Hence it is as mis-leading to label Malebranche simply as a Cartesian as it would be to label Berkeley simply as an empiricist. Both men developed theocentric metaphysical systems, and these systems bear marked resemblances in some points, though there are also notable differences, due at least in part to the association of the one system with Cartesianism and of the other with British empiricism.

10. The philosophy of Malebranche enjoyed a considerable success. Thus the Oratorian Thomassin (1619–95) is generally recognized as having been influenced by Malebranche, even if he does not name the latter when he speaks of the vision in God. Among the Benedictines François Lamy (1636–1711), who attacked Spinoza's idea of God, was influenced by Malebranche. And the Jesuit Yves Marie André (1675–1764), author of a life of Malebranche, exposed himself to considerable difficulties through his championship of the latter's cause. According to André, the Aristotelian-Thomist doctrine of the sense-origin of our know-ledge destroys science and morals. The mathematician and physicist René Fédé, author of *Méditations métaphysiques sur l'origine de l'âme* (1683), can be reckoned as a disciple of Male-branche, though in some respects he inclined to Spinozism. In general, the French disciples of Malebranche endeavoured to defend him against the charge that his philosophy led to or was akin to Spinozism, and also to use his system against the influence of empiricism which was beginning to be felt on the Continent.

A translation of the *Recherche de la vérité* was published in England in 1694; and in the following year Locke wrote *An Examination of Malebranche's Opinion of Seeing All Things in God*, in which he criticized this opinion adversely. This work was not published until 1706, two years after Locke's death. Meanwhile John Norris (1657–1711) had shown his acceptance of Male-branche's opinion in *An Essay Towards the Theory of the Ideal or Intelligible World* (1701–4) in the second part of which he criticized Locke's empiricism.

Ideas of Malebranche were also used by Italian writers against empiricism in the eighteenth century. One can mention especially

Mattia Doria, author of a *Difesa della metafisca contro il signor G. Locke* (1732), and Cardinal Gerdil[1] who published his *Immatérialité de l'âme démontrée contre M. Locke* in 1747 and in the following year a *Défense du sentiment du P. Malebranche sur l'origine et la nature des idées contre l'examen de Locke.*

[1] Cardinal Gerdil was born in Savoy, but he passed most of his life in Italy.

CHAPTER X

SPINOZA (1)

Life—Works—The geometrical method—The influence of other philosophies on Spinoza's thought—Interpretations of Spinoza's philosophy.

1. BARUCH SPINOZA (Benedict Spinoza or de Spinoza or Despinoza) was born at Amsterdam on November 24th, 1632. He came of a family of Portuguese Jews who had emigrated to Holland towards the close of the sixteenth century. His ancestors were perhaps Marranos; that is to say, Jews who in the last decade of the fifteenth century had outwardly accepted Christianity in order to avoid expulsion from their country, while remaining inwardly attached to the Jewish religion. In any case, on arrival in Holland the emigrants made open profession of Judaism; and Spinoza was thus brought up in the Jewish community of Amsterdam according to the Jewish traditions. Though his native language was Spanish (he also learned Portuguese at a very early age), his early education naturally took the form of the study of the Old Testament and the Talmud. He also became acquainted with the Cabalistic speculations which had been influenced by the neo-Platonic tradition, and later he studied the writings of Jewish philosophers such as Moses Maimonides.[1] The elements of Latin he acquired from a German, and he continued his study of the language under Francis Van den Ende, a Christian, under whose tuition he studied also mathematics and the Cartesian philosophy. In addition he learned some Greek, though his knowledge of this language did not equal his knowledge of Latin, and he was acquainted with French, Italian and, of course, Hebrew and Dutch.

Though educated in the Jewish religious tradition, Spinoza soon found himself unable to accept the orthodox Jewish theology and interpretation of the Scriptures, and in 1656, when only twenty-four years old, he was solemnly excommunicated, that is, excluded from the Jewish community. As a means of livelihood he took to grinding lenses for optical instruments, and he was thus enabled to lead the retired and quiet life of a scholar and philosopher. In

[1] For Maimonides (1135–1204), see vol. II, pp. 203–4.

1660 he went to reside near Leyden, and while there he entered
into correspondence with Henry Oldenburg, secretary of the Royal
Society in London. In 1663 he moved to the neighbourhood of
The Hague, where he was visited by Leibniz in 1676. Spinoza
never occupied an academic post. In 1673 he was offered the chair
of philosophy of Heidelberg, but he refused it, mainly no doubt
because he wished to preserve complete freedom. But in any case
he was never the man to seek the limelight. He died of consump-
tion in 1677.

2. Only two works by Spinoza were published during his life-
time, and of these only one appeared under his own name. His
exposition 'in geometrical form' of part of Descartes' *Principles of
Philosophy* (*Renati des Cartes Principiorum philosophiae partes
prima et secunda more geometrico demonstratae. Accesserunt
Cogitata metaphysica*) appeared in 1663, while his *Theological-
Political Treatise* (*Tractatus theologico-politicus*) was published
anonymously in 1670. The *Opera posthuma*, which were published
shortly after Spinoza's death, include his *Treatise on the Correction
of the Understanding* (*Tractatus de intellectus emendatione*) which
was written during his residence near Leyden, the *Ethics demonstrated according to the Geometrical Order* (*Ethica ordine geometrico
demonstrata*), which is his most important work,[1] and the *Political
Treatise* (*Tractatus politicus*). *His Short Treatise on God, Man and
his Well-Being* (*Tractatus brevis de Deo et homine ejusque felicitate*)
was discovered in 1851 and is generally known as the *Short
Treatise*. The complete works of Spinoza include also one or two
essays and a collection of his correspondence.

3. The most conspicuous idea of Spinoza's philosophy is that
there is only one substance, the infinite divine substance which is
identified with Nature; *Deus sive Natura*, God or Nature. And a
striking feature of this philosophy as it is presented in the *Ethics*
is the geometrical form of its presentation. This work is divided
into five parts in which the following subjects are treated in turn:
God, the nature and origin of the mind, the origin and nature of
the emotions, the power of the intellect or human freedom. At
the beginning of the first part we find eight definitions, followed
by seven axioms. The second part starts with seven definitions
and five axioms, the third with three definitions and two postulates, the fourth with eight definitions and one axiom, and the

---

[1] In references this work will be referred to as *E*.
'P.' signifies Part, 'def.' definition and 'prop.' proposition.

fifth with two axioms.[1] And in each case these definitions and axioms or postulates are succeeded by numbered propositions with proofs, ending with the letters Q.E.D., and corollaries.

We can distinguish between this geometrical form of presentation and the central idea of the unity of God and Nature in one infinite substance. Consideration of the first topic I shall leave to the next section; while in the present section I shall make some remarks about the influences which contributed to the formation of Spinoza's central metaphysical idea.

It can hardly be denied that Cartesianism exercised an influence on the mind of Spinoza and that it was to some extent at least an instrument in the formation of his philosophy. In the first place it provided him with an ideal of method. In the second place it provided him with a good deal of his terminology. For example, a comparison of Spinoza's definitions of substance and attribute with those of Descartes reveals clearly enough his indebtedness to the French philosopher. In the third place he was doubtless positively influenced by Descartes' treatment of certain particular points. For instance, he may well have been influenced by Descartes' assertion[2] that in philosophy we should inquire only into efficient and not into final causes, as also of his use of the ontological argument for the existence of God. In the fourth place Cartesianism probably helped to determine the nature of the problems with which he dealt; for example, the problem of the relation between mind and body.

But though it is reasonable to say that Spinoza was influenced by Descartes, it does not follow immediately that his monism was derived from the latter's philosophy. Nobody would wish to claim, of course, that he derived his monism from Cartesianism in the sense of borrowing or adopting it from Descartes. For the latter was not a monist. But it has been argued that what Spinoza did was to develop the logical implications of Cartesianism in a monist direction. We have seen that Descartes defined substance in such a way that the definition applied literally to God alone. It is understandable, therefore, that some historians should claim that Spinoza adopted monism under the influence of this definition. After all, it certainly appeared to a number of people at the time that Spinozism was the result of a logical and consistent

---

[1] In the second, third, fourth and fifth parts the definitions and axioms are preceded by prefaces.
[2] *Principles of Philosophy*, 1, 28.

re-thinking of Cartesianism. And though the Cartesians strenuously resisted any attempt to hang Spinoza round the neck of Descartes, it is arguable that their opposition to Spinozism was rendered all the more vehement by an uneasy feeling that it could be plausibly represented as a logical development of Descartes' philosophy. In a letter to Oldenburg Spinoza remarked that 'the stupid Cartesians, being suspected of favouring me, endeavoured to remove the aspersion by abusing everywhere my opinions and writings, a course which they still pursue'.[1] But though from the theoretical point of view the philosophy could have been developed through reflection on that of Descartes,[2] it by no means follows necessarily that as a matter of historical fact Spinoza arrived at his central metaphysical idea in precisely this way. And there are reasons for thinking that he did not do so.

In the first place there is reason for thinking that Spinoza was at least predisposed towards pantheistic monism by his study of certain Jewish writers before he devoted attention to Cartesianism. His Jewish upbringing was, of course, ultimately responsible for his use of the word 'God' for the ultimate reality, though it is obvious that he did not borrow the identification of God with Nature from the Old Testament writers, who certainly did not make any such identification. But when still a youth Spinoza came to think that belief in a personal transcendent God who created the world freely is philosophically untenable. He admitted that theological language expressing this belief has a valuable function to perform for those who cannot appreciate the language of philosophy; but he regarded its action as being that of leading people to adopt certain lines of action rather than as that of conveying true information about God. Against Maimonides he argued that it is idle to look for philosophical truth in the Scriptures, since it is not there to be found, save for a few simple truths, though he maintained at the same time that there can be no important contradiction between true philosophy and the Scriptures, because they do not speak the same language. Philosophy gives us the truth in purely rational, not in pictorial, form. And as philosophy tells us that the ultimate reality is infinite, this reality must contain all being within itself. God cannot be something apart from the world. This idea of God as the infinite Being

---

[1] *Letter 68.*
[2] I do not mean to imply that Cartesianism implies Spinozism as a logically inevitable conclusion.

which expresses itself in and yet comprises within itself the world seems to have been suggested at least to Spinoza by his reading of Jewish mystical and Cabalistic writers.

We have, indeed, to be careful not to exaggerate, or even to emphasize, the influence of the Cabalistic writings on Spinoza's mind. In point of fact he had little sympathy for them. 'I have read and known certain Cabalistic triflers whose insanity provokes my unceasing astonishment.'[1] He found in these writings childish ideas rather than divine secrets. But, as Dunin-Borkowski, for example, has argued, it does not follow that the remote seeds of Spinoza's pantheistic monism were not planted by his acquaintance with these writings. And even if we wish to discount the influence of the later writings of the Cabala, there is at least some evidence other than conjecture to suggest that Jewish writers had exercised some formative influence on his thought. Thus, after saying that a mode of extension and the idea of this mode are one and the same thing, though expressed in different ways, Spinoza adds, 'which certain Jews seem to have perceived, but confusedly, for they said that God and His intellect and the things perceived by His intellect were one and the same thing'.[2] Moreover, Spinoza makes one explicit reference[3] to Chasdaï Crescas, a Jewish writer of the late Middle Ages, who maintained that matter in some way pre-exists in God, on the principle that a being cannot be the cause of another thing if it possesses in itself nothing of that thing. And this idea may possibly have helped to predispose Spinoza to the development of his view of extension as a divine attribute. He may also have been influenced by Crescas's determinism: that is, by the latter's denial that any human choice is incapable of being explained in terms of character and motive.

Another probable source of influence on Spinoza was his study of the pantheistically inclined Renaissance philosophers. It is true that the writings of Giordano Bruno do not figure in the catalogue which was made of the works contained in Spinoza's library. But certain passages in the *Short Treatise* seem to make it clear that he did know Bruno's philosophy and that he had been influenced by it in early years. Moreover, Bruno had made use of the distinction between *Natura naturans* and *Natura naturata* which was an important feature of Spinoza's system.

It is scarcely possible to settle in any definitive fashion the controversy concerning the relative degrees of influence exercised on

[1] *Tractatus theologico-politicus*, 9, 34.   [2] *E.*, P. II, prop. 7, note.   [3] *Letter 12*.

Spinoza's mind by his study of Jewish writers and by that of Renaissance philosophers of Nature such as Bruno. But it seems safe to say that he was predisposed towards the identification of God with Nature through both lines of study, and that this central idea was not derived simply through reflection on Cartesianism. It must be remembered that Spinoza was at no time a Cartesian. True, he expounded part of Descartes' philosophy *more geometrico*; but, as a friend explained in an introduction to the exposition,[1] he did not accept this philosophy. What Cartesianism did for him was to give him an ideal of method and a knowledge of a closely knit and systematically developed philosophy which was far superior to the outpourings of Bruno, and still more to the 'insanity' of the 'Cabalistic triflers'. Spinoza was doubtless impressed by Cartesianism; but he never looked on it as the complete truth. And when writing to Henry Oldenburg, who had asked him what he considered to be the chief defects in the philosophies of Descartes and Bacon, he asserted that the first and chief defect was that 'these philosophers have strayed so far from the knowledge of the first cause and origin of all things'.[2]

It has been claimed that Spinoza owed more to Scholasticism in the way of terminology and concepts than had been generally recognized. But though he had some knowledge of Scholasticism, it does not seem to have been intimate or profound. He did not possess that first-hand and extensive acquaintance with Scholastic philosophers which Leibniz possessed. As for Stoicism, its influence is evident in his moral theory. He was acquainted with at least a few of the writings of ancient Stoics, and he was doubtless well aware of the revived Stoicism of the Renaissance. In his political thought he was influenced by Hobbes, though in a letter to Jarig Jellis he drew attention to a difference between Hobbes's views and his own. But though it is interesting to attempt to trace the influence of other philosophers on Spinoza, the fact remains that his system was his own creation. Historical research into contributory influences should not blind one to the powerful originality of his thought.

4. We have seen that Spinoza expounded part of Descartes' philosophy *more geometrico*, though he was not even at that time an adherent of the Cartesian system. And this fact has been held to show that he did not regard as infallible the method which he himself employed in the *Ethics*. But one has, I think, to make a

---

[1] This was done on Spinoza's instructions, as he says in *Letter 13*.   [2] *Letter 2*.

distinction. It is, indeed, obvious that Spinoza did not attach primary importance to the external trappings of this method, such as the formulas of exposition, the use of letters like Q.E.D. and of words like corollary. The true philosophy could be presented without the use of these geometrical adornments and forms. Conversely, a false philosophy could be presented in a geometrical dress. It is, therefore, true to say that Spinoza did not regard the method as infallible if one is thinking simply of externals. But if by the method one means not so much the external geometrical trappings as the logical deduction of propositions from definitions expressing clear and distinct ideas and from self-evident axioms, it seems to me that the method was certainly in Spinoza's eyes an infallible means of developing the true philosophy. If one looks at his definitions, for example, it is true, as far as the wording goes, that they express simply the ways in which Spinoza chooses to understand certain terms. For instance, 'An Attribute I understand to be that which the intellect perceives as constituting the essence of a substance',[1] or, 'By Good I understand that which we certainly know to be useful to us.'[2] But Spinoza was convinced that each definition expressed a clear and distinct idea and that 'every definition or clear and distinct idea is true'.[3] And if the intellect operates with clear and distinct ideas and deduces their logical implications it cannot err; for it is operating according to its own nature, the nature of reason itself. Thus he criticizes Francis Bacon for assuming that 'the human intellect is liable to err, not only through the fallibility of the senses, but also solely through its own nature'.[4]

But those who say that Spinoza did not regard his geometrical method as infallible may have in mind the following point. He regarded the logical deduction from clear and distinct ideas as providing an explanatory account of the world, as rendering the world of experience intelligible. And this point of view involves the assumption that the causal relation is akin to the relation of logical implication. The order of ideas and the order of causes are the same. The logical deduction of conclusions from the appropriate set of definitions and axioms is at the same time a metaphysical deduction and affords us knowledge of reality. Here we have an assumption or hypothesis. And if Spinoza were called upon to justify it, he would have to reply that the assumption is justified by the power of the developed system to give a coherent

[1] E., P. I, def. 4.   [2] E., P. IV, def. 1.   [3] Letter 4.   [4] Letter 2.

and comprehensive explanatory account of the world as we experience it. It is not, therefore, a case of simply assuming that the employment of a certain method infallibly provides us with a true philosophy of the world. It is rather that the employment of the method is justified by results; that is, by the power of the system developed with the aid of this method to do what it professes to do.

It seems to me, however, to be extremely doubtful whether Spinoza would have been willing to speak of hypotheses or assumptions. We read in the *Ethics* that 'the order and connection of ideas is the same as the order and connection of things'.[1] In the proof of this proposition he remarks that its truth is clear from the fourth axiom of the first part of the *Ethics*, namely, 'The knowledge of effect depends on the knowledge of cause, and involves the same.' Spinoza adds, 'For the idea of everything which is caused depends on the knowledge of the cause of which it is an effect.'[2] It is arguable, of course, that even if we grant that to know an effect adequately involves knowing its cause, it does not follow that the causal relation is akin to the relation of logical implication. But the point is that Spinoza appears to have regarded the assertion of this affinity as something clearly true and not as a mere assumption or hypothesis. It would be quite possible for him, of course, to appeal to the coherence and explanatory power of the developed system as evidence of its truth. Further, the exposition of the true philosophy in deductive or synthetic form would not be necessary; he might have chosen another form of presentation. But I feel convinced that Spinoza did not regard the system as resting on an assumption or hypothesis which was capable only of pragmatic or empirical confirmation. Writing to Albert Burgh, he remarked, 'I do not presume that I have found the best philosophy, I know that I understand the true philosophy.'[3] And this remark seems to express his attitude admirably.

In Spinoza's view the proper order of philosophical argument demands that we should start with that which is ontologically and logically prior, namely, with the divine essence or nature, and then proceed by logically deducible stages. He speaks of those thinkers who 'have not observed the order of philosophical argument. For the divine nature, which they ought to have considered before all things, because it is prior to knowledge and nature, they have

---

[1] *E.*, P. II, prop. 7.　　　[2] *Ibid.*　　　[3] *Letter* 76.

thought to be the last in the order of knowledge, and things which are called the objects of the senses they have believed to be prior to all things.'[1]

In adopting this approach Spinoza separated himself both from the Scholastics and from Descartes. In the philosophy of St. Thomas Aquinas, for example, the mind does not start with God, but with the objects of sense-experience, and through reflection on the latter it ascends to the affirmation of God's existence. Thus, as far as philosophical method is concerned, God is not prior in the order of ideas, though He is ontologically prior or prior in the order of nature. Similarly, Descartes begins with the *Cogito, ergo sum*, not with God. Further, neither St. Thomas nor Descartes thought that we can deduce finite things from the infinite Being, God. Spinoza, however, rejects the procedures of the Scholastics and of Descartes. The divine substance must be regarded as prior both in the ontological order and in the order of ideas. At least God must be regarded as prior in the order of ideas when a properly philosophical 'order of argument' is observed.

Two points can profitably be noted at once. First, if we propose to start with the infinite divine substance, and if the affirmation of the existence of this substance is not to be regarded as an hypothesis, it has to be shown that the definition of the divine essence or substance involves its existence. In other words, Spinoza is committed to using the ontological argument in some form or other. Otherwise God would not be prior in the order of ideas. Secondly, if we propose to start with God and to proceed to finite things, assimilating causal dependence to logical dependence, we must rule out contingency in the universe. It does not follow, of course, that the finite mind is capable of deducing the existence of particular finite things. Nor did Spinoza think that it was. But if the causal dependence of all things on God is akin to logical dependence, there is no place for free creation, nor for contingency in the world of material things, nor for human freedom. Any contingency which there may seem to be is only apparent. And if we think that some of our actions are free, this is only because we are ignorant of their determining causes.

[1] *E.*, P. II, prop. 10, note 2.

CHAPTER XI

SPINOZA (2)

Substance and its attributes—Infinite modes—The production of finite modes—Mind and body—The elimination of final causality.

1. In their endeavour to give a rational explanation of the world speculative metaphysicians have always tended towards the reduction of multiplicity to unity. And inasmuch as explanation in this connection means explanation in terms of causality, to say that they have tended towards the reduction of multiplicity to unity is to say that they have tended to explain the existence and natures of finite things in terms of one ultimate causal factor. I use the term 'tend to' because not all speculative metaphysicians have actually postulated one ultimate cause. For example, though the drive towards the reduction of multiplicity to unity is clearly present in the Platonic dialectic, there is at least no adequate proof that Plato ever identified the absolute Good with 'God' in his sense of the term. In the philosophy of Spinoza, however, we find the many beings of experience causally explained by reference to the unique infinite substance which Spinoza called 'God or Nature', *Deus sive Natura*. As we have already seen, he assimilated the causal relation to the relation of logical implication, and depicted finite things as proceeding necessarily from infinite substance. Here he differs sharply from the Christian mediaeval metaphysicians, and for the matter of that from Descartes, who postulated one ultimate cause but who did not attempt to deduce finite things from this cause.

In order to know a thing, one must know its cause. 'The knowledge of effect depends on the knowledge of cause and involves the same.'[1] To explain a thing is to assign its cause or causes. Now, substance was defined by Spinoza as 'that which is in itself and is conceived through itself: I mean that the conception of which does not depend on the conception of another thing from which it must be formed'.[2] But that which can be known through itself alone cannot have an external cause. Substance, then, is what Spinoza calls 'cause of itself': it is explained

[1] *E.*, P. I, axiom 4.   [2] *Ibid.*, def. 3.

through itself and not by reference to any external cause. The definition implies, therefore, that substance is completely self-dependent: it does not depend on any external cause either for its existence or for its attributes and modifications. To say this is to say that its essence involves its existence. 'I understand that to be cause of itself the essence of which involves existence and the nature of which cannot be conceived except as existing.'[1]

In Spinoza's view we have or can have a clear and distinct idea of substance, and in this idea we perceive that existence pertains to the essence of substance. 'If anyone says, then, that he has a clear and distinct, that is, a true idea of substance and nevertheless doubts whether such substance exists, he is like one who says that he has a true idea and yet doubts whether it may not be false.'[2] 'Since existence appertains to the nature of substance, its definition must of necessity involve existence, and therefore from its mere definition its existence can be concluded.'[3] At a later stage, when he has argued that there is one and only one substance, infinite and eternal, and that this substance is God, Spinoza returns to the same line of thought. Since the essence of God 'excludes all imperfection and involves absolute perfection, by that very fact it removes all doubt concerning His existence and makes it most certain, which will be manifest, I think, to such as pay it the least attention'.[4] Here we have the 'ontological argument', liable to the same line of attack to which St. Anselm's argument was open.

If substance were finite, it would be limited, says Spinoza, by some other substance of the same nature, that is, having the same attribute. But there cannot be two or more substances possessing the same attribute. For if there were two or more of them, they would have to be distinguishable from one another, and this means that they would have to possess different attributes. 'An "attribute" I understand to be that which the intellect perceives as constituting the essence of a substance.'[5] Once given this definition it follows that, if two substances possessed the same attributes, they would possess the same essence; and in this case we should have no reason to speak of them as 'two', for we should not be able to distinguish them. But if there cannot be two or more substances possessing the same attribute, substance cannot be limited or finite. It must, therefore, be infinite.

---

[1] *Ibid.*, def. 1.   [2] *Ibid.*, prop. 8, note 2.   [3] *Ibid.*
[4] *E.*, P. I, prop. 11, note.   [5] *E.*, P. I, def. 4.

This piece of reasoning is difficult to follow, and it does not seem to me cogent. The word 'same' appears to be used ambiguously. But Spinoza's idea is obviously that the existence of a plurality of substances would need explanation, and 'explanation' involves reference to a cause. Substance, however, has been defined in such a way that it cannot be said of it that it is the effect of an external cause. We must come in the end to a being which is 'cause of itself', its own explanation, and infinite. For if substance were limited and finite, it could be acted upon, it could be the term of causal activity. But if it is liable to be affected by an external cause, it cannot be understood purely through itself. And this is against the definition of substance. It follows that substance, so defined, must be infinite.

Infinite substance must possess infinite attributes. 'The more reality or being a thing has, the more attributes will it have.'[1] An infinite being must therefore have an infinity of attributes. And this infinite substance with infinite attributes is called 'God' by Spinoza. 'God I understand to be a being absolutely infinite, that is, a substance consisting of infinite attributes, each of which expresses eternal and infinite essence.'[2] And Spinoza goes on to argue that the infinite divine substance is indivisible, unique and eternal and that in God existence and essence are one and the same.[3]

To any one who has made a study of Scholasticism and Cartesianism all this will doubtless sound familiar. The essence-existence language and the term 'substance' were used by the Scholastics, while Spinoza's definitions of substance and attribute were formed in dependence on Descartes' definitions. And we have seen how Spinoza used a form of the 'ontological argument' to demonstrate God's existence. Further, his description of God as infinite being, as infinite substance, as unique, eternal and simple (indivisible and without parts) was the traditional description of God. But one is not entitled to conclude that Spinoza's idea of God was precisely the same as that of the Scholastics or of Descartes. One has only to consider the proposition that 'extension is an attribute of God, or God is an extended thing'[4] in order at once to see a difference. This proposition suggests that Spinoza's view of the relation of God to the world was certainly not the view held by the Scholastics. Nor was it. In Spinoza's opinion, neither

---

[1] E., P. I, prop. 9.
[2] E., P. I, def. 6.
[3] E., P. I, props. 12–14 and 19–20.
[4] E., P. II, prop. 2.

the Scholastics nor Descartes understood what is implied by the nature of an infinite being or substance. If God were distinct from Nature and if there were substances other than God, God would not be infinite. Conversely, if God is infinite, there cannot be other substances. Finite things cannot be understood or explained apart from God's causal activity. They cannot, therefore, be substances in the sense in which Spinoza has defined the term 'substance'. They must, then, be in God. 'Whatever is, is in God, and nothing can exist or be conceived without God.'[1] This proposition could, indeed, be accepted by theistic philosophers if it were taken to mean simply that every finite being is essentially dependent on God and that God is present in all finite things, upholding them in existence. But what Spinoza meant was that finite beings are modifications of God, the unique substance. God possesses an infinity of attributes, each of which is infinite; and of these two are known to us, namely, thought and extension. Finite minds are modes of God under the attribute of thought, and finite bodies are modes of God under the attribute of extension. Nature is not ontologically distinct from God; and the reason why it cannot be ontologically distinct is that God is infinite. He must comprise in Himself all reality.[2]

2. In the logical process of deduction Spinoza does not proceed straight from the infinite substance to finite modes. In between, as it were, come the infinite and eternal modes, immediate and mediate, which are logically prior to the finite modes and about which something must now be said. As a preliminary it is necessary to recall Spinoza's doctrine that of the divine attributes we perceive two, thought and extension. Of the other attributes nothing more can be said, since we cannot know them. One should also notice that in passing from consideration of God as an infinite substance with divine attributes to consideration of the modes of God the mind is passing from *Natura naturans* to *Natura naturata*; that is, from God in Himself to 'creation', though one must not take the last phrases to mean that the world is distinct from God.

The intellect can discern certain changeless and eternal

[1] *E.*, P. I, prop. 15.
[2] The Scholastics were aware of the difficulty involved in asserting that God is infinite and at the same time that Nature is distinct from Him. Their answer was that though the creation of finite things adds to the number of beings (the term 'being' was understood analogically) it does not increase, so to speak, the amount of being. God and finite things are incommensurable, in the sense that their existence adds nothing to the infinite divine being and perfection.

properties of the universe when it considers the universe under the attributes of thought and extension. I take extension first. The logically prior state of substance under the attribute of extension is motion-and-rest. In order to understand what this means one must remember that for Spinoza there can be no question of movement being impressed upon the world by an external cause. Descartes depicted God as conferring, as it were, a certain amount of movement upon the extended world at creation. But for Spinoza movement must be a characteristic of Nature itself; for there is no cause distinct from Nature which could confer or impress movement upon Nature. Motion-and-rest is the primary characteristic of extended Nature, and the total proportions of motion-and-rest remain constant, though the proportions in the case of individual bodies are constantly changing. Using the language of a later time one can say, then, that the total amount of energy in the universe is an intrinsic property of the universe and that it remains constant. The physical universe is thus a self-contained system of bodies in motion. This total amount of motion-and-rest, or of energy, is what Spinoza calls the 'infinite and eternal immediate mode' of God or Nature under the attribute of extension.

Complex bodies are composed of particles. If each particle is looked on as an individual body, things like human bodies or the bodies of animals are individuals of a higher order, that is, they are complex individuals. They may gain or lose particles, and in this sense they change; but so long as the same proportion of motion-and-rest is preserved in the complex structure they are said to retain their identity. Now, we can conceive increasingly complex bodies; 'and if we thus proceed still further to infinity, we can easily conceive that all nature is one individual whose parts, that is, all bodies, vary in infinite ways without any change of the individual as a whole'.[1] This 'individual as a whole', that is, Nature, considered as a spatial system or system of bodies, is the mediate infinite and eternal mode of God or Nature under the attribute of extension. It is also called the 'face of the universe'.

The immediate infinite and eternal mode of God or Nature under the attribute of thought is called by Spinoza 'absolutely infinite understanding'.[2] He apparently means that just as motion-and-rest is the fundamental mode of extension, so understanding

---

[1] *E.*, P. II, prop. 13, lemma 7, note.   [2] *Letter 64.*

or apprehending is the fundamental mode of thought. It is presupposed, for example, by love and desire. 'The modes of thinking, such as love, desire, or any other name by which the modifications of the mind are designated, are not granted unless an idea in the same individual is granted of the thing loved, desired, etc. But the idea can be granted although no other mode of thinking be granted.'[1] If this account of the immediate and eternal mode under the attribute of thought is correct, it means that 'thought' in general includes, as with Descartes, all conscious activity as such, though the fundamental mode of 'thinking', on which the others depend, is apprehending.

Spinoza does not make it clear what the mediate infinite and eternal mode under the attribute of thought is. But since for him the attributes of thought and extension were attributes of the same substance or different aspects of the one substance, his scheme seems to demand that the mediate and eternal mode of substance under the attribute of thought should be the strict counterpart of 'the face of the universe', the total system of bodies. In this case it is the total system of minds. 'It is apparent that our mind, in so far as it understands, is an eternal mode of thinking, which is determined by another mode of thinking, and this one again by another, and so on to infinity: so that they all constitute at the same time the eternal and infinite intellect of God.'[2] Spinoza does not actually say that this is the mediate infinite and eternal mode of thought; but it is not unreasonable to think that this was his view. It should be noted, however, that 'the eternal and infinite intellect of God' belongs to *Natura naturata* and not to *Natura naturans*. We cannot speak of God as He is in Himself as having an intellect, distinct from the infinite system of minds. If we do so, the word 'intellect' has no meaning for us. 'If intellect and will appertain to the eternal essence of God, something quite other must be understood by these two attributes than what is commonly understood by men. For intellect and will, which would constitute the essence of God, must differ *toto caelo* from our intellect and will, nor can they agree in any thing save name, nor any more than the dog as a heavenly body agrees with the dog as a barking animal.'[3]

3. According to Spinoza, 'infinite things in infinite modes must necessarily follow from the necessity of divine nature'.[4] And the

[1] *E.*, P. II, axiom 3.
[2] *E.*, P. V, prop. 40, note.
[3] *E.*, P. I, prop. 17, note.
[4] *Ibid.*, prop. 16.

truth of this proposition is said to be 'manifest' to anyone who considers that from a given definition certain properties necessarily follow. It is assumed, in other words, that substance must have modes; and the conclusion is drawn that as substance is infinite it must have infinite modes. However, whatever the value of Spinoza's 'proof' may be, it is clear that for him finite modes are caused necessarily by God. 'In the nature of things nothing contingent is granted, but all things are determined by the necessity of divine nature for existing and working in a certain way.'[1] Again, 'things could not have been produced by God in any other manner or order than that in which they were produced'.[2] It is true that 'the essence of things produced by God does not involve existence'.[3] For if it did involve existence, they would be causes of themselves. In fact, each would be infinite substance, and this is impossible. Finite things can be called 'contingent', therefore, if by a 'contingent' thing one simply means a thing the essence of which does not involve existence. But they cannot be called 'contingent' if by giving them this name one means that they follow contingently, and not of necessity, from the divine nature. God causes them, but He causes them necessarily, in the sense that He could not omit to cause them. Nor could He produce any other things or order of things than those which He actually causes. It is true, of course, that we may not be able to see how a given thing follows of necessity from the divine nature, but 'nothing can be said to be contingent save in respect to the imperfection of our knowledge'.[4]

At the same time Spinoza states that God is 'free'. This statement may sound surprising at first; but it is a good illustration of the fact that the terms used by Spinoza must be understood in the light of his own definitions and not in the light of the meanings commonly attributed to these terms in ordinary speech. 'That thing is said to be "free" which exists by the mere necessity of its own nature and is determined in its actions by itself alone. That thing is said to be necessary (*necessaria*), or rather compelled (*coacta*), which is determined in its existence and actions by something else in a certain fixed ratio.'[5] God, then, is 'free' in the sense that He is self-determined in His actions. But He is not free in the sense that it was open to Him not to create the world at all or to create other finite beings than those which He has created. 'Hence

---

[1] *E.*, P. I, prop. 29.   [3] *Ibid.*, prop. 33.   [3] *Ibid.*, prop. 24.
[4] *Ibid.*, prop. 33, note 1.   [5] *Ibid.*, def. 7.

it follows that God does not act from freedom of will.'[1] The difference between God, the infinite substance, and finite things is that God is not determined in His existence or actions by any external cause (there is no cause external to God which could act upon Him) whereas finite things, being modifications of God, are determined by Him in respect of their existence, essence and actions.

The foregoing account of God's necessary production of finite things may easily suggest a most misleading interpretation of Spinoza's thought; and one must guard against allowing one's interpretation to be coloured by the picture which the account inevitably tends to conjure up. For if one speaks of God creating finite things and of finite things being caused and determined by God, one inevitably tends to form a picture of a transcendent God who creates necessarily in the sense that His infinite perfection necessarily expresses itself in finite beings which are distinct from Him, even though they flow necessarily from Him. Spinoza states, for example, that 'things were produced by the consummate perfection of God, since they followed necessarily from a given most perfect nature'.[2] And remarks of this kind tend to suggest that Spinoza had in mind an emanation-theory of the neo-Platonic type. But such an interpretation would be based on a misunderstanding of Spinoza's use of terms. God is identified with Nature. We can consider Nature either as an infinite substance, without reference to its modifications, or as a system of modes, the first way of considering Nature being logically prior to the second. If we consider Nature in the second way (as *Natura naturata*), we must recognize, according to Spinoza, that a given mode is caused by a preceding mode or preceding modes, which are themselves caused by other modes, and so on indefinitely. For example, a particular body is caused by other bodies, and these by other bodies, and so on indefinitely. There is no question of a transcendent God 'intervening', as it were, to create a particular body or a particular mind. There is an endless chain of particular causes. On the other hand, the chain of finite causes is logically and ontologically dependent (it comes to the same thing, since the order of ideas and the order of things are said to be ultimately the same) on Nature considered as a self-dependent and self-determined unique substance (*Natura naturans*). Nature necessarily expresses itself in modifications, and in this sense Nature is the

[1] *E.*, P. I, prop. 32, corollary 1.   [2] *Ibid.*, prop. 33, note 2.

immanent cause of all its modifications or modes. 'God is the indwelling and not the transient cause of all things',[1] for all things exist in God or Nature. But this does not mean that God exists apart from the modes and can interfere with the chain of finite causes. The chain of finite causality *is* the divine causality; for it is the modal expression of God's self-determination.

It is a help, then, towards understanding the drift of Spinoza's thought if for the word 'God' one substitutes the word 'Nature'. For example, the sentence, 'Particular things are nothing else than modifications of the attributes of God, or modes by which attributes of God are expressed in a certain and determined manner',[2] becomes clearer if for 'God' one reads 'Nature'. Nature is an infinite system in which there is one infinite chain of particular causes; but the whole infinite chain exists only because Nature exists. In the order of logical dependence one can distinguish the infinite modes from the finite modes and one can say in a sense that God or Nature is the proximate cause of the infinite modes and the remote cause of the finite modes. But this way of speaking is illegitimate, says Spinoza, if by calling God the remote cause of individual things one means to imply that God is in some way unconnected with individual effects. 'We understand by a remote cause one which is in no wise connected with its effect. But all things which are, are in God, and so depend on God that without Him they can neither exist nor be conceived.'[3] Individual things cannot exist apart from Nature and they are thus all caused by Nature. But this is not to say that they cannot be accounted for in terms of particular causal connections, provided that we remember that *Natura naturata* is not a substance distinct from *Natura naturans*. There is one infinite system; but it can be looked at from different points of view.

4. This infinite system is one system: there are not two systems, a system of minds and a system of bodies. But the one system can be looked at from two points of view: it can be conceived under the attribute of thought or under the attribute of extension. To every mode under the attribute of extension there corresponds a mode under the attribute of thought, and this second mode Spinoza calls an 'idea'. Thus to every extended thing there corresponds an idea. But the word 'corresponds' is misleading, though it is difficult to avoid using it. It suggests that there are

---

[1] *E.*, P. I, prop. 18.   [2] *Ibid.*, prop. 25, corollary.
[3] *Ibid.*, prop. 28, note.

two orders, two chains of causes, namely, the order of bodies and the order of ideas. But in reality there is, according to Spinoza, only one order, though it can be conceived by us in two ways. 'The order and connection of ideas is the same as the order and connection of things.'[1] 'Whether we consider Nature under the attribute of extension or under the attribute of thought or under any other attribute, we shall find one and the same order and one and the same connection of causes: that is, the same things follow in either case.'[2] This does not mean that one can explain bodies in terms of ideas. For if, says Spinoza, we are considering individual things as modes of extension, we must explain the whole system of bodies in terms of the attribute of extension. There is no question of attempting to reduce bodies to ideas or ideas to bodies. Indeed, there would be no sense in making this attempt, since there is really only one order of Nature. But if we are considering things as modes under one particular attribute we ought to do so consistently and not change our points of view and language in an irresponsible manner.

If there is only one order of Nature, it follows that it is inadmissible to speak of the human mind as belonging to one order and of the human body as belonging to another order. The human being is one thing. It is true that 'man consists of mind and body'[3] and that 'the human mind is united to the body';[4] but the human body is man considered as a mode of the attribute of extension, and the human mind is man considered as a mode of the attribute of thought. They are, then, two aspects of the one thing. The Cartesian problem of 'interaction' between soul and body is, therefore, no real problem. Just as it would be senseless to ask how there can be interaction between the divine attributes of thought and extension, which are aspects of God, so is it senseless to ask how there can be interaction between mind and body in the particular case of man. If the natures of mind and body are understood, it must also be recognized that the problem of interaction does not and cannot arise. Spinoza thus avoids altogether the problem which so perplexed the Cartesians. And he avoided it not by reducing mind to body or body to mind but by declaring that they are simply two aspects of one thing. It may be doubted, however, whether his elimination of the problem was anything more than a verbal elimination. I cannot discuss here for its own

---

[1] *E.*, P. II, prop. 7.   [2] *Ibid.*, note.
[3] *Ibid.*, prop. 13, corollary.   [4] *Ibid.*, note.

sake the problem of the relation of soul to body; but it is worth
while pointing out that the problem is not eliminated simply by
framing one's language in such a way that the problem does not
arise in this language. For it has to be shown that the data are
more adequately expressed or described in this language than in
any other. It may be said, of course, that Spinoza's doctrine about
the relation between mind and body must be true if his general
doctrine about substance and its attributes is true. This may well
be so; but the word 'if' is here of some importance.

The mind, according to Spinoza, is the idea of the body. That
is to say, the mind is the counterpart under the attribute of
thought of a mode of extension, namely, the body. The body,
however, is composed of many parts, and to each part there
'corresponds' an idea (though it is more accurate to say that each
'pair' are two aspects of one and the same thing). It follows,
therefore, that 'the idea which constitutes the formal being of the
human mind is not simple but composed of many ideas'.[1] Now,
when the human body is affected by an external body, the idea of
the modification in the human body is at the same time an idea
of the external body. Hence 'the human mind can perceive the
nature of many bodies at the same time as the nature of its own
body'.[2] Moreover, the mind regards the external body 'as actually
existing or as present to itself until the body is affected by a
modification which cuts off the existence or presence of that
(external) body'.[3] And if the modification of one's own body
continues when the external body is no longer actually affecting
it, one may continue to regard the external body as present when
it is really no longer present. Further, 'if the human body has
once been affected at the same time by two or more bodies, when
the mind afterwards remembers any one of them it will straight-
way remember the others'.[4] In this way Spinoza explains memory
which, he says, is 'nothing else than a certain concatenation of
ideas involving the nature of things which are outside the human
body, and this concatenation takes place according to the order
and concatenation of the modifications of the human body'.[5]

Besides the 'idea of the body', that is to say, the mind, there
can also be 'the idea of the mind'; for the human being can form
an idea of his mind. He enjoys self-consciousness. We can consider a mode of thinking without relation to its object, and we

[1] E., P. II. prop. 15.   [2] Ibid., prop. 16, corollary 1.   [3] Ibid., prop. 17.
[4] Ibid., prop. 18.   [5] Ibid., note.

then have the idea of an idea. 'Thus if a man knows anything, by that very fact he knows that he knows it, and so on to infinity.'[1] All self-consciousness has a physical basis, in the sense that 'the mind has no knowledge of itself save in so far as it perceives the ideas of the modifications of the body';[2] but that we do enjoy self-consciousness Spinoza does not, of course, dispute.

Spinoza's theory of the relation between mind and body was introduced here as a particular illustration of his theory of attributes and modes. But if one considers his theory of mind and body in itself, its chief interest lies, I think, in his insistence on the physical dependence of mind. If the human mind is the idea of the body, it follows that the perfection of the mind corresponds to the perfection of the body. This is perhaps another way of saying that we depend on perception for our ideas. It also follows that the relative imperfection of an animal's mind depends on the relative imperfection of its body as compared with the human body. Spinoza did not, of course, think that cows, for example, have 'minds' in the sense in which we ordinarily talk about minds. But it follows from his general theory of attributes and modes that to every cow's body there 'corresponds' an idea of that body; that is, a mode under the attribute of thought. And the perfection of this 'idea' or 'mind' corresponds to the perfection of the body. If one detaches this theory of the physical dependence of mind from its general metaphysical framework, one can regard it as a programme for scientific research into the ascertainable dependence of mind on body. Spinoza doubtless regarded his view on this matter as the result of *a priori* logical deduction and not as a generalization from empirical investigations. But from the point of view of one who is disinclined to believe that such matters can be settled by purely deductive reasoning the view is likely to be of interest in the guise of an hypothesis forming a provisional basis for empirical research. To what extent mental activities are dependent on non-mental factors is a question which can hardly be answered *a priori*. But it is an interesting question and an important one.

5. In the concluding section of this chapter I wish to draw attention to an important point in Spinoza's philosophy, namely, his elimination of final causality. At the same time I wish to set this particular point in a wide context; for it seems to me to shed a clear light on the general direction of Spinoza's thought. This

---

[1] *E.*, P. II, prop. 21, note.   [2] *Ibid.*, prop. 23.

section may be said, then, to consist of general reflections on
Spinoza's view of God and the world in the light of his elimination
of final causes.

We have seen that Spinoza's initial idea of God was derived
from the Jewish religion. But he soon rejected orthodox Jewish
theology; and there is reason for thinking, as has been already
remarked, that his mind was influenced in the direction of pantheism by his study both of certain Jewish philosophers and of
Renaissance thinkers like Giordano Bruno. In working out his
system, however, Spinoza made use of terminology and categories
of thought derived from Scholasticism and Cartesianism. His
pantheism took the form, then, of saying that as God is infinite
being He must include within Himself all beings, all reality, and
that as God is infinite substance finite beings must be modes of
this substance. One may say, then, that the pantheistic element
of his thought derives from a process of drawing what seemed to
Spinoza to be the logical consequences of the idea of God as infinite
and completely non-dependent being (that is, as substance in his
sense of the word). And if one isolates this element of his thought,
one can say, I think, that the term 'God' retains something of its
traditional meaning. God is infinite substance possessing infinite
attributes, only two of which are known to us, and there is some
distinction between *Natura naturans* and *Natura naturata*. It is
not empirical Nature which is identified with God, but rather
Nature in a peculiar sense, namely, as the infinite substance, which
lies behind the transitory modes. One great difficulty about this
theory, however, is that of seeing how any logical deduction of
Natura naturata is possible, unless the initial assumption is made
that substance *must* express itself in modes; and this is precisely
the point which ought to be proved, not assumed. It is as though
Spinoza took the traditional idea of substance as that in which
accidents inhere and then applied it without more ado to infinite
being. It is true, of course, that he claimed to have a clear and
distinct idea of the objective essence of substance or God. In a
letter to Hugo Boxell he asserted that he had as clear an idea of God
as he had of a triangle.[1] And he had to make this claim. For if
his definitions did not express objective essences clearly conceived,
the whole system might be simply a system of 'tautologies'. But
it is difficult to see that it follows even from Spinoza's definitions
that substance as he defined it *must* have modes. On the one hand

[1] *Letter 56.*

he started with the idea of God. On the other hand he knew very well by experience, as we all know, that finite beings exist. In developing a deductive system he thus knew in advance the point of arrival, and it seems probable that his knowledge that there are finite beings encouraged him to believe that he had achieved a logical deduction of *Natura naturata*.

If the terms 'intellect' and 'will' cannot be predicated of God in any sense which has any meaning for us, and if causal connections are of the nature of logical connections, it would seem impossible to talk significantly of God creating the world for any purpose. Spinoza does say that 'things were produced by the consummate perfection of God, since they followed necessarily from a given most perfect nature';[1] and this statement may perhaps seem to imply that it makes sense to talk of God as creating things for a purpose, such as the manifestation of the divine perfection or the wider diffusion of the good. But Spinoza will not allow that there is any sense in speaking of God as acting 'in all things for the furthering of good'.[2] The order of nature follows necessarily from the nature of God, and there could not have been any other order. It is illegitimate, then, to speak of God as 'choosing' to create or as having a purpose in creation. To speak in this way is to turn God into a kind of superman.

Human beings act with an end in view. And this inclines them to interpret Nature in the light of themselves. If they do not know the cause or causes of some natural event, 'nothing remains for them but to turn to themselves and reflect what could induce them personally to bring about such a thing, and thus they necessarily estimate other natures by their own'.[3] Again, since they find many things in Nature useful to them, men are inclined to imagine that these things must have been made for their use by a superhuman power. And when they find inconveniences in Nature, like earthquakes and diseases, they attribute them to the divine anger and displeasure. If it is pointed out to them that these inconveniences affect the pious and good as well as the impious and bad, they talk about the inscrutable judgments of God. Thus 'truth might have lain hidden from the human race through all eternity, had not mathematics, which does not deal with final causes but with the essence and properties of things, offered to men another standard of truth'.[4]

Though human beings act with an end in view this does not

---

[1] *E.*, P. I, prop. 33, note 2.   [2] *Ibid.*   [3] *E.*, P. I, appendix.   [4] *Ibid.*

mean that their actions are not determined. 'Men think themselves free inasmuch as they are conscious of their volitions and
desires, and because they are ignorant of the causes by which they
are led to wish and desire, they do not even dream of their
existence.'[1] Belief that one is free is for Spinoza the result and
expression of ignorance of the determining causes of one's desires,
ideals, choices and actions, just as belief in finality in Nature is
due to ignorance of the real causes of natural events. Thus belief
in final causes in any form is simply the fruit of ignorance. Once
the origin of the belief has been traced it should be clear that
'nature has no fixed aim in view and that all final causes are
simply fabrications of men'.[2] Indeed, the doctrine of final causality
perverts the true notion of causality. For it subordinates the
efficient cause, which is prior, to the so-called final cause. 'And
so it makes that which is first by nature to be last.'[3] And it is
useless to object that if all things follow necessarily from the
divine nature it is impossible to explain the imperfections and
evils in the world. No explanation is required. For what people
call 'imperfections' and 'evils' are so only from the human point
of view. An earthquake endangers human life and property and
so we think of it as an 'evil'; but it is an evil only in relation to us
and from our point of view, not in itself. It requires no explanation, therefore, save in terms of efficient causality, unless we have
reason to think that the world was made for man's convenience;
and we have, Spinoza was convinced, no reason to think this.

One can, I think, consider Spinoza's elimination of final
causality from two points of view. First of all there is what may
be called the vertical aspect. *Natura naturata*, the system of
modes, follows necessarily from *Natura naturans*, infinite substance or God; and the process has no final cause. Secondly, there
is the horizontal aspect. In the infinite system of modes any given
mode and any given event can be explained, in principle at least,
in terms of efficient causality by reference to the causal activity
of other modes. I have purposely spoken of two 'aspects' since
they are connected with one another in Spinoza's system. The
existence of a given mode is due to causal factors in the modal
system, but it is also referable to God, to God, that is, as 'modified'. One can legitimately say that a given event in the modal
system is caused by God, provided that one realizes that this does
not mean that God interferes from without, as it were, in the

---

[1] *E.*, P. I, appendix.   [2] *Ibid.*   [3] *Ibid.*

system. The system of modes is God as modified, and thus to say that X is caused by Y is to say that X is caused by God, that is to say, by God as modified in Y. At the same time one's attention is differently directed, I think, according to whether one considers the one aspect or the other. If one considers the metaphysical aspect, one's attention is directed to the logical priority of *Natura naturans* in relation to *Natura naturata*, and the traditional elements in Spinoza's idea of God are brought into prominence. God as infinite substance appears as supreme and ultimate cause of the empirical world. If on the other hand one considers simply the causal connections between the members of the modal system, the elimination of final causality appears as a programme for research into efficient causes or as a hypothesis in the light of which physical and psychological inquiries are to be pursued.

The system of Spinoza is thus, I suggest, two-faced. The metaphysic of infinite being manifesting itself in finite beings looks back to the metaphysical systems of the past. The theory that all finite beings and their modifications can be explained in terms of causal connections which are in principle ascertainable, looks forward to those empirical sciences which do in fact omit consideration of final causality and try to explain their data in terms of efficient causality, however the phrase 'efficient causality' may be understood. I do not, of course, wish to imply that in considering Spinoza's system as he expounded it one can profitably neglect either aspect. But there are, I think, two aspects. If one stresses the metaphysical aspect, one will tend to think of Spinoza primarily as a 'pantheist', as one who endeavoured to develop consistently, even if not successfully, the implications of the concept of God as infinite and completely non-dependent being. If one stresses what I may perhaps call the 'naturalistic' aspect, one will tend to concentrate on *Natura naturata*, to question the propriety of calling Nature 'God' and of describing it as 'substance', and to see in the philosophical system the sketch of a programme for scientific research. But one must not forget that Spinoza himself was a metaphysician with the ambitious aim of explaining reality or making the universe intelligible. He may have anticipated hypotheses which have commended themselves to many scientists; but he concerned himself with metaphysical problems with which the scientist as scientist is not concerned.

CHAPTER XII

SPINOZA (3)

Spinoza's levels or degrees of knowledge—Confused experience; universal ideas; falsity—Scientific knowledge—Intuitive knowledge.

1. SPINOZA's ideal of knowledge recalls to a certain extent the Platonic ideal of knowledge. And we find in Spinoza as in Plato a theory of degrees of knowledge. Both philosophers present us with ascending degrees of adequacy and of synoptic vision.

In the *Treatise on the Correction of the Understanding*[1] Spinoza distinguishes four levels of what he calls perception. The first and lowest of these levels is perception 'by hearsay', and Spinoza illustrates what he means by an example. 'By hearsay I know my birthday, that certain people were my parents, and the like: things of which I have never had any doubt.'[2] I do not know by personal experience that I was born on a certain day, nor have I probably ever taken steps to prove it. I have been told that I was born on a certain day, and I have become accustomed to regard a certain date as my birthday. I have no doubt that I have been told the truth; but I know this truth only 'by hearsay', through the testimony of others.

The second level of perception as outlined in the *Treatise on the Correction of the Understanding* is the perception of knowledge which we have from vague or confused experience. 'By vague experience I know that I shall die; and I assert this because I have seen my equals undergo death, although they did not all live for the same length of time nor die from the same illness. Again, by vague experience I know also that oil is good for feeding a flame and that water is good for extinguishing it. I know also that a dog is a barking animal, and man a rational animal; and in this way I know nearly all things which are useful in life.'[3]

The third level of perception as given in the *Treatise* is perception wherein 'the essence of one thing is inferred from the essence of another, but not adequately'.[4] For instance, I conclude that some event or thing has a cause, though I have no clear idea of

---

[1] This work will be referred to as *T.*   [2] *T.*, 4, 20.
[3] *Ibid.*   [4] *T.*, 4, 193.

the cause, nor of the precise connection between cause and effect.

Finally, the fourth kind of perception is that whereby a thing is perceived through its essence alone or through a knowledge of its proximate cause'.[1] For example, if in virtue of the fact that I know something I know what it is to know anything, that is to say, if in a concrete act of knowing I perceive clearly the essence of knowledge, I enjoy this fourth degree of perception. Again, if I possess a knowledge of the essence of the mind such that I see clearly that mind is essentially united to a body, I enjoy a higher level of perception than if I merely conclude from my feelings with regard to my own body that there is a mind in me and that it is somehow or other united with this body, though I do not understand the mode of union. This fourth level of knowledge is also enjoyed in mathematics. 'But the things which I have so far been able to know by this knowledge have been very few.'[2]

In the *Ethics*, however, Spinoza gives three, and not four, levels of knowledge. 'Perception by hearsay' is not mentioned as a distinct kind of knowledge, and the second level of perception of the *Treatise* appears in the *Ethics* as 'knowledge of the first kind' (*cognitio primi generis*), opinion (*opinio*) or imagination (*imaginatio*). And it is customary to follow the practice of the *Ethics* and to speak of Spinoza's three degrees or levels of knowledge. Following this practice, I shall now attempt to explain somewhat more fully what Spinoza meant by *cognitio primi generis*, knowledge of the first (and lowest) type.

2. The human body is affected by other bodies, and every modification or state so produced is reflected in an idea. Ideas of this kind are more or less equivalent, therefore, to ideas derived from sensation, and Spinoza calls them ideas of imagination. They are not derived by logical deduction from other ideas,[3] and in so far as the mind consists of such ideas it is passive and not active. For these ideas do not spring from the active power of the mind but reflect bodily changes and states produced by other bodies. There is a certain 'casualness' about them: they reflect experience, indeed, but this experience is 'vague'. An individual body is affected by other individual bodies, and its changing states are

---

[1] *T.*, 4, 19, 4.   [2] *T.*, 4, 22.
[3] To avoid misunderstanding it is important to note that Spinoza uses the term 'idea' to cover what we would call 'propositions'. Given his understanding of the term 'idea', therefore, it is legitimate to speak of deriving ideas from ideas and of ideas as being true or false.

reflected in ideas which do not represent any scientific and coherent knowledge. On the level of sense-perception the human being has knowledge of other human beings, but its knowledge is knowledge of them as individual things which affect it in some way. It has no scientific knowledge of them, and its ideas are inadequate. When I know an external body through sense-perception I know it only in so far as it affects my own body. I know that it exists, at least as long as it is affecting my body, and I know something of its nature; but I have no adequate knowledge of its nature or essence. Moreover, though I necessarily know my own body in so far as it is affected by another body, since the state produced in my body is reflected in an idea, this knowledge is inadequate. Knowledge which is purely dependent on sense-perception is therefore called by Spinoza 'inadequate' and 'confused'. 'I say expressly that the mind has no adequate but only confused knowledge of itself, of its body and of external bodies when it perceives a thing in the common order of nature, that is, whenever it is determined externally, that is, by fortuitous circumstances, to contemplate this or that.'[1] There is, of course, association of ideas; but on the level of sense-perception or confused and 'vague' experience, these associations are determined by associated modifications of our bodies and not by clear knowledge of objective causal relations between things.

It is to be noted that for Spinoza general or universal ideas belong to this level of experience. A human body is frequently affected by, say, other human bodies. And the ideas which reflect the bodily modifications so produced coalesce to form a confused idea of man in general, which is nothing but a sort of confused and composite image. This does not mean that there are no adequate general ideas; it means that the general ideas which are dependent on sense-perception are, according to Spinoza, confused composite images. 'The human body, since it is limited, is only capable of distinctly forming in itself a certain number of images; and if more than this number are formed, the images begin to be confused; and if this number of images which the body is capable of forming in itself is much exceeded, all will become entirely confused one with the other.'[2] In this way arise the ideas of 'being', 'thing', etc. 'And from similar causes have arisen those notions which are called universal or general, such as man, dog, horse, etc.'[3] These common ideas or composite images are not the same

[1] E., P. II, prop. 29, note.   [2] Ibid., prop. 40, note 1.   [3] Ibid.

in all men and vary from individual to individual; but in so far as there is similarity it is due to the fact that human bodies resemble one another in structure and are frequently affected in ways which resemble one another.

There are two points which must be borne in mind if Spinoza's doctrine of 'vague or casual experience' is not to be misunderstood. In the first place, although he denies the adequacy of the first and lowest level of knowledge he does not deny its utility. Speaking of knowledge obtained by 'vague experience', he says: 'And thus I know nearly all things that are useful in life.'[1] Again, when illustrating his theory of levels of knowledge he speaks of the following problem.[2] Three numbers are given, and one has to find a fourth which stands in the same relation to the third as the second stands to the first. He then mentions tradesmen who unhesitatingly multiply the second by the third and divide the product by the first because they have not forgotten the rule once given them by the schoolmaster, though they have never seen any proof of the rule and could give no rational account of their procedure. Their knowledge is not adequate mathematical knowledge; but its practical utility can hardly be denied. In the second place, the inadequacy of an idea does not involve that idea being false when it is taken in isolation. 'There is nothing positive in ideas on account of which they could be called false.'[3] For example, when we look at the sun it seems, says Spinoza, to be 'only some two hundred feet distant from us'.[4] In so far as we consider this impression entirely by itself it is not false; for it is true that the sun appears to us to be near. But once we stop talking about the subjective impression and say that the sun is actually only two hundred feet distant from us, we make a false statement. And what makes it false is a privation, namely, the fact that we lack the knowledge of the cause of the impression and of the true distance of the sun. Yet it is obvious that this privation is not the sole cause of our false statement or 'idea'; for we would not say that the sun is only two hundred feet distant from us unless we had a certain impression or 'imagination'. Spinoza says, therefore, that 'falsity consists in privation of knowledge which is involved by inadequate or mutilated and confused ideas'.[5] Ideas of imagination or confused experience do not represent the true order of causes in Nature: they will not fit into a rational and

---

[1] *T.*, 4, 20.   [2] *E.*, P. II, prop. 40, note 2.   [3] *Ibid.*, prop. 33.
[4] *Ibid.*, prop. 35, note.   [5] *Ibid.*, prop. 35.

coherent view of Nature. And in this sense they are false, though no one of them is positively false if it is taken entirely by itself and considered simply as an isolated 'idea' reflecting a bodily modification.

3. Knowledge of the second kind (*cognitio secundi generis*) involves adequate ideas and is scientific knowledge. Spinoza calls this level the level of 'reason' (*ratio*) as distinguished from the level of 'imagination'. But this does not mean that it is accessible only to scientists. For all men have some adequate ideas. All human bodies are modes of extension, and all minds are, according to Spinoza, ideas of bodies. All minds, then, will reflect some common properties of bodies; that is, some pervasive features of extended Nature or common properties of extension. Spinoza does not particularize; but we can say that 'motion' is one of these common properties. If a property is common to all bodies in such a way that it is equally in the part and in the whole, the mind necessarily perceives it and its idea of it is an adequate idea. 'Hence it follows that certain ideas or notions are granted common to all men. For all bodies agree in certain things which must be adequately or clearly and distinctly perceived by all.'[1]

These common notions (*notiones communes*) must not be confused with the universal ideas which have been spoken of under the heading of 'imagination'. The latter are composite images, formed by the confusion of 'ideas' which are logically unrelated, whereas the former are logically required for the understanding of things. The idea of extension, for example, or the idea of motion is not a composite image: it is a clear and distinct idea of a universal characteristic of bodies. These 'common notions' are the foundation of the fundamental principles of mathematics and physics. And since the conclusions which can be logically derived from these principles also represent clear and distinct ideas, it is the 'common notions' which make possible systematic and scientific knowledge of the world. But Spinoza apparently did not confine the term 'common notions' to the fundamental principles of mathematics and physics; he used it to cover any fundamental and, in his opinion, self-evident truths.

Knowledge of the second kind (*cognitio secundi generis*) is, says Spinoza, necessarily true.[2] For it is based on adequate ideas, and an adequate idea is defined as 'an idea which, in so far as it is considered without regard to the object, has all the properties or

[1] *E.*, P. II, prop. 38, corollary.　　　[2] *Ibid.*, prop. 41.

intrinsic marks of a true idea'.[1] There is no sense, then, in seeking for a criterion of the truth of an adequate idea outside the idea itself: it is its own criterion, and we know that it is adequate by having it. 'He who has a true idea knows at the same time that he has a true idea, nor can he doubt concerning the truth of the thing.'[2] Truth is thus its own standard and criterion. It follows that any system of propositions which are logically derived from self-evident axioms is necessarily true and that we know that it is true. To doubt the truth of a self-evident proposition is not possible. Nor can one doubt the truth of a proposition which one sees to be logically entailed by a self-evident proposition.

A deductive system of general propositions, representing knowledge of the second kind, is, of course, abstract in character. General propositions about extension or motion, for example, do not say anything about this or that extended thing or moving body. By advancing from the first to the second level of knowledge one passes from logically unrelated impressions and confused ideas to logically related and clear propositions and adequate ideas; but at the same time one abandons the concreteness of sense-perception and imagination for the abstract generality of mathematics, physics and other sciences. Indeed the philosophical system of Spinoza as expounded in the *Ethics* is itself, in great part at least, an example of this second level of knowledge. Essential properties of all bodies, for example, are deduced, but not individual bodies as such. Spinoza was perfectly well aware, of course, that even if the essential characteristics of bodies can be deduced or discovered by logical analysis it would be beyond the power of the human mind to exhibit the whole of Nature, with all its concrete modes, as a logically interrelated system. Philosophical deduction is a deduction of general propositions: it deals with timeless truths rather than with transitory individual modes as such. This means, however, that knowledge of the second kind is not the highest and most comprehensive level of knowledge which is conceivable. As a limiting ideal at least, to which the human mind can only approximate, we can conceive a third level of knowledge, 'intuitive' knowledge, by which the whole system of Nature in all its richness is grasped in one comprehensive act of vision.

4. The third level of knowledge is called by Spinoza intuitive

---

[1] *E.*, P. II, def. 4.   [2] *Ibid.*, prop. 43.

knowledge (*scientia intuitiva*). But it is important to realize that it arises from the second kind of knowledge and that it is not a disconnected stage reached by a leap or by a mystical process. 'Now this kind of knowing proceeds from an adequate idea of the formal essence of certain attributes of God to the adequate knowledge of the essence of things.'[1] This quotation seems to equate knowledge of the third with knowledge of the second kind; but Spinoza's mind seems to be that it is a result of knowledge of the second kind. Elsewhere he says that 'as all things are in God and are conceived through Him, it follows that we can deduce from this knowledge many things which we can adequately know and thereby form that third kind of knowledge'.[2] It seems that Spinoza thought of the logical deduction of the essential and eternal structure of Nature from the divine attributes as providing the necessary framework for seeing all things, that is, the whole of Nature in its concrete reality, as one great system causally dependent on infinite substance. If this is the correct interpretation, it means that in the third level of knowledge the mind returns, as it were, to individual things, though it perceives them in their essential relation to God and not, as in the first level of knowledge, as isolated phenomena. And the passage from the one way of looking at things to the other is made possible only by ascending from the first to the second level of knowledge, which is an indispensable preliminary stage for attaining the third level. 'The more we understand individual things,' says Spinoza, 'the more we understand God.'[3] 'The greatest endeavour of the mind and its greatest virtue is to understand things by the third class of knowledge.'[4] But 'the endeavour or desire of knowing things according to the third class of knowledge cannot arise from the first but (only) from the second class of knowledge'.[5]

As will be seen later, this third class of knowledge is accompanied by the highest satisfaction and emotional fulfilment. Let it be sufficient here to point out that the vision of all things in God is not something which can be fully attained but something to which the mind can approximate. 'The more advanced, then, everyone is in this class of knowledge, the more conscious he is of himself and God, that is, the more perfect or blessed he is.'[6] But these words must be interpreted in the light of Spinoza's

[1] *E.*, P. II, prop. 40, note 2.   [2] *Ibid.*, prop. 47, note.
[3] *E.*, P. V, prop. 24.   [4] *Ibid.*, prop. 25.
[5] *Ibid.*, prop. 28.   [6] *Ibid.*, prop. 31, note.

general philosophy, and, in particular, of his identification of God with Nature. The vision which is in question is an intellectual contemplation of the eternal and infinite system of Nature and of one's own place in it, not a contemplation of a transcendent God, nor perhaps a religious contemplation at all in any ordinary sense. True, there are religious overtones in what Spinoza says; but these derive more from his upbringing and perhaps from a personal piety than from the requirements of his philosophical system.

CHAPTER XIII

SPINOZA (4)

*Spinoza's intention in his account of human emotions and con-
duct—The* conatus; *pleasure and pain—The derived emotions
—Passive and active emotions—Servitude and freedom—The
intellectual love of God—The 'eternity' of the human mind—An
inconsistency in Spinoza's ethics.*

1. AT the beginning of the third part of the *Ethics* Spinoza
remarks that most of those who have written on the emotions and
on human conduct seem to have looked on man as a kingdom
within a kingdom, as something standing apart from and above
the ordinary course of Nature. He himself, however, proposes to
treat man as a part of Nature and to regard 'human actions and
desires exactly as if I were dealing with lines, planes and bodies'.[1]
The problem of the interaction between mind and body was for
Spinoza, as we have already seen, no problem, because he regarded
mind and body 'as one and the same thing, which is conceived now
under the attribute of thought and now under the attribute of
extension'.[2] There is no need, therefore, to become perplexed
about the question how the mind can influence and move the
body. Nor ought we to imagine that there are free choices which
cannot be explained in terms of efficient causes and which belong
to the activity of mind as something really distinct from body.
As mind and body are the same thing, conceived under different
attributes, our mental activities are as determined as our bodily
activities. If we are spontaneously inclined to believe that our
deliberate acts of choice are free, this is simply because we are
ignorant of their causes. Not understanding their causes we think
that they have no causes. It is true that people say that activities
such as the creation of works of art cannot be explained by the
laws of Nature alone in so far as Nature is extended. But these
people 'know not what a body is',[3] nor what it is capable of. The
fabric of the human body 'far surpasses any piece of work made
by human art, to say nothing of what I have already shown,
namely, that from Nature considered under any attribute infinite
things follow'.[4]

[1] *E.*, P. III, preface.   [2] *E.*, P. III, prop. 2, note.   [3] *Ibid.*   [4] *Ibid.*

In the three last parts of the *Ethics*, therefore, Spinoza sets out
to give a naturalistic account of human emotions and human
conduct. At the same time, however, he sets out to show how
freedom from the bondage of the passions can be achieved. And
this combination of causal analysis, based on a theory of determinism, with ethical idealism seems to involve two inconsistent
positions, in a sense which will be discussed later.

2. Every individual thing (and so not merely man) endeavours
to persist in its own being; and this endeavour Spinoza calls
conatus. Nothing can do anything else but that which follows
from its nature: its essence or nature determines its activity. The
power or 'endeavour', then, by which a thing does what it does or
endeavours to do what it endeavours to do is identical with its
essence. 'The endeavour wherewith a thing endeavours to persist
in its being is nothing else than the actual essence of that thing.'[1]
When, therefore, Spinoza says that the fundamental drive in man
is the endeavour to persist in his own being, he is not simply
making a psychological generalization. He is applying a statement which holds good of every finite thing, and the truth of the
statement is, according to him, logically demonstrable. It can be
shown that every thing tends to preserve itself and to increase its
power and activity.

This tendency, that is, the *conatus*, is called by Spinoza 'appetite'
(*appetitus*) when it refers simultaneously to mind and body. But
in man there is consciousness of this tendency, and conscious
appetite is called 'desire' (*cupiditas*). Further, just as the tendency
to self-preservation and to self-perfection is reflected in consciousness as desire, so also is the transition to a higher or lower state of
vitality or perfection reflected in consciousness. The former, that
is to say, the reflection in consciousness of the transition to a state
of greater perfection is called 'pleasure' (*laetitia*), while the
reflection in consciousness of the transition to a state of lower
perfection is called 'pain' (*tristitia*). On Spinoza's general principles an increase in the mind's perfection must be an increase
in the body's perfection, and conversely. 'Whatever increases or
diminishes, helps or hinders the power of action of our body, the
idea thereof increases or diminishes, helps or hinders the power of
thinking of our mind.'[2] The perfection of the mind, according to
Spinoza, increases in proportion as the mind is active, that is to
say, in proportion as the ideas of which it consists are logically

[1] *E.*, P. III, prop. 7.   [2] *Ibid.*, prop. 11.

connected with one another and are not simply reflections of changing states produced by the action of external causes on the body. But it is not clear how this fits in with the general doctrine that the mind is the idea of the body, nor is it clear what is the condition of the body which is reflected in the mind's activity. One may note, however, that it follows from Spinoza's definitions that everyone necessarily pursues pleasure. This does not mean that everyone takes pleasure as the consciously conceived end or purpose of all his actions: it means that one necessarily seeks to preserve and perfect one's being. And this perfecting of one's being, when looked at in its mental aspect, is pleasure. The word 'pleasure' may, of course, suggest simply 'sense-pleasure'; but this is not Spinoza's meaning. For there are as many species of pleasure and pain 'as there are species of objects by which we are affected'.[1]

3. Having explained the fundamental emotions of pleasure and pain in terms of the *conatus*, which is identical with the determined essence of a thing, Spinoza proceeds to derive other emotions from these fundamental forms. For example, love (*amor*) is 'nothing else but pleasure accompanied by the idea of an external cause', while hate (*odium*) is nothing else but 'pain accompanied by the idea of an external cause'.[2] Again, if I imagine another human being, whom I have not hitherto regarded with any emotion, as being affected by an emotion, I am affected with a like emotion. An image of an external body is a modification of my own body, and the idea of this modification involves the nature of my own body as well as the nature of the external body as present. If, therefore, the nature of the external body is similar to the nature of my own body, the idea of the external body involves a modification of my own body similar to the modification of the external body. Hence, if I imagine a fellow human being to be affected by an emotion, this imagination involves a modification of my own body corresponding to this emotion, with the result that I too am affected by this emotion. In this way compassion, for instance, can be explained: 'This imitation of emotions, when it refers to pain, is called compassion.'[3]

Spinoza thus endeavours to derive the various emotions from the fundamental passions or emotions of desire, pleasure and pain. And this explanation holds good both for men and brutes. 'Hence it follows that the emotions of animals, which are called irrational (for we can in no wise doubt that brutes feel, now that we know

E., P. III, prop. 56.   [2] *Ibid.*, prop. 13, note.   [3] *Ibid.*, prop. 27, note 1.

the origin of the mind), differ from the emotions of men only inasmuch as their nature differs from man's nature. Horse and man are filled with the desire of procreation: the desire of the former is equine, while that of the latter is human. So also the lusts and appetites of insects, fishes and birds must vary.'[1] Spinoza intended, of course, to give a logical deduction of the emotions; but we can, if we like, regard his treatment of the passions and emotions as a speculative programme for modern psychological research with a more empirical basis. In a psychology like that of Freud, for example, we find an analogous attempt to explain man's emotional life in terms of a fundamental drive. In any case Spinoza's explanation is thoroughly 'naturalistic'.

This naturalism finds expression in his account of 'good' and 'evil'. 'By good (bonum) I understand here all kinds of pleasure and whatever conduces to it, and more especially that which satisfies our fervent desires, whatever they may be. By bad (malum) I understand all kinds of pain, and especially that which frustrates our desires.'[2] We do not desire a thing because we think it good: on the contrary, we call it 'good' because we desire it. Similarly, we call 'evil' or 'bad' a thing from which we turn away and towards which we feel an aversion. 'Wherefore each one judges or estimates according to his own emotion what is good or bad, better or worse, best or worst.'[3] And because our emotions are determined, so also are our judgments of what is good and what is bad. We do not always realize this; but our failure to recognize it is due to ignorance of causal connections. Once we understand the causal origins of the emotions we understand that our judgments concerning 'good' and 'evil' are determined.

4. It is now necessary to make a distinction which is important for Spinoza's moral theory. All emotions are derived from the fundamental passions of desire, pleasure and pain. And normally they are explicable in terms of association. When the idea of an external thing becomes associated in my mind with pleasure, that is, with the heightening of my vitality or drive to self-preservation and increase of power, I can be said to 'love' that thing. And I call it 'good'. Moreover, 'anything can accidentally be the cause of pleasure, pain or desire'.[4] It depends on my psycho-physical condition what at any given time causes me pleasure or pain, and once the association between a given thing and the causing of

---

[1] E., P. III, prop. 57, note.   [2] Ibid., prop. 39, note.
[3] Ibid.   [4] E., P. III, prop. 15.

pleasure or pain has been set up, I necessarily tend to love or hate
that thing and to call it 'good' or 'bad'. Looked at in this way,
the emotions are passive; they are, properly speaking, 'passions'.
I am dominated by them. 'Different men can be affected by one
and the same object in different manners, and one and the same
man can be affected by one and the same object in different ways
at different times.'[1] Hence what one man loves another hates,
and what one man calls 'good' another man may call 'evil'. But
though we can distinguish different men according to their
different emotions there is no place for moral judgments, in so far
as these imply that a man is free to feel as he likes and to determine freely his judgments of good and evil.

Yet though 'all emotions have reference to pleasure, pain or
desire',[2] not all emotions are passive. For there are active emotions
which are not merely passive reflections of bodily modifications
but which flow from the mind in so far as it is active, that is, in so
far as it understands. The active emotions cannot, however, have
reference to pain; for 'we understand by pain that the mind's
power of thinking is diminished or hindered:[3] it is only emotions
of pleasure and desire which can be active emotions. These will
be 'adequate ideas', derived from the mind, in contrast with the
passive emotions which are confused or inadequate ideas. All
actions which follow from the emotions in so far as the mind is
active or understands, Spinoza refers to 'fortitude' (*fortitudo*); and
he distinguishes in fortitude two parts. The first he calls 'courage'
or 'magnanimity' (*animositas*) and the second 'nobility' (*generosi-
tas*). 'I understand by "courage" the desire by which each endeavours to preserve what is his own according to the dictate of
reason alone.'[4] Temperance, sobriety, presence of mind in danger,
and in general all actions which promote the good of the agent in
accordance with the dictate of reason alone fall under the general
heading of 'courage'. 'By "nobility" I understand the desire by
which each endeavours according to the dictate of reason alone to
help and to join to himself in friendship all other men.'[5] Modesty,
clemency and so on fall under the heading of 'nobility'. One
would expect, therefore, that moral advance would consist for
Spinoza in a liberation from passive emotions and in a changing
of passive emotions, so far as this is possible, into active emotions.
And this is in fact what one finds. Moral advance is thus a parallel

[1] *E.*, P. III, prop. 51.   [2] *Ibid.*, prop. 59.   [3] *Ibid.*
[4] *E.*, P. III, prop. 59, note.   [5] *Ibid.*

of intellectual advance, or rather, it is an aspect of the one advance, since passive emotions are called inadequate or confused ideas and active emotions adequate or clear ideas. Spinoza was essentially a 'rationalist'. One might expect a distinction between feeling and thinking; but Spinoza could make no sharp distinction between them because on his general principles every conscious state, including the 'enjoyment' of an emotion, involves having an idea. The more the idea proceeds from the mind itself as it thinks logically, the more 'active' the emotion will be.

5. 'Human lack of power in moderating and checking the emotions I call servitude. For a man who is submissive to his emotions has not power over himself but is in the hands of fortune to such an extent that he is often constrained, although he may see what is better for him, to follow what is worse.'[1] The last statement may appear to be inconsistent with Spinoza's explanation of the words 'good' and 'bad'. Indeed, he repeats his belief that 'as for the terms "good" and "bad", they indicate nothing positive in things considered in themselves, nor are they anything else than modes of thought or notions which we form from the comparison of things mutually'.[2] But we can and do form a general idea of man, a type of human nature, or, more accurately, an ideal of human nature. And the term 'good' can be understood as meaning that which 'we certainly know to be a means of our attaining the type of human nature which we have set before us', while the term 'bad' can be used to mean 'that which we know certainly prevents us from attaining the said type'.[3] Similarly, we can speak of men as more or less perfect in so far as they approach or are distant from the attainment of this type. If, then, we understand the terms 'good' and 'bad' in this way, we can say that it is possible for a man to know what is good, that is, what will certainly help him to attain the recognized type or ideal of human nature, and yet to do what is bad, that is, what will certainly hinder him from attaining this standard or ideal. The reason why this can happen is that the desires which arise from passive emotions, depending on external causes, can be stronger than the desire which arises from 'a true knowledge of good and evil', in so far as this is an emotion.[4] For example, desire for the attainment of an ideal, envisaged as a future goal, tends to be weaker than desire for a thing which is present and causes pleasure.

Opposed to the bondage of the passive emotions is the life of

---

[1] *E.*, P. IV, preface. [2] *Ibid.* [3] *Ibid.* [4] *E.*, P. IV, prop. 15.

reason, the life of the wise man. This is the life of virtue. For 'to act absolutely according to virtue is nothing else in us than to act under the guidance of reason, to live and to preserve one's being (these three have the same meaning) on the basis of seeking what is useful to oneself'.[1] The certainly useful is that which is truly conducive to understanding, and the certainly harmful or evil is that which hinders us from understanding. To understand is to be freed from the servitude of the emotions. 'An emotion which is a passion ceases to be a passion as soon as we form a clear and distinct idea of it.'[2] For it becomes an expression of the mind's activity rather than of its passivity. Take hatred, for example. This cannot become an active emotion in Spinoza's sense; for it is essentially a passive emotion or passion. But once I understand that men act from a necessity of nature I shall more easily overcome the hatred which I feel for anyone because he has injured me. Moreover, once I understand that hatred depends on nonrecognition of the fact that men are similar in nature and have a common good, I shall cease to wish evil to another. For I shall see that to wish evil to another is irrational. Hatred is felt by those who are governed by confused and inadequate ideas. If I understood the relation of all men to God, I should not feel hatred for any of them.

6. Understanding, therefore, is the path to freedom from the servitude of the passions. And the highest function of the mind is to know God. 'The greatest good of the mind is the knowledge of God, and the greatest virtue of the mind is to know God.'[3] For a man cannot understand anything greater than the infinite. And the more he understands God, so much the more he loves God. It may seem that the opposite should be the case. For in understanding that God is the cause of all things we understand that He is the cause of pain. 'But to this I make answer that, in so far as we understand the causes of pain, it ceases to be a passion, that is, it ceases to be a pain, and therefore in so far as we understand God to be the cause of pain we rejoice.'[4]

It is important to remember that for Spinoza God and Nature are the same. So far as we conceive things as contained in God and as following from the necessity of the divine nature, that is, so far as we conceive them in their relation to the infinite causal system of Nature, we conceive them 'under the species of eternity'

---

[1] *E.*, P. IV, prop. 24.   [2] *E.*, P. V, prop. 3.
[3] *E.*, P. IV, prop. 28.   [4] *E.*, P. V, prop. 18, note.

(*sub specie aeternitatis*). We conceive them as part of the logically connected infinite system. And in so far as we conceive ourselves and other things in this way we know God. Further, from this knowledge arises pleasure or satisfaction of mind. And pleasure accompanied by the idea of God as eternal cause is the 'intellectual love of God'.[1] This intellectual love of God is 'the very love of God with which God loves Himself, not in so far as He is infinite but in so far as He can be expressed through the essence of the human mind considered under the species of eternity'.[2] In fact, 'the love of God for men and the mind's intellectual love towards God is one and the same thing'.[3]

Spinoza declares that this love of God is 'our salvation, blessedness or liberty'.[4] But it is clear that the intellectual love of God must not be interpreted in a mystical sense or in the sense of love for a personal Being. The language is often the language of religion; and the language may perhaps express a personal piety. But, if so, that personal piety was rooted in Spinoza's religious upbringing rather than in his philosophic system. As far as the system alone is concerned, the love in question is more akin to the pleasure or mental satisfaction accompanying a scientist's vision of a complete explanation of Nature rather than to love in the sense of love between persons. And if one remembers that for Spinoza God is Nature, one will not be surprised at his famous saying that 'he who loves God cannot endeavour to bring it about that God should love him in return'.[5] Goethe interpreted this as an expression of Spinoza's boundless disinterestedness. This may be so; but at the same time it is clear that, given Spinoza's conception of God, it was impossible for him to speak of God as 'loving' men in any sense analogous to the normal sense of the word. Indeed, his statement that for a man to desire that God should love him in return would be to desire that 'the God whom he loves should not be God'[6] is perfectly correct, once given his understanding of 'God'.

7. Spinoza declared more than once that the human mind enjoys no existence apart from the body which can be described in terms of duration. He says, for example, that 'our mind can only be said to last, and its existence can be defined by a certain time only in so far as it involves the actual existence of the body'.[7] And it is generally agreed that he rejected the notion of the mind

[1] *E.*, P. V, prop. 32, corollary. [2] *Ibid.*, prop. 36. [3] *Ibid.*, corollary. [4] *Ibid.*, note.
[5] *Ibid.*, prop. 19. [6] *Ibid.*, proof. [7] *Ibid.*, prop. 23, note.

persisting everlastingly as a distinct entity after death. Indeed,
if the human mind consists of ideas which are the ideas of bodily
modifications, and if mind and body are one and the same thing,
viewed now under the attribute of thought and now under that
of extension, it is difficult to see how the mind could possibly
survive as a distinct entity after the body had disintegrated.

At the same time Spinoza spoke of the mind as being in some
sense 'eternal'; and it is not easy to understand precisely what he
meant by this. The statement that 'we are certain that the mind
is eternal in so far as it conceives things under the species of
eternity'[1] seems, if taken by itself, to suggest that only those
minds which enjoy the third degree of knowledge are eternal and
that they are eternal only in so far as they enjoy this intuition of
all things *sub specie aeternitatis*. Yet he also speaks in a way
which implies no such restriction but which seems to mean that
eternity belongs in some sense to the essence of the mind, that is,
every mind. 'The human mind,' he says, 'cannot be absolutely
destroyed with the human body, but there is some part of it which
remains eternal.'[2] Again, 'we feel and know that we are eternal'.[3]

I doubt whether a thoroughly satisfactory elucidation of
Spinoza's meaning is attainable which will do justice to all his
various pronouncements on the topic. In any case it is not
sufficient to say simply that Spinoza rejected the idea of the mind's
everlasting duration and that he affirmed eternity as a quality of
the mind 'here and now'. For it is by no means clear what is
meant by saying that the mind is eternal here and now. Indeed,
it is the very point which stands in need of explanation. But since
Spinoza was careful about terms one ought to be able to gain some
light from looking at his definition of eternity. 'I understand
eternity to be existence itself, in so far as it is conceived to follow
necessarily from the definition of an eternal thing.'[4] Spinoza then
explains that 'the existence of a thing, as an eternal truth, is conceived to be the same as its essence'. One can say, then, that the
human mind is 'eternal' in so far as it is conceived to follow
necessarily from the nature of substance or God. Since connections in Nature are akin to logical connections, one can regard
the infinite system of Nature as a logical and timeless system, and
in that system each human mind, expressing the idea or truth of a
mode of extension, is a necessary moment. In the infinite system

---

[1] *E.*, P. V, prop. 31, note.   [2] *Ibid.*, prop. 23.
[3] *Ibid.*, note.   [4] *E.*, P. I, def. 8.

I have an inalienable place. In this sense every human mind is 'eternal'! And in so far as a given mind rises to the third level or degree of knowledge and views things *sub specie aeternitatis* it is conscious of its eternity.

Spinoza seems to have meant something of this sort when he called the human mind eternal in essence. He may have meant something more; but, if he did, one does not seem to be in a position to say what it was. It is perhaps just conceivable that a relic, as it were, of the theory that the mind's 'centre' is divine and eternal appears in his statements; but the safest way of interpreting his meaning is to interpret it in the light of his definition of eternity. Duration applies only to finite things thought of as succeeding one another. And in terms of duration my mind does not survive bodily death. From the point of view of duration it was once true that I shall exist, it is now true that I exist, and it will be true that I have existed. But if one leaves the point of view of duration and looks at things as following necessarily from the eternal substance, God, without any reference to time—much as one looks at the conclusions of a mathematical theorem as following necessarily and timelessly from the premisses—one can say that my existence is in some sense an eternal truth. That is why Spinoza speaks of the mind's eternity as lacking any relation to time: the mind is eternal just as much 'before' as 'after' the existence of the body as a distinct finite entity.[1] 'We do not attribute duration save as long as the body lasts';[2] but the mind can be considered as a necessary moment in God's consciousness of Himself, just as the intellectual love of God is a moment of God's love of Himself, when both are considered *sub specie aeternitatis*. Whether all this is fully intelligible is another question. But Spinoza's point seems to be that the mind, in so far as it actively understands, is 'an eternal mode of thinking' and that all eternal modes of thinking 'constitute at the same time the eternal and infinite intellect of God'.[3] This much at least is clear, that Spinoza rejected the Christian doctrine of immortality. And one can hardly suppose that when he called the mind 'eternal' he meant no more than that the wise enjoy the third degree of knowledge while they enjoy the third degree of knowledge. In some sense, it seems, all human minds were for him eternal in essence. But the precise sense in which this should be understood remains obscure.

[1] Cf. *E.*, P. V, prop. 33, note.   [2] *Ibid.*, proof.   [3] *E.* P. V, prop. 40, note.

8. There are marked affinities between Spinoza's moral theory and the Stoic ethics. His ideal of the wise man and the emphasis he lays on knowledge and on understanding the place of individual things in the whole divine system of Nature, his belief that this knowledge protects the wise man from undue disturbance of mind in face of the vicissitudes of life and of the blows of fate or fortune, the emphasis he lays on life according to reason and on the acquisition of virtue for its own sake, all bear a similarity to analogous themes in the Stoic philosophy. Moreover, though we miss in Spinoza the noble statements of Stoic writers about the kinship of all men as children of God, he was no mere individualist. 'Nothing can be desired by men more excellent for their self-preservation than that all should so agree with all that they compose the minds of all into one mind and the bodies of all into one body, that all endeavour at the same time as much as possible to preserve their being, and that all seek at the same time what is useful to them all as a body. From which it follows those men who are governed by reason, that is, men who, under the guidance of reason, seek what is useful to them, desire nothing for themselves which they do not also desire for the rest of mankind. And therefore they are just, faithful and honourable.'[1] A passage like this may not attain the level of nobility sometimes reached by Epictetus and Marcus Aurelius; but it at least shows that when Spinoza affirmed that the tendency to preserve one's own being is the fundamental drive he did not mean thereby to teach or promote atomic individualism. Indeed, his monism, like that of the Stoics, leads logically to some doctrine of human solidarity.

The point of similarity, however, between Spinozism and Stoicism to which I want to draw attention is their common acceptance of determinism. For the denial of human freedom raises an important problem in regard to ethics. In what sense can there be a moral theory if determinism is once accepted? It is at any rate questionable whether there is any sense in exhorting men to act in a particular way if each is determined to act in a certain manner, though Spinoza might, of course, reply that the exhorter is determined to exhort and that the exhortation is one of the factors which determine the conduct of the man exhorted. And is there any sense in blaming a man for performing a given action if he was not free to perform any other action? If, then, one understands by 'moral theory' an exhortatory ethic, in the

---

[1] *E.*, P. IV, prop. 18, note.

sense of one which lays down the way in which human beings ought to act, though they are capable of acting otherwise even in the same set of circumstances, one must say that acceptance of determinism rules out the possibility of a moral theory. If on the other hand by 'moral theory' one means a theory about human conduct which consists of an analysis of the ways in which different types of men behave, it seems, at first sight at least, that a moral theory is perfectly possible even though determinism is accepted.

Spinoza did not, of course, deny that we often 'feel' free, in the sense that we feel responsible for making a given choice or performing some action. It is obvious that we can often give a motive for acting in a certain way, and it is obvious that we do in fact sometimes deliberate about our course of action and finally come to a decision. These psychological facts are so obvious that Spinoza would not have sought to deny them. What he did maintain, however, was that we feel ourselves to be free because we do not understand the causes of our actions and the causes which determine us to desire certain things and to have certain motives. If we imagine a falling stone suddenly endowed with consciousness, it might think that it was falling of its own volition, since it would not perceive the cause of its movement; but it would not be free not to fall, even if it imagined that it was.[1] And it is in view of this determinist position that the claim has been made on Spinoza's behalf that he had no intention of expounding an exhortatory but only an analytic ethic.

There is certainly much to be said in favour of this claim. Writing to Oldenburg, Spinoza remarks that though all are excusable it does not follow that all men are blessed. 'A horse is excusable for being a horse and not a man; but, nevertheless, it must needs be a horse and not a man. He who goes mad from the bite of a dog is excusable, yet he is rightly suffocated. Lastly, he who cannot govern his desires and keep them in check with the fear of the laws, though his weakness may be excusable, yet cannot enjoy with contentment the knowledge and love of God but necessarily perishes.'[2] In other words, even though all men are determined and so 'excusable', there remains an objective difference between those who are the slaves of their passions and those who enjoy 'blessedness', the intellectual love of God. Again, in a letter to Van Blyenbergh Spinoza says that 'in the language of philosophy it cannot be said that God desires anything of any

---

[1] Cf. *Letter 58.*   [2] *Letter 78.*

man, or that anything is displeasing or pleasing to Him: all these are human qualities and have no place in God'.[1] But it does not follow that murderers and almsgivers are equally perfect. Similar statements appear in a letter to von Tschirnhausen. In answer to the objection that in his view all wickedness is excusable, Spinoza retorts: 'What then? Wicked men are not less to be feared and are not less harmful when they are wicked from necessity.'[2] Finally, in the *Ethics* Spinoza remarks that it is only in civil society that commonly accepted meanings are given to terms like 'good', 'bad', 'sin' (which, he says, is nothing else but disobedience punishable by the State), 'merit', 'just' and 'unjust'. And his conclusion is that 'just and unjust, sin and merit, are merely extrinsic notions, not attributes which explain the nature of the mind'.[3]

It is only to be expected, of course, that Spinoza should sometimes speak in another way, for the language of freedom and of moral obligation is too much embedded in our ordinary speech for it to be avoided. And we find him saying, for example, that his doctrine 'teaches us in what manner we should act with regard to the affairs of fortune' and that it 'teaches us not to despise, hate or ridicule anyone, to be angry with or envy no one'.[4] But it is not simply a question of a phrase here or there or of isolated statements. The *Treatise on the Correction of the Understanding* was intended as a guide to the attainment of true knowledge. 'A method must be thought out of healing the understanding and purifying it at the beginning, that it may with the greatest success understand things correctly. From this every one will be able to see that I wish to direct all sciences in one direction or to one end, namely, to attain the greatest possible human perfection: and thus everything in the sciences which does not promote this endeavour must be rejected as useless, that is, in a word, all our endeavour and thoughts must be directed to this end.'[5] It would have been open to Spinoza to say that some people enjoy a lower degree of knowledge and others a higher and that nothing can be done to enable the former to render their ideas adequate and clear and to free themselves from the servitude of the passions. But he evidently supposed that intellectual progress is possible through efforts. And in this case moral progress is achieved, for Spinoza, through purifying confused and inadequate ideas. He explicitly

---

[1] *Letter 23.* [2] *Letter 58.* [3] *E.*, P. IV, prop. 37, note 2.
[4] *E.*, P. II, prop. 49, note. [5] *T.*, 2, 16.

speaks of man as being incited 'to seek means which should lead him to perfection'[1] and of 'striving' to acquire a better nature.[2] The concluding sentences of the *Ethics* are especially significant in this respect. 'If the road I have shown to lead to this (that is, to 'power of the mind over emotions, or the freedom of the mind') is very difficult, it can yet be discovered. And clearly it must be very hard when it is so seldom found. For how could it be that it is neglected practically by all, if salvation were close at hand and could be found without difficulty? But all excellent things are as difficult as they are rare.'[3] Whatever some commentators may say, it is hard to see how this is compatible with a consistent doctrine of determinism. It is all very well to say that it is a change of point of view which is involved rather than a change in con- duct. Change in conduct depends for Spinoza on a change in point of view; and how could one change one's point of view unless one were free? It may be said that some people are determined to change their point of view. But in this case why point out the road to them and try to convince them? It is difficult to avoid the impression that Spinoza tried to have it both ways; to maintain a thorough determinism, based on a metaphysical theory, and at the same time to propound an ethic which makes sense only if deter- minism is not absolute.

[1] *T.*, 2, 13.   [2] *Ibid*.   [3] *E.*, P. V, prop. 42, note.

CHAPTER XIV

SPINOZA (5)

Natural right—The foundation of political society—Sovereignty and government—Relations between States—Freedom and toleration—Spinoza's influence and different estimates of his philosophy.

1. SPINOZA'S approach to political theory closely resembles that of Hobbes, whose *De Cive* and *Leviathan* he had studied. Both believed that every man is conditioned by nature to pursue his own advantage, and both tried to show that the formation of political society, with all the restrictions on human liberty which it involves, is justifiable in terms of rational or enlightened self-interest. Man is so constituted that in order to avoid the greater evil of anarchy and chaos he has to join with other men in organized social life, even at the cost of restrictions to his natural right to do whatever he is able to do.

Spinoza, like Hobbes, speaks of 'natural law' and 'natural right'. But in order to understand Spinoza's use of these terms it is necessary to prescind altogether from the theological background of the Scholastic conception of natural law and natural rights. When Spinoza speaks of 'natural law' he is not thinking of a moral law which answers to man's nature but which obliges him morally as a free being to act in a certain way: he is thinking of the way of acting which any finite thing, including man, is determined by Nature to pursue. 'By the right and ordinance of Nature I merely mean those natural laws by which we conceive every individual to be conditioned by Nature so as to live and act in a given way.'[1] Fishes, for example, are so conditioned by Nature that 'the greater devour the less by sovereign natural right'.[2] In order to understand Spinoza's meaning it is essential to remember that to say that large fish have 'the right' to devour small fish is simply to say that large fish can devour fish and that they are so made that they do so, given the occasion. 'For it is certain that Nature, taken in the abstract, has sovereign right to do anything she can; in other words, her right is co-extensive with her power.'[3]

---

[1] *Theologico-Political Treatise*, 16. This work will be referred to as *T.-P.T.*
[2] *Ibid.* [3] *Ibid.*

The rights of any individual, therefore, are limited only by the limits of his power. And the limits of his power are determined by his nature. Therefore, 'as the wise man has sovereign right ... to live according to the laws of reason, so also the ignorant and foolish man has sovereign right to ... live according to the laws of desire'.[1] An ignorant or foolish man is no more bound to live according to the dictates of enlightened reason 'than a cat is bound to live by the laws of the nature of a lion'.[2]

Nobody can justifiably accuse Spinoza of not having made his 'realistic' position perfectly plain. Whether a given individual is led by enlightened reason or by the passions, he has a sovereign right to seek and to take for himself whatever he thinks useful, 'whether by force, cunning, entreaty or any other means'.[3] The cause of this is that Nature is not limited by the laws of human reason, which aims at man's preservation. Nature's aims, so far as one can speak of Nature's aims, 'have reference to the eternal order of Nature wherein man is but a speck'.[4] If anything seems to us evil or absurd in Nature, it is simply because we are ignorant of the system of Nature and the interdependence of the members of the system and because we want everything arranged according to the dictates of human reason and interest. If we once succeed in transcending anthropomorphic and anthropocentric ways of regarding Nature, we shall understand that natural right is limited only by desire and power and that desire and power are conditioned by the nature of a given individual.

The same doctrine is repeated in the *Political Treatise*. Spinoza there reaffirms his thesis that if we are treating of the universal power or right of Nature, we can recognize no distinction between desires which are engendered by reason and desires which are engendered by other causes. 'The natural right of universal nature, and consequently of every individual thing, extends as far as its power; and accordingly whatever any man does according to the laws of his nature he does by the highest natural right, and he has as much right over Nature as he has power.'[5] Men are led more by desire than by reason. Hence one can say that natural power and right is limited by appetite rather than by reason. Nature 'forbids' only what we do not desire and have no power to obtain or to do.

Since every man has a natural impulse to self-maintenance and

---

[1] *T.-P.T.*, 16.   [2] *Ibid.*   [3] *Ibid.*   [4] *Ibid.*
[5] *Political Treatise*, 2, 4. This work will be referred to as *P.T.*

self-preservation, he is, therefore, naturally entitled to take any means which he thinks will help him to preserve himself. And he is entitled to treat as an enemy anyone who hinders the fulfilment of this natural impulse. Indeed, as they are very liable to the passions of anger, envy and hatred in general, 'men are naturally enemies'.[1]

Spinoza's statement in the *Ethics* that just and unjust, sin and merit are 'merely extrinsic notions'[2] was quoted in the last chapter; and it can now be understood in its appropriate context. In the state of nature it is 'just' for me to take whatever I think useful for my preservation and welfare: 'justice' is measured simply by desire and power. In organized society, however, certain property-rights and certain rules for the transference of property are established, and by common agreement terms like 'just', 'unjust' and 'right' are given definite meanings. When understood in this way they are 'merely extrinsic notions', referring not to properties of actions considered in themselves but to actions considered in relation to norms and rules set up by and resting on agreement. One can add that the binding force of agreements rests on the power to enforce them. In the state of nature a man who has made an agreement with another is entitled 'by nature' to break the agreement directly he comes to think, rightly or wrongly, that it will be advantageous to him to do so.[3] This doctrine is simply a logical application of Spinoza's theory that, if we look at things simply from the point of view of Nature at large, the only limits of 'right' are desire and power.

2. However, 'everyone wishes to live as far as possible securely beyond the reach of fear, and this would be quite impossible so long as everyone did everything he liked and reason's claim was lowered to a par with those of hatred and anger. . . . When we reflect that men without mutual help, or the aid of reason, must needs live most miserably, we shall see plainly that men must necessarily come to an agreement to live together as securely and as well as possible.'[4] Further, 'without mutual help men can hardly support life and cultivate the mind'.[5] One's own power and natural right is thus in constant danger of being rendered ineffective unless one combines with others to form a stable society. One can thus say that natural right itself points to the formation of organized society. 'And if this is why the Schoolmen want to call

[1] *P.T.*, 2, 14.   [2] *E.*, P. IV, prop. 37, note 2.
[3] *P.T.*, 2, 12.   [4] *T-P.T.*, 16.   [5] *P.T.*, 2, 15.

man a sociable animal—I mean because men in the state of nature can hardly be independent—I have nothing to say against them.'[1]

The social compact thus rests on enlightened self-interest, and the restrictions of social life are justified by being shown to constitute a lesser threat to one's welfare than the perils of the state of nature. 'It is a universal law of human nature that no one ever neglects anything which he judges to be good, except with the hope of gaining a greater good or from the fear of a greater evil; nor does anyone endure an evil except for the sake of avoiding a greater evil or gaining a greater good.'[2] No one, then, will make a compact except to gain a greater good or avoid a greater evil. 'And we may, therefore, conclude that a compact is made valid only by its utility, without which it becomes null and void.'[3]

3. In concluding a social compact individuals hand over their natural rights to the sovereign power; and 'the possessor of sovereign power, whether he be one, or many, or the whole body politic, has the sovereign right of imposing any commands he pleases'.[4] It is, indeed, impossible to transfer all power, and so all right; for there are some things which follow necessarily from human nature and which cannot be altered by the command of authority. For example, it is useless for the sovereign to command men not to love what is pleasurable to them. But apart from cases like this the subject is bound to obey the commands of the sovereign. And it is through the laws enacted by the sovereign that justice and injustice arise. 'Wrong-doing cannot be conceived of but under dominion. . . . Like, then, wrong-doing and obedience in their strict sense, so also justice and injustice cannot be conceived of except under dominion.'[5]

Spinoza did not, however, intend to justify tyrannical government. In his opinion, as in that of Seneca, 'no one can long retain a tyrant's sway'.[6] For if the sovereign acts in a thoroughly capricious, arbitrary and irrational manner, he will eventually raise such opposition that he will lose his power to govern. And loss of power to govern means loss of right to govern. In his own best interests, then, the sovereign is unlikely to exceed reasonable limits in the exercise of authority.

In the *Political Treatise* Spinoza discusses three general forms of 'dominion', monarchy, aristocracy and democracy. But it is

---

[1] *P.T.*, 2, 15.   [2] *T-P.T.*, 16.   [3] *Ibid.*
[4] *Ibid.*   [5] *P.T.*, 2, 19 and 23.   [6] *T-P.T.*, 16.

unnecessary to enter upon his treatment of this theme. Of more
interest is his general principle that 'that commonwealth is most
powerful and most independent which is founded and guided by
reason'.[1] The purpose of civil society is 'nothing else but peace
and security of life. And therefore that dominion is the best where
men pass their lives in unity and the laws are kept unbroken.'[2]
In the *Theologico-Political Treatise* he states that the most rational
State is also the freest, since to live freely is 'to live with full
consent under the entire guidance of reason'.[3] And this sort of
life is best secured in a democracy, 'which may be defined as a
society which wields all its power as a whole'.[4] A democracy is
'of all forms of government the most natural and the most consonant with individual liberty. In it no one transfers his natural
right so absolutely that he has no further voice in affairs; he only
hands it over to the majority of a society of which he is a unit.
Thus all men remain equals, as they were in the state of nature.'[5]
In a democracy, says Spinoza, irrational commands are less to be
feared than in any other form of constitution; 'for it is almost
impossible that the majority of a people, especially if it is a large
one, should agree in an irrational design. And, moreover, the basis
and aim of a democracy is to avoid the desires as irrational and to
bring men as far as possible under the control of reason, so that
they may live in peace and harmony.'[6]

4. In discussing the best form of constitution in an *a priori*
fashion Spinoza trod in the footsteps of predecessors like Aristotle.
To look to him for a real sense of historical development is to look
in vain. What distinguishes him from the great Greek writers on
politics and from the Scholastics is the emphasis which he lays
on power. In the state of nature right is limited only by power,
and in civil society sovereignty rests on power. The members of
a State are, indeed, bound to obey the laws, but the fundamental
reason for this is that the sovereign has the power to enforce them.
This is not the whole of the story, of course. Spinoza was in some
respects a tough political 'realist'; but at the same time he
emphasized the function of the State to provide theframework
in which men could live rationally. He considered perhaps that
most men are led by desire rather than by reason and that restraint
is, as it were, the fundamental purpose of law. But his ideal certainly was that law should be rational and that human beings

[1] *P.T.*, 5, 1.   [2] *P.T.*, 5, 2.   [3] *T-P.T.*, 16.
[4] *Ibid.*   [5] *Ibid.*   [6] *Ibid.*

should be guided in their private conduct and in their obedience
to law by reason rather than by fear. All the same, it is on power
that political authority rests, even if this power is never misused.
And if the power disappears, the claim to authority disappears.

The importance attributed by Spinoza to power comes out
clearly in his view of the relations between States. Different
States may enter into agreements with one another, but there is
no authority to enforce such agreements, as there is in the case of
contracts between fellow members of a State. The relations
between States are governed, therefore, not by law but by power
and self-interest. A covenant between different States 'is valid so
long as its basis of danger or advantage is in force. No one enters
into an engagement, or is bound to stand by his compacts, unless
there is a hope of some accruing good, or the fear of some evil: if
this basis is removed, the compact thereby becomes void. This
has been abundantly shown by experience.'[1] States, then, in their
relations with one another are in the position of individuals considered apart from the social compact and from the organized
society to which the compact gives rise. Spinoza appeals to
experience for confirmation of his theory, and in order to recognize
that it gives expression to historical fact one has only to reflect on
the modern discussions about the need for some international
authority.

5. In spite of the emphasis he laid on power, Spinoza's ideal
was, as we have seen, the life of reason. And one of the main
features of a rationally organized society would be, he was convinced, religious toleration. Like Hobbes, he was filled with
horror at the thought of religious wars and divisions, but his idea
of the proper remedy was different from that of Hobbes. For
whereas Hobbes tended to think that the only remedy lay in subordinating religion to the civil power, that is, in a thorough-going
Erastianism, Spinoza emphasized toleration in the matter of
religious beliefs. This attitude followed naturally from his philosophical principles. For he made a sharp distinction between the
language of philosophy and the language of theology. The
function of the latter is not to give scientific information but
rather to impel people to adopt certain lines of conduct. Provided,
therefore, that the line of conduct to which a certain set of religious
beliefs naturally leads is not prejudicial to the good of society, full
liberty should be allowed to those who find help in this set of

[1] *T.-P.T.*, 16.

beliefs. Speaking of the religious freedom enjoyed in Holland, he says that he wishes to show that 'not only can such freedom be granted without prejudice to the public peace but also that without such freedom piety cannot flourish nor the public peace be secure'.[1] And he concludes that 'every one should be free to choose for himself the foundations of his creed and that faith should be judged only by its fruits'.[2]

Right over one's judgments, feelings and beliefs is something that one cannot alienate by any social compact. Every man is 'by indefeasible natural right the master of his own thoughts', and he 'cannot, without disastrous results, be compelled to speak only according to the dictates of the supreme power'.[3] Indeed, 'the true aim of government,' says Spinoza, 'is liberty'. For 'the object of government is not to change men from rational beings into beasts or puppets, but to enable them to develop their minds and bodies in security and to employ their reason unshackled'.[4] Toleration, therefore, should not be confined to the sphere of religion. Provided that a man criticizes the sovereign from rational conviction and not out of a desire to make trouble or to promote sedition, he should be allowed to speak his mind freely. Regard for the public welfare sets a limit to free speech; mere agitation, inciting to rebellion or to disobedience to the law, and disturbance of peace cannot reasonably be allowed. But rational discussion and criticism do good rather than harm. If the attempt is made to crush liberty and to regiment thought and speech, great harm results. It is not possible to suppress all freedom of thought; and, if freedom of speech is suppressed, the result is that fools, flatterers, the insincere and the unscrupulous flourish. Moreover, 'freedom is absolutely necessary for progress in science and the liberal arts'.[5] And this freedom is best secured in a democracy, 'the most natural form of government', in which 'every one submits to the control of authority over his actions but not over his judgment and reason'.[6]

It is as well to have brought out this side of Spinoza's political theory. For undue concentration on those elements of his theory which are common to him and Hobbes may easily give a wrong impression: it tends to conceal the fact that his ideal was the life of reason and that he did not laud power for its own sake, even though he was convinced not only that power does play a most

---

[1] T-P.T., preface. [2] Ibid. [3] T-P.T., 20.
[4] Ibid. [5] Ibid. [6] Ibid.

important part in political life but that it must do so, for metaphysical and psychological reasons. Moreover, although Spinoza
himself clearly did not believe in a definite divine revelation of
statable truths, so that his premises were different from those of
believers in such a revelation, the problem which he discussed is a
real problem for all. On the one hand, faith is in any case something which cannot be forced; and the attempt to enforce it leads
to evil results. On the other hand, complete and unlimited toleration is, as Spinoza saw, impracticable. No government can permit
incitement to political assassination, for example, or unhindered
propaganda for beliefs which lead directly to crime. The problem
for Spinoza, as for those of a later age, is that of combining the
greatest possible amount of freedom with regard for the public
good. It is hardly to be expected that all will agree about the
precise limits of toleration; and in any case this question can
scarcely be settled *a priori* and without reference to historical
circumstances. To give a very obvious example, all reasonable
people agree that in times of war and national crisis liberties may
have to be restricted in a way which would be undesirable at other
times. But the general principles that Governments should foster
rather than destroy liberty and that liberty is required for true
cultural development are as valid now as they were when Spinoza
enunciated them.

6. For a considerable time after his death Spinoza was often
called an 'atheist', and so far as any attention was paid to him he
was generally attacked. The main reason, of course, why he was
called an atheist was his identification of God with Nature. The
charge of atheism has been indignantly repudiated by many of
Spinoza's modern admirers; but the question cannot be settled so
simply, and certainly not by the use of emotive language on either
side. The only proper way of settling it in a rational manner is to
decide on the meaning to be attached to the word 'God' and then
to decide whether Spinoza did or did not deny the existence of
God so understood. But even this procedure is not so simple to
follow in practice as might at first appear. It might reasonably be
argued that if the word 'God' is understood in the Judaeo-Christian
sense, as meaning a personal Being transcending Nature, the
charge of 'atheism' was correct. For it is true that Spinoza denied
the existence of a personal Being transcending Nature. Thus when
his Lutheran biographer, John Colerus, says in his *Life of Benedict
de Spinoza* that the philosopher 'takes the liberty to use the word

"God" and to use it in a sense unknown to all Christians' and that Spinoza's doctrine is therefore atheism, the statement, it might be said, is obviously true if one understands by 'atheism' denial of the existence of God in the sense in which the word is understood by Christians. Spinoza, however, might reply that he defined God as the absolutely infinite Being and that Christians also understood by 'God' the infinite Being, though they did not, in his opinion, understand the implications of this definition. His identification of God with Nature, he might say, was the expression not of atheism but of a true understanding of what is meant by 'God', if 'God' is defined as the absolutely infinite Being. Still, the fact remains that Christians, whether philosophers or not, affirm God's transcendence and do not identify God with Nature; and if the term 'God' is understood in the way in which all Christians understand it, whether they are philosophers or not, it can be said that Spinoza was an 'atheist' in that he denied the existence of God as so understood. It is difficult to see why the charge of atheism, if so interpreted, should raise indignation. Writers who wax indignant over the charge are presumably either thinking of the abusive epithets which were sometimes added to it or protesting against the use of the term 'God' in an exclusively Christian sense.

But it was not only by the theologians that Spinoza was criticized and belittled. In his *Dictionary* Bayle not only represented Spinoza as an atheist but also condemned his philosophy as absurd. And Diderot took more or less the same line in his article on Spinoza in the *Encyclopaedia*. Indeed, the philosophers of the French Enlightenment in general, though they respected Spinoza as a man and were glad of the opportunity of presenting the example of a virtuous yet highly unorthodox thinker, did not extend their respect to his philosophy. They regarded it as obscure sophistry and a juggling with geometrical and metaphysical terms and formulae. Hume remarked that 'the fundamental principle of the atheism of Spinoza' lies in his monism, and he called this a 'hideous hypothesis'.[1] But as he coupled this with the assertion that 'the doctrine of the immateriality, simplicity, and indivisibility of a thinking substance is a true atheism and will serve to justify all those sentiments for which Spinoza is so universally infamous', one may feel a certain doubt about Hume's horror at Spinoza's 'hypothesis'. It is clear, however, that he considered

---

[1] *Treatise of Human Nature*. I. 4, 5.

both Descartes' doctrine of an immaterial thinking substance and Spinoza's theory of a unique substance to be unintelligible.

Attacked by theologians on the one hand and by philosophers on the other, the philosophy of Spinoza hardly appeared worthy of serious consideration. In the course of time, however, the tide of opinion turned. In 1780 Lessing had his famous conversation with Jacobi in which he expressed his appreciation of and indebtedness to Spinoza. Herder too appreciated Spinoza, and Novalis described him in an oft-quoted phrase as 'a God-intoxicated man'. Heine wrote warmly of Spinoza, and Goethe spoke of the Jewish philosopher's influence upon him, of the calm and resignation which the *Ethics* brought to his soul and of the wide and disinterested view of reality which the work opened up. The German romantics in general (I do not mean to imply that Goethe can properly be labelled a 'romantic', though he was able to give expression to romanticism) found or thought they found in Spinoza a kindred soul. For them, with their feeling for the totality and their inclination to a poetic and quasi-mystical view of Nature, Spinoza was the 'pantheist' who did not place God in a remote transcendence but saw in Nature a theophany or immanent manifestation of God. And German philosophers like Schelling and Hegel, the philosophers of the romantic movement, brought Spinozism into the main stream of European philosophy. For Hegel, Spinoza's system was an integral and important stage in the development of European thought. Spinoza's idea of God as substance was inadequate; for God should be conceived as Spirit. But the charge of atheism was unfounded. 'Spinozism,' says Hegel, 'might really just as well or even better have been termed Acosmism, since according to its teaching it is not to the world, finite existence, the universe, that reality and permanency are to be ascribed, but rather to God alone as the substantial.'[1] In England Coleridge wrote enthusiastically of Spinoza, and Shelley began a translation of the *Tractatus theologico-politicus*.

While he was regarded by his earlier critics as an atheist and by the romantics as a pantheist, the tendency of a number of modern writers is to represent Spinoza as a speculative forerunner of a completely scientific view of the world. For he made a sustained attempt always to give a naturalistic explanation of events without having recourse to explanations in terms either of the

[1] *Lectures on the History of Philosophy*, translated by E. S. Haldane and F. H. Simons, vol. III, p. 281.

supernatural and transcendent or of final causes. Those who stress this aspect of Spinoza's thought do not forget that he was a metaphysician and that he aimed at giving an 'ultimate' explanation of the world. But they think that his idea of Nature as one organic cosmos which can be understood without postulating anything outside Nature can be considered a vast speculative programme for scientific research, though the method required by scientific research is not the method which Spinoza employed in his philosophy. For them, therefore, the central idea of Spinozism is the idea of Nature as a system which can be scientifically investigated. The Hegelian interpretation of Spinoza is put on one side, and one can say perhaps that the 'atheistic' interpretation comes once more to the fore, provided that one remembers that if these writers used the word 'atheism' in this connection it would not have for them the abusive overtones which it had for Spinoza's early theological critics.

It is difficult to say precisely how much truth there is in each of these lines of interpretation. To read the spirit and atmosphere of the romantic movement into Spinoza's thought is certainly incorrect, and if one had to choose between a romantic and a naturalistic interpretation, one would certainly do better by preferring the latter. Yet though Spinoza's thought seems to have moved far away from its Jewish origins in the direction of a naturalistic monism, his doctrines of the infinite Godhead, and of the unknown divine attributes, suggest that the religious origins of his thought were by no means completely obscured by its later development. Moreover, we must remember that Spinoza was not interested simply in tracing causal connections and exhibiting the infinite series of causes as a self-enclosed system. His chief work was not entitled the *Ethics* for nothing: he was interested in the attainment of true peace of mind and of freedom from the servitude of the passions. In a famous passage at the beginning of the *Treatise on the Correction of the Understanding* he speaks of his experience of the vanity and futility of riches, fame and pleasure, of the search for supreme happiness and the greatest good. For 'the love towards a thing eternal and infinite alone feeds the mind with pleasure, and it is free from all pain; so it is much to be desired and to be sought out with all our might'.[1] Again, 'I wish to direct all sciences in one direction, or to one end, namely, to attain the greatest possible human perfection: and thus everything

[1] *T.*, I, 10.

in the sciences which does not promote this endeavour must be rejected as useless, that is, in a word, all our endeavours and thoughts must be directed to this one end.'[1] And in a letter to Van Blyenbergh he says: 'Meanwhile I know (and this knowledge gives me the highest contentment and peace of mind) that all things come to pass by the power and unchangeable decree of a Being supremely perfect.'[2]

But one must not let oneself be misled by the use of phrases such as 'the intellectual love of God' into interpreting Spinoza as though he were a religious mystic like Eckhart. Indeed, in interpreting Spinoza it is essential to remember that terms and phrases must be understood in the sense of his definitions and not in the sense which they bear in 'ordinary language'. In Spinoza's philosophy terms are given a technical sense, and this is often different from the meaning which we would naturally and spontaneously attach to them. The notion that the philosophy of Spinoza was a philosophy of religious mysticism arises only if one persists in neglecting his definitions of terms like 'God' and 'love' and the light shed on those definitions by the system as a whole.

[1] *T.*, 2, 16.   [2] *Letter 21*.

CHAPTER XV

LEIBNIZ (1)

Life—The De arte combinatoria *and the idea of harmony—*
Writings—Different interpretations of Leibniz's thought.

1. GOTTFRIED WILHELM LEIBNIZ was born at Leipzig in 1646, his father being professor of moral philosophy in the university. A precocious boy, Leibniz studied both Greek and Scholastic philosophy, and he tells us, speaking of himself at about the age of thirteen, that he read Suárez with as much facility as people are accustomed to read romances. At the age of fifteen he entered the university and studied under James Thomasius. Making the acquaintance of 'modern' thinkers like Bacon, Hobbes, Gassendi, Descartes, Kepler and Galileo, he found in them examples of a 'better philosophy'. And according to his reminiscences he debated within himself during solitary walks whether to retain the Aristotelian theory of substantial forms and final causes or to adopt mechanism. Mechanism prevailed, though he later tried to combine Aristotelian elements with new ideas. Indeed, the influence of his early studies of Aristotelianism and Scholasticism is obvious in his later writings; and of all the leading philosophers of the pre-Kantian 'modern' period it was probably Leibniz who possessed the most extensive knowledge of the Scholastics. He was certainly much better acquainted with them than was Spinoza. And his baccalaureate thesis (1663) on the principle of individuation was written under the influence of Scholasticism, though of the nominalist direction.

In 1663 Leibniz went to Jena, where he studied mathematics under Erhard Weigel. He then gave himself to the study of jurisprudence and took the doctorate in Law at Altdorf in 1667. The offer of a university chair at Altdorf was refused, as Leibniz said that he had very different things in view. Having been given a post in the court of the Elector of Mainz, he was sent on a diplomatic mission to Paris in 1672, where he made the acquaintance of men like Malebranche and Arnauld. In 1673 he visited England, meeting Boyle and Oldenburg. Returning to Paris, he remained there until 1676, the final year of his stay being memorable for his discovery of the infinitesimal calculus. Though

Leibniz was unaware of the fact, Newton had already written on the same subject. But the latter was very slow to publish his results and did not do so until 1687, whereas Leibniz published his in 1684. Hence the unprofitable dispute about priority in discovery.

On his way back to Germany Leibniz visited Spinoza. He had already been in correspondence with Spinoza, and he was extremely curious about the latter's philosophy. The precise relations between Leibniz and Spinoza are not very clear. The former criticized and continued to criticize the latter's theories, and when he had studied Spinoza's posthumously published works he made persistent attempts to compromise Descartes by representing Spinozism as the logical outcome of Cartesianism. The philosophy of Descartes, according to Leibniz, leads by way of Spinozism to atheism. On the other hand, it is clear that Leibniz's insatiable curiosity in intellectual matters produced in him a lively interest in Spinoza's doctrine, even if he made no very profound study of it, and that he found it stimulating. Moreover, in view of Leibniz's diplomatic character it has even been suggested that his strong repudiation of Spinozism was partly inspired by his desire to maintain a reputation for orthodoxy. But though Leibniz was a diplomat, a courtier and a man of the world, which Spinoza was not, and though he had an eye to edifying his various patrons and eminent acquaintances, there is no real reason, I think, for believing that his opposition to Spinozism was insincere. He had already arrived at some of the main ideas of his own philosophy by the time he studied Spinoza, and though certain affinities between their respective philosophies stimulated his interest and probably also his eagerness to dissociate himself publicly from Spinoza, the differences between their respective positions were far-reaching.

Owing to his association with the House of Hanover, Leibniz found himself involved in compiling the history of the family; that is, the Brunswick family. But his interests and activities were manifold. In 1682 he founded at Leipzig the *Acta eruditorum*, and in 1700 he became the first president of the Society of the Sciences at Berlin, which later became the Prussian Academy. In addition to an interest in founding learned societies he occupied himself with the problem of uniting the Christian Confessions. First of all he endeavoured to find common ground for agreement between Catholics and Protestants. Later, when he realized that the difficulties were greater than had been anticipated, he tried, though again without success, to prepare the way for the reunion of the Calvinist and Lutheran bodies. Another of his schemes was a plan for an alliance between Christian States, the formation of a kind of United Europe; and after having failed to interest Louis XIV of France, he addressed himself in 1711 to the Tsar Peter the Great. He also endeavoured to bring about an alliance between the Tsar and the Emperor. But his plans for inducing Christian monarchs to abandon their quarrels and to join in alliance against the non-Christian world, were as abortive as his schemes for the reunion of the Christian Confessions. One may mention also that Leibniz took a considerable interest in the information about the Far East which was beginning to percolate into Europe, and that he warmly defended the Jesuit missionaries in China in connection with the rites controversy.

Leibniz was one of the most distinguished men of his time, and he enjoyed the patronage of many eminent people. But the closing years of his life were embittered by neglect, and when the Elector of Hanover became George I of England in 1714 Leibniz was not chosen to accompany him to London. His death in 1716 passed unnoticed even in the Academy which he had founded at Berlin, the French Academy being the sole learned body to do honour to his memory.

2. It is against the background of this varied activity and many-sided interests that one has to see Leibniz's career as a philosophical writer. His history of the House of Brunswick falls, of course, into a class apart. Planned in 1692 and carried on intermittently until his death, though never completed, it was not published until 1843-5. Between his philosophical work, however, and his interest in founding learned societies, in uniting Christian bodies and in furthering an alliance of Christian States there is a much closer connection than might appear at first sight.

In order to grasp this connection it is necessary to bear in mind the part played in Leibniz's thought by the idea of universal harmony. The idea of the universe as a harmonious system in which there is at the same time unity and multiplicity, co-ordination and differentiation of parts, seems to have become a leading idea, probably the leading idea, of Leibniz at a very early age. For example, in a letter to Thomasius, written in 1669 when Leibniz was twenty-three, after mentioning sayings like 'Nature does nothing in vain' and 'everything shuns its own destruction',

he remarks: 'Since, however, there is really no wisdom or appetite
in Nature, the beautiful order arises from the fact that Nature is
the clock of God (*horologium Dei*).'[1] Similarly, in a letter to Magnus
Wedderkopf, written in 1671, Leibniz affirms that God the Creator
wills what is most harmonious. The idea of the cosmos as a
universal harmony had been prominent in the writings of Renaissance philosophers like Nicholas of Cusa and Giordano Bruno, and
it had been emphasized by Kepler and John Henry Bisterfeld,
whom Leibniz mentions appreciatively in the *De arte combinatoria*
(1666). He was to develop it later in terms of his theory of
monads, but it was present in his mind long before he wrote the
Monadology.

In the *De arte combinatoria* Leibniz proposed the development
of a method suggested by the writings of Raymond Lull, the
mediaeval Franciscan, and by modern mathematicians and
philosophers. He envisaged first of all the analysis of complex
terms into simple terms. 'Analysis is as follows. Let any given
term be resolved into its formal parts, that is, let it be defined.
Then let these parts be resolved into their own parts, or let
definitions be given of the terms of the (first) definition, until (one
reaches) simple parts or indefinable terms.'[2] These simple or
indefinable terms would form an alphabet of human thoughts.
For, as all words and phrases are combinations of the letters of the
alphabet, so can propositions be seen to result from combinations
of simple or indefinable terms. The second step in Leibniz's plan
consists in representing these indefinable terms by mathematical
symbols. If, then, one can find the right way of 'combining' these
symbols, one will have formed a deductive logic of discovery,
which would serve not only for demonstrating truths already
known but also for discovering new truths.

Leibniz did not think that all truths can be deduced *a poriri*:
there are contingent propositions which cannot be deduced in this
way. For example, that Augustus was Roman emperor or that
Christ was born at Bethlehem are truths known by research into
the facts of history, not by logical deduction from definitions.
And in addition to particular historical statements of this kind
there are also universal propositions the truth of which is known

[1] G., 1, 25. The letter G in references to Leibniz's writings signifies C. I.
Gerhardt's edition of *Die philosophischen Schriften von G. W. Leibniz* (7 vols.,
1875–90). Where possible page references are also given to *The Philosophical Works
of Leibniz*, edited by G. M. Duncan (1890). This work, which contains only a
selection of Leibniz's writings, is signified by the letter D.
[2] *De arte combinatoria*, 64; G., 4, 64–5.

by observation and induction, not by deduction. Their truth 'is
founded not in the essence (of things) but in their existence; and
they are true as though by chance'.[1] I shall return later to Leibniz's
distinction between contingent and necessary propositions: at
the moment it is sufficient to notice that he made a distinction.
But it is important to understand that by propositions *quarum
veritas in essentia fundata est* he did not mean simply the propositions of formal logic and pure mathematics. His ideal of deductive
and scientific logic was certainly largely due to that influence of
mathematics which can be seen in the thought of other rationalist
philosophers of the period; but, like them, he thought that the
deductive method could be used to develop systems of true
propositions in other spheres than logic and mathematics. He
anticipated, in general idea, later symbolic logic; but the development of systems of pure logic and mathematics was but one aspect
of his total plan. The deductive method can, he thought, be
utilized in developing the essential ideas and truths of metaphysics, physics, jurisprudence and even theology. The discovery
of the proper mathematical symbolism would provide a universal
language, a *characteristica universalis*, and by using this language
in the different branches of study human knowledge could be
indefinitely developed in such a way that there would be no more
room for rival theories than there is in pure mathematics.

Leibniz thus dreamed of a universal science, of which logic and
mathematics would form only parts. And he was led to extend
the scope of the deductive method beyond the frontiers of formal
logic and pure mathematics largely because of his conviction that
the universe forms a harmonious system. In the *De arte combinatoria*[2] he draws attention to Bisterfeld's doctrine of the essential connections between all beings. A deductive system of logic
or of mathematics is an illustration or example of the general
truth that the universe is a system. Hence there can be a deductive
science of metaphysics, a science of being.

The fact that the implementation of Leibniz's grandiose scheme
postulates the analysis of complex truths into simple truths and
of definable terms into indefinable terms helps to explain his
interest in the founding of learned societies. For he conceived the
idea of a comprehensive encyclopaedia of human knowledge, from
which the fundamental simple ideas could be, as it were, extracted;
and he hoped that it would prove possible to enlist the aid of

[1] *De arte combinatoria*, 83; G., 4, 69.   [2] 85; G., 4, 70.

learned societies and academies in this undertaking. He also hoped that the Religious Orders, particularly the Jesuits, would co-operate in the construction of the projected encyclopaedia.

Leibniz's logical dream also helps to explain the attitude which he adopted on the subject of Christian reunion. For he thought that it should prove possible to deduce a number of essential propositions in theology on which all Confessions might agree. He never actually attempted to work out this plan, but in his *Systema theologicum* (1686) he endeavoured to find common ground on which Catholic and Protestants could agree. His ideal of harmony was, of course, more fundamental than the idea of logically deducing a kind of highest common factor for the Christian Confessions.

This ideal of harmony obviously shows itself also in Leibniz's dream of a union of Christian princes. It was manifested too in his view of the development of philosophy. The history of philosophy was for him a perennial philosophy. One thinker may over-emphasize one aspect of reality or one truth and his successor another aspect or truth; but there is truth in all systems. Most schools of philosophy, he thought, are right in the greater part of what they affirm, but wrong in the greater part of what they deny. For instance, mechanists are right in affirming that there is efficient mechanical causality but wrong in denying that mechanical causality subserves purpose. There is truth in both mechanism and finalism.

3. The publication of Locke's *Essay*, with its attack on the doctrine of innate ideas, prompted Leibniz to prepare a detailed reply during the period 1701-9. The work was not completely finished, and its publication was for various reasons deferred. It appeared posthumously in 1765 under the title *New Essays on Human Understanding* (*Nouveaux essais sur l'entendement humain*). The only other large work by Leibniz is his *Essays in Theodicy* (*Essais de Théodicée*). This work, a systematic answer to Bayle's article 'Rorarius' in his *Historical and Critical Dictionary*, was published in 1710.

Leibniz's philosophy, that is, what is sometimes called his 'popular philosophy', was not expounded in any large systematic tome. One has to look for it in letters, in articles, in periodicals, and in brief works like the *Discourse on Metaphysics* (*Discours de métaphysique*, 1686), which he sent to Arnauld, the *New System of Nature and of the Interaction of Substances* (*Système nouveau de la*

nature et de la communication des substances, 1695), *The Principles
of Nature and of Grace* (*Principes de la nature et de la grâce*, 1714)
and the *Monadology* (*Monadologie*, 1714), which was written for
Prince Eugene of Savoy. But he left behind him a mass of manu-
scripts which remained unpublished until comparatively recently.
In 1903 L. Couturat published his important collection, *Opuscules
et fragments inédits*, and in 1913 there appeared at Kazan *Leibni-
tiana, Elementa philosophiae arcanae, de summa rerum*, edited by
J. Jagodinski. The complete edition of the writings of Leibniz,
including all available letters, which was begun by the Prussian
Academy of Sciences in 1923, was planned to comprise forty
volumes. Political events unfortunately slowed down the con-
tinuance of this great project.

4. Most philosophies have given rise to divergent interpretations. In the case of Leibniz there have been pronounced differences. For example, according to Couturat and Bertrand Russell
the publication of Leibniz's notes has shown that his metaphysical
philosophy was based on his logical studies. The doctrine of
monads, for instance, was closely connected with the subject-
predicate analysis of propositions. On the other hand, there are
inconsistencies and contradictions in his thought. In particular,
his ethics and theology are at variance with his logical premises.
The explanation, in Bertrand Russell's opinion, is that Leibniz,
having an eye to edification and to the maintenance of his reputation for orthodoxy, shrank from drawing the logical conclusions
of his premises. 'This is the reason why the best parts of his
philosophy are the most abstract, and the worst those which most
nearly concern human life.'[1] Indeed, Earl Russell does not
hesitate to make a sharp distinction between Leibniz's 'popular
philosophy' and his 'esoteric doctrine'.[2]

Jean Baruzi, however, in his *Leibniz et l'organisation religieuse
de la terre d'après des documents inédits*, maintained that Leibniz
was primarily a religious-minded thinker, animated above all by
zeal for the glory of God. Another interpretation was that of
Kuno Fischer, who saw in Leibniz the chief embodiment of
the spirit of the Enlightenment. Leibniz combined in himself
the different aspects of the Age of Reason, and in his schemes
for Christian reunion and for the political alliance of Christian
States we can see the expression of the point of view of rational

[1] *A Critical Exposition of the Philosophy of Leibniz*, p. 202.
[2] *History of Western Philosophy*, pp. 606 and 613.

enlightenment as distinct from fanaticism, sectarianism and narrow nationalism. Again, for Windelband, as also for the Italian idealist Guido de Ruggiero, Leibniz was essentially the precursor of Kant. In the *New Essays* Leibniz showed his belief that the life of the soul transcends the sphere of distinct consciousness or clear awareness, and he foreshadowed the idea of the deeper unity of sensibility and understanding, which the rationalists of the Enlightenment had tended to separate with undue sharpness. On this matter he influenced Herder. 'More important still was another effect of the work of Leibniz. It was no less a thinker than Kant who undertook to build up the doctrine of the *Nouveaux Essais* into a system of epistemology.'[1] On the other hand, Louis Davillé, in his *Leibniz historien*, emphasized the historical activity of Leibniz and the pains he took in gathering materials in various places—in Vienna and Italy, for example—for his history of the House of Brunswick.

That there is truth in all these lines of interpretation scarcely needs saying. For they would not have been seriously proposed by their authors had there not been foundations in fact for each of them. It is, for example, undoubtedly true that there is a close connection between Leibniz's logical studies and his metaphysics; and it is also true that he wrote down reflections which indicate some apprehension about possible reactions to the conclusions of the lines of thought he was developing, were he to make those conclusions public. On the other hand, though it is an exaggeration to picture Leibniz as a profoundly religious figure, there is no real reason to think that his theological and ethical writings were insincere or that he had no genuine concern for the realization of religious and political harmony. Again, it is undeniable that Leibniz embodied many of the aspects of the Age of Reason, while it is also true that he endeavoured to overcome some of the features characteristic of the philosophers of the Enlightenment. Further, in some important ways he certainly prepared the way for Kant, while he was, on the other hand, also an historian.

But it is difficult to pigeon-hole Leibniz in any one compartment. The logical side of his philosophy is undoubtedly important, and Couturat and Russell did good service in drawing attention to its importance; but the ethical and theological parts of his philosophy are also real parts. There may be, indeed, as Russell maintains, inconsistencies and even contradictions in

[1] Windelband, *A History of Philosophy* (translated by J. H. Tufts), p. 465.

Leibniz's thought; but this does not mean that we are entitled to make a radical distinction between his 'esoteric' and his 'exoteric' thought. Leibniz was doubtless a complicated personality; but he was not a split personality. Again, Leibniz is too outstanding and many-sided a thinker for it to be legitimate to label him simply as 'a thinker of the Enlightenment' or as 'a precursor of Kant'. And as for Leibniz as historian, it would be strange to emphasize this aspect of his activity at the expense of his activity as logician, mathematician and philosopher. Moreover, as Benedetto Croce has argued, Leibniz lacked the sense of historical development which was shown by Vico. His tendency to panlogism smacks far more of the rationalist spirit of the Enlightenment and of its comparative neglect of history than of the historical outlook represented by Vico, even though his monadology was in a sense a philosophy of development. In fine, an ideal presentation of Leibniz would do justice to all aspects of his thought while over-emphasizing no one element at the expense of others. But, so far as the achievement of this ideal is a practical possibility, it would have to be the work of a Leibnizian expert thoroughly acquainted with the whole of the relevant literature and without any particular axe of his own to grind. It seems likely, however, that Leibniz will in practice always be a subject for controversy. Perhaps this is inevitable in the case of a man who never really attempted a fully systematic synthesis of his thought.

CHAPTER XVI

LEIBNIZ (2)

The distinction between truths of reason and truths of fact—
Truths of reason or necessary propositions—Truths of fact or
contingent propositions—The principle of perfection—Substance
—The identity of indiscernibles—The law of continuity—The
'panlogism' of Leibniz.

1. IN this chapter I propose to discuss some of Leibniz's logical
principles. And the first point to be explained is the fundamental
distinction between truths of reason and truths of fact. For
Leibniz every proposition possesses the subject-predicate form or
can be analysed into a proposition or set of propositions of this
form. The subject-predicate form of proposition is thus fundamental. And truth consists in the correspondence of a proposition
with reality, possible or actual. 'Let us content ourselves with
seeking truth in the correspondence of the propositions in the mind
with the things in question. It is true that I have also attributed
truth to ideas in saying that ideas are true or false; but then I
mean in reality the truth of propositions affirming the possibility
of the object of the idea. In the same sense we can say also that a
being is true, that is to say the proposition affirming its actual or
at least possible existence.'[1]

But propositions are not all of the same kind, and a distinction
must be made between truths of reason and truths of fact. The
former are necessary propositions, in the sense that they are either
themselves self-evident propositions or reducible thereto. If we
really know what the propositions mean, we see that their
contradictories cannot conceivably be true. All truths of reason
are necessarily true, and their truth rests on the principle of contradiction. One cannot deny a truth of reason without being
involved in contradiction. Leibniz also refers to the principle of
contradiction as the principle of identity. 'The first of the truths
of reason is the principle of contradiction or, what comes to

---

[1] *New Essays*, 4, 5, p. 452 (page references to the *New Essays* are to the translation by A. G. Langley, listed in the Appendix); *G.*, 5, 378.

the same thing, that of identity.'[1] To take an example given by Leibniz himself, I cannot deny the proposition that the equilateral rectangle is a rectangle without being involved in contradiction.

Truths of fact, on the other hand, are not necessary propositions. Their opposites are conceivable; and they can be denied without logical contradiction. The proposition, for example, that John Smith exists or that John Smith married Mary Brown is not a necessary but a contingent proposition. It is, indeed, logically and metaphysically inconceivable that John Smith should not exist while he is existing. But the proposition the opposite of which is inconceivable is not the existential statement that John Smith exists but the hypothetical statement that if John Smith exists, he cannot at the same time not exist. The true existential statement that John Smith actually exists is a contingent proposition, a truth of fact. We cannot deduce it from any a priori self-evident truth: we know its truth a posteriori. At the same time there must be a sufficient reason for the existence of John Smith. It would have been possible for there never to have been a John Smith. 'Truths of reason are necessary and their opposite is impossible: truths of fact are contingent and their opposite is possible.'[2] But if John Smith actually exists, there must be a sufficient reason for his existence; that is, if it is true to say that John Smith exists, there must be a sufficient reason why it is true to say that he exists. Truths of fact, then, rest on the principle of sufficient reason. But they do not rest on the principle of contradiction, since their truth is not necessary and their opposites are conceivable.

Now, for Leibniz contingent propositions or truths of fact are analytic in a sense which will be explained presently. If we are using his language, therefore, we cannot simply equate truths of reason with analytic and truths of fact with synthetic propositions. But since what he calls 'truths of reason' can be shown by us to

---

[1] G., 4, 357. In the New Essays (4, 2, 1, pp. 404–5) Leibniz speaks of propositions such as 'each thing is what it is' and 'A is A' as affirmative identicals. Negative identicals belong either to the principle of contradiction or to the disparates (e.g. heat is not the same thing as colour). 'The principle of contradiction is in general: a proposition is either true or false. This contains two true statements; one that the true and the false are not compatible in one and the same proposition, or that a proposition cannot be true and false at once; the other that the opposition or the negation of the true and the false are not compatible, or that there is no mean between the true and the false, or rather: it is impossible for a proposition to be neither true nor false' (G., 5, 343).

[2] Monadology, 33; G., 6, 612; D., p. 223.

be analytic, that is, since in the case of truths of reason we can show that the predicate is contained in the subject while in the case of truths of fact we are unable to demonstrate that the predicate is contained in the subject, we can to that extent say that Leibniz's 'truths of reason' are analytic and his 'truths of fact' synthetic propositions. Moreover, we can make the following broad distinction between the range of truths of reason and that of truths of fact. The former embrace the sphere of the possible, while the latter embrace the sphere of the existential. There is, however, one exception to the rule that existential propositions are truths of fact and not of reason. For the proposition that God exists is a truth of reason or necessary proposition, and denial of it involves for Leibniz a logical contradiction. To this subject I shall return later. But apart from this one exception no truth of reason asserts existence of any subject. Conversely, if, except in the one case just mentioned, a true proposition asserts existence of a subject, it is a truth of fact, a contingent proposition, and not a truth of reason. Leibniz's distinction between truths of reason and truths of fact needs, however, some further elucidation, and I propose to say something more about each in turn.

2. Among truths of reason are those primitive truths which Leibniz calls 'identicals'. They are known by intuition, their truth being self-evident. They are called 'identicals', says Leibniz, 'because they seem only to repeat the same thing without giving us any information'.[1] Examples of affirmative identicals are 'each thing is what it is', and 'A is A', 'the equilateral rectangle is a rectangle'. An example of a negative identical is 'what is A cannot be non-A'. But there are also negative identicals which are called 'disparates', that is, propositions which state that the object of one idea is not the object of another idea. For example, 'heat is not the same thing as colour'. 'All this,' says Leibniz, 'can be asserted independently of all proof or of reduction to opposition or to the principle of contradiction, when these ideas are sufficiently understood not to require here analysis.'[2] If we understand, for instance, what the terms 'heat' and 'colour' mean, we see at once, without any need of proof, that heat is not the same thing as colour.

If one looks at Leibniz's examples of primitive truths of reason, one notices at once that some of them are tautologies. For example, the propositions that an equilateral rectangle is a

[1] *New Essays* 4, 2, 1, p. 404; *G.*, 5, 343.   [2] *New Essays*, pp. 405–6; *G.*, 5, 344.

rectangle, that a rational animal is an animal and that *A* is *A* are clearly tautological. This, of course, is the reason why Leibniz says that identicals seem to repeat the same thing without giving us any information. Indeed, it appears to have been Leibniz's view that logic and pure mathematics are systems of propositions of the kind which are now sometimes called 'tautologies'. 'The great foundation of mathematics is the principle of contradiction or identity, that is, that a proposition cannot be true and false at the same time, and that, therefore, *A* is *A* and cannot be non-*A*. This single principle is sufficient to demonstrate every part of arithmetic and geometry, that is, all mathematical principles. But in order to proceed from mathematics to natural philosophy another principle is required, as I have observed in my *Theodicy*. I mean the principle of sufficient reason, that is, that nothing happens without a reason why it should be so rather than otherwise.'[1]

Leibniz was, of course, well aware that definitions are required in mathematics. And, according to him, the proposition that three is equal to two plus one is 'only the definition of the term three'.[2] But he would not allow that all definitions are arbitrary. We must distinguish between real and nominal definitions. The former 'show clearly that the thing is possible',[3] while the latter do not. Hobbes, says Leibniz, thought that 'truths were arbitrary because they depended on nominal definitions'.[4] But there are also real definitions, clearly defining the possible, and propositions derived from real definitions are true. Nominal definitions are of use; but they can be the source of knowledge of the truth 'only when it is well established otherwise that the thing defined is possible'.[5] 'In order to be assured that what I conclude from a definition is true, I must know that this notion is possible.'[6] Real definitions are thus fundamental.

In a science such as pure mathematics, therefore, we have self-evident propositions or fundamental axioms, definitions and propositions deduced therefrom; and the whole science concerns the sphere of the possible. There are here several points to notice. First, Leibniz defined the possible as the non-contradictory. The proposition that roundness is compatible with squareness is a contradictory proposition, and this is what is meant when it is said that the idea of a round square is contradictory and

---

[1] Second letter to S. Clarke, 1; *G.*, 7, 355–6; *D.*, p. 239.
[2] *New Essays*, 4, 2, 1, p. 410; *G.*, 5, 347.
[3] *Thoughts on Knowledge, Truth and Ideas*; *G.*, 4, 424–5; *D.*, p. 30.
[4] *Ibid.*   [5] *Ibid.*   [6] *G.*, 1, 384 (in a letter to Foucher).

impossible. Secondly, mathematical propositions are but one instance of truths of reason; and we can say that all truths of reason are concerned with the sphere of possibility. Thirdly, to say that truths of reason are concerned with the sphere of possibility is to say that they are not existential judgments. Truths of reason state what would be true in any case, whereas true existential judgments depend on God's choice of one particular possible world. The exception to the rule that truths of reason are not existential judgments is the proposition that God is a possible Being. For to state that God is possible is to state that God exists. Apart from this exception no truths of reason affirm existence of any subject. A truth of reason may hold good in regard to existent reality: we use mathematics in astronomy, for example. But it is not mathematics which tells us that the stars exist.

One must not be misled by Leibniz's example of heat not being the same thing as colour. If I say that heat is not the same thing as colour, I no more assert that heat or colour exist than I assert that triangular bodies exist when I say that a triangle has three sides. Similarly, when I say that man is an animal, I assert that the class 'man' falls under the class 'animal'; but I do not assert that there are existent members of the class. Statements like these concern the sphere of the possible; they concern essences or universals. Except in the one case of God truths of reason are not statements affirming the existence of any individual or individuals. 'That God exists, that all right angles are equal to each other, are necessary truths; but it is a contingent truth that I exist or that there are bodies which show an actual right angle.'[1]

I have said that Leibniz's truths of reason or necessary truths cannot be equated without more ado with analytic propositions because for him all true propositions are in a sense analytic. But contingent propositions or truths of fact are, for him, incapable of being reduced by us to self-evident propositions, whereas truths of reason are either self-evident truths or capable of being reduced by us to self-evident truths. We can say, then, that truths of reason are finitely analytic, and that the principle of contradiction says that all finitely analytic propositions are true. If, therefore, one means by analytic propositions those which are finitely analytic, that is, those which human analysis can show to be necessary propositions, we can equate Leibniz's truths of reason

[1] *On Necessity and Contingency* (to M. Coste); *G.*, 3, 400; *D.*, p. 170.

with analytic propositions understood in this sense. And as Leibniz speaks of truths of fact as being 'incapable of analysis'[1] and as not necessary, we can for all intents and purposes speak of truths of reason as analytic propositions, provided that one remembers that for Leibniz truths of fact can be known *a priori* by the divine mind, though not by us.

3. Connection between truths of reason is necessary, but connection between truths of fact is not always necessary. 'Connection is of two sorts: the one is absolutely necessary, so that its contrary implies contradiction, and this deduction occurs in eternal truths like those of geometry; the other is only necessary *ex hypothesi* and, so to speak, by accident, and it is contingent in itself, when the contrary does not imply contradiction.'[2] It is true that there are interconnections between things: the occurrence of event *B* may depend upon the occurrence of event *A*, and, given *A*, the occurrence of *B* may be certain. Then we have a hypothetical proposition, 'if *A*, then *B*'. But the existence of the system in which this connection finds a place is not necessary but contingent. 'We must distinguish between an absolute and a hypothetical necessity.'[3] Not all possibles are compossible. 'I have reason to believe that not all possible species are compossible in the universe, great as it is, and that this holds not only in regard to things which exist contemporaneously but also in regard to the whole series of things. That is to say, I believe that there are necessarily species which never have existed and never will exist, not being compatible with this series of creatures which God has chosen.'[4] If God chooses, for example, to create a system in which *A* finds a place, *B*, if logically incompatible with *A*, will be necessarily excluded. But it is excluded only on the assumption that God chooses the system in which *A* finds a place; He might have chosen the system in which *B*, and not *A*, finds a place. In other words, the series of existents is not necessary, and so all propositions affirming the existence either of the series as a whole, that is, the world, or any member of the series is a contingent proposition, in the sense that its contrary does not involve logical contradiction. There are different possible worlds. 'The universe is only the collection of a certain kind of compossibles, and the actual universe is the collection of all existent possibles. . . . And as there are different combinations of possibles, some better than

[1] *Scientia Generalis Characteristica*, 14; *G.*, 7, 200.   [2] *G.*, 4, 437.
[3] Fifth letter to S. Clarke, 4; *G.*, 7, 389; *D.*, p. 254.
[4] *New Essays*, 3. 6, 12, p. 334; *G.*, 5, 286.

others, there are many possible universes, each collection of compossibles making one of them.'[1] And God was under no absolute
necessity to choose one particular possible world. 'The whole
universe might have been made differently, time, space and
matter being absolutely indifferent to motions and figures. . . .
Though all the facts of the universe are now certain in relation to
God, . . . it does not follow that the truth which pronounces that
one fact follows from another is necessary.'[2] Physical science,
therefore, cannot be a deductive science in the same sense in
which geometry is a deductive science. 'The laws of motion which
actually occur in Nature and which are verified by experiments
are not in truth absolutely demonstrable, as a geometrical proposition would be.'[3]

Now, if this were all that Leibniz had to say, the matter would
be fairly simple. We could say that there are on the one hand
truths of reason or analytic and necessary propositions, like the
propositions of logic and pure mathematics, and on the other
hand truths of fact or synthetic and contingent propositions, and
that with one exception all existential statements fall into the
second category. Nor would Leibniz's view that each contingent
truth must have a sufficient reason cause any difficulty. When A
and B are both finite things, the existence of B may be explicable
in terms of the existence and activity of A. But the existence of
A itself requires a sufficient reason. In the end we must say
that the existence of the world, of the whole harmonious system
of finite things, requires a sufficient reason why it exists. And this
sufficient reason Leibniz finds in a free decree of God. 'For truths
of fact or of existence depend upon the decree of God.'[4] Again,
'the true cause why certain things exist rather than others is to be
derived from the free decrees of the divine will. . . .'[5]

But Leibniz complicates matters by implying that contingent
propositions are in a sense analytic; and it is necessary to explain
in what sense they can be called analytic. In *The Principles of
Nature and of Grace* and the *Monadology*, both dated 1714,
Leibniz was concerned with using the principle of sufficient reason
to prove the existence of God. But in earlier papers he speaks in
logical rather than in metaphysical terms and explains the
principle of sufficient reason in terms of the subject-predicate

[1] *G.*, 3, 573 (in a letter to Bourguet).
[2] *On Necessity and Contingence* (to M. Coste); *G.*, 3, 400; *D.*, pp. 170–1.
[3] *Theodicy*, 345; *G.*, 6, 319.   [4] *G.*, 2, 39.
[5] *Specimen inventorum de admirandis naturae generalis arcanis*; *G.*, 7, 309.

form of proposition. 'In demonstration I use two principles, of which one is that what implies contradiction is false, (while) the other is that a reason can be given for every truth (which is not identical or immediate), that is, that the notion of the predicate is always contained, explicitly or implicitly, in the notion of its subject, and that this holds good no less in extrinsic than in intrinsic denominations, no less in contingent than in necessary truths.'[1] For example, Caesar's resolve to cross the Rubicon was certain *a priori*: the predicate was contained in the notion of the subject. But it does not follow that we can see how the notion of the predicate is contained in that of the subject. In order to have an *a priori* certain knowledge of Caesar's resolve to cross the Rubicon we should have to know perfectly not merely Caesar but the whole system of infinite complexity in which Caesar plays a part. 'For, paradoxical as it may appear, it is impossible for us to have knowledge of individuals. . . . The most important factor in the problem is the fact that individuality includes infinity, and only he who is capable of comprehending it can have the knowledge of the principle of individuation of this or that thing.'[2] The ultimate sufficient reason and ground of certainty of a truth of fact is to be found in God, and an infinite analysis would be required in order to know it *a priori*. No finite mind can perform this analysis; and in this sense Leibniz speaks of truths of fact as 'incapable of analysis'.[3] Only God can possess that complete and perfect idea of the individuality of Caesar which would be necessary in order to know *a priori* all that will ever be predicated of him.

Leibniz sums up the matter in this way. 'It is essential to distinguish between necessary or eternal truths and contingent truths or truths of fact; and these differ from each other almost as rational numbers and surds. For necessary truths can be reduced to those which are identical, as commensurable quantities can be brought to a common measure; but in contingent truths, as in surd numbers, the reduction proceeds to infinity without ever terminating. And thus the certainty and the perfect reason of contingent truths is known to God alone, who embraces the infinite in one intuition. And when this secret is known, the difficulty about the absolute necessity of all things is removed, and it is apparent what the difference is between the infallible and the necessary.'[4] One can say, then, that while the principle of

[1] *G.*, 7, 199–200. [2] *New Essays*, 3, 3, 6, p. 309; *G.*, 5, 268.
[3] *G.*, 7, 200. [4] *Specimen* (cf. note 5, p. 279); *G.*, 7, 309.

contradiction states that all finitely analytic propositions are true,
the principle of sufficient reason says that all true propositions are
analytic, that is, that the predicate is contained in its subject. But
it does not follow that all true propositions are finitely analytic,
as are truths of reason ('analytic' propositions proper).

A natural conclusion to draw from this is that for Leibniz the
difference between truths of reason and truths of fact, that is,
between necessary and contingent propositions, is essentially
relative to human knowledge. In this case all true propositions
would be necessary in themselves and would be recognized as such
by God, though the human mind, owing to its limited and finite
character, is able to see the necessity only of those propositions
which can be reduced by a finite process to what Leibniz calls
'identicals'. And Leibniz certainly implies this on occasion.
'There is a difference between analysis of the necessary and
analysis of the contingent. Analysis of the necessary, which is
that of essences, goes from the posterior by nature to the prior
by nature and ends in primitive notions, and it is thus that
numbers are resolved into units. But in contingents or existents
this analysis from the subsequent by nature to the prior by nature
proceeds to infinity, without a reduction to primitive elements
being ever possible.'[1]

This conclusion would not, however, represent Leibniz's position
accurately. It is true that when an individual finite subject like
Caesar is considered as a possible being, that is, without reference
to its actual existence, the complete notion of this individual comprises all its predicates save existence. 'Every predicate, necessary
or contingent, past, present or future, is comprised in the notion
of the subject.'[2] But there are two points to notice. In the first
place, the meaning which Leibniz attached to the statement that
voluntary actions, like Caesar's resolve to cross the Rubicon, are
contained in the notion of the subject cannot be understood without introducing the notion of the good, and so of final causality.
In the second place, existence, which Leibniz regarded as a
predicate, is unique in that it is not comprised in the notion of any
finite being. The existence of all actual finite beings is therefore
contingent. And when we ask why these beings exist rather than
those, we have again to introduce the idea of the good and the
principle of perfection. This subject will now be discussed (and it
raises its own difficulties); but it is as well to have pointed out in

[1] *G.*, 3, 582 (in a letter to Bourguet).   [2] *G.*, 2, 46.

advance that for Leibniz existential propositions are unique. Caesar's resolve to cross the Rubicon was indeed comprised in the notion of Caesar; but it does not follow that the possible world in which Caesar is a member is necessary. Granted that God selected this particular possible world, it was *a priori* certain that Caesar would resolve to cross the Rubicon; but it was not logically or metaphysically necessary for God to select this particular world. The only existential proposition which is necessary in the strict sense is the proposition affirming God's existence.

4. If from among possible worlds God has freely selected one particular world for creation, the question can be raised, why did God choose this particular world? Leibniz was not content to answer simply that God made this choice. For to answer in this way would be equivalent to 'maintaining that God wills something without any sufficient reason for His will', which would be 'contrary to the wisdom of God as though He could operate without acting by reason'.[1] There must, therefore, be a sufficient reason for God's choice. Similarly, though Caesar chose freely to cross the Rubicon, there must be a sufficient reason for his making this choice. Now, though the principle of sufficient reason tells us that God had a sufficient reason for creating this actual world and that there was a sufficient reason for Caesar's decision to cross the Rubicon, it does not by itself tell us what the sufficient reason was in either case. Something more, that is, a complementary principle to the principle of sufficient reason, is required; and Leibniz finds this complementary principle in the principle of perfection.

In Leibniz's opinion, it is ideally possible to assign a maximum amount of perfection to every possible world or set of compossibles. Therefore, to ask why God chose to create one particular world rather than another is to ask why He chose to confer existence on one system of compossibles, possessing a certain maximum of perfection, rather than on another system of compossibles, possessing a different maximum of perfection. And the answer is that God chose the world which has the greatest maximum of perfection. Further, God has created man in such a way that he chooses what seems to him to be the best. The reason why Caesar chose to cross the Rubicon was that his choice seemed to him to be the best. The principle of perfection states, therefore, that God acts for the objectively best and that man acts with a

---

[1] Third letter to S. Clarke, 7; *G.*, 7, 365; *D.*, p. 245. Leibniz is talking about the spatial situations of bodies, but he refers to his 'axiom' or 'general rule'.

view to what seems to him to be the best. This principle, as Leibniz saw clearly, meant the reintroduction of final causality. Thus of physics he says that 'so far from excluding final causes and the consideration of a Being acting with wisdom, it is from this that everything must be deduced in physics'.[1] Again, dynamics 'is to a great extent the foundation of my system; for we there learn the difference between truths the necessity of which is brute and geometric and truths which have their source in fitness and final causes'.[2]

Leibniz is careful, especially in his published writings, to make this view square with his admission of contingency. God chose the most perfect world freely; and Leibniz even speaks of God choosing freely to act with a view to the best. 'The true cause why certain things exist rather than others is to be derived from the free decrees of the divine will, the first of which is to will to do all things in the best possible way.'[3] God was not under any absolute compulsion to choose the best possible world. Again, though it was certain that Caesar would resolve to cross the Rubicon, his decision was a free decision. He made a rational decision, and therefore he acted freely. 'There is contingency in a thousand actions of nature; but when there is no judgment in the agent there is no liberty.'[4] God has so made man that he chooses what appears to him to be the best, and for an infinite mind man's actions are certain *a priori*. Yet to act in accordance with a judgment of the reason is to act freely. 'To ask whether there is freedom in our will is the same as to ask whether there is choice in our will. Free and voluntary mean the same thing. For the free is the same as the spontaneous with reason; and to will is to be carried to action by a reason perceived by the intellect. . . .'[5] If freedom, then, is understood in this sense, Caesar chose freely to cross the Rubicon in spite of the fact that his choice was certain *a priori*.

These statements by Leibniz leave some important questions unanswered. It is all very well to say that God chose freely to act for the best. But must there not be, on Leibniz's own principles, a sufficient reason for this choice; and must not this sufficient reason be found in the divine nature? Leibniz admits that this is so. 'Absolutely speaking, it must be said that another state (of things)

[1] *On a General Principle Useful in the Explanation of the Laws of Nature* to Bayle); *G.*, 3, 54; *D.*, p. 36.   [2] *G.*, 3, 645 (in a letter to Remond).
[3] *Specimen* (cf. note 5, p. 279); *G.*, 7, 309–10.   [4] *Theodicy* 34; *G.*, 6, 122.
[5] *Animadversions on Descartes' Principles of Philosophy*, on Article 39; *G.*, 4, 362; *D.*, p. 54.

could exist; yet (it must also be said) that the present state exists
because it follows from the nature of God that He should prefer
the most perfect.'[1] But if it follows from the nature of God that
He should prefer the most perfect, does it not also follow that the
creation of the most perfect world is necessary? Leibniz admits
this too up to a point. 'In my opinion, if there were no best
possible series, God would certainly have created nothing, since
He cannot act without a reason or prefer the less perfect to the
more perfect.'[2] Further, Leibniz speaks of possibles as having
'a certain need of existence and, so to speak, some claim to
existence', and he draws the conclusion that 'among the infinite
combinations of possibles and of possible series that one exists by
which the most of essence or of possibility is brought into existence'.[3] This seems to imply that creation is in some sense
necessary.

Leibniz's answer is to be found in a distinction between logica
or metaphysical necessity on the one hand and moral necessity on
the other. To say that God chose freely to act for the best is not
to say that it was uncertain whether He would act for the best or
not. It was morally necessary that He should act for the best, and
so it was certain that He would act in this way. But it was not
logically or metaphysically necessary for Him to choose the best
possible world. 'One can say in a certain sense that it is necessary
... that God should choose what is best. ... But this necessity is
not incompatible with contingency; for it is not that necessity
which I call logical, geometric or metaphysical, the denial of
which involves contradiction.'[4] Similarly, given the world and
human nature as God created them, it was morally necessary that
Caesar should choose to cross the Rubicon; but it was not logically
or metaphysically necessary for him to make this choice. He
decided under the prevailing inclination to choose what appears
to be the best, and it was certain that he would make the decision
he did make; but to choose in accordance with this prevailing
inclination is to choose freely. 'The demonstration of this predicate
of Caesar (that he decided to cross the Rubicon) is not as absolute
as those of numbers or of geometry but presupposes the series of
things which God has chosen freely and which is founded on the
first free decree of God, namely to do always what is most perfect,
and on the decree which God has made, in consequence of the

---

[1] Grua, *Textes inédits*, 1, 393.   [2] *G.*, 2, 424–5 (in a letter to des Bosses).
[3] *On the Ultimate Origin of Things*; *G.*, 7, 303; *D.*, p. 101.
[4] *Theodicy*, 282; *G.*, 6, 284.

first, in regard to human nature, which is that man will always do, though freely, what appears best. Now every truth which is founded on decrees of this kind is contingent, although it is certain.'[1]

The difficulty might be raised that God's existence is necessary and that He must be necessarily good if He is good at all. The necessary Being cannot be contingently good. But Leibniz made a distinction between metaphysical perfection and moral perfection or goodness. The former is quantity of essence or reality. 'The good is what contributes to perfection. But perfection is what involves the most of essence.'[2] As God is infinite being, He necessarily possesses infinite metaphysical perfection. But 'goodness' is distinct from metaphysical perfection: it arises when the latter is the object of intelligent choice.[3] Since, therefore, intelligent choice is free, it seems that there is a sense in which God's moral goodness, arising from a free choice, can be called 'contingent' for Leibniz.

If one understands by free choice purely arbitrary and capricious choice, it is, of course, impossible to make Leibniz consistent. But he explicitly rejected any such conception of freedom as being 'absolutely chimerical, even in creatures'.[4] 'In maintaining that the eternal truths of geometry and morals, and consequently also the rules of justice, goodness and beauty, are the effect of a free or arbitrary choice of the will of God, it seems that He is deprived of His wisdom and justice, or rather of His understanding and will, having left only a certain unmeasured power from which all emanates and which deserves the name of Nature rather than that of God.'[5] God's choice must have a sufficient reason, and the same is true of man's free acts. What this sufficient reason is, is explained by the principle of perfection, which says that God always and certainly, though freely, chooses the objectively best and that man certainly, though freely, chooses what appears to him to be the best. Creation is not absolutely necessary; but, if God creates, He certainly, though freely, creates the best possible world. Leibniz's principle of contingency is thus the principle of perfection. 'All contingent propositions have reasons for being as they are rather than otherwise. . . ; but they do not have necessary demonstrations, since these reasons are founded only on the principle of contingency, or of the existence of things, that is, on

[1] G., 4, 438.   [2] G., 7, 195.   [3] Cf. Grua, *Textes inédits*, I, 393.
[4] Third letter to S. Clarke, 7; G., 7, 365; D., p. 245.   [5] G., 4, 344

what is or appears the best among several equally possible things.'[1] The principle of perfection is, therefore, not identical with the principle of sufficient reason. For the former introduces the notion of the good, whereas the latter by itself says nothing about the good. Even an inferior world would have its sufficient reason, though this could not be the principle of perfection. The principle of sufficient reason needs some complement to make it definite; but this complement need not have been the principle of perfection. If the latter principle says that all propositions, the infinite analysis of which converges on some characteristic of the best possible world, are true, it still remains that they need not, absolutely speaking, have been true. For God was not logically or metaphysically compelled to choose the best possible world.

At the same time Leibniz's logical theory, especially his view that all predicates are contained virtually in their subjects, seems difficult to reconcile with freedom, if by 'freedom' one means something more than spontaneity. Leibniz himself thought that it could be reconciled, and we are not, I think, entitled to speak as though he denied in his logical papers what he affirmed in his published writings. His correspondence with Arnauld shows that he was conscious of the fact that his subject-predicate theory, when applied to human actions, was unlikely to meet with a favourable reception, were it clearly set forth in a work like the *Monadology*. And he may have allowed readers to attach a meaning to terms like 'freedom' which they would hardly have been able to attach to them, had they been aware of his logical views. But though Leibniz may have exercised a certain prudence, it does not follow that he considered his 'esoteric philosophy' and his 'popular philosophy' to be incompatible: it simply means that in some works he withheld the full explanation of what he meant. He was afraid of being accused of Spinozism, but it does not follow that he was secretly a Spinozist. None the less, it is difficult to see how, on Leibniz's logical principles and given his notion of possibles as pressing forward, as it were, to existence, God was not compelled by His very nature to create the best possible world. Presumably the predicate, God's decision to create this world, was contained in the subject, and it is not easy to understand how, on Leibniz's principles, God's choice was anything else but necessary. It is true that for him existence is not comprised in the notion of any subject save God; but what precisely does it mean to say that

[1] G., 4, 438.

God was under a moral necessity, and not under an absolute necessity, of choosing the best possible world? God's choice of the principle of perfection, the principle of contingency, must itself have had its sufficient reason in the divine nature. If so, it seems to me that the principle of perfection must be in some sense subordinate to the principle of sufficient reason.

Possibly one of the reasons why some people seem inclined to think that Leibniz had his tongue in his cheek when he spoke as though contingency is not simply relative to our knowledge is that they regard unpredictability as being essential to the notion of free choice. Leibniz spoke of choices and decisions as being *a priori* certain and yet free. These two characteristics are incompatible, and Leibniz, as a man of outstanding ability, must have seen that they were incompatible. Therefore we must take it that his real mind was revealed in his private papers and not in his published writings. This view ignores the fact, however, that Leibniz was by no means alone in regarding predictability as compatible with freedom. The Jesuit Molina (d. 1600) had held that God, and God alone, knows man's future free acts through His 'supercomprehension' of the agent, while the followers of the Dominican Bañez (d. 1604) had held that God knows man's future free acts in virtue of His decree to predetermine the free agent to act, though freely, in a certain way in certain circumstances. One may think that neither of these views is true, but the fact remains that they had been put forward and that Leibniz was well acquainted with Scholastic controversies. Like the Scholastics, Leibniz accepted the traditional view that God created the world freely and that man is free. In his analysis, however, of the meaning of these propositions he approached the matter from a logical point of view and interpreted them in the light of his subject-predicate logic, whereas the Bannesians, for example, had approached the matter from a predominantly metaphysical point of view. We can no more say that Leibniz denied freedom than we can say that the Bannesians denied freedom; but if one understands by 'freedom' something which they did not understand by the term and which Leibniz called 'chimerical', one can say that it is difficult to see how their analysis of freedom does not amount to an explaining-away. In this sense one can speak of a discrepancy between Leibniz's logical studies and his popular writings. But this discrepancy is no more a proof of insincerity than would be an exhortatory sermon by a follower of Bañez in which no explicit mention was made of God's predetermining decrees or by a follower of Molina who did not refer to the 'supercomprehension' of the infinite mind.

5. The foregoing remarks are not meant, of course, to deny the influence of Leibniz's logical studies on his philosophy. And if we turn to his general idea of substance, we find a clear instance of such influence. Leibniz did not obtain his idea of substance from the analysis of propositions, nor did he think that our conviction that there are substances is a result of the forms of language. 'I believe that we have a clear but not a distinct idea of substance, which comes, in my opinion, from the fact that we have the internal feeling of it in ourselves, who are substances.'[1] It is not, I think, true to say that Leibniz derived the idea of substance or the conviction that there are substances by arguing from the subject-predicate form of the proposition. At the same time he connected his idea of substance with his logical studies; and these in turn reacted on his philosophy of substance. We can say, then, with Bertrand Russell, that Leibniz 'definitely brought his notion of substance into dependence upon this logical relation',[2] namely the relation of subject to predicate, provided that we do not understand this as meaning that for Leibniz we are led simply by the forms of language into thinking that there are substances.

In the *New Essays*[3] Philalethes gives Locke's view that because we find clusters of 'simple ideas' (qualities) going together but are unable to conceive their existing by themselves, we assume a substratum in which they inhere and to which we give the name 'substance'. Theophilus (that is, Leibniz) replies that there is reason for thinking in this way, since we conceive several predicates as belonging to one and the same subject. He adds that metaphysical terms like 'support' or 'substratum' mean simply this, namely, that several predicates are conceived as belonging to the same subject. Here we have a clear instance of Leibniz connecting the metaphysic of substance with the subject-predicate form of the proposition. An allied example is cited in the following paragraph.

A substance is not simply the subject of predicates: it also pertains to the notion of substance that it is an enduring subject of which different attributes are successively predicated. Now, our idea of an enduring substance is derived primarily from inner

---

[1] *G.*, 3, 247 (in a letter to T. Burnett).
[2] *A Critical Exposition of the Philosophy of Leibniz*, p. 42.
[3] 2, 23, 1, p. 225; *G.*, 5, 201–2.

experience, that is, of a permanent self. But there must also be, according to Leibniz, an *a priori* reason for the persistence of substance as well as the *a posteriori* reason provided by our experience of our continuing self-identity. 'Now, it is impossible to find any other (*a priori* reason) except that my attributes of the earlier time and state, as well as my attributes of the later time and state, are predicates of the same subject. But what is meant by saying that the predicate is in the subject, if not that the notion of the predicate is found in some way in the notion of the subject?'[1] Leibniz thus connects the persistence of substances under changing modifications or accidents with the virtual inclusion of the notions of successive predicates in the notions of the subjects. Indeed, a substance is a subject which virtually contains all the attributes which will ever be predicated of it. Translated into the language of substance, this theory of the inclusion of predicates in their subjects means that all the actions of any substances are virtually contained in it. 'This being so, we may say that the nature of an individual substance or complete being is to have a notion so complete that it suffices to comprehend, and to render deducible from it, all the predicates of the subject to which this notion is attributed.'[2] The quality of being a king, which belongs to Alexander, does not give us a complete notion of the individuality of Alexander; and, indeed, we cannot have a complete notion of it. 'But God, seeing the individual notion or haecceity of Alexander, sees in it at the same time the foundation and the reason of all the predicates which can truly be attributed to him, as for example, whether he would conquer Darius and Porus, even to knowing *a priori*, and not by experience, whether he would die a natural death or by poison, which we can know only by history.'[3] In fine, 'in saying that the individual notion of Adam involves all that will ever happen to him, I mean nothing else but what all philosophers mean when they say that the predicate is in the subject of a true proposition'.[4]

A substance, then, is a subject which contains virtually all the predicates which it will ever have. But it could not develop its potentialities, that is to say, it could not pass from one state to another while remaining the same subject, unless it had an inner tendency to this self-development or self-unfolding. 'If things were so formed by the mandate (of God) as to render them fit to accomplish the will of the legislator, then it must be admitted that

[1] *G.*, 2, 43.   [2] *G.*, 4, 433.   [3] *Ibid.*   [4] *G.*, 2, 43.

a certain efficacy, form or force . . . was impressed on things from which proceeds the series of phenomena according to the prescription of the first command.'[1] Activity, then, is an essential characteristic of substance. In fact, though a different system of things might have been created by God, 'the activity of substance is rather of metaphysical necessity and would have had a place, if I am not mistaken, in any system whatever'.[2] Again, 'I hold that naturally a substance cannot exist without action.'[3] I do not mean to suggest that Leibniz derived his notion of substance as essentially active simply from reflection on the virtual inclusion of predicates in their subjects; but he connected his theory of substance as actively self-unfolding with his theory of the subject-predicate relation. And in general it is not so much that he derived his metaphysic from his logic as that he brought the two into connection with one another, so that the one influenced the other. They form different aspects of his philosophy.

6. Leibniz tried to deduce from the principle of sufficient reason the conclusion that there cannot be two indiscernible substances. 'I infer from the principle of sufficient reason, among other consequences, that there are not in Nature two real, absolute beings indiscernible from each other; because if there were, God and Nature would act without reason in ordering the one otherwise than the other.'[4] By 'absolute beings' Leibniz means substances, and his contention is that each substance must differ internally from every other substance. In the total system of substances God would have no sufficient reason for placing two indiscernible substances one in one position in the series and the other in a different position. If two substances were indistinguishable from one another, they would be the same substance.

The principle of the identity of indiscernibles was important in Leibniz's eyes. 'Those great principles of sufficient reason and of the identity of indiscernibles change the state of metaphysics.'[5] The principle was for him bound up with the notion of universal harmony, implying a systematic and harmonious unity of different beings, any two of which are internally different from one another, even though the difference may in some cases be infinitesimal and imperceptible. But the precise status of the principle is not

---

[1] On Nature in Itself, 6; G., 4, 507; D., p. 116.
[2] G., 2, 169 (in a letter to de Volder).
[3] New Essays, preface, p. 47; G., 5, 46.
[4] Fifth letter to S. Clarke, 21; G., 7, 393; D., p. 259.
[5] Fourth letter to S. Clarke, 5; G., 7, 372; D., p. 247.

very clear. According to Leibniz, it is possible to conceive two indiscernible substances, though it is false and contrary to the principle of sufficient reason to suppose that two indiscernible substances exist.[1] This seems to imply that the principle of the identity of indiscernibles is contingent. Abstractly or absolutely speaking, two indiscernible substances are conceivable and possible, but it is incompatible with the principle of sufficient reason, interpreted in the light of the principle of perfection, which is a contingent principle, that they should exist. God, having freely chosen to act for the best, would have no sufficient reason for creating them. Elsewhere, however, Leibniz seems to imply that two indiscernibles are inconceivable and metaphysically impossible. 'If two individuals were perfectly alike and equal and, in a word, indistinguishable in themselves, there would be no principle of individuation; and I even venture to assert that there would be no individual distinction or different individuals under this condition.'[2] He goes on to say that this is why the notion of atoms is chimerical. If two atoms possess the same size and shape, they could be distinguished only by external denominations. 'But it is always necessary that besides the difference of time and place there should be an internal principle of distinction.'[3] For different external relations implied for Leibniz different attributes in the related substances. He may have thought that a substance can be defined only in terms of its predicates, with the consequence that two substances could not be spoken of as 'two' and as 'different' unless they had different predicates.[4] But the difficulty then arises, as Bertrand Russell points out, of seeing how there can be more than one substance. 'Until predicates have been assigned, the two substances remain indiscernible; but they cannot have predicates by which they cease to be indiscernible, unless they are first distinguished as numerically different.'[5] If, however, we assume that Leibniz's real view is that two indiscernibles are conceivable and metaphysically possible, though it is incompatible with the principle of perfection that they should actually exist, this difficulty might be overcome. But it is difficult to see how two indiscernibles are conceivable within the framework of Leibniz's philosophy of substance, predicates and relations.

[1] Fifth letter to S. Clarke, 21; *G.*, 7, 394; *D.*, p. 259.
[2] *New Essays*, 2, 27, 3, p. 239; *G.*, 5, 214.
[3] *New Essays*, 2, 27, 1, p. 238; *G.*, 5, 213.
[4] Cf. *New Essays*, 2, 23, 1–2, p. 226; *G.*, 5, 201–2.
[5] *A Critical Exposition of the Philosophy of Leibniz*, p. 59.

7. In a letter to Bayle, Leibniz speaks of 'a certain principle of general order', which is 'absolutely necessary in geometry but also holds good in physics', since God acts as a perfect geometrician. He states the principle in the following way. 'When the difference of two cases can be diminished below any magnitude given in the data or in what is posited, it must also be possible to diminish it below any magnitude given in what is sought (*in quaesitis*) or in what results. Or, to express it more familiarly, when the cases (or what is given) continually approach each other and are finally merged in one another, the results or events (or what is sought) must do so too. This depends again on a more general principle, namely: when the data form a series, what is sought does so also (*datis ordinatis etiam quaesita sunt ordinata*).'[1] Leibniz gives examples from geometry and physics. A parabola can be considered as an ellipse with an infinitely distant focus or as a figure which differs from some ellipse by less than any given difference. The geometrical theorems which are true of the ellipse in general can then be applied to the parabola, when considered as an ellipse. Again, rest can be considered as an infinitely small velocity or as an infinite slowness. What is true of velocity or of slowness will then be true of rest when considered in this way, 'so much so that the rule of rest ought to be considered as a particular case of the rule of motion'.[2]

Leibniz thus applied the idea of infinitesimal differences to show how there is continuity between, for example, the parabola and the ellipse in geometry and between motion and rest in physics. He applied it also in his philosophy of substance in the form of the law of continuity, which states that there are no leaps or discontinuities in Nature. 'Nothing is accomplished all at once, and it is one of my great maxims, and one of the most completely verified, that Nature makes no leaps: a maxim which I called the law of continuity.'[3] This law holds good 'not only of transitions from place to place but also of those from form to form or from state to state'.[4] Changes are continuous, and leaps are apparent only, though, says Leibniz, the beauty of Nature demands them so that there can be distinct perceptions. We do not see the infinitesimal stages of change, and so there seems to be discontinuity where there is none in reality.

The law of continuity is complementary to the principle of the

<hr />

[1] *On a General Principle Useful in the Explanation of the Laws of Nature* (to Bayle); *G.*, 3, 52; *D.*, p. 33.   [2] *Ibid.*, G., 3, 53; *D.*, p. 34.
[3] *New Essays*, preface, p. 50; *G.*, 5, 49.   [4] *G.*, 2, 168 (in a letter to de Volder).

identity of indiscernibles. For the law of continuity states that in the series of created things every possible position is occupied, while the principle of the identity of indiscernibles states that every possible position is occupied once and once only. But as far as the created world of substances is concerned, the law of continuity is not metaphysically necessary. It is dependent on the principle of perfection. 'The hypothesis of leaps cannot be refuted except by the principle of order, by the help of the supreme reason, which does everything in the most perfect way.'[1]

8. It can hardly be denied, I think, that there is a close connection between Leibniz's logical and mathematical reflections on the one hand and his philosophy of substances on the other. As we have seen, it is legitimate to speak, in regard to certain important points at any rate, of a tendency to subordinate the latter to the former and to interpret, for example, the theory of substance and attributes in the light of a particular logical theory about propositions. There is a close connection between the logical theory of analytic propositions and the metaphysical theory of windowless monads or substances, that is, of substances which develop their attributes purely from within according to a pre-established series of continuous changes. And in the law of continuity, as applied to substances, we can see the influence of Leibniz's study of infinite analysis in mathematics. This study is also reflected in his idea of contingent propositions as requiring infinite analysis, that is, as being only infinitely analytic and not finitely analytic like truths of reason.

On the other hand, Leibniz's 'panlogism' is only one aspect of his thought, not the whole of it. He may, for example, have connected his idea of substance as essentially active with his idea of a subject as that in which an infinity of predicates are virtually contained; but this is not to say that he actually derived his idea of activity or force from logic. It is difficult to see how any such derivation would be plausible or possible. Moreover, apart from his own reflections on the self and on the existent world, Leibniz was acquainted not only with the writings of men like Descartes, Hobbes and Spinoza but also with those of Renaissance thinkers who had anticipated several of his leading ideas. The fundamental idea in Leibniz's philosophy was probably that of the universal harmony of the potentially infinite system of Nature, and this idea was certainly present in the philosophy of Nicolas

---

[1] G., 2, 193 (in a letter to de Volder)

of Cusa in the fifteenth and again in that of Bruno in the sixteenth century. Further, the ideas that no two things are exactly alike and that each thing mirrors the universe in its own way had both been put forward by Nicholas of Cusa. Leibniz may have brought these and allied ideas into relation with his logical and mathematical studies: he could hardly do otherwise, unless he was prepared to admit a fundamental dichotomy in his thought. But this does not justify us regarding him as simply a 'panlogist'. For the matter of that, even if one can show how certain metaphysical theories were derivable from Leibniz's logic, it does not necessarily follow that they were actually so derived. And though there may be inconsistencies between some of Leibniz's logical theories and some of his metaphysical speculations, and even though he may have consciously refrained from publishing some of his conclusions to all and sundry, it is rash to conclude that his mature published writings contain only a popular and edifying philosophy in which he did not really believe. He was a complex and many-sided figure; and even if his logical studies form in some ways the characteristic note of his thinking, the other aspects of his thought cannot be simply disregarded. Moreover, if we remember that he never worked out a system in the way that Spinoza had tried to do, it becomes easier to understand his inconsistencies. It may very well be the case that, as Bertrand Russell has maintained, some of Leibniz's logical reflections would more readily lead to Spinozism than to the monadology; but it does not follow that Leibniz was not sincere in his rejection of Spinozism. He was convinced, for example, that Spinozism is not supported by experience and that his own monadology did gain some support from experience. To this monadology I shall now turn.

CHAPTER XVII

LEIBNIZ (3)

*Simple substances or monads—Entelechies and prime matter—
Extension—Body and corporeal substance—Space and time—
The pre-established harmony—Perception and appetite—Soul
and body—Innate ideas.*

1. LEIBNIZ connected the psychological origin of the idea of substance with self-consciousness. 'To think a colour and to observe
that one thinks it are two very different thoughts, as different as
is the colour from the ego which thinks it. And as I conceive that
other beings may also have the right to say "I", or that it could be
said for them, it is through this that I conceive what is called
"substance" in general.'[1] And it is also the consideration of the
ego itself which furnishes other metaphysical notions, like cause,
effect, action, similarity, etc., and even those of logic and ethics.
There are primitive truths of fact as well as primitive truths of
reason; and the proposition 'I exist' is a primitive truth of fact,
an immediate truth, though it is not the only one. These primitive
truths of fact are 'immediate internal experiences of an immediacy
of feeling':[2] they are not necessary propositions but propositions
'founded on an immediate experience'.[3] I am certain, then, that
I exist, and I am aware of myself as a unity. Hence I derive the
general idea of substance as a unity. At the same time, the connection of the idea of substance with the self-consciousness of the
ego militates against the Spinozistic conception of a unique substance of which I am but a mode. However much some of Leibniz's
logical speculations may have pointed towards Spinozism, his
lively awareness of spiritual individuality made it impossible for
him to entertain seriously the general metaphysic of Spinoza. He
was not prepared to follow Descartes in making the *Cogito* the one
fundamental existential proposition; but he agreed that 'the
Cartesian principle is valid', though 'it is not the only one of its
kind'.[4]

It is not possible to demonstrate by any argument giving

[1] *On the Supersensible Element in Knowledge and on the Immaterial in Nature*
(to Queen Charlotte of Prussia); *G.*, 6, 493; *D.*, p. 151.
[2] *New Essays*, 4, 2, 1, p. 410; *G.*, 5, 347. [3] *New Essays*, 4, 7, 7, p. 469; *G.*, 5, 392.
[4] *New Essays*, 4, 2, 1, p. 410; *G.*, 5, 348.

absolute certainty that the external world exists,[1] and 'the existence of spirit is more certain than that of sensible objects'.[2] We certainly discover between phenomena connections which enable us to predict, and there must be some cause of this constant connection; but it does not follow as an absolutely certain conclusion that bodies exist, for an external cause, like Berkeley's God, might present to us orderly successions of phenomena.[3] However, we have no real reason to suppose that this is the case, and we are morally, though not metaphysically, certain that bodies exist. Now, we observe that visible bodies, the objects of the senses, are divisible: that is to say, they are aggregates or compounds. This means that bodies are composed of simple substances, without parts. 'There must be simple substances, since there are compound substances, for the compound is only a collection or *aggregatum* of simple substances.'[4] These simple substances, of which all empirical things are composed, are called by Leibniz 'monads'. They are 'the true atoms of nature and, in a word, the elements of things'.[5]

The use of the word 'atom' must not be taken to mean that the Leibnizian monad resembles the atoms of Democritus or Epicurus. The monad, being without parts, does not possess extension, figure or divisibility.[6] A thing cannot possess figure or shape unless it is extended; nor can it be divisible unless it possesses extension. But a simple thing cannot be extended; for simplicity and extension are incompatible. This means that monads cannot come into existence in any other way than by creation. Nor can they perish in any other way than by annihilation. Compound substances can, of course, come into existence and perish by aggregation and dissolution of monads; but the latter, being simple, do not admit of these processes. In this respect there is, indeed, a certain resemblance between monads and the atoms of the philosophers; but the atoms of Epicurus possessed shape, even though they were asserted to be indivisible. Moreover, whereas the atomists first conceived atoms and then interpreted the soul in terms of the atomic theory, as composed of smoother, rounder and finer atoms, Leibniz may have been said to have conceived the monad on an analogy with the soul. For each is in some sense a spiritual substance.

---

[1] *New Essays*, Appendix 12, p. 719; *G.*, 7, 320.
[2] *New Essays*, 2, 23, 15, p. 229; *G.*, 5, 205.   [3] *G.*, 1, 372-3 (in a letter to Foucher).
[4] *Monadology*, 2; *G.*, 6, 607; *D.*, p. 218.   [5] *Monadology*, 3; *G.*, 6, 607; *D.*, p. 218.
[6] *Ibid.*

But though monads are without extension and without differences of quantity and figure, they must, according to the theory
of the identity of indiscernibles, be qualitatively distinguishable
from one another. They differ, in a sense to be explained later, in
the degree of perception and appetition which each possesses.
Each monad differs qualitatively and intrinsically from every other
monad; yet the universe is an organized and harmonious system
in which there is an infinite variety of substances combining to
form a perfect harmony. Each monad develops according to its
own inner constitution and law; it is insusceptible of increase or
diminution through the activity of other monads, since the simple
cannot have parts added to it or subtracted from it. But each
one, being gifted with some degree of perception, mirrors the
universe, that is, the total system, in its own way.

Leibniz thus reaffirmed the existence of a plurality of individual substances; and on this point he agreed with Descartes.
But he did not agree with the latter's conception of matter as
geometrical extension. Corporeal mass is an aggregate, and we
must postulate real substantial unities: bodies cannot be composed of the geometer's points. 'If there were not real substantial
unities there would be nothing substantial or real in the mass. It
was this which forced Cordemoy to abandon Descartes and to
embrace Democritus' doctrine of atoms in order to find a true
unity.'[1] Leibniz himself had toyed for a time with the atomic
theory. 'At first, when I had freed myself from the yoke of
Aristotle, I occupied myself with consideration of the void and
atoms.'[2] But he became convinced of the unsatisfactory character
of the theory. For the atoms of Democritus and Epicurus were
not true unities. Possessing size and shape, they could not be the
ultimate factors discoverable by analysis. Even if their physical
indivisibility were postulated, they would still be divisible in
principle. The ultimate constitutents of things must, therefore,
be 'points', though not mathematical points. They must be, then,
metaphysical points, distinct both from physical points, which are
indivisible in appearance only, and from mathematical points,
which do not exist and cannot together form bodies. Further,
these metaphysical points, which are logically prior to body, must
be conceived after the analogy of souls. There must be some
internal principle of differentiation, and Leibniz decided that

[1] *A New System of Nature*, 11; G., 4, 482; D., p. 76.
[2] *A New System of Nature*, 3; G., 4, 478; D., p. 72.

these substantial units are distinguished from one another by the degree of 'perception' and 'appetite' which each possesses. He frequently called them 'souls', therefore, though in order to be able to distinguish between souls in the ordinary sense and other substantial units he came to employ the word 'monad' as a general term. '*Monas* is a Greek word which signifies unity or that which is one.'[1]

2. It is necessary to introduce here a point which is of the greatest importance for an understanding of Leibniz's theory of monads. Each substance or monad is the principle and source of its activities: it is not inert but has an inner tendency to activity and self-development. Force, energy, activity are of the essence of substance. 'The idea of energy or virtue, called by the Germans *Kraft* and by the French *la force*, and for the explanation of which I have designed a special science of dynamics, adds much to the understanding of the notion of substance.'[2] Indeed, substance can be defined as 'being, capable of action'.[3] Substance is not simply activity itself: activity is the activity of a substance. This means that there is in the monad a principle of activity or a primitive force, which can be distinguished from the actual successive activities of the monad.

Leibniz thus reintroduced the idea of entelechy or substantial form. When he had reached his conception of a substantial unit containing some kind of active principle 'it became necessary to recall and, as it were, reinstate the substantial forms so much decried nowadays, but in a way which rendered them more intelligible and distinguished the use to which they should be put from the abuse which they had suffered. I found, then, that the nature of substantial forms consists in force. . . . Aristotle calls them "first entelechies". I call them, perhaps more intelligibly, primitive forces which comprise in themselves not only the act or complement of possibility but also an original activity.'[4] Again, 'the name of "entelechies" might be given to all simple substances or created monads; for they have within themselves a certain perfection (ἔχουσι τὸ ἐντελές). There is a certain sufficiency (αὐτάρκεια) which makes them the source of their internal actions and, so to speak, incorporeal automata.'[5] This entelechy or sub-

---

[1] *The Principles of Nature and of Grace*, 1; G., 6, 598; D., p. 209.
[2] *On the Reform of Metaphysics and of the Notion of Substance;* G., 4, 469; D. p 69.   [3] *The Principles of Nature and of Grace*, 1; G., 6, 598; D., p. 209.
[4] *A New System of Nature*, 3; G., 4, 478–9; D., p. 72.
[5] *Monadology*, 18; G., 6, 609–10; D., p. 220.

stantial form is not to be conceived as a mere potentiality for acting, which requires an external stimulus to make it active: it involves what Leibniz calls a *conatus* or positive tendency to action, which inevitably fulfils itself unless it is hindered. It is, indeed, necessary to distinguish primitive active force from derivative active force, the latter being a tendency to some determinate motion, by which the primitive force is modified.[1] And mention of the primitive force does not suffice for the explanation of phenomena. For instance, it is absurd to think that it is a sufficient explanation of any given phenomenal change if we say that it is due to the substantial form of the thing; and Leibniz declares that he is agreed with those who say that the doctrine of forms should not be employed in determining the particular causes of events and of sensible things. General metaphysical notions cannot provide us with adequate answers to scientific questions. At the same time abuse of the theory of forms by some Scholastic Aristotelians is no reason, said Leibniz, for rejecting the theory in itself. The inadequacy of rival philosophies makes it necessary to reintroduce the Aristotelian theory, provided that it is interpreted in dynamic terms, that is, in terms of force or energy, and provided that it is not used as a substitute for scientific explanations of causal events. In reintroducing substantial forms or entelechies Leibniz did not turn his back on the 'modern' mechanical view of Nature, though he considered it insufficient. On the contrary, he insisted that the finalistic and the mechanistic views of Nature are complementary.

Though each monad contains a principle of activity or substantial form, no created monad is without a passive component which Leibniz calls 'prime' or 'first matter'. Unfortunately he uses the terms 'matter', 'prime matter' and 'secondary matter' in several senses, and one cannot always assume that the same term has the same meaning in different places or contexts. However, prime matter, as attributed to every created monad, must not be understood as involving corporeality. 'For prime matter does not consist in mass or impenetrability and extension, although it has an exigency for it.'[2] It pertains to the essence of created substance and is more akin to the Scholastic 'potentiality' or 'potency' than to matter in any ordinary sense. 'Although God can by His absolute power deprive substance of secondary matter,

[1] *New Essays*, Appendix 7, p. 702; *G.*, 4, 396.
[2] *G.*, 3, 324 (in a letter to des Bosses).

He cannot deprive it of prime matter; for He would then make it to be pure act, which He alone is.'[1] To say that there is prime matter in every created substance is to say that the created substance is limited and imperfect; and this imperfection and passivity is shown in confused perceptions. Monads 'are not pure forces: they are the foundations not only of actions but also of resistances or passivities, and their "passions" lie in confused perceptions'.[2]

3. Reality thus consists ultimately of monads, each of which is an unextended metaphysical point. These monads combine, however, to form compound substances. But how is it that extended body results from a union of some sort between unextended monads? Leibniz's answer to this question seems to me extremely obscure. Extension, he says, is a reducible and relative notion: it is reducible to 'plurality, continuity and co-existence or the existence of parts at one and the same time'.[3] These concepts, however, differ formally: existence and continuity are distinct. Extension is, therefore, derived and not primitive: it cannot be an attribute of substance. 'It is one of the primary errors of the Cartesians that they conceived extension as something primitive and absolute and as what constitutes substance.'[4] Extension is thus more the way in which we perceive things than an attribute of things themselves. It belongs to the phenomenal order. It is 'nothing but a certain indefinite repetition of things in so far as they are similar to each other or indiscernible'.[5] As we have already seen, no two monads are indiscernible; but to represent multiplicity one must represent them as similar and to that extent as indiscernible, that is, one must 'repeat' them. This supposes, however, that they possess some quality which is repeated or, as Leibniz also puts it, 'diffused'. And this quality is resistance, which is the essence of matter and implies impenetrability. Here Leibniz is using the term 'matter' (that is, prime or first matter) in a rather different sense from that in which we have already found him using it. He is now using it to mean the passive principle in substance. 'The resistance of matter contains two things, impenetrability or antitypia, and resistance or inertia; and in

[1] G., 3, 324–5.
[2] G., 6, 636 (in a letter to Remond), cf. Monadology, 47–9; G., 6, 614–15; D., p. 225.
[3] G., 2, 169 (in a letter to de Volder).
[4] G., 2, 233–4 (in a letter to de Volder).
[5] Refutation of Spinoza (edit. Foucher de Careil), p. 28; D., p. 176; cf. G., 4, 393–4.

these . . . I place the nature of the passive principle or matter.'[1] Again, 'passive force properly constitutes matter or mass. . . . Passive force is that resistance by which a body resists not only penetration but also motion. . . . Thus there are in it two resistances or masses: the first is called antitypia or impenetrability, the second resistance or what Kepler calls the natural inertia of bodies.'[2]

If we start with the conception of many substances or monads, we can consider simply the passive element in them or what Leibniz calls 'prime matter', consisting in impenetrability and inertia. By considering this quality alone we consider substances so far as they are indiscernible; we consider the quality as 'repeated'. And extension is the indefinite repetition of things in so far as they are similar to one another or indiscernible. We are here in the sphere of abstraction. The conception of prime matter is already an abstraction; for passivity is only one constituent principle in substance. And extension is a further abstraction; for the conception of extension as indefinite repetition presupposes the abstraction of prime matter.

4. The idea of prime matter is not the same thing as the idea of body. Prime matter is passivity, but body comprises active force as well as passivity. If the two are taken together, that is, if the active and passive principles are taken together, we have 'matter taken as a complete being (that is, secondary matter in distinction from primary, which is something purely passive and consequently incomplete)'.[3] Secondary matter is thus matter considered as endowed with active force: it is also the same thing as body. 'Matter is that which consists in antitypia or that which resists penetration, and so naked matter is merely passive. Body, however, possesses besides matter also active force.'[4] Secondary matter is also called 'mass' by Leibniz: it is an aggregate of monads. One can say, then, that secondary matter, mass and body mean the same thing, namely, an aggregate of substances or monads. Leibniz also refers to it as an organic body or an organic machine. It is made into an organic body, however; that is, into a truly unified body instead of a mere aggregate or accidental collection of monads, by possessing a dominant monad which acts as the entelechy or substantial form of its organic body. This compound

---

[1] *G.*, 2, 171 (in a letter to de Volder).
[2] *New Essays*, Appendix 7, p. 701; *G.*, 4, 395.
[3] *New Essays*, 4, 3, 6, p. 428; *G.*, 5, 359.
[4] *New Essays*, p. 722.

of the dominant monad and an organic body is called by Leibniz a corporeal substance. 'I distinguish (i) the primitive entelechy or soul; (ii) primary matter or primitive passive force; (iii) the monad, completed by these two; (iv) mass or secondary matter or the organic machine, to which innumerable subordinate monads concur; (v) the animal, or corporeal substance, which is made into one machine by the dominant monad.'[1]

If one looks to Leibniz for an absolutely consistent use of terms, one will look in vain. However, certain points are clear enough. The ultimate realities are monads or simple substances. These, of course, are invisible: what we perceive are aggregates of monads. And when an aggregate has a dominant monad, it is an organic body and forms, together with the dominant monad, what Leibniz calls a corporeal substance. A sheep, for example, is an animal or a corporeal substance, not a mere aggregate of monads. What it means for a monad to 'dominate' over an organic body can hardly be considered apart from the theme of perception, and I postpone treatment of this for the moment. But it is worth while pointing out here that in each corporeal substance, and indeed in every mass or aggregate, there is, according to Leibniz, an infinite number of monads. In a sense, then, Leibniz affirmed the existence of an actual infinite, or rather, of actual infinities. 'I am so much in favour of the actual infinite that instead of admitting that Nature abhors it, as is commonly said, I hold that it affects it everywhere in order better to work the perfections of its author. So I believe that there is no part of matter which is not, I do not say divisible, but actually divided; and consequently the least particle must be regarded as a world full of an infinity of different creatures.'[2] But Leibniz did not admit that the conclusion follows that there is an actually infinite number of monads in any aggregate. For there is no infinite number. To say that there is an infinity of monads is to say that there are always more of them than can be assigned. 'Notwithstanding my infinitesimal calculus, I admit no true infinite number, though I confess that the multitude of things surpasses every finite number, or rather every number.'[3] From the statement, therefore, that in any aggregate there is an infinity of monads one cannot draw the conclusion that every aggregate is equal, on the ground that each is composed of an infinite number of simple substances. For there is no sense

[1] G., 2, 252 (in a letter to de Volder).
[2] Reply to a letter of M. Foucher; G., 1, 416; D., p. 65.
[3] G., 6, 629.

in speaking of equal infinite numbers. The aggregate is not an infinite whole made up of an infinite number of parts. There is only one true infinite, and this is 'the Absolute, which is anterior to all composition and is not formed by addition of parts'.[1] And Leibniz refers to the distinction made by 'the Schools' between the 'syncategorematic infinite, as they call it', and the categorematic infinite.[2] The former is the indefinite, not the true infinite. 'Instead of an infinite number we ought to say that there are more than any number can express.'[3]

It should also be noticed that substances in the sense of aggregates of monads are for Leibniz phenomenal. 'For everything except the component monads is added by perception alone, from the very fact of their being simultaneously perceived.'[4] But to say that aggregates are phenomena is not to say that they are dreams or hallucinations. They are well-founded phenomena, their real basis being the co-existence of the monads of which they are aggregates. What is meant is that stones and trees, for example, though they appear to the senses to be unitary things, are really aggregates of simple unextended substances. The world of everyday life, so to speak, the world of sense-perception, and indeed also of science, is phenomenal. The monads or ultimate realities are not phenomenal: they do not appear for perception but are known only by a process of philosophical analysis.

5. Space and time, Leibniz insists, are relative. 'As for my own opinion, I have said more than once that I hold space to be something merely relative, as time is. I hold it to be an order of co-existences, as time is an order of successions. For space denotes, in terms of possibility, an order of things which exist at the same time, considered as existing together, without inquiring into their ways of existing. And when one sees various things together, one perceives this order of things among themselves.'[5] Two co-existing things, A and B, stand in a relation of situation, and indeed, all co-existing things stand in relations of situation. If we now consider things simply as co-existing, that is, as standing in mutual relations of situation, we have the idea of space as the idea of an order of co-existence. And if, further, we do not advert to any actually existing things but conceive simply the order of possible relations of situation, we have the abstract idea of space. Abstract space, therefore, is nothing real: it is simply the idea of

[1] *New Essays*, 2, 17, 1, p. 162; *G.*, 5, 144.   [2] *New Essays*, pp. 161–2.
[3] *G.*, 2, 304 (in a letter to des Bosses). [4] *G.*, 2, 517 (in a letter to des Bosses).
[5] Third letter to S. Clarke, 4; *G.*, 7, 363; *D.*, p. 243.

a possible relational order. Time is also relational. If two events, A and B, are not simultaneous but successive, there is a certain relation between them which we express by saying that A is before B and B after A. And if we conceive the order of possible relations of this kind, we have the abstract idea of time. Abstract time is no more something real than is abstract space. There is no real abstract space in which things are situated, and there is no real abstract and homogeneous time in which successions occur. Both, then, are ideal. At the same time co-existence and pre- and post-existence are real. 'Time is neither more or less a being of reason (that is, something ideal or mental) than space. To co-exist and to pre- or post-exist are something real. . . .'[1] This can be expressed by saying that if space and time are phenomenal, they are none the less well-grounded phenomena (*phenomena bene fundata*): the abstract ideas have some objective foundation or basis, namely, relations.

Leibniz does not give any very detailed considerations to time; but he gives an account of the way in which men form the idea of space. First of all they consider that many things exist at once, and they observe in them an order of co-existence. 'This order is their situation or distance.'[2] Now, when one of these co-existent things, A, changes its relation to a number of others (B, C, D) which do not change their mutual relations, and when a new arrival on the scene, X, acquires the same relations to B, C and D which A formerly had, we say that X has taken the place of A. And, in general, the 'places' of co-existents can be determined in terms of relations. It is true that no two co-existents can have identically the same relations; for a relation supposes 'accidents' or 'affections' in the related things, and no two things can have the same individual accidents. In strict accuracy, therefore, X does not acquire the same relations which A formerly had. Nevertheless, we consider them as the same and speak of X occupying the same 'place' which A formerly occupied. We thus tend to think of place as being in some way extrinsic to X and A. Now, 'space is that which results from places taken together':[3] it is that which comprehends all place, the place, one might say, of places. Considered in this way, namely as extrinsic to things, space is a mental abstraction, something existing only in idea. But the relations which form the basis of this mental construction are real.

---

[1] G., 2, 183.   [2] Fifth letter to S. Clarke, 47; G., 7, 400; D., p. 256.
[3] Ibid., D., p. 266.

In view of the fact that Leibniz maintained a relational theory of space and time, it is only natural that he was a vigorous opponent of the theories maintained by Newton and Clarke, who regarded space and time as absolute. For Newton space was an infinite number of points and time an infinite number of instants. He also used a rather queer analogy by speaking of space and time as God's *sensorium*, apparently meaning that there is some analogy between the way in which God, everywhere present, perceives things in the infinite space in which they are situated and the way in which the soul perceives the image formed in the brain. Leibniz made rather heavy weather of this analogy, pressing it in a manner which Clarke considered unjustifiable. 'There is hardly any expression less proper upon this subject than that which makes God to have a *sensorium*. It seems to make God the soul of the world. And it will be a hard matter to put a justifiable sense upon this word according to the use Sir Isaac Newton makes of it.'[1] As for Clarke's own view, that infinite space is a property of God, namely the divine immensity, Leibniz remarks, among other observations, that in this case 'there would be parts in the essence of God'.[2]

Quite apart, however, from these theological speculations of Newton and Clarke, Leibniz roundly rejected their conceptions of absolute space as being 'an idol of some modern Englishmen',[3] the word 'idol' being used in Francis Bacon's sense. If space were an infinite and real being in which things are situated, it would appear that God could have placed things in space otherwise than they are and that one might speak of the universe, if finite, moving forward in empty space. But there would be no discernible difference between one position of the universe in space and another position. God, therefore, would have no sufficient reason for choosing one position rather than another. And the notion of a finite universe moving forward in empty space is fantastic and chimerical; for there would be no observable change whatsoever. 'Mere mathematicians, who are only taken up with the conceits of the imagination, are apt to forge such notions; but they are destroyed by superior reasons.'[4] Absolutely speaking, God could have created a universe of finite extent; but, whether it is finite or infinite, there is no sense in speaking of it as occupying or as

[1] Fourth letter to S. Clarke, 27; *G.*, 7, 375; *D.*, p. 250.
[2] Fifth letter to S. Clarke, 42; *G.*, 7, 399; *D.*, p. 264.
[3] Third letter to S. Clarke, 2; *G.*, 7, 363; *D.*, p. 243.
[4] Fifth letter to S. Clarke, 29; *G.*, 7, 396; *D.*, p. 261.

capable of occupying different positions. If it were finite and if it were turned round, as it were, in infinite space, the two imagined positions would be indistinguishable. According to the law of sufficient reason, then, it would not occupy one position rather than the other. In fact, it is nonsensical to speak of two positions at all; and the temptation to speak in this way arises only when we frame the chimerical notion of infinite empty space as an assemblage of points, no one of which would be in any way distinguishable from any other.

A similar argument can be used against the idea of absolute time. Suppose that somebody asks why God did not create the world a year or a million years sooner; that is, why He applied, as it were, successive events to this rather than to that succession of instants in absolute time. No answer could be given, since there would be no sufficient reason for God's creating the world at one moment rather than another, if the succession of created things is assumed to be the same in any case. This might seem to be an argument in favour of the eternity of the world, were it not for the fact that in proving that there would be no sufficient reason for God's creating the world at instant X rather than at instant Y one also proves that there are no instants apart from things. For the fact that there would be no sufficient reason for God preferring one instant rather than another is due to the instants being indistinguishable. And if they are indistinguishable, there cannot be two of them. The notion of absolute time as composed of an infinite number of instants is thus a figment of the imagination.[1] As for Clarke's idea that infinite time is the eternity of God, it would follow from this that everything which is in time is also in the divine essence, just as, if infinite space is the divine immensity, things in space are in the divine essence. 'Strange expressions, which plainly show that the author makes a wrong use of terms.'[2]

Absolute space and time, extrinsic to things, are therefore imaginary entities, 'as the Schoolmen themselves have acknowledged'.[3] But though Leibniz doubtless succeeded in his object of drawing attention to the paradoxical character of the views on space and time put forward by Newton and Clarke, it does not follow that his own theory is, I do not say adequate, since the last word on space and time has scarcely been said even in the

---

[1] Cf. fourth letter to S. Clarke, 15; *G.*, 7, 373; *D.*, p. 271 (cf. third letter, 6; *G.*, 7, 364; *D.*, p. 244).
[2] Fifth letter to S. Clarke, 44; *G.*, 7, 399; *D.*, p. 264.
[3] Fifth letter to S. Clarke, 33; *G.*, 7, 396; *D.*, p. 261.

post-Einstein era, but self-consistent. On the one hand, monads are not points in space, and they have no real relative situation extending beyond the phenomenal order.[1] 'There is no spatial or absolute distance or propinquity of monads. To say that they are massed together in a point, or disseminated in space, is to make use of certain fictions of our soul.'[2] Space, therefore, belongs to the phenomenal order. On the other hand, space is not purely subjective; it is a *phenomenon bene fundatum*. Monads have an ordered relation of co-existence to other things; and the dominant monad or soul is in some sense, never clearly defined by Leibniz, 'in' the organic body which it dominates. It is all very well to suggest that the position of the dominant monad is defined in some way by the organic body which it dominates; the fact remains that this body is itself composed of monads. And how are their positions defined? If the order of co-existent phenomena which is space and the order of successive phenomena which is time are simply due to 'the mutually conspiring perceptions of monads',[3] space and time are purely subjective. But Leibniz evidently felt that this would not quite do. For the different points of view of different monads presuppose objective relative positions. And in this case space cannot be purely subjective. But Leibniz does not appear to have worked out successfully the relation between the subjective and objective elements in space and time.

Kant was particularly influenced, of course, by the former aspect of Leibniz's theory of space and time, namely its subjectivist aspect. It is true that even Kant admitted on occasion that there must be an objective ground, itself unknown, for actual spatial relations; but his general theory of space and time was more subjectivist, and hence possibly more coherent even though more paradoxical and less acceptable than that of Leibniz. Moreover, though space was subjective for Kant, it resembled more the absolute empty space of Newton than Leibniz's system of relations.

6. The ultimate realities are, then, monads, simple substances conceived according to an analogy with souls. Leibniz was a convinced pluralist. Experience teaches us, he said, that there are individual egos or souls; and this experience is incompatible with the acceptance of Spinozism. The notion that 'there is but one substance, namely God, which thinks, believes and wills one thing

[1] *G.*, 2, 444 (in a letter to des Bosses).
[2] *G.*, 2, 450–1 (in a letter to des Bosses).
[3] *G.*, 2, 450 (in a letter to des Bosses).

in me, but which thinks, believes and wills exactly the contrary
in another (is) an opinion the absurdity of which M. Bayle has
well shown in certain parts of his Dictionary'.[1] And no two of
these monads is exactly alike. Each has its own peculiar characteristics. Moreover, each monad forms a world apart, in the sense
that it develops its potentialities from within. Leibniz did not, of
course, deny that on the phenomenal level there is what we call
efficient or mechanical causality: he did not, for example, deny
that it is true to say that the door slammed because a gust of wind
exercised pressure on it. But we must distinguish between the
physical level at which this statement is true and the metaphysical
level at which we speak about monads. Each monad is like a
subject which virtually contains all its predicates, and the primitive force or entelechy of the monad is, as it were, the law of its
variations and changes. 'Derivative force is the actual present
state while tending to or pre-involving the following state, as
everything present is big with the future. But that which persists,
in so far as it involves all that can ever happen to it, has primitive
force, so that primitive force is, as it were, the law of the series,
while derivative force is the determination which designates a
particular term of the series.'[2] The monads are, to use Leibniz's
term, 'windowless'. Further, there is an infinity of them, though
this statement must be understood in the light of Leibniz's denial
that there can be an actual infinite number. 'Instead of an infinite
number, we ought to say that there are more than any number can
express.'[3]

But though there are innumerable monads or simple substances,
each of which pre-contains all its successive variations, they do
not form a chaotic agglomeration. Though each monad is a world
apart, it changes in harmonious correspondence with the changes in
all other monads according to a law or harmony pre-established by
God. The universe is an ordered system in which each monad has
its particular function. The monads are so related to one another
in the pre-established harmony that each reflects the whole infinite
system in a particular way.

The universe is thus a system in the sense that if one thing
'were taken away or supposed different, all the things in the world
would have been different from those which now are'.[4] Each
monad or substance expresses the whole universe, though some,

---

[1] *Considerations on the Doctrine of a Universal Spirit; G.*, 6, 537; *D.*, p. 146.
[2] *G.*, 2, 262 (in a letter to de Volder). [3] *G.*, 2, 304 (in a letter to des Bosses).
[4] *G.*, 2, 226 (in a letter to de Volder).

as will be seen later, express it more distinctly than others as they enjoy a higher degree of perception. But there is no direct causal interaction between monads. 'The union of soul and body, and even the operation of one substance on another, consists only in this perfect mutual agreement, purposely established by the order of the first creation, in virtue of which each substance, following its own laws, agrees with what the others demand; and the operations of the one thus follow or accompany the operation or change of the other.'[1] According to Leibniz, this doctrine of a pre-established harmony between the changes and variations of non-interacting monads is not a gratuitous theory. It is the only theory which is 'at once intelligible and natural'[2] and it can even be proved *a priori* through showing that the notion of the predicate is contained in that of the subject.[3]

According to Leibniz, then, God pre-established the harmony of the universe 'in the beginning of things, after which everything goes its own way in the phenomena of Nature, according to the laws of souls and bodies'.[4] Speaking about the relation between soul and body, he compares God to a clockmaker who so constructs two clocks that they ever after keep perfect time without there being any need for repair or adjustment to make them synchronize.[5] The simile can be extended to the pre-established harmony in general. 'Common philosophy' supposes that one thing exercises a physical influence on another; but this is impossible in the case of immaterial monads. The occasionalists assume that God is constantly adjusting the clocks which He has made; but this theory, says Leibniz, involves a *Deus ex machina* unnecessarily and unreasonably. There remains, therefore, the theory of the pre-established harmony. One might be inclined to conclude from this that God sets the universe going, as it were, and then has nothing more to do with it. But writing to Clarke, Leibniz protests that he does not maintain that the world is a machine or clock which goes without any activity on God's part. It needs to be conserved by God and it depends on Him for its continued existence; but it is a clock which goes without needing to be mended by Him. 'Otherwise we must say that God bethinks Himself again.'[6]

It should be noted that in the doctrine of the pre-established

---

[1] *G.*, 2, 136 (in a letter to Arnauld).   [2] *G.*, 3, 144 (in a letter to Basnage).
[3] Cf. *G.*, 2, 58 (to Bayle).   [4] *G.*, 3, 143 (to Basnage).
[5] *G.*, 4, 498; *D.*, pp. 90–3.
[6] Second letter to S. Clarke, 8; *G.*, 7, 358; *D.*, pp. 241–2.

harmony Leibniz finds a reconciliation of final and mechanical causality; or, rather, he finds the means of subordinating the latter to the former. Material things act according to fixed and ascertainable laws; and in ordinary language we are entitled to speak of them as acting on one another according to mechanical laws. But all these activities form part of the harmonious system pre-established by God according to the principle of perfection. 'Souls act according to the laws of final causes, by appetitions, ends and means. Bodies act in accordance with the laws of efficient causes or of motion. And the two realms, that of efficient causes and that of final causes, are in harmony with each other.'[1] Finally, history moves towards the establishment of 'a moral world within the natural world'[2] and so towards harmony between 'the physical kingdom of nature and the moral kingdom of grace'.[3] Thus 'nature leads to grace, and grace, while making use of nature, perfects it'.[4]

7. We have seen that each monad reflects in itself the whole universe from its own finite point of view. To say this is to say that each monad enjoys perception. For Leibniz defines perception as 'the internal state of the monad representing external things'.[5] Further, each monad will have successive perceptions corresponding to changes in the environment, more particularly in the body of which it is the dominant monad, if it is a dominant monad, or in the body of which it is a member. But owing to the lack of interaction between monads the change from one perception to another must be due to an internal principle. And the action of this principle is called 'appetition' by Leibniz. 'The action of the internal principle which causes the change or the passage from one perception to another may be called appetition.'[6] As this is present in every monad, we can say, therefore, that all monads have perception and appetite.[7] But this must not be taken to mean that for Leibniz every monad is conscious or that every monad experiences desires in the sense in which we experience them. When he says that every monad has perception he simply means that owing to the pre-established harmony each monad reflects internally the changes in its environment. It is not required that this representation of the environment should be

---

[1] *Monadology*, 79; *G.*, 6, 620; *D.*, p. 230.
[2] *Monadology*, 86; *G.*, 6, 622; *D.*, p. 231.　[3] *Monadology*, 87; *G.*, 6, 622; *D.*, p. 231
[4] *The Principles of Nature and of Grace*, 15; *G.*, 6, 605; *D.*, p. 215.
[5] *The Principles of Nature and of Grace*, 4; *G.*, 6, 600; *D.*, p. 211.
[6] *Monadology*, 15; *G.*, 6, 609; *D.*, pp. 219–20.　　　[7] *G.*, 3, 622 (to Remond).

accompanied by consciousness of the representation. And when he says that each monad has appetite he means fundamentally that the change from one representation to another is due to an internal principle in the monad itself. The monad has been created according to the principle of perfection, and it has a natural tendency to mirror the infinite system of which it is a member.

Leibniz draws a distinction, therefore, between 'perception' and 'apperception'. The former, as already mentioned, is simply 'the internal condition of the monad representing external things' while apperception is 'consciousness or the reflective knowledge of this internal state'.[1] The latter is not enjoyed by all monads, nor at all times by the same monad. There are, therefore, degrees of perception. Some monads possess simply confused perceptions, without distinctness, without memory and without consciousness. Monads in this condition (the dominant monad of a plant, for example) may be said to be in a state of slumber or swoon. Even human beings are sometimes in this condition. A higher degree of perception is found when perception is accompanied by memory and feeling. 'Memory furnishes souls with a sort of consecutiveness which imitates reason but which ought to be distinguished from it. We observe that animals, having the perception of something which strikes them and of which they have had a similar perception before, expect, through the representations of their memory, that which was associated with it in the preceding perception and experience feelings similar to those which they had at that time. For instance, if we show dogs a stick, they remember the pain it has caused them and whine and run.'[2] The living corporeal substance which enjoys perception accompanied by memory is called an 'animal', and its dominant monad can be called a 'soul' to distinguish it from a 'naked monad'. Finally, there is apperception or perception accompanied by consciousness. At this level perception becomes distinct, and the perceiver is aware of the perception. Souls which enjoy apperceptions are called 'rational souls' or 'spirits', to distinguish them from souls in a wider sense. It is only rational souls or spirits which are capable of true reasoning, which depends on a knowledge of necessary and eternal truths, and of performing those acts of reflection which enable us to conceive 'the ego, substance, monad,

---

[1] *The Principles of Nature and of Grace*, 4; *G.*, 6, 600; *D.*, p. 211.
[2] *Monadology*, 26; *G.*, 6, 611; *D.*, pp. 221-2.

soul, spirit, in a word, immaterial things and truths'.[1] 'These reflective acts furnish the principal objects of our reasonings.'[2]

In attributing apperception to human beings Leibniz did not, of course, mean to suggest that all our perceptions are distinct, still less that 'true reasoning is habitual'. Even in conscious life many perceptions are confused. 'There are a thousand indications which lead us to think that there are constantly numberless perceptions in us, but without apperception and without reflection.'[3] For example, the man who lives near a mill generally has no distinct awareness of his perception of the noise. And even when he has, he is aware of one global perception, as it were, though this is composed of a multitude of confused perceptions. Similarly, a man walking by the sea-shore may be conscious of the sound of the waves in general; but he is not conscious of the *petites perceptions* of which this general perception is composed. Again, 'in three-fourths of their actions (men) act simply as brutes'.[4] Few people are in a position to give the scientific cause why there will be daylight tomorrow: most people are led simply by memory and the association of perceptions to expect daylight tomorrow. 'We are simple empirics in three-fourths of our actions.'[5] Further, although appetite in the rational soul reaches the level of will, this does not mean that we are devoid of the 'passions' and impulses which are found in animals.

Leibniz opposed this theory of varying degrees of perception to the sharp distinction drawn by Descartes between spirit and matter. In a sense all things are living for Leibniz, since all things are ultimately composed of immaterial monads. At the same time there is room for distinctions between different levels of reality in terms of degrees of clarity of perception. If we ask why one monad enjoys a lower degree and another a higher degree of perception the only answer can be that God has so ordered things in accordance with the principle of perfection. Thus Leibniz says that when conception takes place in the case of human beings the monads which before were sensitive souls 'are elevated to the rank of reason and to the prerogative of spirits'.[6] Again, souls 'are not rational until by conception they are destined for human life; but when they are once made rational and rendered capable of consciousness and of society with God, I think that they never lay

[1] *The Principles of Nature and of Grace*, 5; *G.*, 6, 601; *D.*, p. 211.
[2] *Monadology*, 30; *G.*, 6, 612; *D.*, p. 222.   [3] *New Essays*, preface, p. 47; *G.*, 5, 46.
[4] *The Principles of Nature and of Grace*, 5; *G.*, 6, 600; *D.*, p. 211.
[5] *Monadology*, 28; *G.*, 6, 611; *D.*, p. 222.   [6] *Monadology*, 82; *G.*, 6, 621; *D.*, p. 231.

aside the character of citizens in the Republic of God'.[1] In a sense Leibniz's theory might seem to lend itself to interpretation in an evolutionary sense. In a letter to Remond (1715) he remarks that 'since one can conceive that by the development and change of matter the machine which forms the body of a spermatic animal can become a machine such as is necessary to form the organic body of a man, the sensitive soul must be capable of becoming rational owing to the perfect harmony between the soul and the machine'.[2] He adds, however, that 'as this harmony is pre-established, the future state is already in the present, and a perfect intelligence would recognize long before in the present animal the future man in the case of both soul and body. Thus a pure animal will never become man, and human spermatic animals which do not arrive at the great transformation by conception, are pure animals.' One can say that there are hints of an evolutionary theory in Leibniz; but he was thinking in terms of a monadology which was foreign to the mind of the pioneers of the scientific hypothesis of transformistic evolution.

8. The relation of soul to body is that of a dominant monad to an assemblage of monads; but it is not at all easy to give a precise account of what is the relation for Leibniz. Certain basic ideas must, however, be presupposed by any interpretation. First, the human soul is an immaterial substance, and the human body also consists of immaterial monads, its corporeality being a *phenomenon bene fundatum*. Secondly (and this statement follows from the first), there is no interaction in the sense of direct physical influence between the monads composing the human being. Thirdly, the harmony or agreement between the changes in the individual monads composing the human being is due to the pre-established harmony. Fourthly, the relation between the human soul or dominant monad and the monads composing the human body must be explained in such a way as to make it possible to attach a meaning to the statements that soul and body form one being and that in some sense the soul rules the body.

According to Leibniz, 'the creature is said to act externally in so far as it is perfect and to suffer from another (that is, to be acted upon by another) in so far as it is imperfect. Thus action is attributed to the monad in so far as it has distinct perceptions, and passion in so far as it has confused perceptions.'[3] Thus in so

[1] Letter to Wagner, 5; *G.*, 7, 531; *D.*, p. 192.   [2] *G.*, 3, 635.
[3] *Monadology*, 49; *G.*, 6, 615; *D.*, p. 225.

far as the human soul has distinct perceptions it is said to be
active, and in so far as the monads composing the human body
have confused perceptions they are said to be passive. In this
sense the body is said to be subject to the soul and the soul to
dominate or rule the body. Again, although there is no interaction
in the strict sense between soul and body, the changes in the
inferior monads composing the human body take place, according
to the pre-established harmony, with a view to or for the sake of
the changes in the soul, which is a superior monad. The human
soul or spirit acts in accordance with its judgment about the best
thing to do, and its judgment is objective in proportion as its
perceptions are clear and distinct. It can be said, then, to be
perfect in so far as it has clear perceptions. And the changes in the
inferior monads composing the body are correlated by God with
the changes in the superior monad or human soul. In this sense,
therefore, the soul, in virtue of its greater perfection, can be said
to dominate the body and to act upon the body. This is what
Leibniz means when he says that 'one creature is more perfect
than another in that there is found in it that which serves to
account *a priori* for what takes place in another, and it is in this
way that it is said to act upon the other'.[1] In establishing the
harmony between monads God correlates the changes in the
inferior monads with the changes in the more perfect monads, and
not the other way round. It is legitimate, says Leibniz, to speak
in ordinary language of the soul acting on the body and of interaction between them. But philosophical analysis of the meaning
of such phrases reveals that they mean something rather different
from what they are popularly taken to mean. If we speak, for
example, of the body acting on the soul, what is meant is that the
soul has confused and not clear perceptions; that is to say, the
perceptions are not clearly seen to proceed from an internal
principle but appear to come from without. In so far as the soul
has confused perceptions, it is said to be passive rather than active
and so to be acted upon rather than to rule the body. But this
must not be taken to mean that there is any physical interaction
between soul and body.

Now, it is quite clear that it is not always the same monads
which compose the human body: the latter is always, as it were,
shedding some monads and gaining others. And the question
arises, in what sense can one legitimately speak of this changing

[1] *Monadology*, 50; *G.*, 6, 615; *D.*, p. 225.

assemblage of monads as 'a body'? It scarcely seems sufficient to say that the monads form one body because there is a dominant monad, if one simply means by 'dominant monad' a monad enjoying clear perceptions. For the dominant monad or soul is distinct from the monads which form the human body. It will not do to say, for example, that the monads composing the body of an individual A are A's body because the monad which is the soul of A has clearer perceptions. For the monad which is the soul of B also has clearer perceptions than the monad composing the body of A. Yet the latter do not form the body of B. What, then, is the peculiar bond which unites the monads composing A's body to A's soul and which makes it necessary to speak of the former as A's body and not as B's body? We must at least have recourse to an idea mentioned above and say that a certain changing set of monads form the body of A in so far as the variations occurring in those monads have their 'a priori reasons' in the variations occurring in the monad which is the soul of A. One can also say perhaps that the monads composing the human body have points of view or perceptions which, according to the pre-established harmony, resemble or approximate to, though confusedly, the point of view of the dominant monad, and that they thus have a peculiar relation to it. But it would seem that the chief reason for saying that these rather than those monads compose A's body must be that the changes in the one set of monads, though not in the other set, are explicable, in terms of final causality, through reference to the changes occurring in A's soul.

In his letters to Father des Bosses, Leibniz speaks of a 'substantial bond' (*vinculum substantiale*) which unites monads to form one substance. But this suggestion cannot legitimately be used to show that the philosopher was dissatisfied with his account of the relation between monads which are said to form one thing. For he made the suggestion in response to a question how the Catholic doctrine of transubstantiation could be stated in terms of his philosophy. In a letter written in 1709 he suggested that 'your transubstantiation' might be explained in 'my philosophy' by saying that the monads composing the bread are taken away as far as their primitive active and passive forces are concerned, and that the presence of the monads composing the Body of Christ is substituted, though the derivative forces of the monads composing the bread remain (to allow for the dogma that the accidents of the bread remain after transubstantiation). But in later letters he put forward the theory of the *vinculum substantiale*. Thus in a letter written in 1712 he said that 'your transubstantiation' can be explained without supposing that the monads composing the bread are removed. One might say instead that the *vinculum substantiale* of the bread is destroyed and that the *vinculum substantiale* of the Body of Christ is applied to the same monads which were formerly united into one substance by the substantial bond of the bread. The 'phenomena' of the bread and wine will, however, remain.

It is to be noted, however, that Leibniz speaks of 'your transubstantiation' and that he says that 'we who reject transubstantiation have no need of such theories'.[1] One cannot, therefore, conclude that he himself held the doctrine of the *vinculum substantiale*. He did, however, declare that he made a distinction between an inorganic body, which is not properly a substance, and an organic natural body which, together with its dominant monad, forms a true substance or *unum per se*.[2] And it is difficult to see how this use of Scholastic language is really warranted by the theory of monads.

9. It is well known that in the *New Essays* Leibniz criticized Locke's attack on the doctrine of innate ideas. Indeed, given his denial of interaction between monads and his theory of the preestablished harmony, one would naturally expect Leibniz to say that all ideas are innate, in the sense that they are all produced from within, in virtue, that is, of a principle internal to the mind. As a matter of fact, however, he used the term 'innate' in a special sense which enabled him to say that only some ideas and truths are innate. For example, he says that 'the proposition, the sweet is not the bitter, is not innate according to the sense we have given to the term "innate truth" '.[3] It is necessary, then, to inquire how Leibniz understood the terms 'innate idea' and 'innate truth'.

The reason given by Leibniz for saying that the proposition, the sweet is not the bitter, is not an innate truth is that 'the feelings of sweet and bitter come from the external senses'.[4] Now, he obviously cannot mean by this that the feelings of sweet and bitter are caused by the physical action of external things. In other words, the distinction between ideas which are innate and ideas which are not innate cannot be a distinction between ideas which, to put it crudely, are impressed from without and ideas

---

[1] G., 2, 399 (to des Bosses).
[2] Cf. *On the Doctrine of Malebranche*, 3; G., 3, 657; D., p. 234.
[3] *New Essays*, 1, 1, 18, p. 84; G., 5, 79.   [4] *Ibid.*

which are born from within: there must be some intrinsic difference
between the two kinds of ideas. And in order to discover this
difference one has to refer back to what has already been said on
the subject of interaction. The mind or dominant monad can have
clear perceptions, and in so far as it has clear perceptions it is
said to be active. But it can also have confused perceptions, and
in so far as it has them it is said to be passive. The reason for
calling it 'passive' is that the '*a priori* reasons' for the confused
perceptions in the dominant monad are to be found in changes in
the monads composing the human body. In ordinary language,
however, we can say that certain ideas are derived from sensation
and are due to the action of external things on the sense-organs,
just as Copernicans are entitled to speak in ordinary language of
the sun rising and setting. For phrases of this kind express the
phenomena or appearances.

Leibniz also implies that ideas of sense, that is, ideas which are
not innate, are marked by externality in the sense that they
represent external things. 'For the soul is a little world in which
distinct ideas are a representation of God and in which confused
ideas are a representation of the universe.'[1] But this statement
has to be qualified. It may seem that the idea of space is marked
by externality and that it is thus a confused idea of sense. But
Leibniz explicitly says that we can have a distinct idea of space,
and also, for example, of motion and rest, which come from
'common sense, that is to say, from the mind itself, for they are
ideas of the pure understanding' and are 'capable of definition
and demonstration'.[2] In speaking of confused ideas of sense
Leibniz is thinking rather of ideas of 'scarlet', 'sweet', 'bitter',
and so on; that is, of ideas of apparently external qualities which
presuppose extension and spatial externality and which cannot
in their phenomenal character belong to monads. 'Sweet' and
'bitter', therefore, are confused ideas, and the proposition, the
sweet is not the bitter, is not an innate truth, since these confused
ideas 'come from the external senses'.

Certain ideas, however, are derived from the mind itself, and
not from the external senses. For example, the ideas of squareness and circularity are derived from the mind itself. Again, 'the
soul comprises being, substance, unity, identity, cause, perception,
reason and many other notions which the senses cannot give'.[3]

[1] *New Essays*, 2, 1, 1, p. 109; *G.*, 5, 99.
[2] *New Essays*, 2, 5, p. 129; *G.*, 5, 116.
[3] *New Essays*, 2, 1, 2, p. 111; *G.*, 5, 100.

These ideas are derived from reflection and are thus innate ideas. They are, moreover, presupposed (and here Leibniz approaches the position of Kant) by sense-knowledge.

To make the matter clearer attention should be drawn to the following point. In the proposition, the square is not a circle, the principle of contradiction, which is an innate truth of reason, is applied to ideas derived from the mind itself and not from the senses; it is applied, in short, to innate ideas. The proposition can, therefore, be called an innate truth. But it does not follow that the proposition, the sweet is not the bitter, is also an innate truth, on the ground that the principle of contradiction is here applied to the ideas of sweet and bitter. For these ideas are not innate. The proposition is 'a mixed conclusion (*hybrida conclusio*) in which the axiom is applied to a sensible truth'.[1] In spite, then, of the fact that in the proposition the sweet is not the bitter, an application is made of the principle of contradiction, this true proposition is not an innate truth in Leibniz's technical sense.

If logic and mathematics are 'innate', the obvious difficulty arises that children are not born with a knowledge of the propositions of logic and mathematics. But Leibniz never imagined that they were. Innate ideas are innate in the sense that the mind derives them from itself; but it does not follow that every mind starts with a stock, as it were, of innate ideas and truths or even that every mind ever comes to an explicit knowledge of all those truths which are derivable from itself. Further, Leibniz did not deny that experience may be necessary in order to attend to or come to a conscious awareness of innate ideas and truths. There are 'truths of instinct', which are innate and which we employ by a natural instinct. For example, 'everybody employs the rules of deduction by a natural logic without being aware of it'.[2] We all have some instinctive knowledge of the principle of contradiction, not in the sense that we all necessarily possess an explicit knowledge of the principle but in the sense that we all instinctively use the principle. For an explicit knowledge of the principle it may very well be that experience is required, and we certainly come to learn geometry, for example, in this way; we do not possess an explicit knowledge of geometry from the start. But Leibniz refused to admit that 'every innate truth is known always and by all'[3] or that ' all that one learns is not innate'.[4] A child may come

---

[1] *New Essays*, I, I, 18, p. 84; *G.*, 5, 79.   [2] *New Essays*, I, 2, 3, p. 88; *G.*, 5, 83.
[3] *New Essays*, I, 2, 11, p. 93; *G.*, 5, 87.   [4] *New Essays*, I, I, 23, p. 75; *G.*, 5, 71.

to have an explicit knowledge of a geometrical theorem on the occasion of a diagram being drawn on the blackboard; but this does not mean that it acquires the idea of, say, a triangle, through the senses. For a geometrical triangle cannot be seen: the figure on the board is not a geometrical triangle.

For Leibniz, therefore, innate ideas are virtually innate. This does not mean simply that the mind has the power to form certain ideas and then to perceive the relations between them. For the opponents of innate ideas would admit this. It means in addition that the mind has the power of finding these ideas in itself.[1] For example, by reflection on itself the mind comes to conceive the idea of substance. To the philosophic axiom that there is nothing in the soul which does not come from the senses one must accordingly add 'except the soul itself and its affections. *Nihil est in intellectu quod non fuerit in sensu, excipe: nisi ipse intellectus.*'[2] Leibniz therefore rejects the idea that the mind is originally a blank tablet or *tabula rasa*, if this means that 'truths would be in us as the figure of Hercules is in the marble when the marble is wholly indifferent to the reception of this figure or of some other'.[3] It is more like a piece of marble which is so veined that the figure of Hercules can be said to be virtually contained in it, although labour is required on the sculptor's part before this figure can be revealed. 'Thus it is that ideas and truths are for us innate as inclinations, dispositions, habits or natural propensities and not as actions, although these potentialities are always accompanied by some actions, often insensible, which correspond to them.'[4]

One of the ideas which Leibniz asserts to be innate in the sense described is the idea of God. 'I have always held, as I still hold, to the innate idea of God, which Descartes maintained.'[5] This does not mean that all men have a clear idea of God. 'What is innate is not at first known clearly and distinctly as such; often much attention and method is necessary in order to perceive it. Students do not always do so, still less every human being.'[6] To say that the idea of God is innate thus means for Leibniz, as it meant for Descartes, that the mind can arrive at this idea from within and that by internal reflection alone it can come to know the truth of the proposition that God exists. But Leibniz's arguments for God's existence can be left to the next chapter.

[1] *New Essays*, 1, 1, 22, p. 75; *G.*, 5, 70.   [2] *New Essays*, 2, 1, 2, p. 111; *G.*, 5, 1⌒0.
[3] *New Essays*, preface, p. 46; *G.*, 5, 45.   [4] *Ibid.*
[5] *New Essays*, 1, 1, 1, p. 70; *G.*, 5, 66.   [6] *New Essays*, 1, 2, 12, p. 94; *G.*, 5, 88.

CHAPTER XVIII

LEIBNIZ (4)

*The ontological argument—The argument to God's existence from
eternal truths—The argument from truths of fact—The argument
from the pre-established harmony—The problem of evil—Progress
and history.*

1. LEIBNIZ recognized the validity, or possible validity, of several
lines of argument for the existence of God. 'You will remember
that I have shown how ideas are in us, not always in such a way
that we are conscious of them, but always in such a way that we
can draw them from our own depths and make them perceivable.
And this is also my belief concerning the idea of God, the possibility and existence of which I hold to be demonstrated in more
than one way. . . . I believe also that nearly all the means which
have been employed to prove the existence of God are good and
might be of service, if we would perfect them. . . .'[1] I shall consider
first of all what he says about the so-called 'ontological argument'.

It will be remembered that the ontological argument, if taken
as a purely formal argument, is an attempt to show that the
proposition 'God exists' is analytic and that its truth is evident
a priori. That is to say, if anyone understands the notion of the
subject, God, he will see that the predicate, existence, is contained
in the subject. The notion of God is the notion of a supremely
perfect Being. Now, existence is a perfection. Therefore existence
is comprised in the notion of God; that is to say, existence belongs
to the essence of God. Therefore God is definable as the necessary
Being or as the Being who necessarily exists. He must therefore
exist; for it would be a contradiction to deny existence of the
Being who necessarily exists. Thus by analysing the idea of God
we can see that God exists.

Kant later objected against this line of argument that existence
is not a perfection and that existence is not predicated of anything
in the way in which a quality is predicated of a subject. But
Leibniz believed that existence is a perfection[2] and he spoke of it
as a predicate.[3] He was thus favourably disposed towards the

[1] *New Essays*, 4, 10, 7, p. 505; *G.*, 5, 419–20.
[2] *On the Cartesian Demonstration of the Existence of God*; *G.*, 4, 401–2; *D.*, p. 132.
[3] *New Essays*, 4, 1, 7, p. 401; *G.*, 5, 339.

argument, and he agreed that it would be absurd to speak of God as a merely possible Being. For if the necessary Being is possible He exists. To speak of a merely possible necessary Being would be a contradiction in terms. 'Assuming that God is possible, He exists, which is the privilege of divinity alone.'[1] At the same time Leibniz was convinced that the argument as it stood was not a strict demonstration, since it was assumed that the idea of God is the idea of a possible Being. To say that if God is possible, He exists, does not by itself show that God is possible. Before the argument can be conclusive, it has to be demonstrated that the idea of God is the idea of a possible Being. He therefore spoke of the argument without this demonstration as imperfect. For example, 'the Scholastics, not excepting their Doctor Angelicus, have misunderstood this argument and have taken it as a paralogism. In this respect they were altogether wrong, and Descartes, who studied the Scholastic philosophy for quite a long time at the Jesuit college of La Flèche, had great reason for re-establishing it. It is not a paralogism, but it is an imperfect demonstration, which assumes something that must still be proved in order to render it mathematically evident; that is, it is tacitly assumed that this idea of the all-great or all-perfect Being is possible and implies no contradiction.'[2] According to Leibniz, there is always a presumption on the side of possibility; 'that is to say, everything is held to be possible until its impossibility is proved'.[3] But this presumption is not sufficient to turn the ontological argument into a strict demonstration. Once, however, it has been demonstrated that the idea of a supremely perfect Being is the idea of a possible Being, 'it could be said that the existence of God was demonstrated geometrically *a priori*'.[4] In Leibniz's opinion the Cartesians had paid insufficient attention to demonstrating the possibility of the supremely perfect Being. No doubt he was right; but as has been already mentioned in connection with Descartes, the latter did make some attempt in his reply to the second set of *Objections* to show that God is possible by arguing that there is no contradiction in the idea of God. And this is the line of argument which Leibniz himself adopted. It is true, however, that Descartes had made the attempt as a kind of afterthought, when faced by objections.

[1] *New Essays*, 4, 10, 7, p. 504; G., 5, 419.
[2] *New Essays*, 4, 10, 7, pp. 503–4; G., 5, 418–19.
[3] *On the Cartesian Demonstration of the Existence of God*; G., 4, 405; D., p. 134.
[4] *On the Cartesian Demonstration of the Existence of God*; G., 4, 405; D., p. 136.

The possible was for Leibniz the non-contradictory. In undertaking, therefore, to prove that the idea of God is the idea of a possible Being he was undertaking to show that the idea does not involve any contradiction. This really means showing that we have a distinct idea of God as supreme and infinite perfection; for if the 'idea' proved to be self-contradictory it might be questioned whether we ever had any idea, properly speaking. We can, for example, use the words 'square circle'; but in what sense have we an idea of a square circle? The question is whether analysis of the idea of God shows that it consists of two or more incompatible ideas or not. Leibniz accordingly asserts that 'we must prove with all imaginable accuracy that there is an idea of an all-perfect Being, that is to say, of God'.[1]

Writing in 1701 to the editor of the *Journal de Trévoux* Leibniz first asserts that if necessary Being is possible, it exists. He then equates necessary Being with Being of itself and proceeds as follows: 'If Being of itself is impossible, all beings by others are so also, since they exist ultimately only through Being of itself. Thus nothing could exist. . . . If necessary Being is not, no being is possible. It seems that this demonstration has not been carried so far up to this time.'[2] This may seem like a switch-over to an *a posteriori* argument. But Leibniz does not argue, so far as words are concerned, from existent contingent being to Being of itself, but from the possibility of a contingent being. It might, of course, be said that we know its possibility only because we are acquainted with existent contingent beings, that is, because we know that there are true affirmative contingent propositions. And the sentence 'thus nothing could exist' suggests the further sentence 'but something does exist' with the conclusion 'therefore contingent being is possible'. Verbally, however, Leibniz keeps within the sphere of possibility. Still, he adds to this piece of reasoning the statement, 'However, I have also laboured elsewhere to prove that the perfect Being is possible.'

This last sentence presumably refers to a paper entitled 'That the most perfect Being exists', which Leibniz showed to Spinoza in 1676. 'I call every simple quality which is positive and absolute or expresses whatever it expresses without any limits a *perfection*.'[3] A quality of this sort is indefinable or irresolvable. Therefore the

---

[1] *On the Cartesian Demonstration of the Existence of God*; G., 4, 405; *D.*, p. 133.
[2] *On the Cartesian Demonstration of the Existence of God*; G., 4, 406; *D.*, p. 138.
[3] *New Essays*, Appendix 10, pp. 714–15; G., 7, 261–2.

incompatibility of two perfections cannot be demonstrated, since demonstration would require the resolution of the terms. Nor is their incompatibility evident *per se*. But if the incompatibility of perfections is neither evident nor demonstrable, there can be a subject of all perfections. Existence is a perfection. Therefore the Being which exists in virtue of its essence is possible. Therefore it exists.

This argument presupposes that existence is a perfection. It also seems to be liable to an objection seen by Leibniz himself, namely, that 'it does not follow that a thing is possible because we do not see its impossibility, our knowledge being limited'.[1] This objection might also be brought against the argument for God's possibility adduced by Leibniz in the *Monadology*. 'God, or the necessary Being, alone has this privilege that He must exist if it is possible. And since nothing can hinder the possibility of that which possesses no limitations, no negations and consequently no contradiction, this alone is sufficient to establish the existence of God *a priori*.'[2] This line of argument, namely that the idea of the supremely perfect Being is the idea of a Being without any limitations and that this is the idea of a Being without contradiction and so of a possible Being, is fundamentally the same as the argument in the paper which Leibniz showed to Spinoza. And it is open to the same line of objection, namely, that one is not entitled to equate negative possibility (that is, absence of discerned contradiction) with positive possibility. We should first have to possess a clear, distinct and adequate idea of the divine essence.

2. Another *a priori* argument for God's existence given by Leibniz is the argument from eternal and necessary truths, which had been the favourite argument of St. Augustine. Mathematical propositions, for example, are necessary and eternal, in the sense that their truth is independent of the existence of any contingent things. The statement that given a figure bounded by three straight lines it has three angles is a necessary truth, whether there are any triangles in existence or not. These eternal truths, says Leibniz, are not 'fictions'.[3] They therefore require a metaphysical ground, and we are forced to say that they 'must have their existence in a certain subject absolutely and metaphysically necessary, that is, in God'.[4] God therefore exists.

This is a rather difficult argument to understand. We are not

---

[1] *On the Cartesian Demonstration of the Existence of God*; *G.*, 4, 402; *D.*, p. 135.
[2] *Monadology*, 45; *G.*, 6, 614; *D.*, p. 224.
[3] *On the Ultimate Origin of Things*; *G.*, 7, 305; *D.*, p. 103.　　　　　　[4] *Ibid.*

to suppose, says Leibniz, that 'eternal truths . . . depend on the divine will. . . . The reason of truths lies in the ideas of things, which are involved in the divine essence itself.'[1] Again, 'the understanding of God is the region of eternal truths or of the ideas on which they depend'.[2] But in what sense can eternal truths be said to 'exist' in the divine understanding? And if they do exist in the divine understanding, how can we know them? It may be said that the eternal truths are hypothetical (for example, 'given a triangle, the sum of its three angles is 180°') and that they belong to the sphere of possibility, so that Leibniz's argument from necessary propositions is a particular case of the argument from possibles to God as their ultimate ground. And such an interpretation seems to gain support from the statement that 'if there is a reality in the essences or possibilities or in the eternal truths, this reality must be founded in something existing and actual; consequently in the existence of the necessary Being in whom essence involves existence or with whom it is sufficient to be possible in order to be actual'.[3] But some clear statement is required of what it means to say that analytic propositions possess reality and of their precise relation to the divine understanding.

3. Leibniz also uses the principle of sufficient reason to argue from truths of fact to the existence of God. For any given event or for the existence of any given thing in the series of finite beings an explanation could be given in terms of finite causes. And the process of explanation in terms of finite causes might proceed to infinity. In order to explain A, B and C it might be necessary to mention D, E and F, and to explain these latter one might have to mention G, H, I; and so on without end, not only because of the infinite series going back into the past but also because of the infinite complexity of the universe at any given moment. But 'as all this detail only involves other contingents, anterior or more detailed, each one of which needs a like analysis for its explanation, we make no advance, and the sufficient or final reason must be outside the sequence or series of this detail of contingents, however infinite it may be. And thus it is that the final reason of things must be found in a necessary substance, in which the detail of changes exists only eminently, as in their source. And this it is that we call God. Now this substance being the sufficient reason of all this detail, which also is linked together throughout, there

[1] G., 7, 311 (Specimen).   [2] Monadology, 43; G., 6, 614; D., p. 224.
[3] Monadology, 44; G., 6, 614; D., p. 224.

is but one God, and this God suffices.'[1] This, Leibniz observes, is an *a posteriori* argument.[2]

In his paper *On the Ultimate Origin of Things* Leibniz remarks that truths of fact are hypothetically necessary, in the sense that a posterior state of the world is determined by a prior state. 'The present world is necessary, physically or hypothetically, but not absolutely or metaphysically.'[3]   In considering his theory of propositions we saw that for Leibniz all truths of fact or existential propositions save one (namely, the proposition 'God exists') are contingent, that is, not metaphysically necessary. The ultimate origin of 'the chain of states or series of things, the aggregate of which constitutes the world',[4] must therefore be sought outside the series: we must pass 'from physical or hypothetical necessity, which determines the posterior states of the world by the prior, to something which is absolute or metaphysical necessity, the reason for which cannot be given'.[5] By the last remark Leibniz means that no extrinsic reason (or cause) can be given for God's existence: the necessary Being is its own sufficient reason. If by 'reason' is meant 'cause', God has no cause; but His essence is the *ratio sufficiens* of His existence.

According to Kant, this argument depends upon the ontological argument. Kant's statement has been frequently repeated; but frequent repetition does not make it true. It is, of course, true that 'if the world can only be accounted for by the existence of a necessary Being, then there must be a Being whose essence involves existence, for this is what is meant by a necessary Being'.[6] But it does not follow that the possibility of a necessary Being is presupposed by the line of argument based on the existence of finite and contingent things. Leibniz himself accepted the ontological argument, as we have seen, provided that a missing link was supplied; but his *a posteriori* argument for God's existence does not involve the ontological argument.

4. Leibniz also argued *a posteriori* to God's existence from the pre-established harmony. 'This perfect harmony of so many substances which have no communication with each other can only come from a common cause.'[7] Thus we have 'a new proof of the existence of God, which is one of surprising clearness'.[8] The argument to God's existence simply from the order, harmony and

[1] *Monadology*, 37–9; G., 6, 613; D., p. 223.   [2] *Monadology*, 45; G., 6, 614; D., p. 224.
[3] *On the Ultimate Origin of Things*; G., 7, 303; D., p. 101.   [4] *Ibid.*   [5] *Ibid.*
[6] Bertrand Russell, *History of Western Philosophy*, pp. 610–11.
[7] *A New System of Nature*, 16; G., 4, 486; D., p. 79.   [8] *Ibid.*

beauty of Nature 'appears to possess only a moral certainty', though it acquires 'a necessity wholly metaphysical by the new kind of harmony I have introduced, which is the pre-established harmony'.[1] If Leibniz's theory of windowless monads is once accepted, the harmonious correlating of their activities is certainly remarkable. But Leibniz's 'new proof' of God's existence is so dependent on the previous acceptance of his denial of all interaction between monads that it has never won wide support in the form he gave it.

5. As has been mentioned in the last chapter, God, according to Leibniz, always acts for the best, so that this world must be the best of all possible worlds. Absolutely speaking, God could have created a different world, but, morally speaking, He could create only the best possible world. This is the metaphysical optimism of Leibniz, which excited the ridicule of Schopenhauer, for whom this world, so far from being the best, is rather the worst of all possible worlds and a standing objection to the existence of a beneficent Creator. And, given this optimistic position, it was clearly incumbent on Leibniz to explain how it is that the evil in the world does not constitute its refutation. He gave considerable attention to this subject, and in 1710 he published his *Theodicy, Essays on the Goodness of God, the Freedom of Man and the Origin of Evil*.

Leibniz distinguished three kinds of evil. 'Evil may be taken metaphysically, physically and morally. Metaphysical evil consists in mere imperfection, physical evil in suffering, and moral evil in sin.'[2] What he meant by 'metaphysical evil' will be explained presently. At the moment I wish to draw attention to two general principles enunciated by Leibniz. First of all, evil itself consists in a privation, not in a positive entity. Hence it has, properly speaking, no efficient cause, for it consists 'in that which the efficient cause does not bring about. That is why the Schoolmen are wont to call the cause of evil *deficient*.'[3] 'St. Augustine has already put forward this idea.'[4] Secondly, God does not will moral evil at all but only permits it, while physical evil or suffering He does not will absolutely but only hypothetically, on the hypothesis, for example, that it will serve as a means to a good end, such as contributing to the greater perfection of the sufferer.

---

[1] *New Essays*, 4, 10, 10, p. 507; *G.*, 5, 421.
[2] *Theodicy*, 21, p. 136 (page references to the *Theodicy* are to the translation by E. M. Huggard, listed in the Appendix); *G.*, 6, 115.
[3] *Theodicy*, 20; *G.*, 6, 115.   [4] *Theodicy*, 378, p. 352; *G.*, 6, 340.

Metaphysical evil is imperfection; and this is the imperfection involved in finite being as such. Created being is necessarily finite, and finite being is necessarily imperfect; and this imperfection is the root of the possibility of error and evil. 'We, who derive all being from God, where shall we find the source of evil? The answer is that it must be sought in the ideal nature of the creature, in so far as this nature is contained in the eternal verities which are in the understanding of God independently of His will. For we must consider that there is an *original imperfection in the creature* before sin, because the creature is limited in its essence; whence it follows that it cannot know all, and that it can deceive itself and commit other errors.'[1] The ultimate origin of evil is thus metaphysical, and the question arises, how God is not responsible for evil by the mere fact that He created the world, thus giving existence to limited and imperfect things. Leibniz's answer is that existence is better than non-existence. In so far as we are entitled to distinguish different moments in the divine will, we can say that God willed 'antecedently' simply the good. But since the imperfection of the creature does not depend on the divine choice but on the ideal essence of the creature, God could not choose to create without choosing to create imperfect beings. He chose, however, to create the best possible world. Considered simply in itself the divine will wills simply the good, but 'consequently', that is, once given the divine decision to create, it wills the best possible. 'God wills *antecedently* the good and *consequently* the best.'[2] But He could not will 'the best' without willing the existence of imperfect things. Even in the best of all possible worlds creatures must be imperfect.

In treating the problems of physical and moral evil Leibniz presupposed his metaphysical position. This, of course, he had every right to do; for it was precisely his metaphysical position which gave rise to the problem. (He might, however, have given more consideration to the fact that the doctrine of the pre-established harmony makes these problems even more acute than they are in any case in a theistic philosophy.) Presupposing that the world is the best possible, he observes that 'one must believe that even sufferings and monstrosities are part of order';[3] they all belong to the system, and we have no reason to suppose that another world would be a better world. There is, moreover, more physical

---

[1] *Theodicy*, 20, pp. 135–6; *G.*, 6, 115.
[2] *Theodicy*, 23, p. 137; *G.*, 6, 116.
[3] *Theodicy*, 241, p. 276; *G.*, 6, 261.

good than physical evil in the world. Further, physical sufferings
are 'results of moral evil'.[1] They serve many useful purposes; for
they act as a penalty for sin and as a means of perfecting the good.
As for animals, 'one cannot reasonably doubt the existence of pain
among animals, but it seems as if their pleasures and their pains
are not so keen as they are in man; for animals, since they do not
reflect, are susceptible neither to the grief that accompanies pain
nor to the joy that accompanies pleasure'.[2] Leibniz's general contention is, however, that there is incomparably more good than
evil in the world, and that the evil there is in the world belongs to
the whole system, which must be taken as a totality. The shadows
set the lights in clearer relief. From the metaphysical point of
view Leibniz tends to make evil necessary. 'Now since God made
all positive reality which is not eternal, He would have made the
source of evil (imperfection), if that did not lie rather in the
possibility of things or forms, which God did not make, since He
is not the author of His own understanding.'[3] When treating of
concrete physical evils, he writes in a way which to many minds
would seem superficial and 'edifying' in a pejorative sense. Indeed,
in the preface to the *Theodicy* he says, 'I have endeavoured in all
things to consider edification.'[4]

The chief problem considered by Leibniz is, however, that of
moral evil. In the *Theodicy* he writes diffusely about this subject,
with many references to other philosophers and to the Scholastic
theologians. Indeed, he shows an astonishing knowledge of
Scholastic controversies, like that between the 'Thomists' and the
'Molinists'. This diffusiveness makes it somewhat difficult to sum
up his position, in spite of the fact that he wrote an abridgement
or summary of the *Theodicy*. But a more important reason for the
difficulty one finds in stating Leibniz's position in succinct form is
that he appears to combine two divergent points of view.

One of the difficulties confronting every theist who tries to
grapple with the problem of evil is that of showing how God is not
responsible for the moral evil in the world which He created and
which He conserves in existence. In answering this difficulty
Leibniz employs the Scholastic theory of evil as privation. 'The
Platonists, St. Augustine and the Schoolmen were right in saying
that God is the cause of the material element of evil which lies
in the positive, and not of the formal element which lies in

---

[1] *Theodicy*, 241, p. 276; *G.*, 6, 261.　　[2] *Theodicy*, 250, p. 281; *G.*, 6, 266.
[3] *Theodicy*, 380, p. 353; *G.*, 6, 341.　　[4] *Theodicy*, p. 71; *G.*, 6, 47.

privation.'¹ Moral evil is a privation of right order in the will. If
A murders *B* by shooting him, his action is physically the same as
it would have been if he had shot *B* in legitimate self-defence; but
in the first case there is a privation of right order which would not
have been present in the second case. This privation is then connected by Leibniz with what he calls 'metaphysical evil'. 'And
when it is said that the creature depends upon God in so far as it
exists and in so far as it acts, and even that conservation is a
continual creation, this is true in that God gives always to the
creature and produces continually all that is positive, good and
perfect in it. . . . The imperfections, on the other hand, and the
defects in operations spring from the original limitation which
the creature could not but receive with the first beginning of its
being, through the ideal reasons that restrict it. For God could
not give the creature all without making it a God; therefore there
must needs be different degrees in the perfections of things, and
limitations also of every kind.'² This implies that a man's evil
actions are the unfolding, as it were, of the imperfection and
limitation of his essence as contained in the idea of him in the
divine understanding. In this sense they would seem to be
necessary, even metaphysically necessary. They do not, however,
depend on the divine will, save in the sense that God chose to
create. And though He created the best possible world freely, He
could not create even this world without creating imperfect beings.
Further, if Leibniz had pressed his idea of possibles as demanding
existence and as competing, as it were, for existence, he might
have gone on to say that the existence of the world is necessary
and that therefore God cannot be held responsible for the evil in
the world.

But these developments of his thought would have taken
Leibniz very close to Spinozism. And in point of fact he never
did develop his ideas in this way. He chose instead to emphasize
divine and human freedom and to find place for human responsibility and for sanctions after death. God created the world
freely; but He willed positively the positive element, not the
element of privation or evil, so far at any rate as moral evil is
concerned. This last is to be ascribed to the human agent who
will be justly rewarded or punished after death. Writing against
Descartes' idea of immortality without memory Leibniz asserts
that 'this immortality without memory is altogether useless,

¹ *Theodicy*, 30, p. 141; *G.*, 6, 120.   ² *Theodicy*, 31, pp. 141–2; *G.*, 6, 121.

viewed ethically, for it destroys all reward, all recompense and all punishment. . . . In order to satisfy the hope of the human race, it must be proved that the God Who governs all is wise and just, and that He will leave nothing without recompense and without punishment. These are the great foundations of ethics. . . .'[1] But if eternal sanctions were to be justified, freedom must be asserted.

Yet here again Leibniz was involved in great difficulty. According to him, all the successive predicates of a given subject are virtually comprised within the notion of that subject. Now, a substance is analogous to a subject, and all its attributes and actions are virtually contained in its essence. All a man's actions are therefore predictable in principle, in the sense that they can be foreseen by an infinite Mind. How, then, can they properly be called free? In the *Theodicy* Leibniz stoutly asserts the reality of freedom, and he points out that certain Scholastic writers 'of great profundity' developed the idea of God's predetermining decrees in order to explain the divine foreknowledge of future contingents and that they asserted freedom at the same time. God predetermines men to choose this or that freely. He then adds that the doctrine of the pre-established harmony will explain the divine knowledge without there being any need either to introduce further immediate predetermination by God or to postulate the *scientia media* of the Molinists. And this doctrine is perfectly compatible with freedom. For even though it is *a priori* certain that a man will make a certain choice, he will choose not out of constraint but because he is inclined by final causes to choose in that way.

It would be profitless to discuss at greater length the question whether freedom is compatible with Leibniz's logical and metaphysical premises unless one first defined 'freedom'. If one understands by freedom 'liberty of indifference', it is inadmissible in Leibniz's system, as he himself several times asserts; he calls it a chimerical idea. According to Leibniz, 'there is always a prevailing reason which prompts the will to its choice, and for the maintenance of freedom for the will it suffices that this reason should incline without necessitating'.[2] Metaphysical and moral necessity must be distinguished, and determination must not be identified with the former: there can be a determination which is compatible with freedom but which is not the same as absolute necessity, since the contrary of what is determined is not contradictory and

[1] *G.*, 4, 400; *D.*, p. 9.   [2] *Theodicy*, 45, p. 148; *G.*, 6, 127.

logically inconceivable. Where some would speak of psychological determinism, Leibniz speaks of 'freedom'. And if one defines freedom as 'spontaneity joined to intelligence',[1] this is doubtless compatible with Leibniz's logical and metaphysical premisses. But it may be doubted whether it is compatible with his acceptance in the *Theodicy* of the ideas of sin and eternal sanctions. The plain man at least is inclined to think that there can hardly be question of 'sin' and of retributive punishment except in the case of agents who ought to have acted otherwise and who could have acted otherwise, not merely in the sense that another course of action would have been logically possible but also in the sense that it would have been practically possible.

It is difficult, therefore, to avoid the impression that there is a discrepancy between the implications of Leibniz's logical and metaphysical premisses and the orthodox theological pronouncements of the *Theodicy*. On this matter I must confess that I agree with Bertrand Russell. At the same time there is not, I think, any good ground for accusing Leibniz of insincerity or of suggesting that his theology was dictated simply by motives of expediency. After all, he was well acquainted with certain theological and metaphysical systems in which the term 'freedom' was interpreted in a peculiar sense, and it is not as though he was the first among non-Spinozists to regard 'freedom' as compatible with 'determination'. The theologians and metaphysicians in question would have said that the plain man's notion of freedom is confused and needs clarification and correction. And Leibniz doubtless thought the same. Whether the distinction he draws between metaphysical and moral necessity is sufficient to enable one to attach an unambiguous meaning to the term 'freedom' is matter for dispute.

6. By saying that the world is the best of all possible worlds Leibniz did not mean to imply that it has at any given moment attained its maximum state of perfection: it is constantly progressing and developing. The harmony in the universe 'makes all things progress towards grace by natural methods'.[2] In speaking of progress towards grace Leibniz seems to have in mind the elevation of certain sensitive souls, according to the plan of the pre-established harmony, to the rank of spirits or rational souls, a rank which makes them 'images of the Divinity itself',[3] capable of knowing the system of the universe and of 'entering into a sort

[1] G., 7, 108 (*Initia Scientiae Generalis*, H).
[2] *Monadology*, 88; G., 6, 622; D., p. 231.
[3] *Monadology*, 83; G., 6, 621.

of society with God'. The harmonious union of spirits composes the 'city of God,' 'a moral world within the natural world'.[1] God considered as architect of the mechanism of the universe and God considered as monarch of the city of spirits is one and the same Being, and this unity is expressed in the 'harmony between the physical kingdom of nature and the moral kingdom of grace'.[2] Just as Leibniz envisaged the possibility of a given monad ascending the scale of monads in the progressive fulfilment of its potentialities, so he regarded the system of monads as progressing towards an ideal term of development. This development or progress is unending. Speaking of the next life, he observes that 'supreme felicity, by whatever beatific vision or knowledge of God it be accompanied, can never be full; for, since God is infinite, He cannot be wholly known. Therefore our happiness will never, and ought not to consist in full joy where there would be nothing to desire, rendering our mind stupid, but in a perpetual progress to new pleasures and to new perfections.'[3] This conception of unending progress and self-perfection is found again in Kant, who was also influenced by Leibniz's idea of the city of God and of the harmony between the moral kingdom and the kingdom of nature as the goal of history. These ideas represent the historical element in Leibniz's philosophy. He emphasized not only the timeless truths of logic and mathematics but also the dynamic and perpetual self-unfolding and self-perfection of individual substances linked together in a bond of harmony. He tried to connect the two sides of his philosophy by interpreting his monads as logical subjects; but the fact remains that it was through the historical side of his philosophy rather than through the logical and mathematical that he breaks through, as it were, the bounds of the rationalist Enlightenment. Yet the historical aspect of his thought was at the same time subordinate to the mathematical. Nothing new ever emerges: all is in principle predictable: all development is analogous to the working-out of a system of logic or mathematics. It is true that for him history is governed by the principle of fitness or perfection rather than by the principle of contradiction; but the tendency to subordinate the former to the latter is always present.

---

[1] *Monadology*, 86; *G.*, 6, 622.   [2] *Monadology*, 87; *G.*, 6, 622.
[3] *The Principles of Nature and of Grace*, 18; *G.*, 6, 606; *D.*, p. 217.

APPENDIX

A SHORT BIBLIOGRAPHY

1. WITH very few exceptions, articles have not been mentioned in the following Bibliography. For further bibliographical material recourse may be had to *Die Philosophie der Neuzeit bis zum Ende des XVIII Jahrhunderts* by M. Frischeisen-Köhler and W. Moog (mentioned below); to the *Répertoire Bibliographique* (supplement to the *Revue philosophique de Louvain*, formerly *Revue néoscolastique de philosophie*); to *Bibliographia Philosophica*, 1934–45, Vol. I, *Bibliographia Historiae Philosophiae*, edited by G. A. De Brie (Utrecht and Brussels, 1950); to the *Bibliography of Philosophy* published quarterly at Paris (Vrin) for the International Institute of Philosophy (first number Jan.–March 1954); and to the *Bulletin analytique* (*3 Partie, Philosophie*) published at Paris by the *Centre de Documentation* of the *Centre Nationale de la Recherche Scientifique*.

2. The letters *E.L.* in brackets, following the word 'London' after the title of a book, mean that the book in question belongs to the Everyman's Library, published by Messrs. J. M. Dent and Sons Ltd. No dates for these books are given here, as the numbers of the series are frequently reprinted. (And the format is being changed.)

3. The attention of students may be specially drawn to the works on individual philosophers published in the Pelican Philosophy Series edited by Professor A. J. Ayer. Written by experts, their cheapness makes them of obvious utility to students. Volumes mentioned below are described as Penguin Books, the date being added. The place of publication (Harmondsworth, Middlesex) is not given.

General Works

Abbagnano, N. *Storia della filosofia:* II, *parte prima*. Turin, 1949.

Adamson, R. *The Development of Modern Philosophy, with other Lectures and Essays*. Edinburgh, 1908 (2nd edition).

Alexander, A. B. D. *A Short History of Philosophy*. Glasgow, 1922 (3rd edition).

Bréhier, E. *Histoire de la philosophie:* II, *la philosophie moderne; 1re partie, XVIIe et XVIIIe siècles*. Paris, 1942. (Bréhier's work is one of the best histories of philosophy, and it contains brief, but useful, bibliographies.)

Carré, M. H. *Phases of Thought in England*. Oxford, 1949.

Castell, A. *An Introduction to Modern Philosophy in Six Problems.* New York, 1943.

Catlin, G. *A History of the Political Philosophers.* London, 1950.

Collins, J. *A History of Modern European Philosophy.* Milwaukee, 1954. (This work by a Thomist can be highly recommended. It contains useful bibliographies.)

De Ruggiero, G. *Storia della filosofia: IV, la filosofia moderna.* 1, *l'età cartesiana; 2, l'età dell' illuminismo.* 2 vols. Bari, 1946.

De Ruvo, V. *Il problema della verità da Spinoza a Hume.* Padua, 1950.

Deussen, P. *Allgemeine Geschichte der Philosophie: II, 3, von Descartes bis Schopenhauer.* Leipzig, 1920 (2nd edition).

Devaux, P. *De Thalès à Bergson. Introduction historique à la philosophie.* Liége, 1948.

Erdmann, J. E. *A History of Philosophy: II, Modern Philosophy,* translated by W. S. Hough. London, 1889, and subsequent editions.

Falckenberg, R. *Geschichte der neuern Philosophie.* Berlin, 1921 (8th edition).

Ferm, V. (editor). *A History of Philosophical Systems.* New York, 1950. (This work consists of essays, of uneven merit, by different writers on different periods and branches of philosophy.)

Fischer, K. *Geschichte der neuern Philosophie.* 10 vols. Heidelberg, 1897–1904. (This work includes separate volumes on Descartes, Spinoza and Leibniz, as listed under these names.)

Fischl, J. *Geschichte der Philosophie,* 5 vols. II, *Renaissance und Barock, Neuzeit bis Leibniz;* III, *Aufklärung und deutscher Idealismus.* Vienna, 1950.

Frischeisen-Köhler, M. and Moog, W. *Die Philosophie der Neuzeit bis zum Ende des XVIII Jahrhunderts.* Berlin, 1924, reproduction, 1953. (This is the third volume of the new revised edition of Ueberweg's *Grundriss der Geschichte der Philosophie.* It is useful as a work of reference and contains extensive bibliographies. But it is hardly suited for continuous reading.)

Fuller, B. A. G. *A History of Philosophy.* New York, 1945 (revised edition).

Hegel, G. W. F. *Lectures on the History of Philosophy,* translated by E. S. Haldane and F. H. Simson. Vol. III. London, 1895. (Hegel's history of philosophy forms part of his system. His outlook influenced several of the older German historians, such as Erdmann and Schwegler.)

Heimsoeth, H. *Metaphysik der Neuzeit.* Two parts. Munich and Berlin, 1927 and 1929. (This work is contained in the *Handbuch der Philosophie* edited by A. Baeumler and M. Schröter.)

A SHORT BIBLIOGRAPHY

335

Hirschberger, J. *Geschichte der Philosophie:* II, *Neuzeit und Gegenwart.* Freiburg i. B., 1952. (This is an objective account by a Catholic writer who is a professor at the University of Frankfurt-a-M.)

Höffding, H. *A History of Philosophy* (modern), translated by B. E. Meyer. 2 vols. London, 1900 (American reprint, 1924). *A Brief History of Modern Philosophy*, translated by C. F. Sanders. London, 1912.

Jones, W. T. *A History of Western Philosophy:* II, *The Modern Mind.* New York, 1952.

Lamanna, E. P. *Storia della filosofia:* II, *Dall'età cartesiana alla fine dell' Ottocento.* Florence, 1941.

Leroux, E. and Leroy, A. *La philosophie anglaise classique.* Paris, 1951.

Lewes, G. H. *The History of Philosophy:* II, *Modern Philosophy.* London, 1867.

Maréchal, J. *Précis d'histoire de la philosophie moderne, de la renaissance à Kant.* Louvain, 1933; revised edition, Paris, 1951.

Marías, J. *Historia de la filosofía.* Madrid, 1941.

Mellone, S. H. *Dawn of Modern Thought.* Oxford, 1930. (This work deals with Descartes, Spinoza and Leibniz, and forms a short and useful introduction.)

Meyer, H. *Geschichte der abendländischen Weltanschauung:* IV, *von der Renaissance zum deutschen Idealismus.* Würzburg, 1950.

Miller, H. *An Historical Introduction to Modern Philosophy.* New York, 1947.

Morris, C. R. *Locke, Berkeley, Hume.* Oxford, 1931. (A useful, short introduction.)

Rogers, A. K. *A Student's History of Philosophy.* New York, 1954 (3rd edition reprinted). (A straightforward textbook.)

Russell, Bertrand. *History of Western Philosophy and its Connection with Political and Social Circumstances from the Earliest Times to the Present Day.* London, 1946, and reprints. (This volume is unusually lively and entertaining; but its treatment of a number of important philosophers is both inadequate and misleading.)

Sabine, G. H. *A History of Political Theory.* London, 1941. (A valuable study of the subject.)

Schilling, K. *Geschichte der Philosophie:* II, *Die Neuzeit.* Munich, 1953. (Contains useful bibliographies.)

Seth, J. *English Philosophers and Schools of Philosophy.* London, 1912.

Sorley, W. R. *A History of English Philosophy.* Cambridge, 1920 (reprint 1937).

Souilhé, J. *La philosophie chrétienne de Descartes à nos jours.* 2 vols. Paris, 1934.

Thilly, F. *A History of Philosophy*, revised by L. Wood. New York, 1951.

Thonnard, F. J. *Précis d'histoire de la philosophie*. Paris, 1941 (revised edition).

Turner, W. *History of Philosophy*. Boston and London, 1903.

Vorländer, K. *Geschichte der Philosophie:* II, *Die Philosophie der Neuzeit bis Kant*, edited by H. Knittermeyer. Hamburg, 1955.

Webb, C. C. J. *A History of Philosophy*. London (Home University Library), 1915, and reprints.

Windelband, W. *A History of Philosophy, with especial reference to the Formation and Development of its Problems and Conceptions*, translated by J. H. Tufts. New York and London, 1952 (reprint of 1901 edition). (This notable work treats the history of philosophy according to the development of problems.)

Windelband, W. *Lehrbuch der Geschichte der Philosophie*, edited by H. Heimsoeth with a concluding chapter, 'Die Philosophie im 20 Jahrhundert mit einer Uebersicht über den Stand der philosophiegeschichtlichen Forschung'. Tübingen, 1935.

Wright, W. K. *A History of Modern Philosophy*. New York, 1941.

Chapters II–VI: Descartes

Texts

Œuvres de Descartes, edited by C. Adam and P. Tannery. 13 vols. Paris, 1897–1913. (This is the standard edition, to which references are generally made.)

Correspondance de Descartes, edited by C. Adam and G. Milhaud. Paris, 1936 ff. (Standard edition.)

The Philosophical Works of Descartes, translated by E. S. Haldane and G. R. T. Ross. 2 vols. Cambridge, 1911–12 (corrected edition, 1934; reprint, New York, 1955). (The first volume contains *Rules, Discourses, Meditations, Principles*, though in the case of a large number of sections dealing with astronomical and physical matters only the headings are given; *Search after Truth, Passions of the Soul* and *Notes Against a Programme*. The second volume contains seven sets of *Objections* with Descartes' replies, a letter to Clerselier, and a letter to Dinet.)

Œuvres et lettres, with introduction and notes by A. Bridoux. Paris, 1937.

A Discourse on Method (together with the *Meditations* and excerpts from the *Principles*), translated by J. Veitch, with an introduction by A. D. Lindsay, London (*E.L.*).

Discourse on Method. New York, 1950.

Discours de la méthode. Text and commentary by E. Gilson. Paris, 1939 (2nd edition).

Discours de la méthode, with a preface by J. Laporte and introduction and notes by M. Barthélemy. Paris, 1937.

Discours de la méthode, with introduction and notes by L. Liard. Paris, 1942.

The Meditations concerning First Philosophy. New York, 1951.

Meditationes de prima philosophia, with introduction and notes by G. Lewis. Paris, 1943.

Entretien avec Burman. Manuscrit de Göttingen. Text edited, translated and annotated by C. Adam. Paris, 1937.

The Geometry of René Descartes, translated by D. E. Smith and M. L. Latham. New York, 1954.

Lettres sur la morale. Text revised and edited by J. Chevalier. Paris, 1935 (and 1955).

Descartes: Selections, edited by R. M. Eaton. New York, 1929.

Descartes' Philosophical Writings, selected and translated by M. K. Smith. London, 1953.

Descartes: Philosophical Writings. A selection translated and edited by E. Anscombe and P. T. Geach, with an introduction by A. Koyré. London, 1954.

Studies

Adam, C. *Descartes, sa vie, son œuvre.* Paris, 1937.

Alquié, F. *La découverte métaphysique de l'homme chez Descartes.* Paris, 1950.

Balz, A. G. A. *Descartes and the Modern Mind.* New Haven (U.S.A.), 1952.

Beck, L. J. *The Method of Descartes.* Oxford, 1952. (A valuable study of the *Regulae.*)

Brunschvicg, L. *Descartes.* Paris, 1937.

Cassirer, E. *Descartes.* New York, 1941.

Chevalier, J. *Descartes.* Paris, 1937 (17th edition).

De Finance, J. *Cogito cartésien et réflexion thomiste.* Paris, 1946.

Devaux, P. *Descartes philosophe.* Brussels, 1937.

Dijksterhuis, E. J. *Descartes et le cartésianisme hollandais. Études et documents.* Paris, 1951.

Fischer, K. *Descartes and his School.* New York, 1887.

Gibson, A. B. *The Philosophy of Descartes.* London, 1932. (This work and the volume, mentioned below, by Dr. Keeling, form excellent studies for English readers.)
Great Thinkers: VI, *Descartes* (in *Philosophy,* 1935).

Gilson, E. *Index scolastico-cartésien.* Paris, 1912.
La liberté chez Descartes et la théologie. Paris, 1913.
Études sur le rôle de la pensée médiévale dans la formation du système cartésien. Paris, 1930.

Gouhier, H. *La pensée religieuse de Descartes*. Paris, 1924.

Gueroult, M. *Descartes selon l'ordre des raisons*. 2 vols. Paris, 1953.
  Nouvelles réflexions sur la preuve ontologique de Descartes. Paris, 1955.

Haldane, E. S. *Descartes: His Life and Times*. London, 1905.

Jaspers, K. *Descartes und die Philosophie*. Berlin, 1956 (3rd edition).

Joachim, H. M. *Descartes' Rules for the Direction of the Mind*. Oxford, 1956.

Keeling, S. V. *Descartes*. London, 1934. (See remark under Gibson.)

Laberthonnière, L. *Études sur Descartes*. 2 vols. Paris, 1935.
  Études de philosophie cartésienne. Paris, 1937. (These volumes are contained in the *Œuvres de Laberthonnière*, edited by L. Canet.)

Laporte, J. *Le rationalisme de Descartes*. Paris, 1950 (2nd edition).

Leisegang, H. *Descartes*. Berlin, 1951.

Lewis, G. *L'individualité selon Descartes*. Paris, 1950.
  Le problème de l'inconscient et le cartésianisme. Paris, 1950.

Mahaffy, J. P. *Descartes*. Edinburgh and London, 1892.

Maritain, J. *Three Reformers: Luther, Descartes, Rousseau*. London, 1928.
  The Dream of Descartes, translated by M. L. Andison. New York, 1944.

Mesnard, P. *Essai sur la morale de Descartes*. Paris, 1936.

Natorp, P. *Descartes' Erkenntnistheorie*. Marburg, 1882.

Oligiati, F. *Cartesio*. Milan, 1934.
  La filosofia di Descartes. Milan, 1937.

Rodis-Lewis, G. *La morale de Descartes*. Paris, 1957.

Serrurier, C. *Descartes, l'homme et le penseur*. Paris, 1951.

Serrus, C. *La méthode de Descartes et son application à la métaphysique*. Paris, 1933.

Smith, N. K. *Studies in the Cartesian Philosophy*. London, 1902.
  New Studies in the Philosophy of Descartes. London, 1953.

Versfeld, M. *An Essay on the Metaphysics of Descartes*. London, 1940.

There are a number of volumes of essays on Descartes by different authors, such as:

Cartesio nel terzo centenario del Discorso del metodo. Milan, 1937.

Congrès Descartes. Travaux du IXe Congrès International de Philosophie, edited by P. Bayer. Paris, 1937.

Causeries cartésiennes. Paris, 1938.

Descartes. Homenaje en el tercer centenario del Discurso del Método.
3 vols. Buenos Aires, 1937.
Escritos en Honor de Descartes. La Plata, 1938.

Note. For Gassendi (*Opera*, Lyons, 1658, and Florence, 1727) see
The Philosophy of Gassendi by G. S. Brett (New York, 1908). For
Mersenne (*Correspondance*, published by Mme P. Tannery, edited
and annotated by C. De Waard and R. Pintard, 3 vols., Paris,
1945–6) see *Mersenne ou la naissance du mécanisme* by R. Lenoble
(Paris, 1943).

Chapter VII: Pascal

Texts

Œuvres complètes, edited by L. Brunschvicg, E. Boutroux and F.
Gazier. 14 vols. Paris, 1904–14.
Greater Shorter Works of Pascal, translated by E. Caillet and J. C.
Blankenagel. Philadelphia, 1948.
Pensées et opuscules, with an introduction and notes by L. Brunsch-
vicg. Paris, 1914 (7th edition); re-edited, 1934.
Pensées, edited in French and English by H. F. Stewart. London,
1950.
Pensées, translated by W. F. Trotter, with an introduction by T. S.
Eliot. London (*E.L.*).

There are many editions of the *Pensées*; for example, those by
H. Massis (Paris, 1935), J. Chevalier (Paris, 1937), V. Giraud (Paris,
1937), Z. Tourneur (Paris, 1938), and the palaeographic edition by
Z. Tourneur (Paris, 1943).

Discours sur les passions de l'amour de Pascal. Text and commentary by A. Ducas. Algiers, 1953.

Studies

Benzécri, E. *L'esprit humain selon Pascal.* Paris, 1939.
Bishop, M. *Pascal, the Life of Genius.* New York, 1936.
Boutroux, E. *Pascal.* Paris, 1924 (9th edition).
Brunschvicg, L. *Le génie de Pascal.* Paris, 1924.
            Pascal. Paris, 1932.
Caillet, E. *The Clue to Pascal.* Philadelphia, 1944.
Chevalier, J. *Pascal.* London, 1930.
Falcucci, C. *Le problème de la vérité chez Pascal.* Toulouse, 1939.
Fletcher, F. T. H. *Pascal and the Mystical Tradition.* Oxford, 1954.
Guardini, R. *Christliches Bewusstsein. Versuche über Pascal.*
            Leipzig, 1935.

Guitton, J. *Pascal et Leibniz.* Paris, 1951.
Jovy, E. *Études pascaliennes.* 5 vols. Paris, 1927–8.
Lafuma, L. *Histoire des Pensées de Pascal (1656–1952).* Paris, 1954.
Laporte, J. *Le cœur et la raison selon Pascal.* Paris, 1950.
Lefebvre, H. *Pascal.* Paris, 1949.
Mesnard, J. *Pascal, His Life and Works.* New York, 1952.
Russier, J. *La foi selon Pascal.* 2 vols. Paris, 1949.
Sciacca, M. F. *Pascal.* Brescia, 1944.
Serini, P. *Pascal.* Turin, 1942.
Sertillanges, A-D. *Blaise Pascal.* Paris, 1941.
Soreau, E. *Pascal.* Paris, 1935.
Stewart, H. F. *The Secret of Pascal.* Cambridge, 1941.
      Blaise Pascal. London (British Academy Lecture), 1942.
      The Heart of Pascal. Cambridge, 1945.
Stöcker, A. *Das Bild vom Menschen bei Pascal.* Freiburg i. B., 1939.
Strowski, F. *Pascal et son temps.* 3 vols. Paris, 1907–8.
Vinet, A. *Études sur Blaise Pascal.* Lausanne, 1936.
Webb, C. C. J. *Pascal's Philosophy of Religion.* Oxford, 1929.
Woodgate, M. V. *Pascal and his Sister Jacqueline.* St. Louis (U.S.A.), 1945.

Archives de Philosophie (1923, Cahier III) is devoted to *Études sur Pascal.* Paris.

Chapter VIII: Cartesianism

Texts

Geulincx. *Opera philosophica,* edited by J. P. N. Land. 3 vols. The Hague, 1891–3.

Studies

Balz, A. G. A. *Cartesian Studies.* New York, 1951.
Bouillier, F. *Histoire de la philosophie cartésienne.* 2 vols. Paris, 1868 (3rd edition).
Covotti, A. *Storia della filosofia. Gli occasionalisti: Geulincx-Malebranche.* Naples, 1937.
Hausmann, P. *Das Freiheitsproblem bei Geulincx.* Bonn, 1934.
Land, J. P. N. *Arnold Geulincx und seine Philosophie.* The Hague, 1895.
Prost, J. *Essai sur l'atomisme et l'occasionalisme dans la philosophie cartésienne.* Paris, 1907.
Samtleben, G. *Geulincx, ein Vorgänger Spinozas.* Halle, 1885.

Terraillon, E. *La morale de Geulincx dans ses rapports avec la philosophie de Descartes.* Paris, 1912.
Van der Haeghen, V. *Geulincx. Études sur sa vie, sa philosophie et ses ouvrages.* Ghent, 1886.

Chapter IX: Malebranche

Texts

Œuvres complètes, edited by D. Roustan and P. Schrecker. Paris, 1938 ff. (Critical edition.)
Œuvres complètes. 11 vols. Paris, 1712.
Entretiens sur la métaphysique et sur la religion, edited by P. Fontana. Paris, 1922.
Entretiens sur la métaphysique et sur la religion, edited with an introduction and notes by A. Cuvelier. Paris, 1945.
Dialogues on Metaphysics and on Religion, translated by M. Ginsberg. London, 1923.
Méditations chrétiennes, edited by H. Gouhier. Paris, 1928.
De la recherche de la vérité, edited with an introduction by G. Lewis. 2 vols. Paris, 1945.
Traité de morale, edited by H. Joly. Paris, 1882 (republished 1939).
Traité de l'amour de Dieu, edited by D. Roustan. Paris, 1922.
Entretien d'un philosophe chrétien et d'un philosophe chinois, edited with an introduction and notes by A. Le Moine. Paris, 1936.

Studies

Church, R. W. *A Study in the Philosophy of Malebranche.* London, 1931. (Recommended.)
Delbos, V. *Étude sur la philosophie de Malebranche.* Paris, 1925.
De Matteis, F. *L'occasionalismo e il suo sviluppo nel pensiero di N. Malebranche.* Naples, 1936.
Ducassé, P. *Malebranche, sa vie, son œuvre, sa philosophie.* Paris, 1942.
Gouhier, H. *La vocation de Malebranche.* Paris, 1926.
              La philosophie de Malebranche et son expérience religieuse. Paris, 1948 (2nd edition).
Gueroult, M. *Étendue et psychologie chez Malebranche.* Paris, 1940.
Laird, J. *Great Thinkers:* VII, Malebranche (article in *Philosophy,* 1936).
Le Moine, A. *Les vérités éternelles selon Malebranche.* Paris, 1936.
Luce, A. A. *Berkeley and Malebranche.* London, 1934.
Mouy, P. *Les lois du choc des corps d'après Malebranche.* Paris, 1927.
Nadu, P. S. *Malebranche and Modern Philosophy.* Calcutta 1944.

There are several collections of papers on Malebranche; for example, *Malebranche nel terzo centenario della sua nascita* (Milan, 1938) and *Malebranche. Commémoration du troisième centenaire de sa naissance* (Paris, 1938).

Chapters X–XIV: Spinoza

Texts

Werke, edited by C. Gebhardt. 4 vols. Heidelberg, 1925. (Critica edition.)

Opera quotquot reperta sunt, edited by J. Van Vloten and J. P. N. Land. 2 vols., The Hague, 1882, 1883; 3 vols., 1895; 4 vols., 1914.

The Chief Works of Benedict de Spinoza, translated with an introduction by R. H. M. Elwes. 2 vols. London, 1883; revised edition, 1903. (Vol. I contains the *Tractatus theologico-politicus* and the *Tractatus politicus*. Vol. II the *De intellectus emendatione*, the *Ethica* and *Select Letters*.) Reprinted in one volume, New York, 1951.

The Principles of Descartes' Philosophy (together with *Metaphysical Thoughts*), translated by H. H. Britan. Chicago, 1905.

Short Treatise on God, Man and his Well-Being, translated by A. Wolf. London, 1910.

Spinoza's Ethics and De intellectus emendatione, translated by A. Boyle, with an introduction by G. Santayana. London (*E.L.*).

Spinoza: Writings on Political Philosophy, edited by A. G. A. Balz. New York, 1937.

Spinoza: Selections, edited by J. Wild. New York, 1930.

The Correspondence of Spinoza, edited by A. Wolf. London, 1929.

Studies

Bidney, D.   *The Psychology and Ethics of Spinoza: A Study in the History and Logic of Ideas*. New Haven (U.S.A.), 1940.

Brunschvicg, L.   *Spinoza et ses contemporains*.   Paris, 1923 (3rd edition).

Ceriani, G.   *Spinoza*. Brescia, 1943.

Chartier, E.   *Spinoza*. Paris, 1938.

Cresson, A.   *Spinoza*. Paris, 1940.

Darbon, A.   *Études spinozistes*, edited by J. Moreau. Paris, 1946.

De Burgh, W. G.   *Great Thinkers:* VIII, Spinoza (article in *Philosophy*, 1936).

Delbos, V.   *Le problème moral dans la philosophie de Spinoza*. Paris, 1893.

         Le spinozisme. Paris, 1916.

Dujovne, L. *Spinoza. Su vida, su época, su obra y su influencia.* 4 vols. Buenos Aires, 1941–5.

Dunin-Borkowski, S. von *Spinoza.* 4 vols. Münster i. W. Vol. I (*Der junge De Spinoza*), 1933 (2nd edition); Vols. II–IV (*Aus den Tagen Spinozas: Geschehnisse, Gestalten, Gedankenwelt*), 1933–6.

Dunner, J. *Baruch Spinoza and Western Democracy.* New York, 1955.

Fischer, K. *Spinoza. Leben, Werke, Lehre.* Heidelberg, 1909.

Friedmann, G. *Leibniz et Spinoza.* Paris, 1946 (4th edition).

Gebhardt, C. *Spinoza: Vier Reden.* Heidelberg, 1927.

Hallett, H. F. *Aeternitas, a Spinozistic Study.* Oxford, 1930.

Hallett, H. F., *Benedict de Spinoza. The Elements of his Philosophy.* London, 1957.

Hampshire, S. *Spinoza.* Penguin Books, 1951.

Joachim, H. H. *A Study of the Ethics of Spinoza.* Oxford, 1901.
　　　　　　Spinoza's Tractatus de intellectus emendatione: a Commentary. Oxford, 1940.

Kayser, R. *Spinoza, Portrait of a Spiritual Hero.* New York, 1946.

Lachièze-Rey, P. *Les origines cartésiennes du Dieu de Spinoza.* Paris, 1932; 2nd edition, 1950.

McKeon, R. *The Philosophy of Spinoza.* New York, 1928.

Parkinson, G. H. R. *Spinoza's Theory of Knowledge.* Oxford, 1954.

Pollock, Sir F. *Spinoza, His Life and Philosophy.* London, 1899 (2nd edition), reprinted 1936.

Ratner, J. *Spinoza on God.* New York, 1930.

Roth, L. *Spinoza, Descartes and Maimonides.* Oxford, 1924.
　　　　Spinoza. London, 1929, reprint 1954.

Runes, D. D. *Spinoza Dictionary.* New York, 1951.

Saw, R. L. *The Vindication of Metaphysics: A Study in the Philosophy of Spinoza.* London, 1951.

Siwek, P. *L'âme et le corps d'après Spinoza.* Paris, 1930.
　　　　Spinoza et le panthéisme religieux. Paris, 1950 (new edition).
　　　　Au cœur du Spinozisme. Paris, 1952.

Vernière, P. *Spinoza et la pensée française avant la Révolution.* 2 vols. Paris, 1954.

Wolfson, H. A. *The Philosophy of Spinoza.* 2 vols. Cambridge (U.S.A.), 1934. One vol. edition, 1948.

There are a number of collections of essays on Spinoza; for example, *Spinoza nel terzo centenario della sua nascita* (Milan, 1934) and *Travaux du deuxième Congrès des Sociétés de Philosophie Françaises et de Langue Française: Thème historique: Spinoza. Thème de philosophie générale: L'idée de l'Univers* (Lyons, 1939).

For some Marxist views on Spinoza, see *Spinoza in Soviet Philosophy*, edited by G. L. Kline (London, 1952).

Students of Spinoza will find material in the *Chronicum Spinozanum*, founded in 1920 by the *Societas Spinozana*. (First number, The Hague, 1921.)

Chapters XV–XVIII: Leibniz

(In the titles of some books *Leibniz* is spelt *Leibnitz*. I have used the spelling *Leibniz* throughout.)

Texts

Sämtliche Schriften und Briefe, edited under the auspices of the Prussian Academy of Sciences. This critical edition is to consist of 40 vols. The first volume appeared in 1923.

Die mathematischen Schriften von G. W. Leibniz, edited by C. I. Gerhardt. 7 vols. Berlin, 1849–63.

Die philosophischen Schriften von G. W. Leibniz, edited by C. I. Gerhardt. 7 vols. Berlin, 1875–90.
(The critical edition, mentioned above, being still incomplete, Gerhardt's edition is frequently used in references.)

The Philosophical Writings of Leibniz, selected and translated by M. Morris. London (*E.L.*).

The Philosophical Works of Leibniz, translated with notes by G. M. Duncan. New Haven (U.S.A.), 1890. (This volume contains an extensive and useful selection.)

Leibniz: Selections, edited by P. Wiener. New York, 1930.

G. W. Leibniz. Philosophical Papers and Letters. A selection translated and edited with an introduction by L. E. Loemker. 2 vols. Chicago, 1956.

G. W. Leibniz: Opuscula philosophica selecta, edited by P. Schrecker. Paris, 1939.

Leibniz. Œuvres choisies, edited by L. Prenant. Paris, 1940.

Leibniz: The Monadology and other Philosophical Writings, translated with introduction and notes by R. Latta. Oxford, 1898.

Leibniz: The Monadology, translated with commentary by H. W. Carr. Los Angeles, 1930.

Leibniz's Discourse on Metaphysics, Correspondence with Arnauld, and Monadology, translated by G. R. Montgomery. Chicago, 1902.

Leibniz: Discourse on Metaphysics, translated by P. G. Lucas and L. Grint. Manchester, 1953.

Leibniz. Discours de métaphysique, edited with notes by H. Lestienne. Paris, 1945.

New Essays concerning Human Understanding, translated by A. G. Langley. Lasalle (Illinois), 1949 (3rd edition).

Theodicy, Essays on the Goodness of God, the Freedom of Man and the Origin of Evil, translated by E. M. Huggard, with an introduction by A. Farrer. Edinburgh and London, 1952.

Opuscules et fragments inédits de Leibniz, edited by L. Couturat. Paris, 1903.

G. W. Leibniz, Textes inédits, edited by G. Grua. 2 vols. Paris, 1948.

G. W. Leibniz. Lettres et fragments inédits sur les problèmes philosophiques, théologiques, politiques de la réconciliation des doctrines protestantes (1669–1704), edited with an introduction and notes by P. Schrecker. Paris, 1935.

Leibniz-Clarke Correspondence, edited by H. G. Alexander. Manchester, 1956.

Studies

Barber, W. H. *Leibniz in France from Arnauld to Voltaire: A Study in French Reactions to Leibnizianism, 1670–1760*. Oxford, 1955.

Baruzi, J. *Leibniz, avec de nombreux textes inédits*. Paris, 1909.

Belaval, Y. *La pensée de Leibniz*. Paris, 1952.

Boehm, A. *Le 'Vinculum Substantiale' chez Leibniz. Ses origines historiques*. Paris, 1938.

Brunner, F. *Études sur la signification historique de la philosophie de Leibniz*. Paris, 1951.

Carr, H. W. *Leibniz*. London, 1929.

Cassirer, E. *Leibniz' System in seinen wissenschaftlichen Grundlagen*. Marburg, 1902.

Couturat, L. *La logique de Leibniz*. Paris, 1901.

Davillé, L. *Leibniz historien*. Paris, 1909.

Fischer, K. *Gottfried Wilhelm Leibniz*. Heidelberg, 1920 (5th edition).

Friedmann, G. *Leibniz et Spinoza*. Paris, 1946 (4th edition).

Funke, G. *Der Möglichkeitsbegriff in Leibnizens System*. Bonn, 1938.

Getberg, B. *Le problème de la limitation des créatures chez Leibniz*. Paris, 1937.

Grua, G. *Jurisprudence universelle et théodicée selon Leibniz*. Paris, 1953.

Gueroult, M. *Dynamique et métaphysique leibniziennes*. Paris, 1934.

Guhrauer, G. E. *G. W. Freiherr von Leibniz*. 2 vols. Breslau, 1846 (Biography).

Guitton, J. *Pascal et Leibniz*. Paris, 1951.

Hildebrandt, K. *Leibniz und das Reich der Gnade*. The Hague, 1953.

Huber, K. *Leibniz*. Munich, 1951.

Iwanicki, J. *Leibniz et les démonstrations mathématiques de l'existence de Dieu*. Paris, 1934.

Jalabert, J. *La théorie leibnizienne de la substance.* Paris, 1947.

Joseph, H. W. B. *Lectures on the Philosophy of Leibniz.* Oxford, 1949.

Kabitz, W. *Die Philosophie des jungen Leibniz.* Heidelberg, 1909.

Le Chevalier, L. *La morale de Leibniz.* Paris, 1933.

Mackie, J. M. *Life of Godfrey William von Leibniz.* Boston, 1845.

Matzat, H. L. *Untersuchungen über die metaphysischen Grundlagen der Leibnizschen Zeichenkunst.* Berlin, 1938.

Merz, J. T. *Leibniz.* Edinburgh and London, 1884; reprinted New York, 1948.

Meyer, R. W. *Leibniz and the Seventeenth-Century Revolution,* translated by J. P. Stern. Cambridge, 1952.

Moureau, J. *L'univers leibnizien.* Paris, 1956.

Olgiati, F. *Il significato storico di Leibniz.* Milan, 1934.

Piat, C. *Leibniz.* Paris, 1915.

Politella, J. *Platonism, Aristotelianism and Cabalism in the Philosophy of Leibniz.* Philadelphia, 1938.

Russell, Bertrand. *A Critical Exposition of the Philosophy of Leibniz.* London, 1937 (2nd edition).

Russell, L. J. *Great Thinkers:* IX, Leibniz (in *Philosophy,* 1936).

Saw, R. L. *Leibniz.* Penguin Books, 1954.

Schmalenbach, H. *Leibniz.* Munich, 1921.

Stammler, G. *Leibniz.* Munich, 1930.

Wundt, W. *Leibniz.* Leipzig, 1909.

There are several collections of essays on Leibniz; for example, *Gottfried Wilhelm Leibniz. Vorträge der aus Anlass seines 300 Geburtstages in Hamburg abgehaltenen wissenschaftlichen Tagung* (Hamburg, 1946); *Leibniz zu seinem 300 Geburtstag, 1646–1946,* edited by E. Hochstetter (Berlin, 1948); and *Beiträge zur Leibniz-forschung,* edited by G. Schischkoff (Reutlingen, 1947).

INDEX

(The principal references are printed in heavy figures. References followed by an asterisk refer to bibliographical information. A reference in ordinary type to a continuous series of pages, e.g. 167–74, does not necessarily indicate continuous treatment.)

Ratner, J. 343*

reason: Pascal 158, 160, 163–6, 170–2

distinguished from imagination: Spinoza 234

life according to: Spinoza 242 ff, 248, 253, 256 ff

practical R. 60 n.; postulates of practical R. 59 ff

sharing in divine R. 193

reflection: Leibniz 311 f, 318 f; Locke 26

reform 39

Reformation, the 2

Regius, Henricus 65, 83, 174

Régis, Pierre-Sylvain 175

Regnier, Henri 174

regress of causes, infinite 101

Reid, Thomas 37 f

Reimarus, Samuel 42

relations: Malebranche 188, 194 f

religion: Hobbes 45, 257: Pascal 161, 165, 171; Spinoza 257 f; also 34, 36, 42 f, 53, 55

religious beliefs of philosophers: Descartes 66, 153; Pascal 153 to 173 passim; Spinoza 31 f, 208, 237, 245, 262 f; also 6, 24, 34, 271. See also revelation

Renaissance, the 7 ff, 18, 24, 52

Renaissance philosophers and Spinoza 209 f, 226

on universal harmony 267, 293 f also 1 f

Renouvier, Charles 149, 154

representative theory of perception: Descartes 109, 125 f

research 229, 262

resignation 148 f, 178

resistance essential to matter 300 f

responsibility 249, 329

rest, state of 131, 133, 183. See also under motion

reunion of Christendom: Leibniz 265 f, 269 ff

revelation: Descartes 20, 147, 152; Pascal 31, 153, 169; Malebranche 182, 197 f, 202, also 16, 19, 34 ff, 43, 53, 159

Revolution of 1688, the 46 f

riches: Spinoza 262

rights, natural: Hobbes 45; Locke 40, 46; Spinoza 252 ff, 255–8

Robespierre 48

Rodis-Lewis, G. 338*

Rogers, A. K. 335*

Rohault, Jacques 175 f

Romantic movement in Germany and Spinoza 261 f

Roth, L. 343*

Rousseau, Jean-Jacques: political theory 14, 40 f, 47 ff; also 4 f

Ruggiero, Guido de 271, 334*

ruler of State 255 f

rules for thinking and for seeking truth: Descartes 64 f, 69, 74 ff; Malebranche 187; Spinoza 250

Runes, D. D. 343*

Russell, Bertrand 270 f, 288, 291, 294, 331, 335*, 346*

Russell, L. J. 346*

Russier, J. 340*

Ruvo, V. de 334*

Sabine, G. H. 335*

salvation: Spinoza 245, 251

Samtleben, G. 340*

sanctions: Leibniz 329 ff; also 52

Sartre, Jean-Paul 150 f

Saw, R. L. 343*, 346*

scepticism: Pascal and 156, 158, 167, 170 f; also 19 f, 29, 42, 69, 90 n., 176

Schelling, F. W. 261

Schilling, K. 335*

Schmalenbach, H. 346*

Scholastic philosophy and Descartes 3, 70, 128

Descartes on 10, 68, 71

Leibniz and 210, 264, 287, 299, 303, 306, 316, 321, 326, 328, 330

and Locke 26

Malebranche 181

Pascal on 159

Spinoza 210, 213, 216, 217 and n., 226, 254, 256

See also mediaeval philosophy

Schopenhauer, Arthur 326

Schwegler, Albert 334* (under Hegel)

Sciacca, M. F. 340*

science: Descartes 70 ff, 83, 138, 149; Spinoza 250, 261 f; also 18

Aristotelian theory 70 f

all SS. one 70 ff

a universal S.: Leibniz 268